The ~~Good~~ Best Life

A City Girl Thrives in the Jungle

Follow Jesus
Sue Westrum

Sue Westrum

ISBN 978-1-64258-329-8 (paperback)
ISBN 978-1-64258-330-4 (digital)

Christian Faith Publishing, Inc.
832 Park Avenue
Meadville, PA 16335
www.christianfaithpublishing.com

Printed in the United States of America

All proceeds from the sale of my book will be donated to missions.

Dedication

There is a very real sense in which God wrote this book. In January 2016, deep in my heart, God said to me, "Sue, I want you to write a book. Type up all the stories about how I worked in the Berik society, how I planned and nurtured your life, how I've taught you to glorify Me with thanksgiving. Be My instrument, just as you were in Indonesia and in the 15 years since I brought you back to the US. I'll lead you, give you the ideas I want in the book." And so, each day for the last 21 months, as I sat at my computer, with my hands on the keyboard, I prayed, *OK, Father, here I am. Give me Your thoughts again today. Show me what You want in this chapter.* Some days, not having a solid idea of how the chapter would flow, I felt an eagerness to be the first reader at the end of the day—to learn what God wanted included.

Thus, I dedicate this book to my God, my Savior, my Guide, eagerly waiting now to see the unfolding of His plans for these stories of what He has done.

I also dedicate this book to my sons and their wives—David and Tanya, Scott and Chris, Yaufun and Sharon, George and Doris—who love Jesus and are seeking Him in all things, to our grandchildren—Stephan, Nadia, Carlie, Josh, Nate, Nathan and Betsy, David, Benji, Jonny, Rebecca, and Looki—and to our great-grandchildren—Aaron and Wes.

I further dedicate it to you, dear reader, one of those God has planned to read this story of His magnificent love. I pray you'll be drawn closer to Him, with an increased desire to follow the plan He has designed just for you.

Contents

INDONESIA

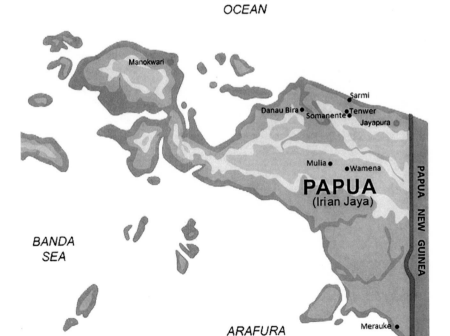

Acknowledgments

First and foremost, I want to thank my husband, Peter, for his patience these past 21 months as I've read through all the prayer letters we've written during the past 49 years, reviewed scribbled entries on 53 years of hard-copy calendars, organized my notes on possible topics for inclusion in the book, made chapter outlines, and finally drafted the chapter stories. He was a never-ending invaluable resource for me—able to recall names, anthropological data, and details of events I had long forgotten. He prayed for and encouraged me daily, patiently listened to all my verbal ramblings about what I was struggling with wondering what to do next. Peter diligently helped me by being the first to read and suggest edits for each chapter as it came from my printer.

Second, I want to acknowledge and thank my sister, Mary. She's the one who was always there for me throughout the years we lived overseas, always ready to listen as I vented frustrations and struggles over both large and small issues (like dealing with the flies—I once killed 33 with one swat of a flyswatter). Mary kept me on track as I wrote about the events involving our mother.

I want to express my sincere appreciation to Kim, Susan, Brenda, Alyssa, Sadie, Caleb, and Shelby, who read chapter drafts and gave their suggestions for improvement and weren't afraid to share when the text was confusing and unclear, and also to Teresa who proofed the entire manuscript, being particularly patient with me regarding the placement of commas.

I'm deeply grateful to our relatives and many friends who have loved and prayed for us and to those who have supported us financially—some for more than four decades! Thank you to our co-workers who lived and worked beside us in Indonesia, enabling us to complete the work God called us all to do. I would like to have written the details about how we came to know and love each of you as the years went by—in fact, I began to do so—but realized that the book was growing too long. I thank you here and trust that as you read, you'll recognize the stories in which you loved on us.

Thank you, Ann, Anton and Joanne, Art and Pam, Bart and Ruth, Ben and Brenda, Bill and Carol, Bill and Janet, Bill and Mary, Bob, Bob and Dallas, Bob and Joan, Bob and Joyce, Bob and Pat, Bryan and Stacey, Bud and Phyllis, Buddy and Betsy, Burt, Bus and Jean, Carolyn, Chris and Terri, Christine, Chuck and Ruth, Corky and Jack, Crist and Norma, Dale and Connie, Dan and Mary, Darryl and Kathy, Darryl and Lois, Dave and Alair, Dave and Jan, Dave and Jean, Dave and Joann, Dave and Paula, Dave and Sandy, Deanna, Dick and Edie, Dick, Dick and Joan, Dick and Kay, Don, Don and Bernice, Don and Dianne, DonnaRae, Doug and Jan, Doug and Marilyn, Dwight and Margaret, Ed and Nitya, Eric and Julie, Evie, Fahlin and Mary, Fay, Gary and Carol, Gary and Mary, George and Evelyn, Glen and Ellen, Gloria and Lowell, Harry and Shirley, Helen, Hogie and Connie, Jan and Gerry, Jan and Lance, Jan, Jerry and Carol, Jim and Glady, Jim and PeggyRose, Jim and Shirley, Jim and Sue, Jim and Vera, Joe and Helen, Joe and Joy, John and Ann, John and Denise, John and Irene, John and Linda, John and Rachel, John and Trudy, Ken and Jody, Ken and Linda, Ken and Marilyn, Ken and Maxine, Ken and Pat, Kevin, Larry and Linda, Leo and Francis, Leta, Lew and Cheryl, Lois, Louis and Connie, Margaret, Marge, Marlin and Karen, Marion, Marvin and Joyce, Mary, Myron and Nancy, Nate and Sheri, Norm and Sheila, Otto and Dolly, Pam, Peggy, Pete and Sheryl, Phil and Barbara, Phil and Dee, Phil and Gayle, Phil and Sandy, Phil and Sheryl, Rachel and John, Ramona, Rex and Judy, Rex and Lisa, Rick and Gayle, Rob, Rod and Char, Ron and Gloria, Ron and Susan, Sally and Bill, Shelly, Sheryl, Ted, Theresa, Tim and Bonnie, Tim and Fran, Tom, Valera, and Wayne.

I thank God for bringing each of you into our lives, enabling us through your love and ministry.

Moving to the Jungle

August and September 1973

Be energetic in your life of salvation, rev-
erent and sensitive before God.
That energy is God's energy, an
energy deep within you,
God Himself willing and working at what
will give Him the most pleasure.
—Philippians 2:13, The Message

I couldn't eat. I couldn't sleep. My body was running in overdrive—my heart pumping with excitement. We were ready. Our 14-month-old son, David, had had his baby shots; the doctor had cleared us to move to a jungle village. We eagerly anticipated flying in a floatplane for the first time, the first leg of our journey into the unknown and the adventure that awaited us.

It was August 27, 1973. We had been living in Jayapura, the capital of Irian Jaya, Indonesia's easternmost province on the island of New Guinea, for the past 11 months. My husband, Peter, had arranged with MAF (Missionary Aviation Fellowship) to take us by single-engine floatplane from Jayapura to the north coast town of Sarmi. After two years of preparation, we were moving to the jungle to live in a village inhabited by 100 of the 1,000 Berik people who lived on the banks of the Tor River, the mouth of which flowed into the Pacific Ocean just east of Sarmi.

On that bright and sunny day, and 90 degrees in the shade as usual, we headed to the dock on Lake Sentani. After our pilot, Bob, loaded all the essential supplies we'd need for the coming month, we boarded the plane.

11

Peter sat next to Bob in the front of the six-seater plane; I sat in the middle row with David on my lap.

Taking off from the lake, we flew west for an hour over jungle so thick that hikers could only walk there if they carried a machete to chop their way through the undergrowth of plants and vines. I recalled World War II stories we had heard about the area when Allied troops had built bridges across the rivers along the north coast of the island. At one point, they had taken 7,000 Japanese prisoners of war on a hike through the jungle below us, right through the area where we would be living.

As Pilot Bob circled the small town of Sarmi and flew over the nearby bay, examining the waves and swells of the sea, we saw people running from town to the beach near our expected landing site on the east side of town. They were waving, and we could tell they were shouting. Making the approach for landing, Bob abruptly decided the waves were too high and the site wasn't suitable. He put the plane into a steep climb. As we flew over to the west side of Sarmi, we were amazed to see the dark-skinned, kinky black-haired people make a U-turn and run down the beach, through town, and to the beach on the other side, where Bob landed the plane on the relatively smooth water.

The people stood on the beach, waving, smiling, and shouting greetings. Among all the strangers, we recognized Sunarjo, a friend we knew from Jayapura, who was also waving a greeting. As the pilot taxied the plane toward the shore, Sunarjo led the pack of barefooted people—men and women, young and old—wading through the breaking waves to meet us. They eagerly helped Pilot Bob unload our goods, each person taking one or two items, then turning and walking effortlessly right back to the beach, as if walking across a soft grassy yard. We took off our tennis shoes and socks, put them in a plastic bag, took a deep breath, and slowly lowered ourselves into the water that alternated between being ankle- or knee-deep as the waves broke around us.

Sunarjo carried David, and Peter guided me as I held my skirt up out of the water and hung tightly onto him. Immediately, we could feel the shells and stones and other debris biting and threatening to cut the soft, tender soles of our feet. The undercurrent of the waves sucked the sand out from under our feet, but Peter managed to keep us upright as we made our way onto the beautiful sandy shore. *Thank You, Lord, for bringing us safely to this place. Thank You for these wonderful people You sent to help.* We thanked Bob for the thrilling ride and said, "Good-bye, Bob. We'll be eager to see you again in a couple of months. God bless as you serve."

"God bless and keep you during these first months out here," he said as he waved good-bye.

The Goat House

Choosing one of several large logs on the beach, we sat down to collect our thoughts, take another deep breath, dry our feet, and put our socks and shoes on. We were amazed as we noticed the people pick everything up and begin the parade into town. Peter and I breathed the ocean air in deeply, looked at each other, and almost in harmony mouthed, "Let's go." I put on my sunglasses, picked up David's diaper bag, opened my umbrella, and with Sunarjo once again carrying David, we were on our way. As we walked along the beach, we heard the plane's engine start. We stopped and stared as the aircraft and Pilot Bob, the only other English-speaking person within 50 miles of us, took off, leaving us to God's care and the amazing months and adventure ahead.

We resumed our long trek to town. After only a few minutes walking on the treeless beach, in the hot equatorial sun—already sweating and breathing more quickly than before—I said, "Peter, I can't keep up with these folks hiking in this soft sand, in this heat."

"That's OK," he answered. "We can slow down. We're such a novelty to them they'll stick with us." Of course, he was right. For them, it was the event of the year to have a large metal bird drop out of the sky, land on the water, and have a white man, woman, and baby get out, saying they would be staying in town while making arrangements to travel by canoe to a village up the Tor River. About 15 more minutes into our walk, I was elated and relieved to see a truck come straight toward us down the beach. The driver had come for us. Praise God! We rode, in relative comfort, on the two-hour drive into Sarmi. The driver brought us to a little kiosk, a small open-air building with tables and chairs, where we could relax and have a tepid drink. No ice here.

A routine part of traveling away from one's usual residence in Indonesia is acquiring a *surat jalan* (letter of permission to travel) from the local police station. Peter knew this was a serious government regulation, so he had taken care of it well in advance of our flight. The officials in Sarmi had been notified of our anticipated visit and had sent a delegation to meet us on the beach. Having arrived in town and seeing that I had a place to rest with David, Sunarjo and the delegation escorted Peter to the police station to officially register our arrival. He then asked for their help in finding a place for us to stay for two or three weeks.

It was necessary for us to remain that long because Dr. Jerry, a mission doctor, would only give me permission to move to the village if we promised to take a minimum of two weeks' rest in Sarmi before making the arduous trip up the river. Why? Because I was pregnant with our second child and had been experiencing all-day morning sickness for the last three months. I was also recovering from a bout with a nasty, debilitating tropical disease, dengue fever. Satan had delayed our move but couldn't stop us. We knew God had a plan for us and was orchestrating our days. We were committed to taking time for the necessary rest.

Crowds of people had stayed with me and David as we waited for Peter to return from the police station. They just watched us and pointed at us, jabbering away in a couple of languages. I understood the Indonesian but didn't recognize the other tongue. Since I knew they had never in their lives seen a little boy whose skin was so white, I surmised much of their chatter was evidence of being quite intrigued by my son.

When Peter and Sunarjo came back to the kiosk to get me and David, they were excited. "Praise God, Sue!" Peter exclaimed. "We won't have to stay in a small multiunit guesthouse. God's given us an abandoned house to stay in. We can have some quiet and privacy." The few people who remained, watching our every move, walked with us about three blocks to the house. By Sarmi standards, the house was quite nice—cement block walls; cement floor, instead of dirt; window openings with shutters; three or four rooms, two with a bedframe and cottonwood-seed mattress; each room with a 20-watt light bulb hanging from the ceiling that worked when the power was on parts of each day; an inside bathroom with an Asian-style "hole in the floor" toilet; a kitchen sink and a one-burner kerosene stove.

The house had some challenges, however, but Peter quickly took care of them. The house was already occupied—by goats!

Peter chased them out and fashioned some lumber to substitute for a door. Sunarjo ran to the market to provide a broom and bucket. We swept and cleaned the place up, checked the stove to be sure it was usable, hung our mosquito net over our bed and David's playpen where he would sleep, and collapsed under the protection of the net for the night, our first overnight on our way to our jungle home.

Satan Tried to Stop Us

Peter's job in Sarmi the next day was to contract with someone who had a large boat with outriggers and a motor to take us up the river to the

Berik village of Tenwer. "Hurrah, Sue! Sunarjo and I found a boat and motor. We can leave as soon as the owner makes one more trip," Peter exclaimed when he came back. However, it wasn't going to be that easy. Satan was not happy to have us traveling across the open ocean and up the Tor River into his previously unchallenged territory. Two days later, we received the news that the boat and motor Peter had arranged to use had encountered huge waves as the motorist was attempting to navigate the dangerous mouth of the river, where the raging water of the Pacific Ocean met the flooding water of the Tor River as it forced its way to mix with the ocean water. The boat and motor were lost at sea. Peter needed to start over and make another contract.

Despite satan's efforts, our delay was a happy time for little David. He loved to walk. Several times each day, he'd come to one of us carrying our flip-flops, umbrella, and sunglasses. He'd tug on our hands, pull us toward the "door," and out we would go. God gave me the energy and stamina, though I was still weak and we walked slowly, while David tried to chase every small creature he saw walking on the path before him. We especially enjoyed being out after 4:00 p.m. when the sun was lower in the sky and it felt relatively cooler. As we walked past villagers' homes, I was delighted to see the multicolored cheery moss roses growing in many yards. I made a mental note to plant some in our village yard when we were settled.

Then satan tried again to delay us. I started spotting, threatening to miscarry the baby. There was no doctor or medical facility available to help us there in Sarmi—as there had been in the US when I had previously miscarried. God's special gift to me was that I had no fear. But when the bleeding increased, I alerted Peter, "You'll need to do what's necessary if I can't function."

"Oh my! Really? What would I have to do?" he asked. I had medication and instructions from the doctor and proceeded to explain what injections he might have to give in case I was unconscious or hemorrhaging. We reviewed sterile procedure, dosage, frequency, and so on. Then we prayed. *Lord, You brought us here. You led us. We're Yours and know You have planned Your best for us and for the people to whom You've called us. We ask for Your healing, but we accept Your plan.*

God answered and gave us that special peace that passes understanding. And He intervened. The next day, the bleeding stopped. Had God been testing us? A couple of days later, God reassured us—I felt our baby kick and move about for the first time. *Thank you, Lord, for keeping us in Your care.*

Satan Doesn't Give Up

Finally, another day, another boat and motor, another motorist. On September 25, one month after we'd arrived in Sarmi, the sun came up at 6:00 a.m.—as it does every day on the equator. Strong, muscular Irianese men, who were skilled and proficient in loading *barang* (baggage), stacked our things safely on the slated wood floor of the boat. Sunarjo assisted as they carefully placed our kerosene refrigerator, lying on its side, balanced on the sides of the craft. We were ready—again. Peter told the motorist about his near-drowning experience in a heavily loaded boat six months before, when he and 12 others had made a survey trip up the Tor. He reminded him of the boat and motor that had been lost the previous month. And Peter made it very clear that the motorist was to unload the boat BEFORE attempting to go through the mouth of the river. The motorist agreed.

Our little family of three and Sunarjo were off, across the open ocean, to our new home in the jungle, where no white woman or child had ever been before. *Father, we praise You. You've brought us several steps closer to the place You've designed for us since eternity past. Today we travel up the river with You. We're in Your keeping.*

It was an interesting "boat." It was actually a large ironwood dugout canoe, with added wood planks to increase the height of the sides and a 50-horsepower motor mounted on the back. The canoe measured about 30 feet long and was three feet wide at the center, with outriggers extending out six feet on either side. There were 10 of us and all our provisions on board. The local authorities deemed that many people were necessary to guide and protect us. After riding the swells and waves straight east along the north coast for several hours, the motorist beached the canoe in a protected bay. David and I got out and enjoyed the walk along the beach as we looked for seashells. Everyone else unloaded and shuttled all the baggage across the sand and a short distance up the river past the river's dangerous mouth where the fast-flowing river water encountered the crashing ocean waves. We held our breath as we watched the motorist bring the empty and much lighter canoe safely through the turbulent, roaring, frothy mouth of the Tor River. We loaded up again and continued on our hazardous journey up the river. The spotter, riding in the bow of the canoe, fulfilled the essential job of alerting the motorist to whirlpools, floating branches and logs, and people floating downriver on homemade rafts. It took us two hours to reach the village of Omte where, although we were totally unexpected, the people welcomed us for the night.

That evening, David got sick for the first time in his life. He started vomiting, then had severe diarrhea, and his temperature rose to 104 degrees. Was satan trying to discourage us? Perhaps get us to turn back? Stay out of his territory? We were up with David all night, sponging him with river water, and praying. *Oh Lord, this child is Yours. You gave him to us to care for. He's in Your hands. Show us what You want us to do.* Again, God gave us His special peace.

In the morning, we continued on our way up the tortuously winding river, brown with silt and mud, as it snaked its way through the jungle. We waved at individuals and even families poling their way down the river on log rafts. As we passed villages, the natives lined the banks of the river to get their first glimpse of the white woman and baby who were entering their domain.

David lay on my lap. Reaching over the side of the canoe with one hand, trusting there wouldn't be a crocodile there looking for lunch, I rinsed each dirty diaper in the river and hung it over the canvas covering that protected us from the blistering hot equatorial sun. I had two dozen cloth diapers with me; I used them all. So I just put the least wet diaper on David when he needed changing—again. I was busy caring for him, trying to keep him hydrated, but had time to wonder at the beauty of the jungle growth sparkling in the sun.

Drums, Bows, and Arrows

Finally, arriving midafternoon in Tenwer, the village that was to be our home for the coming years, the people welcomed us by whooping and hollering, pounding on drums, jumping up and down with their bows and arrows—snapping their bowstrings—and smiling.

Some of the people, especially the children, stood off to the side, peeking out from behind other people or bushes, just staring at our white skin, which was so different than their own dark chocolate skin color. Several of the men—the welcome committee—stood in a group at the edge of the river, patiently waiting for us to get out of our canoe. Our tennis shoes and socks were wet with clumps of gooey mud by the time we made it to the top of the muddy riverbank. The committee motioned for us to follow them and led the way down the path toward the village where I would get my first look at the native-style house that had been prepared for our family.

The crowd of bystanders joined the jubilant parade. As I took in the scene all around me, I rejoiced and thanked God for His goodness and for giving us this highest privilege of following Him to the ends of the earth.

Our First Jungle Home

September 1973

For every house is built by someone,
but the builder of all things is God.
    —Hebrews 3:4, English Standard Version

Several people came right up to us as we walked along the narrow jungle path that day our family arrived for the first time in the village of Tenwer. They were attracted, I assumed, by David's straight very blond hair that seemed to glisten in the sun and was a stark contrast to the villagers' kinky black hair. Many people reached out to pet our arms, smiling as they found that our skin was soft like theirs. With so many new sights, sounds, and smells bombarding my senses, I thought, *I never dreamed I'd wind up in an equatorial jungle where no woman, or baby, from the outside world had ever been before!* I prayed, *I'm in Your hands, Lord. Help me adjust!*

The village chief, Petrus, a slim man of slight stature who had a smile that spread to his whole face, walked beside us. He was friendly and outgoing, and he commanded the respect of all those under his authority. The previous March when Peter visited Tenwer on the survey trip, Petrus had shown him a partially built house and said he could have it for his family. Peter gratefully accepted. He and Sunarjo returned to Tenwer in June and worked hard with the Berik men to prepare the house for me and Baby David. I was eager to put in some womanly finishing touches on the house that would be our home for the next several years.

The House

Except for the size, the fact that our house had walls on all four sides and that we had a front door made of sheets of corrugated aluminum roofing, our house was very similar to Berik houses. Compared to village huts that measured about 400 square feet, our house was quite large—about 1,000 square feet. It included a storeroom and space to do our language and clinic work. Made entirely of local materials, the house stood on ironwood stilts and posts about three feet off the ground.

Ironwood is the wood of choice for the stilts and main support posts of a jungle house because it's so hard that when it dries, it's impossible to pound even a nail into it. Thus, termites can't demolish the house, but they can build their nests, which are also extremely hard. One time, we needed an ax to chop away a termite nest the size of a couple of basketballs.

Since ironwood sinks in water, the men couldn't float the ironwood poles down the river as can be done with other kinds of wood, so strong Berik men had carried the large round ironwood poles from the jungle to the house site. Some of the poles were 12 or more feet long as the roof of our house was perched on the poles that extended three feet over the top of the walls. Peter had heard these strong, muscular men huffing and grunting as they approached the village on the jungle path and dropped their heavy load in what was to be our front yard. Not only were the men strong, they were also skilled; they squared those round poles, down to near-perfect four by fours, using only machetes. I couldn't imagine any of our Western men trying to keep up with them in that extremely difficult work.

Peter told me that the whole time he and Sunarjo were in the village working on the house, they were delighted with how the villagers came each day to help. Even the women and children worked, removing the grass from the yard, leaving just hard-packed dirt, and cleaning up the surroundings. We learned the Berik like a clean dirt yard; it's a deterrent to snakes and other creepy crawly creatures.

Tall (as much as 65 feet) and skinny (only four to six inches in diameter), betel nut trees provide the flooring in Berik homes. The men chopped the tree down and, using an ax, split the bark on each side of the tree as it lay on the ground. It's then possible to "skin" the tree by removing the bark from its trunk. They carried the heavy U-shaped pieces of bark to the building site. Then laying the pieces on the ground, the men split each piece into strips before placing them on the flooring platform of the house. It takes a lot of betel nut trees and work to fill 1,000 square feet. The bark strips in our house were placed to extend 12 or more inches past the outside walls of the house, thus providing a grand ledge for people to stand on and watch what's going on inside. I well remember Sunday afternoons when we would sit in our living room and read a book or do something relaxing. The people would stand on that outer ledge platform, lean on the waist-high wall, and silently just watch us. I wondered what they were thinking, and I often felt like saying, "Is the show interesting?" The strips of bark were securely tied one to another, and to the supporting wood poles underneath, with jungle vine to keep the strips from moving or slipping.

I liked my strips-of-bark floor. It was easy to clean. I just took a bucket of water and, with a dipper, threw the water onto the floor and swept it with a jungle broom. Being amazingly creative, the Berik make their brooms by using jungle vines to tie 100 or more spines from palm branches together. The water and dirt just run through the cracks between the strips of bark and onto the ground under the house. Chickens come running and cackling to see what goodies have fallen to the ground for them. For us though, a bark floor had one drawback. We had folding chairs at our dining table. Before we could sit down, we had to look at the floor and carefully place the chair legs in the center of the bark strips. Neglecting careful placement resulted in the chair falling through the cracks—with me sitting on the floor.

Finally, when building a house, the Berik use the stems of palm fronds to provide both the outer and inner sides of the walls. They remove the leaves from the palm branches and cut the center stems to a uniform length. Since the palm stems are concave, they can be nested and compacted together and placed standing on end. This makes a sturdy and quite pretty brown wall. The young palm leaves are woven together with bamboo and used as shingles to make a rain-proof thatched roof. There are no ceilings in Berik homes.

Our First Night in the Jungle

When I saw our new home for the first time, my heart sang, *Oh Lord, thank You for this wonderful house for us to live in here in the village. Be with us as we learn to fit in. And please heal our little David. Give us wisdom in caring for him now.*

By the time we were able to start getting settled in the house that first day, it was late in the afternoon. It would be dark within the hour. It's amazing living on the equator. Within about 10 minutes every day, the sun would rise at 6:00 a.m. and set at 6:00 p.m. At about 5:55 p.m. on any given day, I used to say, "Peter, it seems that each time I blink my eyes, it gets a little darker!"

That first night in the village, we knew we had to quickly get set up before darkness fell. As Peter took me on a tour of the house, about a dozen Berik followed us from room to room, watching our every move, all the while chattering away to one another. We couldn't understand a word they said.

We set up our Katadyn water filter in the kitchen and filled it with river water so we'd have plenty of safe drinking water in the morning. After unrolling our two-inch foam mattresses, placing them on the bed frames Sunarjo had built, and hanging our mosquito nets, Peter lit a kerosene gas camping lantern. We fixed a light meal on the two-burner kerosene stove we had brought in and ate hungrily after a long and tiring but very exciting day of travel. At last, we grabbed our flashlights to keep them under the net with us all night and fell exhausted into bed.

Yes, satan had tried to discourage us, hoping we would turn back and not enter his domain. But truly, we didn't feel discouraged; turning back never occurred to us. We were on a high with excitement that finally, after two years of preparation, we had arrived. Years later, I said to Peter one day, "Why did we keep going? Were we naïve? Or stupid?" No, the answer is clear. We knew our call. We knew without a shadow of doubt that we were in the center of God's will for us. We knew God was leading.

It was quiet and peaceful all night. We actually enjoyed the sounds of the jungle surrounding us—frogs croaking, cicadas chirping, and people talking around their fires. We slept well. I had had no further difficulties with my pregnancy. Baby David slept all night; his temperature came down, and the vomiting and diarrhea stopped. We woke in the morning at sunrise, giving praise to the Lord who heals.

Little did we know what the people had planned for us two nights later.

Settling in and Surprise Welcome

September 1973

And remember! I will be with you
always, to the end of the age.

—Matthew 28:20,
Holman Christian Standard Bible

As dawn broke that first morning, we were awakened by the village coming alive—roosters crowing, people talking, children playing, babies crying, dogs barking. We quickly crawled out from under the mosquito net and got dressed. The people were alert to our every move, and when they realized we were up, three or four people came right into the house and watched us and followed us around. We had determined that for the first few days, we would not hide our stuff or activities from them—it was best to let them see who we were and how we did things. We had our own personal devotions, prayer time together, and breakfast. *I wonder what they are thinking about our food and books (Bibles) and about seeing us talk quietly with our eyes closed?*

Our priorities for our first three months in the village were to get to know the people, observe their culture and way of life, and start to learn to speak the Berik language. We were ready for the day and ready to get to work. We set out to tour the village together. Our house was across the path from Petrus, the village chief, and his family and was at the far end of the village. Petrus walked with us. We listened to what he said to the people and what they said to him, assuming that they were greeting one another. Or perhaps Petrus was introducing us, saying, "Here they are. Mr. Peter said he would come back and bring his wife and baby son. We're glad he did. Now we need to help them, for they're going to live with us in our village."

Peter had told me about a Berik lady called Mama Lodia. He said she was thin and quite short, standing only about as high as his chest. She was very outgoing and had an ear-to-ear inviting smile. When Peter was leaving Tenwer after his first visit to the village, Mama Lodia was the one who had come up to him and, putting her arms around his waist, had said, "Mr. Peter, you come back here. Bring your wife and baby, and we'll take care of you."

Now, as we toured the village that first day, I was very eager to meet Mama Lodia. I didn't have to wait long; she came running to us and gave me a big hug. She was exactly as I had imagined her, a live wire. She joined us on our village tour and smiled broadly as we tried to repeat short phrases we heard the people say. Not only did we not understand what they were saying, as we heard a long stream of speech; we didn't know where the word breaks were or when a new sentence began. If people didn't laugh when we spoke Berik, we felt elated, thinking, *We must have guessed the meaning of that phrase correctly.* When they laughed, we knew we probably made a mistake and needed to guess again. Learning to speak an unwritten language can be fun, challenging, satisfying, and frustrating all at the same time.

Finishing our walk, we went "home" for lunch and, following equatorial custom, for a nap that is an absolute must when the temperature is about 95 degrees and the humidity runs about 100% daily.

The next day, we were grateful that Peter was able to set up the kerosene refrigerator we had brought to the village. The small freezer was just big enough to hold one ice cube tray, a pound of ground beef, and a couple of ice packs to use for medical emergencies. We were sooo thankful to have cold water to drink and to be able to keep leftovers from our noon meal one day to have for supper the next day.

After another busy and satisfying day, we were once again exhausted. Just before the sun made its rapid descent over the horizon, Peter lit the kerosene pressure lantern; we had supper and looked forward to turning in early.

Surprise

The people—men, women, and children—gave us their official welcome that night. They came to celebrate—by singing and dancing enthusiastically while pounding on drums outside our house—from 7:30 p.m. to 5:30 a.m.! We were thrilled—when it started. Six hours later, we wondered how long they could possibly keep going and how long I would be able to stay awake.

One man brought his BIG homemade one-string stand-up base. Other men brought their drums, made in an hourglass shape, from hollowed-out hardwood and covered on one end with lizard skin. It was like stepping out of this world into a *National Geographic* magazine picture. It was mesmerizing to watch the men pound their drums and set the beat for themselves, the singers, and all the other dancers.

Berik drums are about 28 inches long and are narrower in the center where there's a carved geometrical design. The handle at the center is much like a cup handle through which the men thread a piece of jungle vine. Slipping the vine around his left wrist and holding the drum in the middle with his left hand, each man placed the bottom of the drum between his thighs just above his knees.

We watched the drummers pounding on the lizard skin on top and jumping four to six steps forward, then four to six steps backward, singing all the while. We were amazed at their energy and stamina! Try imitating them—and imagine keeping it up hour after hour.

Baby David slept through it all. Peter and I sat on the wooden steps of our house much of the night, realized we really were actually living in this alien world, and observed as many details as we could as we listened to the "music." We had a small reel-to-reel tape recorder that we had brought with us so we could send tapes to my sister and our parents, thus keeping them informed and involved in our lives. As we recorded that night, we jabbered away to our families, sharing everything we were experiencing.

All of a sudden, I was startled and frightened by a loud bloodcurdling, high-pitched tonal screech. I jumped right off the step where I was sitting. In the dark, I couldn't tell who had emitted such a noise or why. My heart was racing, but as I squinted and peered into the blackness trying to see all those black faces, I finally saw they were smiling, having fun. My heart rate slowed down, and remembering that God had promised to be with us always, I relaxed.

I was certain our parents would be frightened when they heard it, thinking we were in danger for our lives. Not wanting to worry them, I recorded, "Well, that was really something! But you needn't be concerned that the people are about to attack us; they are smiling and friendly. We feel safe and secure here, where God has placed us."

We just couldn't stay up with them all night, so about 3:00 a.m., we went to bed, and in spite of the continued pounding and periodic screeches, we slept a couple of hours. Though their numbers had diminished, we found that some people were still at it when dawn began to break the pitch-black of the night sky.

We knew, from this surprising beginning, that the Berik people were truly happy we had come to live with them, that they would bond with us, and that they were sincere in welcoming us to into their society. And we knew life in our new home would always be an adventure.

A City Girl's Beginnings

1939 to 1946

*Long before He laid down earth's foun-
dations, He had us in mind,
had settled on us as the focus of His love,
to be made whole and holy by His love.*
—Ephesians 1:4, The Message

I never dreamed I'd wind up in the jungles of Indonesian New Guinea—
that faraway, legendary, equatorial land of snow-covered mountain
peaks, malaria-infested swamps, fast-flowing rivers with crocodiles . . . and
headhunters.

You see, I'm a city girl. I was born near Chicago, raised in Minneapolis,
and worked as a stewardess out of San Francisco and New York City. And
God, from eternity past, had a plan for my life, and to this day, He continues to unveil it to me. He is not done with me yet. YIPPEE!

November 16, 1939

With a lusty cry, all seven pounds two ounces of me announced my
arrival in this world in Joliet, Illinois, on November 16, 1939. Also on that
day, the US press announced the arrival of the infamous Al Capone from
Alcatraz prison back into free society. World War II had started 11 weeks
earlier with Nazi Germany's invasion of Poland. The world was in turmoil.
President Franklin D. Roosevelt faced extreme challenges.

By contrast that year, Kate Smith soared to the top of the charts singing Irving Berlin's "God Bless America," the New York World's Fair opened,

Gone with the Wind won the Academy Award, and the first air-conditioned automobile, a Packard, was being exhibited in Chicago, Illinois—just miles from St. Joseph's Hospital in Joliet where my parents, Ed and Lucille Palmer, rejoiced in the arrival of their first baby.

My Dad

My dad, Edgar Eric, was the fourth of five children—Ray, Sarah, Inez, Edgar, and Irving—born to Anton and Jenny Palmer and worked for Land O' Lakes Creameries in Chicago. We lived there for six months, and then he was transferred to Minneapolis where he rose years later to the position of manager of the Poultry and Egg Division. I have happy memories of him bringing new products home for us to test, i.e., boneless turkeys to roast for Thanksgiving. Though there was rationing during those war years, we were always blessed with plenty of eggs, chicken, and butter on the table.

My dad was a golfer, a good golfer. I treasure one of his golf trophies that stands right here on my desk today. He talked about Arnold Palmer so fondly and so often that I was sure he was a relative.

I loved my dad. He taught me to NOT smoke.

"Daddy," I said one day when I was in kindergarten, "teach me how to make smoke rings like you do when you smoke. Pleeeeeaaaaase."

He didn't reprimand me and say, "You can't do that, silly girl." Instead, he said, "OK. But you've got to do it RIGHT. Now watch." He put his cigarette in his mouth and drew in deeply. "You've got to suck real deep and hold the smoke in your mouth. Then you make a circle with your lips." He demonstrated. "Finally, you let out a little puff of smoke . . . a nice ring. You can make lots of rings if each puff is a little one." He demonstrated. I watched, spellbound and excited. "Now you try," he said.

I was thrilled! I took the cigarette, placed it between my lips, and found the smoke made my eyes water. No matter. I sucked in deep. What a surprise! I thought I'd die coughing! Daddy hugged me. When I finally settled down and could breathe again, I looked up at him, and even though I was so young, I understood. I think I knew then that I'd never ever want to touch a cigarette again. In his wisdom that day, I felt his love.

Minneapolis, Minnesota

And I loved living in Minneapolis, the City of Lakes. We lived right across the street from Lake Hiawatha. My mother often took me to the park by the lake where we spent hours in the water in the summertime and ice-skating on the lake in the winter. Every summer during the Minneapolis Aquatennial, we went to many of the lakes to watch swimming, water-skiing, boating, and canoeing competitions.

I also have special memories of Minnesota winters—sledding, tobogganing, making angels in the snow, building snowmen and ice forts, and seeing the ice sculptures at the St. Paul Winter Carnival. Every Christmas, we had a beautiful birch Yule log, with lots of fresh evergreen garland and seven tall, thick red candles on the mantel over the fireplace. I loved staring at the flickering flames in the evening.

My Grandma Sanders

My mother, Lucille Loraine, was the youngest of three children—Raymond Jr., Erwin, and Lucille—who were born to Raymond and Mary Sanders. I never knew my grandpa Sanders; he was a victim of the 1918–1919 flu pandemic, when my mother was three years old. During the summers, I'd visit my grandma Sanders at her home in Chicago. I felt like a big girl when I went to spend time with Grandma because I traveled by train—ALONE. My mom or dad would put me on the train in the care of one of the porters, and Grandma or Uncle Ray would meet me at the Chicago station. Eight hours of fun for me. I well remember those porters. They were friendly, jovial, caring, fun . . . and dark as could be, wearing oh so white uniforms. I felt, and was, safe and secure under their care. They'd take me upstairs in the Vistadome car. Many of the other passengers up there would talk to me and play games with me. The porters would also take me to the dining car to eat. Oh, how my mouth would water when the aroma of all that delicious food—cookies and cakes, chicken and hamburgers—bid me welcome. Money to pay for my meals was in an envelope with my name on it, pinned to the back of my sweater.

Several memories of my visits to Grandma's are still vivid today. Just like I'd seen the elevator girls in the department stores do, I'd go in Grandma's pantry and close the door. Then I'd open it and call out, "Going up! Second floor—women's and children's clothing . . . Good morning. Step right in." Close the door and wait. Open the door. "Second floor. All out. Watch your step!" Sometimes Grandma would come and get in the pantry and "go up" with me and then out on second floor. I loved her for it. She was a good cook, but I didn't like her favorite cooked vegetable. I'd say, "But, Grandma, I don't like 'cookda' carrots."

"You just don't know what's good," she'd respond.

I clearly remember that she had a picture taken of me on my fourth birthday, on the mantel above her fireplace. I was wearing a nurse's uniform. I would longingly stare at that picture and tell everyone who would listen to me, "I'm going to be a nurse when I grow up!" Though I didn't realize or think about it in those days, God had His hand on my life.

Besides dreaming about being a nurse, I'd sit on the piano bench at Grandma's lovely baby grand piano there in her living room and would dream of being able to play beautiful music. My mother had learned to play on that piano. I wanted to be like her.

Every time I was in Chicago, I'd beg whoever would listen to me to take me to see Buckingham Fountain. I was enthralled by the dancing water displaying the ever-changing variety of brilliant colors and the rhythmic splashing of the water by which I hope to be sprayed.

At night, Grandma and I slept together in a BIG bed. At least she slept . . . and snored. But all I had to do was push on her shoulder, and she'd turn over and stop snoring, and I could go back to sleep. One night, I had a dream that I was on a crowded elevator that didn't have any walls. As we went up and up, the people fell off the sides one by one. Suddenly, Grandma was patting me on the head, asking, "Susie, what happened?" I'd fallen out of bed and was sitting on the floor. We laughed, and she held me close as we went back to sleep.

I remember Grandma taking me to see Sonya Henie, three-time Olympic champion, skate in the Ice Follies. And when I was 10 years old, she took me on a tour to Yellowstone Park. It was a bonding time for the two of us, as for ten days, we rode the bus, saw the wonders of God's creation, talked, and ate and slept together. I felt her love. I loved my grandma Sanders.

My Grandma and Grandpa Palmer

And I loved my grandma and grandpa Palmer who were born in Sweden and immigrated to Minnesota as young marrieds. Grandma was a tall, bulky, hardworking, and strong lady who spent hours daily in her vegetable and flower gardens. I especially liked the abundance of lilacs growing in her yard—white, lavender, dark purple, single and double blossoms. I think I got my love of flowers and crawling around in the yard and garden, pulling weeds, from her. Every summer, I'd spend time with her, canning fruits and veggies in her big kitchen. My favorite was the Bing cherries. She had an underground cellar where she stored everything to be eaten throughout the winter. The door to the cellar was outside—just like the one at Dorothy's house in *The Wizard of Oz*. I often asked, "Grandma, can I go down in the cellar and get something for supper tonight?" She always said yes. I'd go outside where the entrance into the cellar was on the ground. I'd lift one of the two big heavy doors and try hard not to let it drop with a crash. I'd struggle to get the other heavy wood door open too and then very carefully go down the ladder into that dark and dank earth cellar. I always brought up a pint jar of those Bing cherries that were on the little shelves right next to the ladder.

Grandpa Palmer was a skilled craftsman, building houses and indoor decorative cabinets. He was well-known in the community. Those were the days, he told me, that written contracts were not necessary. "A man's word, with a handshake, is all that's needed." Oh, for the good old days!

Starting School

School days were happy days. My first memory is of my fifth birthday when I was in kindergarten. Our teacher held me on her lap, and all the kids sang to us, both of us, for it was her birthday too. I felt oh so special, smiling and giggling as the kids turned all their attention on us. Unfortunately, I didn't get to know the kids well, for I was out sick much of the first four months of the school year. My tonsils were continually infected; it was hard for me to eat and swallow. Finally, the doctor said my tonsils had to come out. I remember being in the hospital with a very sore throat after the surgery. The nurses kept after me to swallow sips of water and to suck on ice cubes. I wasn't interested—until they brought me ice cream. I ate all they'd give me. "Neat. Wish we could do that too," my kindergarten classmates enviously commented when I told them about it back in school.

I was a skinny kid. There must have been a lot of skinny kids in the grammar school I attended for first, second, and third grades, for the school principal sent out a notice to all the parents, saying, "Don't send your child to school in the morning unless she or he has eaten a good healthy breakfast."

My mother had been trying to get me to eat more, and now with this ultimatum, she did all she could to get me to fall in line. But I just couldn't force myself. So one day, she kept me home. I cried and cried. And then to my great dismay, an eighth-grade boy arrived at our house. The principal had sent him to bring me to school where she was determined to get me to eat. I was terrified. I remember the boy almost dragging me by the hand. The principal was waiting for me in the kitchen with the biggest breakfast I'd ever seen: scrambled eggs, a slice of sausage, cereal, peaches, toast, orange juice, milk. She set me on a high stool at the counter. "Susan. You'll sit here until you eat everything. You've got to understand that you can't learn if you don't eat." She stood over me like an angry policeman. I was so scared I could hardly move, let alone eat. When I put a bit of food in my mouth, my throat felt like a closed gate, and I started to gag. But she kept me there for what seemed like a couple of hours and then finally sent me home, with that terrible memory indelibly etched in my brain.

My Sister, Mary

The major hallelujah event of the first seven years of my life was the birth of my baby sister, Mary. My mother attended a liturgical church; I always went with her. Every week at church, and often during the week, I prayed for God to give me a baby sister or baby brother. When my mother told me my prayer was being answered, my excitement knew no bounds. As my seventh birthday approached, and Mother was now nine months pregnant, I thought maybe I'd get the best gift ever—that "my" baby would be born in time for my birthday.

Mother made plans for a big party for me—20 seven-year-olds were invited. She arranged for a college girl to come to help her during the festivities, and preparations moved along. I helped Mother bake a cake shaped like a lamb. It was covered with white icing and shredded coconut and looked ever so real. On the afternoon of November 16, that little lamb sat in all its splendor on the dining room table for all to see. And the children began to arrive. The college girl never showed up.

But Mother did a great job, keeping control of all of us through all the games, opening of gifts, and serving the cake and ice cream. I realize now that she must have been exhausted at the end of the day. Mary was born three days later, on November 19, 1946. She was, and still is, one of God's wonderful gifts to me.

Happy Days Shattered

1946 to 1956

*Friends, when life gets really difficult,
don't jump to the conclusion
that God isn't on the job.*
—1 Peter 4:12, The Message

"We're moving," my mother said. "We've been renting the first floor of the house we've been living in. Now we'll have our own home, and you'll have your very own room, and Mary will have hers." It was 1948, the summer after I finished third grade. I was a Brownie; I liked working on and earning my badges. I liked my school and all I was learning. At first, I didn't like the idea of moving. But after I saw the house, on Colfax Avenue in the Minnehaha Parkway area of south Minneapolis, I changed my mind.

The house had a large backyard. Mother encouraged me, "In the winter, we'll shovel the snow off the grass, connect a hose to the basement laundry tub, run it outside through the basement window, and flood the backyard . . . We'll have our own private ice-skating rink. Wouldn't that be special?"

It sounded good to me, and since I really enjoy cleaning and organizing things, I jumped right in and helped pack boxes, clean the new house, and find a place for everything as we unpacked. The house was almost three times the size of our rental; Mother redecorated every room. My own special private abode was at the top of the stairs on the second floor. Happy and continually smiling, I planned my own décor. I chose bright, clean white to paint the doors, windows and doorframes, radiator and its wooden cover, and the wainscoting.

My gorgeous wallpaper, with soft sky-blue background and vines of small red roses, was my constant delight. The paper was hung so the vines climbed up the wall from the wainscoting behind the headboard of my bed, across the ceiling, and down to the wainscoting on the opposite wall. I remember lying in bed, counting the roses passing overhead. Every spring, I lay on my right side to look out my window and watch mama robin build her nest, feed her babies, and gently nudge them out of their comfy home a couple of weeks later. I was happy and content in my room, with my own desk, a set of the *World Book Encyclopedia*, and my own closet—which amazed me because it had a light inside. I felt special—none of my friends had a closet big enough to walk into, thus needing a light.

Many happy activities consumed my out-of-school hours during those years when I was nine to 13 years old, in grades four through eight: studying piano and playing in recitals, taking ice-skating lessons, and spending summers at camp in northern Minnesota. One summer, I was at camp a full nine weeks; I stayed for every camp session as other campers came and went. I especially remember that summer because Mother sent me "goody boxes" in the mail—a whole shoebox full of treats. Few campers received more than letters; I felt special that I had things to share with the others.

It was at camp that I learned to ride a horse. One summer, my riding counselor invited me to ride one of her horses in competition at the Minnesota State Fair at the end of August. What a challenge. I didn't place but sure had a good time, even sleeping three nights in the horse barn on the fair grounds.

In the winter, I could practice my ice-skating spins and figure eights right at home after school. For three years, Mother even enrolled Mary and me in a figure skating club. We met and got to know—and envy—the older really skilled girls as they jumped and spun round and round, faster and faster. In my heart, I dreamed of my future. *Oh, I wish I could do something really well, like they can. I wonder what I'll be when I grow up.*

Suddenly, Life Shattered

I was 11 years old, in the sixth grade at a parochial school. One of my school friends' sister was in a play at her college, and her family invited me to go with them. *A chance to be at a college?* I thought. "Yes," I said. "I'd love to go."

When they brought me home that evening, my mother said, "Your dad's gone. He won't be back."

I was shocked and crushed. Time stood still for me; I just stood there looking at her. Her face spoke of the distress and anger she was feeling inside. "He's taken all his clothes and the car. We're on our own now."

I suppose I shouldn't have been so surprised because for the previous two years, I had often heard them arguing and shouting at each other. But I never dreamed they wouldn't work it out. I ran upstairs and looked in the closet in my parents' bedroom. Yes, all my dad's stuff was gone. I cried and cried, and I cried myself to sleep that night. *All my friends have a dad. Now they won't like me. I won't fit in. What'll I do if the kids won't talk to me anymore? What'll I do without a dad?*

In the weeks that followed, the lawyers worked out the details for the divorce. I didn't tell anyone my dad didn't sleep at home anymore. I felt ashamed and inferior. When I found out there was one other girl whose dad had also left her and her mom, I felt so sorry for her. I wanted to be friends with her, but I was determined that no one would find out about me. I didn't want them to know I didn't measure up to their standards anymore.

Throughout sixth and seventh grades, I was active in the Girl Scouts. We girls took turns bringing a snack to enjoy during our meetings. When it was my turn, I asked my dad, who worked for Land O' Lakes Creameries, if he would provide ice cream for us. He was happy to do so. He would deliver the ice cream just before our meeting started, right after school. He'd pull up in his car, right in front of the school's main door, and I'd run down the steps and out to the car—in front of all the kids coming out of school to go home. They'd see me with my dad. It felt so good. It was the perfect cover-up; the kids thought I had a dad just like everyone else.

My Best Friend

Bernadette knew how hard it was for me; she was my best friend. We had gone to first through third grades together, during those years when I lived in the Lake Hiawatha house. I loved being at Bernadette's house, with her parents and two sisters and their baby brother. Bernadette's dad worked hard for the railroad, and her mom cooked great meals. I remember the titillating aromas that came out of her kitchen as she prepared a large evening meal for her family each afternoon. The whole family always welcomed me, even though every time I arrived at their house, I'd run into the kitchen, find the dessert that was set aside and covered, and beg for a taste in advance. I felt like I belonged, never rejected. Though I didn't realize it

35

at the time, God had provided for me. Mary and I still went to church with our mother each week, but I didn't think about Him being interested in my ordinary daily life.

Sometimes I got to stay overnight at Bernadette's house. It had two bedrooms on the main level, and we girls shared the big upstairs room, with one big double bed. The four of us girls snuggled together and slept well. I belonged. I was accepted. I fit in. When my family moved to the Colfax house, I was comforted by the fact that my mother and Bernadette's mother were good friends; Bernadette and I were able to continue to spend time together. As life's challenges became more difficult for my mother, Bernadette's mother became a second mother to me. Though I didn't know it, God knew I would need another mother. And He provided for me.

I moved on to high school. Socially, I was very shy and not at all athletic. That period of time, when I was 14 to 16 years old, in ninth through eleventh grades, life became more and more unstable for me.

Even later, in my adult life, it was very difficult to think about or to share my memories of those years. I responded to the pain by seeking God's comfort. *If I can do everything He wants, if I can be good, maybe He'll love me.* I went to church every morning and tried desperately not to disappoint those in authority over me. I wanted, and needed, their acceptance and approval. I withdrew into myself, became shy, just wanting to stay in the background. I dated only rarely. *Who'd want me? I've nothing interesting to talk about. I'm not good at sports. Not skilled. Not pretty.* I was afraid of being hurt, afraid of being rejected.

Evie Loved on Me

The final divorce settlement stipulated that Dad had custody of Mary and me every Sunday afternoon from 12:30 p.m. to 7:30 p.m. Because he wasn't permitted on the property, Dad just pulled his car up in front of the Colfax house; Mary and I would run out to the car. We looked forward to the special activities he planned to do with us—swimming, going to the park, going for picnics, and playing games.

Then Dad married again; Evie was so kind to me. I was confused. I tried so hard not to like her, for I had been taught that divorce and remarriage were wrong. Deep down, I thought I needed to reject her, not talk to her, not thank her, and not respond to her kindness. When I enjoyed our times together, and the good food and treats she made for us, I felt guilty. To counteract my guilt, I tried to be mean to her. But Evie accepted me, spoke gently to me, encouraged me, and tried to draw me out of my shell. The conflict within me was strong and deep, sometimes overpowering. But I couldn't deny or hide my excitement in September 1955 when my little baby brother, Jim, was born.

God Helped Mother Adjust

I didn't realize it as I was living through it, but God was at work. He enabled me to adjust to my new life. Slowly, my inner conflicts subsided. God kept me from breaking down, from giving up. I can see now that God used the trials to strengthen me. He implanted in me the desire to succeed, to do well in my studies, to be "good." He was preparing me for the plan He had had for me from eternity past.

Mother and I worked well together. I learned to care for our home, and she taught me how to can our fruit and vegetables. I cleaned, helped with the laundry, and shoveled snow. I loved working outside in the garden and especially liked our hedge of lavender and purple lilacs. Each spring, I tried to keep a fragrant lilac bouquet in the house.

And God helped Mother adjust. He motivated her and enabled her to supplement the alimony she received. She went back to school, received high grades, and completed all the requirements to run a nursery school in our home. She named it Kiddie Kollege. Our upstairs master bedroom became the "quiet" play and activity room. Mother transformed the largest section of the basement into two areas: one for "rough" play and finger painting, the other for daily opening activities.

I enjoyed being there and helping whenever I had a day off from school. Even in the dead of the cold, cold winters, the 20 children—dressed in snowsuits, boots, scarves, and mittens—came down the stairs from the outside and found their own little bench and clothes hook on the wall above. Each child learned to take off all their outdoor wear, hang up their snowsuits, and put their boots in the cubicle under their seat on the bench.

Then, sitting down, with hands folded, they waited for my mother, or the other teacher who worked with her, to call the roll. She sang each child's name—the second syllable five steps higher on the scale than the first syllable. "Peg-gy," she sang.

Peggy answered with the same tune, "Here I—am."

And so it went for each child. I felt so proud of my mother and how she was overcoming, of how she related to the children and of how they responded to her. Everything she prepared for the children was attractive to them, especially the giraffe slide in the backyard—the kids slid right down his neck.

To me, Mother's most amazing accomplishment each day was picking up all those kids in the morning and taking them home at noon—in our station wagon. Imagine—20 four-year-olds in one vehicle. Mother had benches made for the middle and back seats. So 10 kids were in the back—five on the seat and five on the bench; eight kids were in the middle, and two were in front. Mother led them in singing as she drove from house to house.

Mother sought other at-home jobs, such as pouring paint, to help make ends meet. A hobby store hired her to prepare small two-ounce jars of paint to sell in their store. Mother brought home gallon jugs of various colors of paint and boxes and boxes full of empty two-ounce jars. Sometimes in the evenings, Mary and I would help. We'd take the jars out of the box, take the lids off, and line the jars up on the edge of the counter in the laundry room. Mother would fill a serving pitcher that had a metal cover with a trigger-controlled spout. She became very proficient in dispensing just two ounces of paint into each jar. Mary and I would follow along behind her, screwing on the lids and applying the appropriate labels. We put the filled bottles back into the box and started emptying the next box. Fun—for a while. Tiresome. Sometimes sloppy. Satisfying to be involved and to know we were useful and helping.

More Rough Times Hit

In spite of all Mother's success in overcoming the challenges she faced, more and more distressing events occurred, and she became clinically depressed. She worked hard during the days but was unable to sleep at night. Her doctor prescribed sleeping pills and then "pepper-upper" pills, which helped for a while. But her condition worsened. When I was unable to do enough to help or to please her, she began to lash out at me, demanding more and accusing me of not being a good daughter. Her depression increased to the point of suicidal thoughts. Her anger with me increased to the point that one Sunday, when Mary and I were getting ready to go with Dad, she yelled, "You wait! I'll take all those pills while you're gone. When you come home, you'll find me dead on the floor! And you'll know it's all your fault!"

What should I do? I screamed deep inside. My heart beat hard and fast in my chest; my eyes filled with fear and tears.

"Go on! Get out of here," she shouted.

And so we went with Dad, as usual, that day. Totally afraid to tell him or Evie what was going on, I pretended everything was OK for the full seven hours we were gone from home, fearing what I'd find upon our return.

To my great relief, when we got home, Mother was alive, but she just glared at me. I went quietly to my room, and she stayed by herself. Then that week, I figured out what I could do in the future. I knew where she kept her pills—by now, there were several bottles with various contents—so I decided the next time she threatened suicide, I would slip upstairs just before we left the house, get the pills, and take them with me for our afternoon time with Dad and Evie. I planned to put them back when Mary and I got home in the evening. Almost every week for some months, Mother would threaten, and I'd take the pills with me. Evidently, she never intended to actually swallow them; she never told me she'd found them missing. I didn't know or understand all that was happening in her life or the mental stress she was suffering. The demonlike thoughts that plagued Mother became more intense. Pressure was building, like the rumblings in a volcano before it explodes.

Excruciating

The most excruciating experience of my life was the day Mother took me to a school for wayward girls. I was 12 years old. Mother calmly told me, "You're bad. That's what's wrong with you. I'm going to put you in a school for bad girls. They'll teach you to behave, teach you to respect your mother." I begged her not to do it. But she arranged for someone to care for Mary, packed a suitcase for me, put it in the car, and told me to get in.

I cried and begged during the whole hour and a half drive to the school, south of Minneapolis. "Please don't put me away! Please don't leave me! I'll be good, I promise. I'll do everything you want. Please keep me." My tears were to no avail.

As we approached the school, I saw the beautiful stone buildings set on the hill above us. I continued to cry. Mother drove up the winding tree-lined drive and parked. She took my suitcase out of the car and grabbed my hand, taking me up the stairs and through the big double doors of the main building of the school. Inside, in the reception room, I saw some chairs under a window in a little alcove on the far side of the room; I quickly went over there to sit, hoping to be invisible. Mother told the receptionist who we were and also came to sit in the alcove to wait. I continued to beg and sob. It seemed to me the worst thing that could ever happen to me was, in fact, happening. My dad had left me. Now, if I had no mom either, what would I do? I felt rejected, about to be abandoned. I was so afraid. I looked into her eyes, took her arm, and said, "Please don't leave me. I'll be good. I promise." It seemed she was wavering just a little.

The head mistress came into the room. "OK, Mrs. Palmer. I'll take her now," she said. I became hysterical. I begged the woman, "Pleeeease. Give me just five more minutes with my mom. Pleeeease! Just five more minutes."

The woman conceded. For the full five minutes, I continued to cry and beg my mother to keep me. I promised over and over to be good. Mother gave in. And took me home. I was exhausted. I fell asleep in the car on the way.

For decades after that, I was unable to talk about what had happened, unable to tell anyone. The hurt and emotion were too deep, too ingrained. The lump in my throat and watery eyes would come too quickly.

A New Horizon

Amazingly, Mother seemed to heal from her distress; her accusations decreased, and we settled into somewhat of a truce. And then, in the spring of 1956, events in Mother's life became even more severe. Her brother, my uncle Ray, came from California to see us and to help. It had become necessary for Mother to leave the state of Minnesota. Uncle Ray urged her to move to California to make a new start, to live near him and his wife, my aunt Carol. Uncle Ray assisted in all that was necessary, selling the house, helping to dispose of many items, and arranging for a moving company to pack and move our furniture.

In July, Mother fixed up the station wagon, with a mattress in the back where Mary and I could sleep or sit and play games while she drove. We loaded our suitcases and a box of snacks and set out for the Golden State of California, for new horizons and new beginnings.

A New Beginning
Comes to a Sudden End

1956 to 1958

I have loved you with an everlasting love.
—Jeremiah 31:3b, English Standard Version

Exciting California

Completing our cross-country trip, Mary and I squealed in delight with our first view of the waves of the mighty Pacific Ocean breaking onto the wide sandy beaches of Los Angeles. We were eager to run across the beach, straight into the water and those waves. "All in good time," Mother said. "First, we need to get over to Uncle Ray and Aunt Carol's home and let them know we arrived safely. Also, I need a little break after this long drive."

Uncle Ray and Aunt Carol received us into their lovely home in Pacific Palisades, where we stayed while orienting to beauty we hadn't seen before. A variety of palm trees—some short and squatty reminding me of big pineapples, some tall and skinny like two-story telephone poles. A wild abundance of flowers with exotic shapes and colors and names too long for me to pronounce and remember. A wonderful climate, just perfect for running on the beach and trying to learn to body surf in the waves. When we'd go out for a drive, I stared in wonder when Uncle Ray pointed out movie stars' homes.

Mother set about finding her own home for us. Being a buyers' market, she quickly found a house; we settled in, and Mary and I got registered in our new schools. Mary's school was within walking distance of our house, and the bus stop for my new high school was nearby. I remember sitting in homeroom one day shortly after school started and doing a double take when I looked at one of my new classmates. I said to the girl next to me, "That girl over there looks like someone I saw on the *Mickey Mouse Club* TV show last night."

"It is," she responded. "That's Diane Lennon. She and her sisters sing and perform together. Larry Welk, one of our other classmates, got his dad, Lawrence Welk, to give them an audition. I think they're going to start singing on his show too. They're really good." Later, I learned that the youngest Lennon sister, Janet, was the same age as my sister Mary. Somehow that thought provided a special connection between me and Mary; I wanted, needed, and cherished my connections with her.

Being in the same class with Diane—we called her "DeeDee"—made California seem like an adventure land, way out of my league. I had become extremely shy; one teacher commented that I acted like I was afraid of my own shadow. But I was content to stay in the background and just observe all my new experiences. I studied hard, and though I had good grades in all classes, I found I was not interested or skilled in the arts—English, composition, literature. But I was fascinated by and excelled in the sciences, like chemistry and biology—which were great preparation for a nursing career.

After high school graduation in 1957, I applied to two nursing schools, a four-year credit program and a three-year hospital program. In the end, when I learned that I would be working in the hospital with patients within three months of the start of school, I chose the hospital program. The four-year program required two years of classwork before beginning clinical work. Even though at the time I wasn't seeking God's will in such choices, years later, I learned God's wisdom in leading me in this way.

Confused, Accepted, and Rejected

Mother's periods of depression and anger were cyclic. At times, she appeared happy, seemed to be coping well with her new life in California, and was kind and encouraging to me. One afternoon, she was in the car with me when I was driving home from visiting friends. I was stopped at a stoplight at the top of a hill when our car was suddenly hit from behind. As we got out of our car, the man who hit us came forward to admit his wrongdoing. Nevertheless, I was scared, shaking and worried. Mother was supportive and comforted me as she taught me to get the man's name and insurance company. After the police left, Mother said to me, "OK. Now you drive home."

"I can't. I'm too upset."

"It's OK. You can do it." In this, Mother was kind, loving, and wise. She knew that if I didn't drive again right away, I would have a major fear to overcome in the coming weeks. I thanked her for having faith in me.

At other times, Mother made unwise choices. As her problems became increasingly complex, she again became combative and antagonistic, turned to drinking in excess, and then shifted to agnostic and even atheistic thinking.

As I attended nursing classes and began to work in the hospital, relating to and caring for people who were hurting and facing crises in their lives, I felt planted in the place of my destiny—and hopeful for the future. A fellow I had met during my last semester in high school added to my sense of peace and hope, a feeling of being accepted. Alan was a medical student who worked in the hobby shop where I went to buy parts for my senior science project, displaying the action of insulin in the body. At first, Mother liked Alan, and though she wasn't going to church, she was happy that I began to attend church with him. She welcomed him to our home, encouraged us when we built my wooden project display in the backyard, and invited him to eat with us. After I started nursing school, Mother was pleased when Alan took me to the university to learn about his lab research project. She was in tune with my desire to go into the medical field. When I was at school during the week, my feelings of acceptance were solid. But then, without warning, she began to complain about and criticize Alan. The emotions I felt at school were in direct contrast to what I felt when at home on my days off. "I know you two are up to no good," she fanaticized. She started to read my mail. I was deeply offended by this and felt angry. I hid my mail. I felt like I was walking on eggs, not knowing when something unpleasant would happen.

And then, once again, Mother began to talk about my dad. "Your dad doesn't love you. I know he'll quit sending money. Then what will we do?" It seemed she irrationally jumped from one topic of intimidation to another, without basis or connection between the issues.

I was confused and disturbed. I desperately longed for my mother's approval and acceptance. When I didn't get it, I searched for a way to be close to God. Through my own efforts, I worked hard to be good enough for Him to love and accept me. But I didn't understand God's way. I didn't have a firm foundation.

Though my parents, grandparents, aunts, and uncles had taught me good guidelines and spiritual rules for life, they didn't include teaching me to know Jesus in a personal way. Dad once said to me, "Sue, my mother stuffed enough religion down my throat by the time I was 10 to last me a lifetime."

That first year in nursing school while taking a course in medical ethics, I began to question what I had been taught in a liturgical church; I found that I didn't have a sustaining faith in God. In primary and secondary school, I knew and studied ABOUT Jesus. I had prayed to Him and thanked Him for my sister Mary. But I didn't know Him personally. When I found I couldn't agree with the principles I was taught in the ethics course, I stopped following religious practices altogether, and during the next eight years, I wandered and drifted away from God. *If those principles are what God wants, I can't follow Him. I used to believe all that religious stuff. Not anymore. Too restrictive for me.*

But God had plans for me. He had loved me with an everlasting love. From eternity past, He planned that He would call me to Himself. Though I didn't realize it during those erratic high school years and my first year in nursing, He was the "Hound of Heaven" after me.

Devastated

After dating about a year, Alan proposed to me. I accepted and proudly displayed a small diamond ring on my left hand. Mother had liked him—at first. But when her drinking increased and her emotional struggles deepened, she began to falsely accuse us of improper behavior. I was crushed. Though I tried and tried to please her—taking on all responsibilities for shopping, laundry, cleaning, and, when I was at home, cooking—I couldn't measure up.

The speed with which her attitudes changed and the extremes of her angry statements were bewildering. I was devastated when she said, "We'd be better off without you around here! Don't bother to come home again."

My heart skipped a beat, felt like it would stop, and then began to beat faster and faster. I felt totally rejected. I cried. I stared at my mother in disbelief. She just walked away.

I called Alan and told him what had happened; we met and talked through this heartbreaking situation. What could I do? I couldn't live full-time at the school. I was only 17—would turn 18 in November—but didn't yet have a marketable skill, so couldn't afford my own room and board. As heart-wrenching as it would be for both of us, the only viable solution we could see was for me to return to Minnesota to live with Dad and Evie.

That very afternoon, I called Dad. "May I come," I sobbed, "and live with you?"

"Give me a couple of days to check with the lawyers," he said. "I think they'll be able to transfer legal guardianship from your mother to me, but we should be sure before you leave California. I'll get back to you."

I cried. Tears of relief. Tears of feeling alone in life. Tears of hope. Tears of feeling unloved. Tears of feeling loved. Tears of rejection. Tears of loss. Tears of hope. For the next 24 hours, it seemed that I held my breath waiting for Dad's call.

The phone rang the next day. "All the legal arrangements are in place," Dad said. "It's OK for you to come to live with me and Evie and Jim."

I cried tears of gladness. "Oh, thank you. Thank you! How should I get there?" Dad and I talked it over. Plane? Bus? Train? We decided that traveling by train would be the safest and most economical.

Alan helped me consider the train schedules, routes, and number of stops. I bought my ticket, planning my departure for two days later. Alan said he'd take me to the depot.

I told Mother my plans. She was furious. "You can't do that! He can't do that! If you leave this house with him, I'll have him arrested for kidnapping!" She left me alone in my room.

I packed a suitcase, carefully choosing what to take; I had to leave most of my things behind, including my collection of Storybook Dolls, my baby grand piano, my set of *World Book Encyclopedia*, most of my clothes. I went to bed but didn't sleep much that night, half expecting the police to come to our house. The next day, Alan came for me. I tried to remain calm as I said good-bye to Mother. But inside, my stomach was churning; by the time he arrived, I'd already been to the bathroom twice. I couldn't eat. My heart was beating at least double time. I was shaking. Alan spoke to Mother quietly and calmly and said good-bye. "You'll never get by with kidnapping!" she said, glaring at us.

Alan picked up my suitcase. And we left. There were no police at the house. All the way to the train depot, I watched out the side and back windows of the car, listening for police sirens. None came.

At the depot, Alan and I said a tearful good-bye. We promised to write regularly and talk on the phone frequently.

I boarded the train, took a deep breath, and turned my mind to a new life in Minneapolis.

A Nurse, At Last!

1958 to 1964

The LORD will work out His plans for my life.
—Psalm 138:8a, New Living Translation

Life in Minnesota

As the train clacked and swayed rhythmically along the tracks running from Los Angeles to Minneapolis, I sat weak with exhaustion and numb with grief, staring out the window, watching in a daze as the Arizona dessert, Colorado mountains, Nebraska plains, Iowa cornfields, and finally Minnesota farmlands passed by. I wasn't hungry, but I did sleep on and off. The trip was uneventful—no police stopped my journey. Though I didn't realize it at the time, decades later, I understand that it was God's grace that kept me safe and, as I got closer to Minneapolis, at peace with thoughts of another new beginning.

Dad picked me up at the train depot and took me home. The second floor of Dad and Evie's home was just one large carpeted wood-paneled room. They gave me that room to be my own private haven. I felt cozy, snug—and safe—there with my own bed, nightstand, lounge chair, lamp, and desk. Three-year-old Jim's room was on the first floor, across the hall from Dad and Evie. They received me with open arms; I felt their compassion and understanding. Evie was there for me when my mother rejected me. Despite all I'd been through with Mother, I felt compelled to immediately move forward and continue pursuing my dream and goal to be a nurse. Looking back, I now believe it was God's grace that kept me from depression and from turning in the wrong direction.

I called Dad's sister, Aunt Inez, who was a nurse. "Aunt Inez," I asked, "which nursing school here in Minneapolis would be the best for me?"

"Go to my school, Susie." She always called me that. "It's a really good school, and I'd be so pleased if you went there too."

And so I chose St. Barnabas Hospital School of Nursing. I applied and was grateful to be accepted and know that, since "St. B" was also a three-year program with an almost identical curriculum to my Los Angeles school, they would accept my transcripts. Classes started one week later. I lived in the dorm during the week and spent my weekends at home throughout my final two years of nurses training. Since St. B was part of a trischool program, student nurses from all three schools attended class together, rotating to a different school each quarter. To my delight, we were in the hospital every day working with patients. We spent about three months emphasizing each discipline—medical, surgical, obstetrics, pediatrics, orthopedics, and so on.

Every two or three days, Alan and I called each other. I believe he was truly happy for the stability I now had. He was attentive in listening to me share all my new hospital experiences. We wrote a couple of times a week, but each of us became busier and busier with our studies. And then just before Christmas, Alan wrote to say it wasn't going to work out for us. He broke off our engagement but said I could keep the ring. I felt hurt and once again rejected, but deep down, I knew it was for the best. There was no way for us to connect face-to-face again. I mailed the ring back to him. Dad and Evie were there for me to help gain a firm perspective. Evie became a mother to me. I know now that God was orchestrating my life and that He provided for me, according to His plan.

I slowly healed from the trauma of leaving California in such an emotional upheaval and of breaking up with Alan. I began to seek out new friends. One of my classmates was an outdoor enthusiast. She had signed up, with a group of college kids from her church, to go on a 10-day canoeing and camping trip in the Boundary Waters Canoe Area Wilderness, in the Superior National Forest in northeastern Minnesota. She invited me to join them. I was so pleased to be accepted and included. I decided to go. The trip was challenging for me as I'd never been hiking before. But I could swim and help cook. I thanked the fellows for portaging the canoes for us as we transferred between the lakes. The beauty of that pristine country was awesome. I was intrigued by the delicacy of the Lady Slipper, Minnesota's state flower. Every morning, the clear mirror-smooth lakes reflected the pinks, yellows, and golds of sunrise; we saw a double image, in sky and lake. It was quiet, but for the sounds of birds calling to one another and frogs "singing" at bedtime. We carried our food and sleeping bags and tents and dug our own outhouse holes. We paddled our canoes for hours each day, soaking in the sun's warmth, and then enjoyed going overboard into the cold northern waters at day's end. That summer of 1959 was a time of healing and fellowship for me.

There IS a God!

I'll never ever forget the first time I witnessed the birth of a baby. During the previous year, though I had basically disconnected myself from God, I hadn't become an atheist. I still believed God existed, but I didn't pay any attention to Him. I remember being in the delivery room one morning, shortly after our introductory obstetrics class.

There was one person, a woman with a very big abdomen, lying on the delivery table. In wonderment, I watched as her baby was born.

The magnitude of what I had just witnessed hit me like a bolt of lightning. Now there were two individual persons, where before there had been just one. Both were crying with the joy of life.

I experienced an actual thrill in my heart. *There IS a God! He's the Creator. A worker of miracles.* Just thinking of it now as I type, my eyes are blurry with tears. I didn't pray or speak to Him that day. But I was changed in the depths of my being to know without a doubt that God exists. Dear reader, I pray that you too KNOW our Creator.

Admitted to the State Mental Hospital

My last three-month rotation in nursing school was in a northern Minnesota state mental hospital studying psychiatric nursing. It was there that I realized I had truly been accepted by my classmates as one of them; I was elected class president. I enjoyed the classes, but it was particularly challenging for me to assist with patients being treated by electroconvulsive therapy for mental illness, which was given at that time without anesthesia. But I accepted what I was taught as the best means of helping those who were in extreme need.

Orange juice. I loved it. Every morning for years, including my years in nursing school, I looked forward to and drank a big glass of orange juice for breakfast. All my classmates, who spent that summer with me working in the state hospital, knew this. One morning as I went through the cafeteria line, I wasn't hungry, and I didn't pick up a glass of orange juice. "What's the matter with you?" my friends asked.

"I don't know, but I don't feel good."

Feeling nauseous, I went back to my room and soon was curled up with abdominal pain. My roommate called the school nurse to come and see me. After checking my belly, she became alarmed and admitted me to the hospital. In the years since then, I've had fun telling people that I was once a patient in a mental hospital. But it was no fun that day. My white blood count shot up way above normal, and I began to have severe pain in the right lower quadrant of my abdomen. It was an emergency situation— the doctors knocked me out with pain relievers and sedation by injection. Since the hospital was not equipped to handle major surgery, arrangements were made to send me by ambulance to Minneapolis where the operation would be performed at my home hospital.

I was lying on a stretcher in the back of a vehicle when the sedation began to wear off. I was feeling no pain; instead, I was feeling silly and definitely not my normal quiet self. I clearly remember propping myself up on my right elbow, smiling, waving, and making faces at passengers in passing cars. I was confused by the strange looks they gave me.

Arriving at the hospital in Minneapolis, I was taken immediately to the operating room. The doctors told me later that I got there just in time; my appendix had been ripe, ready to burst. When one of the nurses, who had made the trip to Minneapolis with me, came to visit me, I told her about the people in the cars who didn't smile back at me.

"Didn't you know," she said, "that you were in an ambulance with big letters 'Moose Lake State Hospital' painted on the side?"

"Oh my! I didn't know. Whatever were they thinking was wrong with me?" We shared a good laugh.

When my rotation in psychiatric nursing came to an end just two weeks later, I had completed all the requirements to become a Registered Nurse. I sincerely hoped Dad and Evie realized how deeply grateful I was for their generosity in putting me through nursing school.

All 23 of us in my nursing class, the class of 1960, looked beautiful in our white uniforms and caps, wearing corsages of red roses, as we came in to the auditorium for graduation exercises. My dream had come true; I was a nurse, at last. God had brought to pass one of the major plans He had for my life.

Flying

St. Barnabas Hospital offered nursing positions to all of us. I accepted a job as a staff nurse on a medical floor. At one point, I was asked to be a private duty nurse for a severely burned man. I found this to be an especially meaningful service, so I often volunteered to be available. My starting salary was $295.00 a month—until my state board exam results came back; then I received $315.00 a month. Yippee! I rented a small one-bedroom apartment and bought a $600.00 used car. I rejoiced. I was on my own, self-sufficient.

Just six months later, I surprised my family and friends. In fact, I surprised myself. I saw an ad in the newspaper saying that a recruiter for in-flight service personnel, for United Airlines, would be in town over the weekend. A number was given to call for an interview. I read the ad over and over and was bitten by a wanderlust bug. I decided I wanted to travel. I wanted to fly. I called, was interviewed, and was amazed that I was accepted. In April 1961, I quit my nursing job and flew to Cheyenne, Wyoming, to take a five-week stewardess training course.

We lived at the Cheyenne airport, on the second floor of an airplane hangar. In addition to classroom time, which included social skills and application of our makeup, we became proficient in all our passenger service duties by waiting on our instructors as they sat in airplane seats, in aircraft mock-ups. Taking tickets. Making announcements. Serving food. Helping mothers with babies. Calming frightened passengers.

Regarding emergency procedures, we practiced everything, except evacuating a plane ditched in a lake in real flying aircraft. We learned to serve in DC-3, DC-6, and DC-7 aircraft. I loved every minute of the entire program.

Graduation exercises were held in a hotel in Denver. We were given one week off to go home, pack whatever we would need in our new location, and report in to the office in our assigned city. Such exciting days for me—yes, it was another new beginning. I flew to Minneapolis where Evie helped me pack. What a blessing she was as she drove with me from Minneapolis to San Francisco and helped me find and move into an apartment not too far from the airport. We truly enjoyed being together. Evie gave me good advice on that trip. Trust God. Be your own person. Give yourself to others. After she flew back to Minneapolis, I began my one-year flying adventure with United.

For six months, I flew within the Continental US to most of the major cities, making short trips to places like Los Angeles and long cross-country trips to Washington DC and New York City. Regulations for flight personnel specified that the stress placed on the human body while working one hour in the air was equivalent to two hours of work on the ground. As a result, we were given ample time off for rest and also generous food allowances for meals in hotels and restaurants. I had plenty of time for sightseeing.

Reconnecting with Mother

The most encouraging outcome of my life in the air was gaining the poise and self-confidence I had so lacked. I felt pretty and respected. I had overcome my shyness and began to feel comfortable initiating conversations, in and out of the airplane. Passengers showed their appreciation by writing "orchid letters" to my supervisor. I flourished.

I got a part-time job as a substitute nurse for a professional nursing bureau. What a challenge! Every time I called in to say I was available to work, I was sent to a different hospital, which of course meant different procedures, charting systems, supervisors, and nursing staff. I learned to be flexible, to adjust, and to flow with unexpected situations. I had no idea how greatly I would need these skills 10 years later.

Life was good, and I felt secure. I often had flights to Los Angeles. My sister Mary had told me that my mother had remarried, that her life was quiet and stable at that time. After thinking about it for a couple of months and feeling that I had overcome my fear of her, I called my mother. "Mom, I'm living in San Francisco now. I'm working as a stewardess for United Airlines, and I often have flights to LA. I'd like to see you again. Could we start over as adults?"

"Yes, Susie, I'd like that." I was pleased, and a little cautious. But we had a good first visit the next week when I had an LA flight. We continued to get together whenever I was in LA, building a new relationship.

Going International

United's motto of "Extra Care" was well exhibited on their flights from San Francisco to Honolulu, Hawaii. They provided Extra Care on the Hawaiian flights by having a Registered Nurse on board every flight. Thus, after six months with United, my supervisor said, "We need more nurses on the Hawaiian routes. Would you be willing to transfer? You'll need to take a swimming test."

"Absolutely. That'd be great. I'll have no problem with the swim test." And so it was that I flew to Honolulu twice a week for six months. What a life of luxury that was! We stayed in first-class hotels and had many free hours to spend at the pool and touring that beautiful state.

Travel internationally? The idea seemed too good to be true. But it wasn't a dream. As an airline employee, I was able to spend my vacation in Europe, visiting London, Paris, Rome, and Holland for the first time—at 10% of normal passenger fares.

Washington DC

Flying for United was a wonderful experience for me, but nursing was in my blood. I once again surprised myself; in May 1962, I turned in my resignation to United. My dad and Evie said they'd be happy to have me live with them again, so I moved back to Minneapolis and took a job as an office nurse for a group of four pediatricians. Only later did I come to realize that this move and the clinic experience I gained was God ordained; God was preparing me for the isolated village-living situation to which He would be calling me.

Then in 1963, a friend who was living in the Washington DC area, told me of the opportunity to work at the National Orthopedic and Rehabilitation Hospital there. It sounded interesting, and so off I went, moving again. I found I enjoyed helping people who, for various reasons, didn't have the full use of their arms or legs. One afternoon, I was kneeling on the floor in front of a patient who had had a stroke and couldn't use his left arm or leg. I was teaching this dear man to tie his shoelace, using just his right hand, when a nurses' aid came running into the room, shouting, "The president's been shot!"

"The president of—what?" I asked.

"President Kennedy! President of the United States!"

It's a moment in time that was branded into my memory. As was the rest of the nation, we were all in shock. "How can that happen?"

Back to Minnesota—Again

In April of 1964, like a boomerang, I went back to Minneapolis again. This time, instead of living with my dad and Evie, I rented an efficiency apartment near the University of Minnesota and applied for a position at the University of Minnesota Hospitals in the intensive care unit. When I interviewed for the job, the director of nursing said, "Yes, Sue, we can use you in ICU. But I'd like to offer you a different position. In view of your training and experience in rehabilitation and pediatrics, I'd like you to take a leadership role in the university's new Children's Rehabilitation Hospital. I'm offering you the position of Head Nurse on the 20-bed pediatric rehab ward. You'd work on a rehab team with doctors and physical, occupational, and speech therapists. The center is scheduled to open in September. You can work in ICU until then, if you like."

I struggled with this surprise offer. *WOW!* I thought. *I never expected something like this. All my former nursing jobs seem to have prepared me for this. Amazing. But what should I do? I've always wanted to be a camp nurse at one of the camps where I was a camper as a child. I've already contacted one of them, and the job is available for me for this summer. Oh my, what do I say to Ms. Anderson?*

Timidly, I responded, "Thank you, Ms. Anderson. I'm delighted and honored by your offer. Would it be possible for me to work in ICU for just three months? I'd like to be a nurse at a children's camp in July and August, before working to open the new hospital." I felt like shouting, "Hallelujah!" when Ms. Anderson agreed.

And so it was that another dream of mine, to be a camp nurse, was fulfilled. And once again that summer, though I didn't realize it at the time, I learned skills that would benefit the future God had for me.

But I had no idea all that awaited me at the rehab hospital.

The Dawn of Love

28 September 1964 to 21 December 1966

We love because He first loved us.
—1 John 4:19, New International Version

Rehab 5

Dad and Evie shared my excitement when I was hired for the position of Head Nurse for the 20-bed children's ward at the University of Minnesota's new Children's Rehabilitation Hospital.

I well remember my first day on the job, September 28, 1964. At the nursing office, the secretary said I should go directly to the Children's Rehab building, the fifth floor. I was shocked when I got there—it was empty; no beds, no mattresses, no curtains, no sheets, no towels, no syringes, no paper, no pens. Nothing. I picked up the phone and called the office, "There's nothing here!" I exclaimed.

"You have to order what you want," the secretary said.

"How do I do that?"

"Oh! I'm sorry. I forgot to give you a pad of supply order sheets. I'll send one over right away."

Boy, did I have fun. *Now let's see, what's first. Well, 20 beds, of course.* I began to fill out an order sheet:

Quantity:	Item:
20	beds
20	mattresses

40	rubber sheets
40	pillows
160	pillow cases
160	sheets

And so it went. I finished the first order page, turned it in, and within the hour, an army of custodial staff brought beds, mattresses, nightstands, tables, chairs, and everything else we needed to care for 20 children. By the end of the day, they were bringing carts full of linens, boxes full of dishes, silverware, syringes, bedpans, etc. "Where do you want this?" each employee asked. Oh my! What an incredibly busy, fun, rewarding, exhausting, and exhilarating day it was for me. It's one of my treasured memories.

The next day, Mrs. Anderson, the desk clerk, started her assignment to Rehab 5, and we worked together, ordering nursing station supplies, putting things away, and labeling shelves. A couple of days later, the newly assigned nurses, aides, and orderlies started work. What a pleasure it was for me to meet with them for the first time and to begin to train our team. Though I didn't recognize it at the time, God was shedding His abundant blessings on me and on our staff.

On October 5 when all the rooms were ready with pretty curtains, the nurses' station set up, and the kitchen and dining room where we would be teaching the children to feed themselves were functional, we opened the ward with two patients. Rewarding months followed as our fifth-floor team became a part of the larger rehab team, made up of the leading rehab physicians; occupational, physical, and speech therapists; and our nursing team. Our job was to teach the children the activities of daily living: bathing, dressing, eating, bowel and bladder training. It was gratifying to be on this team of specialists; we had great respect for one another and our individual areas of expertise. Dr. Fritz, chief of the rehab hospital, became a personal friend with whom I kept in contact until 2013 when he passed away.

Peter Rescued Me!

In June 1964, Peter Westrum had finished two years of service with the US Peace Corps and had started his junior year at the University of Minnesota when fall classes began. He took a job at the university hospitals and, at the end of October, was assigned to work on Rehab 5 as an orderly (male hospital patient-care helper). He was personable, did a great job, and learned rehab principles quickly. The children loved him.

I first felt my heartstrings being tugged toward Peter when he rescued me, a damsel in distress, during a snowstorm at the end of February. I had finished my 3:00 p.m. to 11:00 p.m. shift and bundled up with many layers of warm clothes—as is necessary in Minnesota winters where the temperatures can drop as low as 30 degrees below zero. I left the hospital and went down the long steep 50-step flight of icy, snowy steps to the "River Flats" where employees parked. My heart sank when I saw my car—A FLAT TIRE! *Oh no! What do I do now? I don't even know HOW to change a tire. And it's too cold for me anyway. Who can I call for help?* I sat in my car trying to think of something. It didn't occur to me, in those days, to pray about my dilemma. *I know! I'll call Peter Westrum and see if he'll come and change the tire for me.*

Since there weren't any cell phones back in 1965, and I didn't even know about AAA (the auto club), I climbed those 50 icy stairs, returned to the hospital, and called Peter. "Peter, this is Ms. Palmer. I know it's really late, but I have a really big problem, and I don't know what to do. I don't know who to call for help. Will you help me?"

"Sure," he said. "What do you need?"

I gulped, thinking, *He doesn't know yet what he's getting into.* "Ah," I said and then spoke quickly to get my request out before I lost my nerve, "I just got off work. My car's parked down in the River Flats. When I got down there after my shift just now, I found a flat tire. I don't know how to change it. Would you be willing to come over and change it for me?" Thinking back now, I can hardly believe I had the guts to call him.

"Sure," he said. "I'll meet you at the car." He asked a buddy to drive him over, easily changed the tire, and made sure I got home safely. My knight in shining armor.

As we worked together in the following months, I saw how interested Peter was in people. I remember how he intensely looked people in the eye when talking to them. He was interested in traveling, and he loved helping the children. He led a group of our staff when we took the children to the circus and on picnic outings in the park. Having learned to dance the Filipino bamboo dance, the tinikling, when he was in the Peace Corps, he taught me to dance it with him. The children squealed in delight when we performed for them in the hospital one evening. We gained great respect for each other in being committed to working hard and helping the children.

Pan American Airways

In October 1965, I realized that I would be 26 years old in a month. I wondered, *Am I going to be an old maid? I don't want to spend my whole life here in the ice and snow working in a hospital. Flying around the US as a stewardess for United was fun. But I'd like to spread my wings and see the world. How about the US Air Force? I could be a flight nurse. Or maybe I could fly for Pan American. Oh my. Pan Am doesn't accept women over the age of 27. I better apply now.*

I contacted the US Air Force and Pan Am recruiters. To my dismay, Pan Am turned me down—I couldn't speak a foreign language. That triggered a deep desire within me. I realized I wanted to fly so badly that I was willing to hire a private French teacher at the university. Hoping against hope that this would land me the job, I found that the wife of a French professor was available and willing to help me. For six months, I crammed French words into my head. During our sessions together, she drilled me on pronunciation of flight announcements, and we role-played conversations I might have with passengers.

But, keeping my eggs in both baskets, I kept in contact with the US Air Force, actually signing papers at the end of March 1966 to be a US Air Force flight nurse.

But in May 1966, I passed my French language exam and bargained with God, *I've been ignoring you, God. Ever since the first time I saw a baby born, I've known You're a worker of miracles. I think I need a miracle now. If You'll get me the job with Pan Am, I'll start going to church every Sunday.*

I got the job and chose to work for Pan Am instead of joining the US Air Force because Pan Am didn't require a long-term commitment. And I started going to church—a different one each Sunday.

Our Matchmaking Staff

Training with Pan Am was scheduled to start September 9, 1966, in Miami, Florida; I put in my resignation from the hospital, effective August 19. On August 8, the hospital staff gave me a farewell party. They took me to dinner at Jax's, an exquisite Minneapolis restaurant, and brought cards and gifts—and a corsage, electing Peter to pin it on me. He did so with a kiss—our first. *What's happening now?* I wondered. Later, I would learn that Peter wondered too, but he knew that I didn't share his belief in Jesus as a personal Savior.

Peter had just graduated from the university, with a major in sociology and a minor in chemistry, and he had also resigned from his job on Rehab 5. We were each about to go our own ways—or so we thought. Peter had taken a position to teach high school in Sabah, Malaysia, on the island of Borneo, going out under the auspices of the Lutheran Board of World Missions. On August 12, I gave Peter the final evaluation of his work at the hospital. As I said good-bye to him, at the elevator door, he asked, "Would you go out with me sometime?" I was delighted. "Yes, I'd like that."

Our first real date was to see a play, *The Strangler*. Afterward, we went out for a snack. It was a crunchy walk on peanut shells as we followed the waiter to our table and sat down to enjoy our own bucket of peanuts. A fun place, but the music was so loud we had to shout in order to hear each other.

The next day, I flew to California to see my mother and my sister Mary. I told them, "I have a boyfriend; I really like him." Mary had wanted to visit Minnesota again, and when I couldn't stop talking about Peter, she decided this was the right time. So she returned to Minnesota with me. Peter met us at the airport—with roses and candy. During Mary's visit, Peter took us to Brainerd, Minnesota, to visit the children's camps where Peter and I had worked during the summers. Peter had served in the kitchen at the boys' camp; I had been a nurse at the girls' camp.

Back in Minneapolis, the three of us went for a canoe ride on one of the many beautiful lakes. Mary wound up paddling in the bow of the canoe; I was in the stern with Peter. Mary says she'll never forget that while she sat up there paddling hard, I sat in the back with Peter who was reading poetry to me in our own little world.

New Ideas

Ours was not the ordinary courtship where man sees woman daily or at least weekly for dates. But the days we were together were filled with the activity and excitement of getting to know each other, like morning glories opening at dawn, and to feel the warmth of growing love.

After Mary went back to California, Peter and I went to the Minnesota State Fair together. In the Midway, since Peter would soon be living in Borneo, I took a picture of him pointing to a sign, "Borneo Woman," inviting us to see this oddity. We chose not to visit that freak show, but once I became a Borneo resident myself, I often wondered what qualified that woman to be included there.

We saw each other whenever we were both off work and talked for hours, in person and on the phone, about our spiritual beliefs. I told Peter, "I used to believe a lot of religious stuff, but in college, I had serious questions. I read and talked to others, looking for answers. In fact, I've read the catechisms of all the major Christian denominations. And I've read about the beliefs of world religions, such as Hinduism, Buddhism, Confucianism, and all the other 'isms.' I decided it's all useless, just a crutch for weak people."

Peter didn't criticize or argue with me. He simply said, "I think my idea of Christianity is a little different than yours."

"Yeah sure. So tell me about it." And he did. He told me about a personal God who loves me, about salvation that's available through faith in a Person, NOT salvation acquired by following a list of rules and regulations, as in some religions.

Base Your Life on the Bible? Really?

One day, Peter gave me a copy of the newly published *Living Gospels* by Tyndale House. I said I'd read it. And I did. Soon, he gave me *Living Letters*. I kept reading. Peter explained the Bible is God's Word to His creation. He said he based his life on what the Bible said. "I never heard of anything like that before," I responded.

I made a decision. *I'll read the entire Bible.* Being the extremely detailed and thorough person that I am, I went out and bought two notebooks. I labeled one "Pro" and the other one "Con." "Peter," I said, "I'm going to read the whole Bible. Every time I read something that makes sense, I'm going to write it in the 'Pro' book. When I find things I disagree with, I'll write them in the 'Con' book. When I finish reading the whole Bible, IF the pros outweigh the cons, I'll believe what you're telling me."

Peter prayed and, I think, was smiling and saying to himself, "Silly woman. We'll see what God will do." He was right. God had a different plan; I never completed mine.

Off to New York

As excited as I was to leave to begin my new flying career soon, September 5 was a sad day. Peter and I said good-bye to each other when he left Minneapolis to go to Ann Arbor, Michigan, to study at the University of Michigan's English Language Institute in order to earn a certificate in teaching English as a second language. Three days later, I flew to Miami to take Pan American's five-week stewardess training course. Our lives were exciting and terrible at the same time—exciting because we were both on a new adventure, terrible because we missed each other intensely. We wrote letters daily and frequently talked on the phone. I read the books Peter had given me and began to pray again. *God, are You really there for me? Is the Bible really a book from You? I want to know the truth.*

When I finished my training, Pan Am assigned me to their base in New York City. The day after graduation, they flew me and Jan, another new Pan Am stewardess, to New York. We were to be ready for our first flight in 11 days. Three days later, we signed a contract on an apartment in Kew Gardens, and I flew to Minneapolis to pack my things and to get my car. Peter met me there, and we drove to Ann Arbor for a three-day visit; I really wanted to get a firsthand look at Peter's university life. Also, we needed time to talk face-to-face.

God Talks to Bob? Strange.

As we walked around the university campus one afternoon, we ran into a friend of Peter, and God used that young medical student to reach into my heart. I asked, "Bob, what branch of medicine will you work in when you graduate from med school?"

He answered, "I don't know, Sue. God hasn't told me yet!" I was really surprised! Here was a perfectly normal-looking fellow who actually expected God to talk to him. Though I only met Bob that once and only spoke with him for about five minutes, God used his answer and simple faith and trust mightily as He continued to pursue me.

As I left Peter there in Ann Arbor and drove on to New York, I couldn't get Bob's attitude and belief out of my mind. And I couldn't get Peter out of my mind. I prayed, *Oh God, is Peter and his life in missions what You want for me?*

Softly, deep in my spirit, I had a strong impression that God was saying yes. This kind of answer to prayer had never happened to me before. I felt happy and scared all at the same time. *God, are You really talking to me? Is this what Bob meant when he said that You hadn't told him yet?* I was puzzled but had a strange new peace.

Back in New York, I began my new career flying to exotic places I had formerly only dreamed about: the islands of the Caribbean, Europe, Russia, South America, and Africa. I loved it; I enjoyed the girls I worked with on the plane and took every opportunity to go sightseeing in all the new cities I visited.

Extreme Faith

I was always eager and watching for a chance to visit Ann Arbor. The first week of November, Peter invited me to visit him, to attend a Michigan versus Illinois football game. I didn't have any flights that weekend, so I went. The morning of the game, Peter asked me, "Sue, would you like to hand out spiritual tracts with me to people who come to the game?"

I felt alarmed. "No. I wouldn't want to do something as forward and as embarrassing as that!" Praying was now OK for me, but handing out tracts? Way too extreme. I sat in the car and watched him before we went into the stadium.

"Don't Do That!"

Peter invited me to celebrate Thanksgiving with his sister, Gloria, and her family in Dayton, Ohio. Peter told her, "I think I'll show Sue my slides while she's here—slides from my two years in the Peace Corps, living a simple life in a village in the Philippines."

"Don't do that!" Gloria exclaimed. "If she sees those primitive pictures, you'll never see her again."

But Peter showed the slides, and the effect on me was the exact opposite of what Gloria had predicted. I was impressed that Peter was willing to live in primitive conditions to serve and help people from another country. Instead of being repulsed, I felt an attraction to that simple way of life. Of course, I asked Peter a million questions about life living in a small bamboo hut in a remote village. God was at work seeking me, drawing me and Peter together. I still have my daily calendar from 1966. Two days after Thanksgiving, I wrote on the calendar, "I'm in love!"

Why Are They Happy?

In December, I was able to make another trip to Ann Arbor. On December 11, Peter and I again visited the church he was attending while living there, Grace Bible Church. Again, I was surprised; the people in that church looked HAPPY. They smiled when they sang—and they really sang! They had something I didn't; it made them happy. I wanted it! And they were friendly; they approached me. They wanted to share their joy. I wanted their joy.

The visiting speaker that Sunday was Dr. John Walvoord of Dallas Theological Seminary. He spoke of the importance of reading the Bible daily. He challenged his listeners to receive Christ as their personal Savior AND to make Him Lord of their lives.

My heart started pounding. I resisted.

"If you feel God's working in your heart and you want to know more about Jesus or pray to thank Him for what He's done for you, come up to the front and talk with one of us," he said.

I felt God working all right, but my pride was also at work. *I'm not going up there in front of all these people and make a fool of myself!* I stayed perfectly still in my place. I didn't find out until later that many of Peter's friends, in fact most of the congregation, were praying that God would soften my heart and that I would respond during that Christmas season.

I Give Up!

The next morning, Pan Am called me; I was to work a charter flight from Columbus, Ohio, to San Juan, Puerto Rico. They flew me from Ann Arbor to Columbus. Since I arrived before the rest of the crew, I had a room to myself in the motel. I was alone. I was upset, deeply disturbed; the Lord had used Dr. Walvoord's words to reach me.

Oh, why didn't I bring one of those Bible books from Peter with me? Surely, I can find answers to my questions in the Bible. But I don't have one. Help me think and remember, God. I _need_ *answers to my doubts and questions. I need to know Your truth!*

Then I saw it—right there on the dresser. A Gideon Bible. It drew me like a magnet. I spent the next 20 hours reading and thinking and looking up many of the passages listed in the front of that Bible, for those in doubt or alone or in need of comfort, etc. The Holy Spirit did His work. I felt that God spoke directly to me through His Word that night. Each verse I looked up seemed written just for me. Amazing!

While all this was going on there in Columbus, Peter and many from the Ann Arbor church were praying for me.

Back at the motel, I finally slept and the next day joined the rest of the crew, and we worked the flight to San Juan. That evening, we all went out to dinner together. The captain rented a car—a big one, similar to a limo. It was December 13. I sat by myself in the third row, staring out the window as the city went by, totally unaware of the conversation going on around me. I was upset and could think of nothing but all I had been told that week. I realized I had been searching to be close to God, but I was doing it through my own efforts to be good, not by relying on what God, through Jesus, had already done for me.

Finally, while just looking out the window, I prayed, *OK, God, I give up! I don't understand all I've learned and what You're saying to me, but I don't want to fight you anymore. I believe it's Your Spirit talking to me, getting my attention. I want Jesus. I want Him in my life. Thank you, Jesus, for dying for me. I want You as MY Savior AND Lord. I accept Your Word as THE BOOK upon which I want to base my life.*

I had complete peace. The internal physical and emotional turmoil I had been feeling was gone. Just like that. December 13, 1967, was my spiritual birthday. My name had been written in heaven (*Luke* 10:20). Before that day, I had given intellectual assent to knowledge about Jesus, but now I had made a total heart commitment.

After dinner with the crew, we went back to the motel. I went to my room and eagerly began to read the Bible again. Then I remembered the gold chain and cross I had been carrying around with me ever since Peter had given me *Living Gospels* four months before. I had told him, "IF I ever decide to believe what you're telling me, I'll start wearing that gold cross my mother gave me when I graduated from high school." I had put it away in college, but it symbolized belief to me. And now I realized that God had been preparing and leading me ever since then. I had finally made the leap and let Him in.

The next day, I worked the charter from San Juan to Nassau in the Bahamas. When I got back to the US, I called Peter. I greeted him with "Guess what?"

"You're wearing the cross," he responded.

"Yes! How'd you know?"

"We've been praying for you."

Amazing grace. Answered prayer. *Thank You, Father.*

Peter and the church prayer group praised God for how He'd pursued me and that I had finally responded.

On my flight, as a passenger, back to New York after completing the charter, I wrote a letter to Peter, detailing everything that had happened since I left him in Ann Arbor. I included these thoughts and desires:

My attendance at Grace Bible Church made me realize I was wasting precious time . . . I feel now that I want to win others for Christ too—this surprises me—and I want my mother to be the first . . . Won't that be an exciting day—when she feels this calm and peace that I now feel? Honey, it's all too wonderful and exciting! My narrow love for family and friends has suddenly exploded to love for Him and for everyone.

Going Our Own Ways

Peter graduated with honors from his course at the University of Michigan and went home to Moorhead, Minnesota, to say good-bye to his family. His church held a commissioning service for him, sending him off to Borneo, promising to uphold him in prayer. I was able to arrange my flights so I could make a two-day visit to Moorhead to say good-bye. I savored every minute of my time getting to know Peter's parents and other relatives; we played games, built a snowman, made angels in the snow, and sang Christmas carols.

Peter and I were able to capture hours together to just talk, beginning a habit of praying together and agreeing that "we'll marry someday."

On December 21, we parted. I went back to New York; Peter left for Borneo. He made a stop in Los Angeles to meet my mother and her husband, Glen. It was a pleasant visit for them all. Peter and I continued to write letters daily, but instead of phone calls, we sent tape recordings back and forth.

The past two years had been a period of the dawning of love between Peter and me. But way more than that—far deeper than that—was God's love that had penetrated into the core of my spirit. It was the beginning of my spiritual life.

And God gave me His amazing gift of peace, which has lasted all through the years ever since. It was His peace that took me, without fear, to Borneo. It was His peace that was with me four years later, as we traveled up the Tor River in Indonesian New Guinea, even though our baby David was so sick. It was God's peace and joy that filled my heart when we went to live in a village with the Berik people, whose grandparents had been headhunters.

God had plans for us, the likes of which had not yet dawned on me.

Love Grows

December 1966 to July 1968

*Love never gives up, never loses faith, is always
hopeful, and endures through every circumstance.*
—1 Corinthians 13:7, New Living Translation

Peter was gone. We were now 10,000 miles apart. Peter was in an exotic, wild, and primitive place, at least that's how I thought of Borneo. I was in New York City. We had only letters and tape recordings as ways to communicate with each other. Even sent by air, each letter or tape took two weeks to make the trip. How in the world could a relationship grow under those conditions? God knew. And He had a plan for us.

And love grew, blossoming like sunflowers in late summer. The recorder we used was a small reel-to-reel recorder, similar to a handheld cassette recorder, with two two-and-a-half-inch reels. We received a recorded reel, listened, took notes, rerecorded, and mailed the reel back. Yes, it took four to five weeks to get an answer to a question. Nevertheless, this method served us well.

My life in New York was full and busy. Near the end of my training, Pan Am had sent me on two international flights, working under the watchful eyes of one of our instructors. Now that I was settled in New York, the adventures I had dreamed of became reality—a weekend in Paris or on a Caribbean island or two days in South Africa.

I was growing in the Lord, attending a small Bible church near my apartment. I started a Bible study for stewardesses and, during the summer, worked as a nurse at a Christian camp for handicapped children. When I attended a Christian Life Convention, I was challenged by this guideline,

"Ask yourself if you can thank God for a particular event, person, place, or whatever you do, asking Him to share it with you." I became aware of my sinful attitudes and behavior and determined to turn from them. Shortly thereafter, I had the equivalent of my own personal bonfire. I took several books that I had read, tore them to pieces, and threw them down the incinerator chute in my apartment building. These were books that I could not imagine Jesus reading and enjoying. God was working to mold me into His image.

During one flight back to the US from Africa, after the meal service was finished and the passengers were asleep or reading, one of the other stewardesses asked me what I meant when I spoke of being born again. She had never heard the term before, nor had she met anyone who spoke of themselves in that way. That night, the Lord provided seven other Christians to talk with her on the plane, including one lady who was a missionary to Africa.

And I was amazed at the changes taking place in my attitudes and thinking. Previously, I had felt insecure; now I felt secure. Previously, I had felt unwanted; now I knew I had been chosen by God to be His own. I had felt unloved and unlovable; now I experienced God's love. I had a deep desire to tell others about Jesus and my new birth. I wanted to read the Bible every day and to be with other believers. My life now had purpose.

The Gideons

I continually thanked God for the Gideon Bible that had been there for me, in the motel room in Columbus, when I was struggling with Jesus's call on my life. One day, I thought, *I need to contact the Gideons and let them know their work isn't in vain—at least one person read one of the Bibles they had placed in a motel. I want to share with them how God is working in my life.* I picked up the phone book and looked under G for Gideon. Actually, I was surprised that a number was listed. I dialed it.

"Hello. Bill, New York Gideon Camp, speaking."

"Mr. Bill, you don't know me, but I looked up 'Gideon' in the phone book and found your number. My name is Sue Palmer. I'm a stewardess for Pan Am living here in New York. I just want you to know that God used a Gideon Bible I found in a hotel room to influence me in giving my heart and life to Jesus. I thought you might like to know that people really do read the Bibles you place in hotels, and I want to thank you for the work you Gideons are doing."

Mr. Bill was very gracious. We had a lovely long talk, and he asked me to write a letter telling him all that I had shared on the phone. When I wrote, I mentioned my plans to marry Peter and join him on the mission field. Little did I know what God would do with my simple letter. I was stunned by the responses that followed. Mr. Bill shared my letter with Dr. Walvoord of Dallas Theological Seminary, the man God had used to speak to my heart during the church service in Ann Arbor, Michigan, in 1966. I was amazed when I received a letter from Dr. Walvoord, praising God for how He had worked in my life.

When the president of Gideons International received a copy of my letter from Mr. Bill, the president had the letter printed in the December 1967 issue of *The Gideon*, their quarterly newsletter. As Mr. Bill requested, Peter and I added him to our mailing list so he would be kept up-to-date regarding God's leading in our lives. We added his name and address to our mailing list, sent him our letters, and thought nothing more of it.

Pan Am Perks

Even though frequent letters and tape recordings served us well, Peter and I were eager to see each other face-to-face again. As a Pan Am employee, I was eligible to get 90% discount tickets on international travel during my vacations.

I did a happy dance in March 1967 when my request for an April vacation was granted. Immediately, I went to the Pan Am employee ticket office. "I need tickets to visit Sandakan, Sabah, Malaysia," I said. The clerk spent several minutes searching flight manuals. Then he looked at me and said, "You can't get there from here."

"Oh yes, I can!" I returned. I explained Sandakan is a city in the state of Sabah on the island of Borneo in the country of Malaysia. "Borneo is the second largest island in the world," I said. "It's the home of Mt. Kinabalu, the snow-covered highest peak in Southeast Asia." The man just stared at me, shocked at my enthusiasm to want to visit such a remote place. But finally realizing where Sandakan was, he arranged for my tickets.

It was a wonderful adventure—my first time to Asia. I praised God that I didn't get bumped off any of my desired flights, which is a real possibility when flying standby on reduced fare tickets. My plane stopped in San Francisco and Anchorage, and I enjoyed visiting and touring in Tokyo, Hong Kong, and Manila along the way.

A Taste of Life in Borneo

It was so very special to get a taste of Peter's life teaching Bible, English, literature, chemistry, physics, and civics. I met his students and teaching colleagues, went on picnics and excursions with them, and toured the town of Sandakan. I saw what life in Borneo, just six degrees north of the equator, was really like—shopping in the open markets, eating foods I'd never seen or tasted before, and experiencing the differing cultures of people who lived there in town—Malay-speaking people, three or four different Chinese language groups, and people from the interior who spoke several other indigenous languages. I was grateful that I could make a second visit seven months later, in September.

Thinking back today, as I write this, it's amazing to realize the abundant grace God gave me on those trips. Instead of suffering from extensive culture shock and accompanying debilitation, I was energized and drawn to assist with the many critical ministries there. God was pulling my heart toward missions. Though I didn't realize it at the time, God had been preparing me since grammar school, in His classroom of life: enabling me to adjust to hardships, providing exposure to society in other parts of the US and in Europe, gaining experience in a variety of nursing disciplines.

ELWA

During my first six months flying for Pan Am, I worked flights mainly to the Caribbean and South America. Then my horizons expanded to Europe, and a few months later, I was able to get African trips. Monrovia, Liberia, was a major layover stop for Pam Am.

When I learned that the Sudan Interior Mission had a center in Monrovia, I determined to visit their ELWA station and meet some missionaries. Since English is the official language of Liberia, I had no trouble arranging for a taxi to take me from the hotel where Pan Am crews were housed to the residential area of the ELWA compound that was located right on the Atlantic shore.

Arriving at the main gate, I paid the driver and started walking down the road toward the houses. I stopped at the first house, knocked on the door, and was greeted by Betty, a single girl who was on staff.

I introduced myself, "Hi. My name is Sue Palmer. I'm a stewardess for Pan Am, and I'm in Monrovia for a couple of days on a layover. I'm a new Christian, and I want to meet some missionaries. Are you a missionary?"

Betty smiled. "Yes, I'm a medical missionary. I work in the ELWA hospital." She graciously welcomed me into her home. I learned that ELWA stands for Eternal Love Winning Africa and that they had a large staff ministering to the Liberian people through the hospital and through a radio station.

Betty and I hit it off right away. She invited me to dinner and to stay overnight with her. The next day as we toured the hospital and broadcasting facilities, she introduced me to many of the staff who all oozed love and acceptance and invited me to visit whenever I had layovers in their city.

I met Bart and Ruth and their three small children while on tour that day. During my subsequent visits to ELWA, we became close friends. Peter met them when they were in the US on furlough in 1971; we've maintained our friendship for an amazing 48 years. I felt a special affinity for Ruth who was a nurse anesthetist at the hospital. Bart served as programming director for Radio ELWA that was beaming Christian broadcasts from Liberia across Africa and the Middle East in both trade and tribal languages, proclaiming the love of God through trust in His Son, the Lord Jesus Christ.

Like all kids, Ruth and Bart's children loved airplanes. They asked me innumerable questions about the jets and what it was like to work in the air. "Do you want me to take you on a tour of the plane?" I asked. "Yes!" they shouted. Strict security was not necessary in those days, so we were able to go to the airport, and by showing my badge, I was able to take the family on board. The kids particularly wanted to see the galley, where everything was stored, and to learn how we cooked the food—with no stove.

Celebration Events

Though I wasn't able to visit Minneapolis often, I was elated to be there with Dad and Evie at the end of September, just two weeks after Baby Nancy Jo was born on September 8. Nancy's physical birth brought us such happiness. I felt honored to be able to join in caring for her, God's special gift to our family.

And then in January, I rejoiced in my mother's spiritual birth. I had been talking with her and writing to her about Jesus and the peace He gives. God had spoken to her and reached into her heart through a little book loaned by a friend. She called to tell me she had accepted Jesus as her Savior. "I feel such joy," she said. "I can't wait to get up in the morning to read the Bible and to learn more." Because of the periodic deep mental torment and depression she had suffered, her testimony was especially exciting. That the Lord had made her a new creation was obvious to those close to her. "Therefore, if anyone is in Christ, he is a new creation. The old has passed away; behold, the new has come" (2 Corinthians 5:17, English Standard Version). Mother almost immediately had become actively and diligently involved in a Bible study group, Bible Study Fellowship. I was blessed to be able to arrange my flights so I could fly to Los Angeles so we could spend a week together. It thrilled my heart to see the many Bibles and commentaries she had open on her desk, and each day, she eagerly initiated time for us to discuss her lesson for the week.

Scripture Press

When I returned to New York, a letter from Mr. Jim, an editor with Scripture Press, was waiting for me. He had read my letter in *The Gideon* and had written to Mr. Bill, saying he wanted to invite me to Wheaton, Illinois, for an interview. "We'd like to write up your testimony in our publications, *Power for Living* for adults, *Power Life* for upper teens, and as a comic strip in *Counselor*," Mr. Jim wrote.

I was stunned. I couldn't imagine why anyone would want to know a story about me. I phoned Mr. Jim for clarification. He said he thought their readers would appreciate knowing how God had changed my heart and life. Evidently, the stereotype of stewardesses being bad girls was so strong that one of them getting saved, wanting to follow Jesus with all her heart, was a big deal. They printed my testimony in the July and November 1969 issues of their periodicals.

In His Steps by Charles Sheldon

I love to read. My friends knew I was always looking for a paperback that I could take with me on my flights. One Sunday at church, a lady handed me a small book, *In His Steps*. "I think you'll enjoy this," she said.

She was right. Coupled with the pastor's admonition during the Christian Life Convention, the main theme and question in the book, "What would Jesus do?" had a profound impact on me. I couldn't get that question out of my mind. I started to pray about my dilemma. I told my roommate, "I've been serving hard liquor on my flights. I can't do it anymore. It's impossible for me to imagine Jesus serving cocktails." I prayed about it. In my heart, I just didn't know what I could do. But God had a plan.

Before the passengers boarded at the beginning of each flight, the purser would assign our duties. On my next flight, I said, "I'd like to work the galley." The purser and the other four girls working the flight looked surprised and thanked me profusely. They all really disliked working the galley, that is, cooking the food. But for me, it meant I wouldn't work the beverage service.

I recognized this solution as another gift from God for me. Then as I thought about future flights, I reasoned that I couldn't expect God to give me the same miracle on every flight. I felt that because of the conflict between being the Lord's ambassadress and serving liquor on board the plane, as was required by the airline, God was leading me to resign from my flying position.

The miracle is that from that day forward, the day I determined to live by how God was leading me, I never again had to serve liquor. The girls on my flights were always delighted to have me work the galley. *God, You're so good!*

I Said Yes BEFORE He Asked!

Each year, the Board of World Missions in New York sent Dr. David to Sabah to see the work firsthand and to have face-to-face meetings with the missionaries. During his April 1968 interview with Peter, Peter submitted his request that he be permitted to get married on the field. Dr. David gave 99% permission but said he'd have to clear it with the full board in New York before we could go ahead with any plans. He also explained the board's qualifying stipulations—Peter would have to give up the house and car provided by the mission. We'd be on our own. It's amazing to me that Peter agreed to that. *Thank You, Lord, for a man who loved me that much!*

In May, Dr. David notified Peter that the board had given 100% permission, and Peter officially proposed to me—by cable. If you looked at my answer cable next to Peter's proposal cable, you'd see that I said yes before Peter asked.

Yes, that's because of the international date line. At 4:40 p.m. on Friday, after finishing teaching for the week, Peter sent his cable:

LORD PROVIDING WILL YOU BECOME
MY WEDDED WIFE DATE SET LATER PETER
WESTRUM

I received his cable in New York at 1:57 p.m. the same Friday and at 4:00 p.m. sent my response:

> YES ALWAYS IN HIS WILL YOUR SUE
> EPH 1:6–8

Publicly Declaring My Commitment to Jesus

The Lord continued to nurture me. My new relationship with Jesus culminated in my baptism on June 23, 1968. I'll never forget hearing the congregation singing "Turn Your Eyes Upon Jesus" as I came up out of the water. Mother had flown to New York from Los Angeles to be with me. She had become very active in attending a weekly women's Bible study, "Bible Study Fellowship," and was often up at 3:30 a.m. reading her Bible and working on her assigned worksheet. God had pursued and was also nurturing her.

Since my own church in Queens didn't have a facility for baptism by immersion, I was baptized at Calvary Church in Manhattan and gave the following testimony to the congregation:

How I praise and thank the Lord for bringing me to this night when I can publicly declare and show my union and new life with Christ.

Although born in Illinois, I grew up in Minnesota thinking I had the faith God wanted me to have, but in college, I slipped away from it and lived without recognition of God, a life which I know now was very displeasing to Him. In spite of that, as I look back, I can see how He cared for me all along and prepared me for the future and the job He has for me, the privilege of serving Him as missionary wife, mother, nurse, and teacher in Southeast Asia.

I came to New York in October 1966, and my new life began two months later on December 13 when I recognized that God was asking me to make a decision to follow Christ and to make Him Lord of my life. Since that day 18 months ago, I've learned the truth of 2 Corinthians 5:17, "Therefore, if anyone is in Christ, he is a new creation. The old has passed away; behold, the new has come."

There's a hymn we sing that says, "Things are different now—things I loved before have passed away, things I love far more have come to stay." This is exactly what I've experienced. Christ didn't give me a set of rules and regulations—I accepted His love, and He came to live in my heart, and as a result, my ideas, values, hopes, and desires are changed. Only one thing is important now, to do His will, to please Him.

Besides a new love for God's Word, He has given me a desire for and led me to the fellowship of other born-again Christians and to a church where I can grow in knowledge of Him. He also brought me here to Calvary where at such functions as the Christian Life Convention He has strengthened me and my faith and has overcome for me the obstacles that satan throws at every new believer.

Christ has given me what I never dreamed existed—what only He can give—perfect peace. My prayer tonight is that He might be glorified by this service and that one of you here listening will choose Him and grow to find Him as precious as I do.

As I came up from being immersed in the waters of baptism, the congregation was singing, "Turn Your Eyes Upon Jesus." That has become the desire of my heart—that people who have contact with me will also look to Jesus in their lives.

Surprise!

The congregation of my church had been requesting pictures and information about Peter's work in Borneo, so in preparation for my departure from New York, the congregation gathered for an extra meeting that last week of June. I showed slides, played a taped of greeting that Peter had sent, and added my own comments. Refreshments had been planned as usual. I went in the kitchen to help. I wasn't needed for food preparation, but several ladies surrounded me, talking and asking questions. Suddenly, I realized I was cornered in there, and the door to the meeting hall was shut. One lady, who had been standing with her hands behind her back, said, "Sue, we have something for you, and we'd like you to wear it now." She handed me a beautiful red carnation corsage. I was struck absolutely speechless! I stood there, looking at each lady through the tears in my eyes while the presenter pinned the corsage on me. Then two of the women took me by my hands and led me out into the main room. For the first time in my life, I could think of nothing to do or say. I just stood there taking in the amazingly transformed room—a table with a large cake decorated with a bride and groom and "Showers of Blessings to Peter and Sue" written on it and another table piled with gifts. *Thank You, Lord, for these dear friends You gave me. Thank You for leading me to this church to help disciple me, just*

73

one month after I came to know You as Savior. Thank You that I can be absolutely certain You'll always lead and care for me.

Saturday, July 6, was my final day as an employee with Pan Am. It was a rough day for me as I finished packing and kept thinking about saying good-bye to all my friends at church the next day, my final Sunday to worship and pray with them. Then they did it again—they caught me off guard and took me by surprise. In cahoots with the pastor, they had planned a commissioning service for me, committing me to God's leading and care. What a grand blessing is to be found in the Body of Christ!

On My Way to Borneo

Monday morning, I loaded my car, and before getting on the road to begin my drive to Minnesota, I stopped by the Pan Am employee ticket office to pick up our "honeymoon tickets." Another Pan Am perk. Employees who resign for the purpose of marrying may purchase two tickets, at a 90% discount, for honeymoon travel within 30 days of leaving the company.

I took parts of four days to make the trip to Minneapolis, stopping in Wheaton to have the interview with Mr. Jim at Scripture Press. A pleasant and gracious man, he showed me the periodicals in which he planned to print my story. It was strange to realize I'd be the subject of the teen flyer that looked very much, to me, like a comic strip.

I felt humbled and oh so blessed by a bridal shower given by my nursing school classmates in Minneapolis and also by an open house at the Westrum homestead in Moorhead. When the Eastlunds, Peter's mother's side of the family, met for their annual family reunion a week later, I was able to meet another large group of my future in-laws—before taking my first flight on my way to my wedding in Borneo.

Amazing. I never dreamed I'd live outside the US—let alone in an exotic place like Borneo!

Married in Borneo

1968

Where you go, I will go. Where you live, I will live.
—Ruth 1:16, Expanded Bible

After saying good-bye to my dad and Evie and other relatives and friends in Minnesota, I flew to Los Angeles to say good-bye to my mother and sister. Neither of my parents was able to travel to Borneo to be with us for our wedding. We really wanted one of our parents to be at our wedding, and Peter's four siblings really wanted Peter's mother to be with us, so we agreed to split her around-the-world travel expenses five ways. Gladys met me in Los Angeles, and we traveled together to Malaysian Borneo, making stops in Honolulu and Hong Kong.

Mom Westrum was a good traveler and was so easy to be with. I took her sightseeing around Hong Kong Island and to the New Territories, right up to the Red China border. We went shopping, and she marveled at being able to have a dress made in one day. We thought it would be fun to ride the double-decker buses, so we stood in line. But I wasn't prepared for what happened when the bus stopped. The people all around us pushed to get on the bus; at the same time, others were trying to get off the bus. We were knocked this way and that, and Mom's glasses were knocked off onto the street. I panicked and hollered. I was ignored. *Lord, help us! Help me get her glasses for her! Please don't let anyone step on them! Whatever would she do on the rest of the trip without them?* I shouted at Mom to just get on the bus, and I just stopped in the middle of the crowd and bent over and picked them up—UNBROKEN. Then I was literally carried right onto the bus as part of the moving mass of humanity. *Thank You, Lord! I feel responsible for Mom's well-being. Please help me get her to Sandakan safely.*

Sandakan City, Island of Borneo, At Last

Peter and a large welcoming party of church and school leaders, Peter's fellow teachers, and students met us at the airport. As the plane was landing, Peter asked the Chinese elder of the church regarding protocol, "Who should I greet first? My bride or my mother?" He wisely answered, "Today, you greet your mother first. After the wedding, you'll always greet your wife first."

In spite of jet lag, Mom Westrum kept up so well with all the planned activities: a tour of the city, our apartment, and the school, followed that first day by a lovely dinner reception. My bridesmaids held a shower for us, and over the weekend, Mom joined us on a mission trip to Mile 86. What a trooper she was to ride in that most uncomfortable Land Rover. In her notes about her trip, she commented on the narrow road, wooden plank bridges, steep hills, many 90-degree turns, and our lunch dishes being washed in cold water.

Mom had a friend who was a missionary nurse deep in the jungle past the end of a rarely used gravel "road" at Mile 93. Mom wanted to go see Minnie! Oh my! Eight people climbed into a small boat that had no motor and only one paddle to cross the river. Then we had to WALK half a mile in the HOT sun to Minnie's house. I still felt responsible for Mom's well-being—she had had heart problems. As she walked, her face became beet red; she was sweating profusely and was short of breath. She insisted on continuing. I was nervous and concerned. I prayed, *Oh God, please take care of her! Protect her. Medical help is so far away!*

Minnie's home was on a hill, and there was a cool breeze that refreshed us all as we visited the rest of the afternoon until the sun began to go down behind the tall trees. We walked back to the river, crossed it safely in that little boat, and drove back to the mission station. When we left Mile 86 at 6:00 p.m., it was already DARK. Then the tropical rain poured down on us. The Land Rover leaked like a sieve. Some people, whose vehicles were stuck in the mud along the way, got in the Rover with us. We finally arrived back to Sandakan at 11:00 p.m.

I praised God for the good sleep Mom got that night; she recovered well from, what I dare say, was the most strenuous expedition of her life.

Mom had volunteered to bake our wedding cake for us. I had brought the four cake pans and white plastic pillars for a tall tiered cake. Mom had helped me hand carry two dozen sugar doves for decoration. She worked hard the day before our wedding, baking the cakes in the school home economics lab. "The ovens are too small and too hot!" she said. But she managed; the white frosted cake was delicious and beautiful with the sugar doves on each layer and a gold Christogram on the top.

After the rehearsal dinner at a lovely restaurant, Peter was driving us home in the Land Rover when the RAIN started again. Yes, it rains daily in a tropical rainforest. In fact, I once counted 14 rain bursts, interspersed with sunshine, in one day. When the Rover got stuck in a flash flood, Peter and the fellows had to get out and push the Rover, soaking Peter's wedding trousers. The next day, he waited until an hour before the wedding for his trousers to be returned from the cleaners. Memories are made of this.

August 6, 1968—Our Wedding

Peter's students spent the day decorating and filling the church (the Basel Christian Church of Malaysia) and school (where the reception was held) with tropical plants and flowers, including orchids and gardenias. The school courtyard became a beautiful garden complete with potted plants, even large palm trees. The students lined the stairs and path from the church to the school with lanterns made of lighted candles, held in place by sand, in large brown paper bags. It was a heavenly scene.

In the front of the church, the students built a ceiling-high archway made of tropical greenery, embedded with fresh flowers. The center aisle of the church was lined with 14 white posts, trimmed with green ferns, attached to the pews, with a big white bow. On top of each post, the students placed a white circular shelf on which stood little glass lanterns, the bases of which were gold, blue, green, and red. We saved one lantern of each color and have them on display in our home today. We carefully wrapped and packaged the other 10 lanterns and mailed them to family members in the US, with a note saying, "This is just one way we can share our wedding day with you. Should the electricity ever fail you, or you feel in the mood for having a lamplit evening meal (as we often enjoy doing), use this little lamp and think of us and pray for us over here at the ends of the earth."

Our attendants were from the United States, Malaysia, Hong Kong, Singapore, Scotland, and Taiwan. Our flower girl, the pastor's daughter, led the processional down the white carpet. The principal of the school, Ken, and his wife, Maxine, who were also in Borneo serving as missionaries, stood in for my parents, with Ken walking me down the aisle. I carried a white Bible Peter had given me, with a small spray of gardenias on top.

Two separate programs, printed in English and Chinese, with the dialogue of the entire ceremony, were given to each person in the congregation. Both the English and the Chinese church choirs sang. We wrote our vows and the words of the wedding service and used the symbol of the Christogram throughout—emphasizing the fact of Christian marriage in Christ. Unlike US custom, the most important, official, mandatory part of the ceremony was the signing of our Certificate of Marriage by us, the pastor, and two elders of the church.

During the solo singing of the "Lord's Prayer" by a missionary colleague, a heavy downpour assaulted us. And the wind blew. The wooden shutters on the windows weren't locked in the open position. The wind took over, and the shutters swung shut—BAM! The wind grabbed the shutters again, swinging them open against the outside wooden walls of the church—BAM! Shut—BAM! Open—BAM! Like a bass kettle adding a beat to the hymn—but totally out of rhythm. Then just as suddenly as it started, the storm passed, and all was quiet once again, except for the soloist grandly finishing the singing of the "Lord's Prayer." The sudden storm with the out-of-rhythm banging of the shutters—so like the unexpected events of life—had been framed with the "Lord's Prayer." Should not all of life be so framed?

We formed a receiving line at the door of the church, Peter introducing me to each person as they came by to congratulate us. Malay-, Chinese-, and English-speaking guests alike were gracious, and I smiled at them all. I still remember how sore and tired my facial muscles were by the time the last person went through the line.

The Reception

Thirty of Peter's students served a wedding feast to more than 200 guests. Mom Westrum's cake was on a table in the center of the room with three large colorful papier-mâché bells hanging from the ceiling. Peter's roommate, Owen, was the emcee. He did a great job leading singing, toasts, and speeches by various guests. Peter's mother read telegrams from our parents and family in the US who couldn't be with us. The festivities ended at 11:00 p.m. when I threw my bouquet from the balcony to the eager young girls below.

People often say or imply that it was too bad we couldn't be at home for our wedding. But I ask you, where's "home"? I believe "home" is wherever God places us, for His purposes, to bring glory to Him. God had implanted His desires in my heart—the expectation that my home in the coming decades would be in Asia. I would go and live wherever it was that God sent us. God Himself had brought us to Sandakan, Sabah, Malaysia, on the island of Borneo. I can emphatically tell you that our wedding day couldn't have been as beautiful and wonderful at "home" in the United States where we grew up because it was God's will that we be married "on the field." He poured out on us all the beauty He had placed in equatorial rainforests, and in the friendships there, that only He in His great love can provide.

You Went on Your Honeymoon with WHO?

Pan Am offered honeymoon passes to employees, and their new spouse, when they married. We decided to take advantage of these passes for both of us to travel for two weeks to places we wouldn't be able to afford to visit on our own. We had tickets to fly from Borneo to Singapore, Bangkok, and Calcutta.

Mom Westrum had to get home. Since this was her first time to travel internationally, we couldn't just leave her in Sandakan to fend for herself. So she went with us to Singapore and Bangkok for the first five days of our honeymoon. She was wonderful—and discreet, never demanding our time. In Bangkok, we stayed at a missionary guesthouse and enjoyed touring together, seeing the wonders of Bangkok: the floating markets, palaces, botanical gardens, Buddhist temples, three-wheeler open-air taxis, and a fireworks display.

We joyfully waved good-bye to her when she boarded her plane in Bangkok, flying straight through to Fargo, North Dakota, though she had fueling stops and plane changes in Russia, Copenhagen, New York, Detroit, Milwaukee, and Minneapolis. Peter's mother was an amazing woman. I loved her dearly.

An Indian Guesthouse and Mt. Everest

We continued on to India and Nepal by land, where we saw the magnificent beauty of some of God's highest mountains. We'll never forget our train ride across northern India where we had an overnight stop at the Nepalese border. There was just one small guesthouse at the train station

for travelers. It was August. It was HOT. There were no fans or air-conditioning. Swarms of mosquitos were out in force. The guesthouse provided
a mosquito net—for our single-size bed. I thought I'd roast under there. I
said, "Peter, I can't stay under here. I can hardly breathe. I'm going outside."

"Sue, I'm sorry," he said. "You can't go out there. The only other
guests here are Indian men. You'll have to tough it out and try to get some
sleep before our long bus ride to Katmandu tomorrow." I stuck it out but
sat up most of the night—and praised God when the sun began to rise.

We were the only Westerners on the bus full of friendly people from
both India and Nepal. We enjoyed their company. When the bus stopped at
every small town along the route, venders crowded around the bus, offering
snacks and beverages and trinkets. I was shocked when I finally figured out
there were NO bathroom facilities available anywhere along the way. It was
no problem for Peter or the other men or even for the women. It was a large
problem for me, however. The bus would stop along the highway, outside of
a village. The men would all line up along the road on one side of the bus,
with their backs to the bus—and the women on the other side of the bus. The
women all wore full long skirts and had no problem simply squatting on the
side of the road, their skirts providing total covering. I'd never done that. I
didn't have a full long skirt. So I held it. ALL DAY! By the time we got to our
hotel in Katmandu, I was in excruciating pain. It was my own fault. I was in
culture shock. I paid for it with a very unpleasant bladder infection for the next
two days. I thanked God that I had medication with me and knew what to do.

Besides touring the town, realizing the depth of spiritual need in that
great land, the grand highlight of our time in Nepal was hiking in the
Himalayas and seeing Mt. Everest, even though it was from a distance. A
young boy, 10 or 11 years old, found us on our second day in Katmandu.
He knew a few words of English and managed to convince us that he could
take us to a higher elevation where we could stay overnight at a guesthouse,
get up at 5:00 a.m. the next day, and get a vista view of that mightiest peak
in the world. We took him up on it. He was fun, using every English word
he knew and eagerly learning more from us. As we hiked nine miles that
afternoon, he chanted, "Hiking, hiking, one, two, three, four," over and
over again. We still sometimes chant it even now if we're out walking on a
slope or hill. The beauty and magnificence of what God had created made
the hike, the primitive "guesthouse," and getting up at 5:00 a.m. worth it.
We were quite adventurous in those days.

The highlight of our trip was over. Our trip back to Sandakan was restful and uneventful. We were ready to begin our Borneo ministry together.

15 Months in Borneo

August 1968 to December 1969

Come, let us tell of the LORD'S *great-
ness; let us exalt His name together.*
—Psalm 34:3. New Living Translation

Our Apartment in Sandakan Town

Our Sandakan apartment was on the fifth floor of a five-story building
and was complete with cold running water and electricity, with one
outlet and a bulb hanging from the ceiling in each room. Air-conditioning
was a luxury in Sandakan and was found only in banks and government
buildings. But we were blessed to have a front balcony and windows opening both in the front and back of our apartment, so in the morning and
late afternoon, we enjoyed the breezes passing through. It was a good thing
we were young and agile and full of energy—we didn't mind it that the
building didn't have an elevator.

As I climbed up and down those 75 stairs two or three times a day, I
became acquainted with the spiritual need of our Chinese neighbors, most
of whom worshipped their ancestors. Most residents had a little shelf on the
wall outside their apartment door. Each shelf held pictures of one or more
of their ancestors, an artifact or two, and small metal urns filled with sand
in which joss sticks had been placed. Joss sticks are thin four-inch-long
sticks consisting of a substance that burns slowly with a fragrant (to some
people, but not to me) aroma and which is used as incense. These sticks
are kept burning day and night. Our neighbors spoke only the Chinese

language, so though I couldn't converse with them as I climbed the stairs, I prayed, *Lord, please put my neighbors in touch with Chinese Christians who will share Jesus's love with them.*

A clicking sound almost always could be heard reverberating through our building. The sound came from the plastic pieces of an addicting tile-matching Chinese game, "Mahjong," that's been played by the Chinese for hundreds of years. The people played in their living room, with the door to the stairwell open. We would smile and wave at one another as I went by.

I was learning about another culture for the first time in my life. I found it all intriguing and exciting. Looking back now, I realize it was an amazing gift and provision from God that I didn't become overwhelmed with culture shock. Our God is soo good.

Chinese custom dictates that gift recipients do not open their gifts at gatherings in front of the gift giver, who may be embarrassed if others saw that his or her gift was of lesser value than theirs. Therefore, we opened our wedding gifts when we were alone as we settled into our apartment after our honeymoon. Opening little red envelopes, in which the Chinese give cash gifts, I found it humorous to read, "Please accept my humble gift of only five Malaysian ringgits (about US$1.67)." Malaysian dollar gifts of 20 Malaysian ringgits or 100 Malaysian ringgits were also given as humble gifts. We gratefully used the cash gifts to purchase all the things we needed to set up housekeeping.

Settling in to Married Life

If you had visited us in our Sandakan apartment, the first thing you would have seen as you came through the apartment door would have been Peter's wedding gift to me: a beautiful, intricately hand-carved, cedar hope chest from Hong Kong. It's still my special treasure in our home today. Hanging on the wall above the hope chest, you would have seen our "elephant carpet," which Peter had purchased for his room when he first arrived in Sabah. Because that carpet is almost like a picture of our encounters with elephants as we drove through the jungle to Mile 86 each month, it also holds cherished memories—and hangs in our home today.

My kitchen was small but efficient. The day we were moving in, I quickly learned that neighborhood ants also thought my kitchen was a great place to be. I stood in silence, my mouth hanging open looking at my glass of Kool-Aid I had left on the sink about a half hour earlier. My glass was covered with ants. I followed their trail coming in the kitchen window and marching in a straight line to the glass, and I wondered how, in the weeks to come, I would deal with this intrusion into my domain. But for that first day, I was looking forward to cooking a special meal for Peter, the first since our wedding.

"This is the best chicken I've ever eaten," Peter commented as he took his first bite. But I was in tears. "Sue, what's the matter?"

"But, Peter, how can you say that? I ruined the chicken! It's burned. I couldn't control the heat on the stove. I'm sorry. I wanted this meal to be so wonderful for you."

"But it IS wonderful, the best. Just the way I like it. I really do enjoy chicken well done, dark, and crispy," he said. Though I couldn't believe it that day, as the years went by, I learned it is true—Peter really does like his chicken and meat very well done.

As we were eating that first supper in our apartment together, I asked, "What am I going to do about all the ants in the kitchen?"

"Yes," Peter said, "we'll need to control them. Those pesky beasts will march through our apartment in and out of every door and window, searching for even one crumb of food or one drop of a beverage. The good news is that both Chinese and Western housewives here all use a simple but absolutely essential 'trick' to overcome the problem. Since Sandakan apartments don't have built-in cupboards or closets, we'll buy a freestanding cupboard for the kitchen. It'll be screened on two sides, have two screened doors on the front, and have four-inch-long legs."

I couldn't imagine how this was going to control the ants, but I saw the twinkle in Peter's eyes and knew it would be good. "When we open cans of Campbell's soup and those low squatty cans of pork luncheon meat this week," he said, "don't throw the cans away. Wash them and save them."

At the end of the week, Peter went to a furniture store, bought the needed cupboard, and enlisted three of his students to help him carry it up those 75 steps to our apartment. They put it in the kitchen, being careful to not let it touch the wall. They put four luncheon meat cans on the floor and put four soup cans, which have a smaller diameter, inside the luncheon meat cans. "Now we need your help, Sue," he said. "When we lift the cupboard, you move the cans so we can lower the cupboard legs into the soup cans."

That accomplished, we all stood back and admired our new cupboard proudly standing in its place. "But," I said, "can't determined ants just crawl over those tin cans and up the cupboard legs?"

"Yes, they could," Peter agreed. "But now, add water to the luncheon meat cans. And voila! You have an ant-free cupboard because ants can't swim." A couple of months later, we purchased a small refrigerator, and my kitchen was complete. *Thank you, Lord, for this wonderful blessing!*

Peter built a desk for us in the second bedroom of our apartment. He accomplished this by taking down the door to the room and attaching it to the wall under the window and adding two legs in the front. I was proud of him for being so resourceful.

Teaching

We were married at the halfway point in Peter's commitment to teach for three years at Sung Siew Secondary School (SSSS), a leading Christian high school for 600 students in Sandakan, Sabah, Malaysia. Most of the students were from either Chinese or Malay ancestry; very few came from the indigenous people groups of Sabah, for they lived in the isolated jungle areas. Peter was chairman of the English department and taught Bible, English, literature, chemistry, physics, and civics. All these classes were taught in English to students who had already completed up to eight years of English stream education and who desired to go on to higher level studies, qualifying by passing the Overseas Cambridge exam.

Though I hadn't taken education courses in college, since I was a native speaker of English, I enjoyed tutoring some of Peter's struggling students in English and Bible and helping Peter correct papers. I was contacted by a Japanese woman who was very eager to learn conversational English. She adhered to the Buddhist religion, and I was disappointed that, because of family pressure, she held back from receiving Jesus as her Savior. But I pray God used the seeds that were planted in her heart to reach her.

I enjoyed becoming involved in three Bible study groups—one for students, one for Malay women, and one for nurses.

Nursing in a British Hospital

"Peter, I'd like to use my nursing skills and get hospital experience here in Sandakan. Do you think it's possible for me to get a job?" I asked.

"Sure," Peter replied. "I'll contact the hospital matron; she'll know what you have to do."

It took months, but I jumped through all the hoops, and my US credentials were finally recognized, and I was given a work pass for a position as staff nurse at the 125-bed Duchess of Kent Hospital in Sandakan. I was hired to work 24 hours a week—two day shifts and one evening shift.

It was a unique experience for me to learn the British system of medicine and the terms and phraseology used. This was my first encounter with working in a remote location where it wasn't possible to have what I considered to be adequate hospital supplies. There were no diapers for babies, and each crib was rationed with only one bedsheet a day. Parents were required to supply what was needed, and they washed their baby's clothes. I learned that because of the shortage of doctors, on the obstetrics ward, the doctors were only called in for emergencies; midwives were far more experienced than the doctors for most deliveries. I was pleased to gain experience with tropical diseases seldom seen in the US, such as malaria, typhoid fever, diphtheria, and tetanus. God was preparing me for my future ministries.

My first assignment was with the children being admitted to the hospital. What a challenge it turned out to be. I remember talking to the parents of one very sick little boy. Their first language was *Bahasa Malayu*, the Malay language. At that point, I spoke only English. I hadn't had any linguistic or language learning training. I was doing my best to speak Malay, but I didn't yet know any Malay medical terms. It was scary! As the parents babbled on and on about what had happened, and I tried desperately to understand them, I felt so inadequate. And I realized how dangerous it could be if I wrote down the wrong information. *Help me, Lord!* I prayed. The next day, I asked to be moved to a 24-bed pediatric ward where I could function well without taking patient histories.

Mile 86

Shortly after Peter arrived in Borneo in 1966, he began to assist in the ministry of a Brethren missionary from Canada, Dr. Chris. He and his wife, another Canadian couple, Ned and Vera, and two nurses preached the Gospel and ran a medical mission station for the indigenous Kadazan-speaking people who lived along the Labuk River, 86 miles from Sandakan, near the end of the national highway. The people helped Ned build a small bamboo and nipa leaf house on stilts where he and Vera lived and a combination chapel-clinic building where the nurses lived. They all learned to speak the Kadazan language, and God worked mightily in the hearts and lives of the people, young and old alike.

When Dr. Chris and his group were no longer able to get visas to work in Malaysia, the Basel Christian Church of Malaysia in Sandakan accepted the challenge of continuing the ministry. Unfortunately, no one was able to live at Mile 86 fulltime, so a weekly visiting schedule was established. Peter had become a part of this outreach. During my two visits to Borneo before we were married, I had gotten a taste of the Mile 86 ministries, and I thanked God I could make use of my nursing skills there.

Now that Peter and I were settled into our apartment in Sandakan and ministering together, I was thrilled to be able to partner with the group on their weekly visits to encourage the believers at Mile 86. The trip from Sandakan to Mile 86 took three hours in an open Land Rover—traveling at a top speed of 30 miles an hour. The road, through mountainous jungle, was gravel and clay most of the way and was often very narrow. There were so many of God's creatures living and "singing" in the thick jungle that we could actually hear them above the clatter of the loud, noisy Rover engine. We often saw monkeys, gibbons, wild boar, and snakes. When wild elephants made their appearance alongside or crossing the road, we stopped and gave them the right of way, remaining still and very quiet until they meandered back into the jungle. "We don't mess with them," the driver warned us.

Upon arrival at the little mission station, the people would give us coconut "milk"—actually the natural liquid found inside young coconuts—and fruits—bananas, papayas, or pineapples—for a snack. I was then able to help by opening a clinic for the people, seeing 25 to 35 patients each time we visited. Many people had TB, malaria, or parasites as a normal part of their lives, so they came seeking help for other illnesses. Patients paid a nominal fee for medicine, but those without money gave us rice, fish, or fruit.

After lunch and a rest—a MUST in the tropical heat and humidity—Peter and the men would lead in a time of worship and teaching. Kadazan people, living in many of the villages along the river and deeper into the jungle, would come eager to hear God's Word. I learned that the word *isa* in the Kadazan language means "one" and is used to refer to the first. "Isa" is also their name for Jesus. Can we not learn a simple lesson from the Kadazan? Jesus must be first or number one in our lives.

Exhausted but praising God for the gift of being with His jungle people, we usually arrived back in Sandakan about 9:00 p.m., thanking God for the privilege of working with Him.

Sometimes God led us to stay at Mile 86 for two or three days. Those were the times when I could make house calls, hiking through the jungle and across fallen-tree "bridges" to reach Kadazan homes. One "home" was nothing more than a lean-to structure made of palm branches. *Oh Lord, THANK YOU for the abundant blessings you've showered on me! Use me to show Your love to these people!*

During our Christmas break in 1968, we spent four days at Mile 86 with the believers and our Christian friends with whom we served there. My heart sang as I was able to take part in a baptism service on Christmas Day.

I was very hesitant though about another of Peter's ministries—to prisoners INSIDE the prison. Peter had become involved before I arrived and invited me to join him. "I feel really nervous about that," I said. "Are the people dangerous?" Peter assured me that those he worked with were in jail for minor offences, and he had not had any frightening episodes. So I agreed to go along. After my first visit, I settled down, and we included monthly prison visits in our schedule; Peter was able to preach in Malay during the chapel services there.

Chinese New Year

"Peter! What's all that racket?" I exclaimed in the middle of the night. "What time is it?"

"Just after midnight," Peter sleepily answered. "It's Chinese New Year; you're in for quite a celebration today."

My new Chinese friends had tried to explain this annual holiday to me, and they had warned me about the firecrackers. But I never expected the almost-unbearable noise I was hearing. They hadn't told me even a tenth of the meaning, extent, or magnitude of this Asia-wide celebration. I think they couldn't imagine that anyone could be an adult and not understand its importance, which includes ancestor worship, placating spirits, and the worship of other gods.

I was speechless, observing the cooking, feasting, gift giving, lantern making and dancing—especially the lion dances. The "lion," which seems to me to be more like a dragon than a lion, is made of multicolored—predominantly red—paper. Its head is about twice the size of a live animal and is held high on a pole, swaying up and down and back and forth by the lead dancer. The lion's body and tail is up to 30 feet long and is carried on poles by 10 or more dancers, all weaving side to side, up and down, as they move down the street, frightening small children who scream in fear.

For 24 hours, ALL day and ALL night, firecrackers exploded all over the city by the hundreds and thousands. I'm NOT exaggerating!

Firecrackers, all wrapped in red paper, were sold in long strings, with 50 or 100 firecrackers on a string, and one wick at the end. I saw people standing on their balconies, lighting one string after another, throwing them down onto the street where the people down there were doing the same. By noon, the streets were <u>covered</u> with a carpet of the red paper left from the explosions. By afternoon, I could walk on a soft carpet of red. Amazing! Though people had told me about it before experiencing it, I couldn't even begin to imagine what it was like in reality.

The symphony of NOISE on Chinese New Year included not only the continuous bursts of firecrackers but also cherry bombs, gongs and cymbals, Chinese music, people shouting and dancing, hawkers selling their wares and food, and parties. Yes, Chinese New Year in Borneo was an unforgettable experience for me. But I cry out to God for these beautiful people who have yet to realize their need to know Jesus, the one who has already triumphed over all those spirits and gods they try to scare away and placate.

Actually, the people of Sabah, who live in towns, are of both Chinese and Malay ancestry, and they practice a variety of religions and religious practices. We learned of the challenges in reaching these people as we fellowshipped with our Christian friends who were actively involved in various outreaches, both in and outside the city. Since it was difficult for Christian missionaries to renew their visas to live in the country, it's up to the indigenous and Chinese Christians to live and witness for Christ and spread the Good News of salvation in Him. We were acutely aware of the needs and problems of our friends, students, fellow teachers, nurses, and missionaries there. We prayed regularly for them and entrusted them to the Lord's keeping.

Steam-engine Train Travel

Peter and I have always enjoyed and sought out new places to see and visit. One day, Peter said, "Let's go on a train trip."

"Where?" I asked. "There's a steam-engine train that runs through a gorge in the Crocker Mountains. That should be fun," he replied. I agreed, "Let's go!"

What an adventure! The engine burned wood. As the train wound its way on the snakelike tracks through the gorge, I could look out the open window of the train and see the whole length of the train in front of our car. And I could see the cinders spewing out of the engine's smokestack, blowing straight at me—and in my window as I ducked out of the way or wiped or blew the still-lit cinders off my clothing. Memories are made of this.

Leong Yaufun

The leader of Peter's homeroom class, Yaufun, was an intelligent young man of Chinese descent. He was Peter's star pupil. Yaufun's skills enabled us to meld a task Peter and I wanted to accomplish with a special interest of mine. We had filled shoeboxes with the pictures we had taken documenting our life in Borneo, and we wanted to bring them home, organized in an album we could share with our families.

Second, I love flowers, which are abundant in Borneo, and Peter had said to me, "A woman should have flowers every day." (Any wonder that I loved this man?) We decided we wanted to incorporate the theme of flowers into our lifetime album.

Cross-pollinating our ideas, we expanded our plan to develop a lifelong album of photographs, not only documenting Borneo but our whole life as well. We call it *The Garden of Our Lives*, titling each section with the name of a flower and referencing a Scripture verse:

The Garden of Our Lives	Picture of fountain with grape vines		Isaiah 61:11
Bachelor's Button	Peter Nickolai Westrum	Oct 23 1942 – Aug 8 1966	Psalms 119:9
Lady Slipper	Susan Sarah Palmer	Nov 16 1939 – Aug 8 1966	Genesis 2:18
Morning Glories	The Dawn of Love	Aug 8 1966 – Dec 21 1966	1 John 4:19
Sunflowers	Love Grows	Dec 21 1966 – Aug 6 1968	1 Corinthians 13:7
Gardenia	Marriage & Anniversaries	August 6, 1968	Ruth 1:16
Poppies	Our Children & Grandchildren		Proverbs 22:6
Forget-Me-Nots	People We Love		John 15:12
Palm Trees	Our Life's Work		Ephesians 4:1
Birds of Paradise	Our Spiritual End		Philippians 1:21

When we learned that Yaufun was a talented artist and skilled at calligraphy, we asked him to help us execute our plan. He did a remarkable job designing, painting, and drawing the title pages for the entire project. That one album has now grown to three albums and is another of our highly prized treasures.

As we talked about our lives and plans and looked forward to the future and our lives and future work, God caused me to reflect on my foundational beliefs. In August 1969, I wrote the following:

1. There is a God.
2. A God, such as I believe in, would give humans instruction on how He expects them to live.
3. A loving God, as I believe in, would provide for all of man's needs.
4. Man is sinful. I'm a sinner.
5. When I try to not sin, I fail. The Bible says I'm separated from God and cannot be united to Him through my own efforts.
6. The Bible claims to be God's instruction to man. It's the only word we have that claims to be direct from God. I will, therefore, follow it.
7. The Bible says God has provided Jesus for my needs—the greatest of which is salvation.
8. Jesus claimed to be God. Either He is or He was crazy. I believe He wasn't crazy.
9. No one else has ever claimed to be God or the way to Him. I will, therefore, put my trust in Him and follow Him. He's my only hope.
10. I'll fight satan's attacks by claiming God's Word. I need to continually hear His Word so I can keep close to Jesus.
11. I know I was changed on December 13, 1966. I was sealed. "And don't grieve God's Holy Spirit. You were sealed by Him for the day of redemption" (Ephesians 4:30, Holman Christian Standard Bible).

Celebrating Our Anniversaries

For our first anniversary in Sandakan, I splurged and went to a beauty salon; I had them pile my hair high on my head in a fashionable bun. Peter gave me gardenias, and we dressed up and went out to dinner at the Rec Club where we had celebrated our rehearsal dinner the year before. As we reviewed our first year, we realized that as the years passed, we would begin to forget many of the special events and ministries in which we would be involved. We decided on some annual anniversary activities: get a picture of me wearing my wedding dress, take a family picture, and record a summary of the year's activities on tape. We successfully followed our plan for about 30 years. I confess I've recently encountered a problem with my wedding dress—it seems to have gotten smaller. But you'd never know it by the pictures—you can't see that all those buttons in the back can no longer be buttoned.

Returning to the US

Anticipating the end of Peter's teaching assignment, we packed our things in barrels and shipped them back to the US. In August, just one year after we had moved into our apartment, we received an invitation from a missionary pastor to move into his roomy two-story home in a newly developed area of Sandakan. He needed to be away for three months and wanted us to stay with his family during his absence and help with the household chores. How fortunate for us—no more 75 stairs to climb many times daily, no noisy traffic passing by us, and no US$67.00 rent charged. And the frosting on the cake: hot and cold running water, screens on all the windows, and the use of a car and piano.

As we left our life and the work God gave us in Borneo, we realized how much we would miss our friends and the work of the church in which we had been involved. We were so pleased that the Basel Christian Church took over the full leadership responsibility of the Mile 86 mission clinic and Gospel outreach. We are still amazed, as we see God at work in our lives daily, doing more abundantly than we could ever think or ask (Ephesians 3:20).

Something Worth Giving Our Lives To

January to June 1970

Proclaim among the nations what He has done.
—Psalms 9:11b, New International Version

As we were finishing up our work in Malaysia, we began to pray, asking God to show us what He had next for us. Peter has natural abilities in speaking languages and in relating to people from other cultures, and we had fallen in love with Asian people. We felt God was calling us to language work in Asia. But we didn't know exactly what that would entail or where in Asia that might be. We prayed. Instead of flying directly back to the States, we took a long and slow route—traveling by air, land, and sea—for five months. We decided that once we arrived back in Minnesota, we'd wait there for God to reveal the next adventure He had planned for us.

We left Sandakan by ship and, bobbing on the waves for an exciting week on the Sulu and South China seas, made stops along the Borneo coasts before arriving in Singapore. Trains carried us north up the entire Malay Peninsula to northern Thailand. From there, we alternately took planes and trains in India, Afghanistan, and five Soviet Union Republics, before spending a month in the fascinating epistle land of Turkey and the Gospel land, Israel. Reminded of the Apostle Paul's journeys, we went by ship to Cyprus and, once in Greece, continued onward all through Europe. It was an engrossing relaxing five-month trip, after which we wrote a 15-page report of our experiences in, and impressions of, the Soviet Union.

When we arrived in Zurich, Switzerland, we went straight to the US Embassy where we picked up our mail. We were delighted to receive a letter from a friend who had attended Calvary Bible Church in New York with me when I was living there before Peter and I were married. Writing about her upcoming service with Wycliffe Bible Translators (WBT) and its sister organization, the Summer Institute of Linguistics (SIL), we learned that Wycliffe is a mission organization dedicated to ensuring that every person around the world has access to God's Word in their heart language—the language they understand best.

It sounded challenging and piqued our interest. We had prayed that we would be able to serve overseas as language workers for a larger home-based team of Christians and work with a people group who had never before heard about Jesus, in their OWN language. Peter said, "This group deals with language work. Let's write to them and get more details."

I thought it was a great idea. So we wrote, explaining our overseas experience and desire to serve the Lord in the field of languages in Asia. We asked for information and requested that they send their response and an application to us at the US Embassy in London. We were quite impressed when we arrived in London, picked up our mail, and found that a letter from Wycliffe was there waiting for us.

We crossed the Atlantic, flying on a Boeing 747 for the first time, and landed in New York on April 12, 1970. Though very tired after the long trip, I was full of energy, and my heart was beating fast. I was sooooooooooooo excited! We waited in that long line of returning citizens, and when we stepped up to the immigration window, the official said, "Welcome home!"

WOW! My eyes filled with tears, and I thanked God for the great privilege of being an American. We cleared customs and made our way out-side onto American soil. I felt like kneeling down and kissing the ground. What rich blessings God has given us to belong to this land, the home of the free. Not until one has lived in another country can a person under-stand how bountifully God has showered His blessings on us as a nation.

We made our way by public limousine and train to Gwynedd Valley, Pennsylvania, where our friends, had stored our car for us at their home. We had wheels again! Yeah!

Spending a week to renew "old" friendships, we drove to New York City (NYC) and had our closing interview with Dr. David, the director of the Board of World Missions, under whom Peter had served in Borneo. He was the man who had cabled the mission's permission for Peter to marry halfway through his contracted term. I enjoyed introducing Peter to my former NYC roommates and my friends and colleagues at Camp Hope, where I had worked as a camp nurse.

Journeying west, we visited relatives and friends, giving programs in churches along the way. I remember our being stopped at a roadblock in Ohio where the police were conducting a traffic survey. "Where are you coming from?" the policeman asked. We hesitated, not knowing what he meant. *Coming from where we stayed last night? Coming from New York? From Europe? From where we started in Borneo?*

"Well, where're you going?" he probed further. *Oh help? What's he mean now? Where we're going tonight? Tomorrow? Minnesota to visit relatives? Or California to visit other relatives.* We were sure he didn't mean our eternal goal—heaven. "What's the purpose of this roadblock?" we asked. "That would help us know how to answer."

As the puzzled man stood there, we explained our confusion and had a good laugh together. We went on our way, not knowing whether our responses were helpful for the traffic survey or not.

I Have to Study—What?

A couple of days later, while visiting friends in Wisconsin, I made a phone call to the Wycliffe office in Santa Ana, California. "I'm a nurse," I said, "and I actually don't know anything about languages and translation work. If God is calling me to be a Bible translator, what will I have to study?"

"You'll need to study linguistics," the man responded.

"I never heard of it!" I exclaimed.

He calmly explained, "You'll need to take courses in phonetics, phonology, and morphology."

"I've never heard of any of it." *Oh Lord, help!*

"That's OK," he said. "Just go up to the University of North Dakota in Grand Forks this summer and take the Summer Institute of Linguistics courses, and we'll teach you."

"OK. That'll work for us. We're planning to be in Los Angeles next month. May we stop by the Santa Ana office for an interview then?"

"Excellent," he replied. "Let us know the exact day you'll be coming. We'd love to show you around and orient you to what God's doing and share the vision God's given us for Bible translation. Also, we'll mail applications, one for each of you, to fill out and return to us before you get here."

"Great," I responded. "We'll look forward to receiving those in Minnesota where we'll be headquartering for the coming months."

After a delightful stop in Minneapolis with my dad and Evie, my brother Jim, and three-year-old Nancy Jo, at last we arrived in Moorhead, Minnesota, on May 8. Our plan was to live there with Peter's parents, Gladys and Lloyd, until God opened the way for our next step of Christian ministry.

The applications from Wycliffe were waiting for us when we arrived in Moorhead. Wycliffe's policy is that both husband and wife need to feel God's call and be assured of His leading to overseas mission work. Both of us needed to apply, pass the academic courses and a Bible exam, and successfully complete jungle-living training in our own right. What a challenge! *Oh Lord, I need You every step of the way. I can't do this without You; it's WAY out of my comfort zone. Help!*

I Can't Say Yes to That

The application was a long four-page affair. Peter filled his out without delay and mailed it off. I started working on mine and was perking along pretty well, when I came to a sudden halt. On the third page, I read the question, "Can you definitely say that you do and will be able to depend solely on God alone for all your needs?" I thought, *No, I can't say yes to that.*

I told Peter, "I've never heard of such a thing. Since I got out of college, I've made my own way. I've always had a job. I put in my time, punched a time clock, and got a paycheck for what I did. That's the way life is. Isn't it presumptuous to think God would just give me what I need without working for an earthly employer? I can't finish my application. I'm tabling it until God shows me, in some tangible way, that this is right, and this is what He wants of me." We prayed. We talked only to the Lord—no one else—about my dilemma, and I put the application aside.

The very next day—I kid you not—the doorbell rang. I answered the door. It was a family friend, Dave, who had heard that God was calling us into mission work. I invited him in. He sat down and said, "Sue, I'm eager to hear more about the work to which God's calling you. But first, I have to tell you that I've never experienced anything like this before in my life. I don't understand it, but I felt compelled by God this morning to come over here and give you this." He handed me a check for $50.00!

I called to Peter, who was upstairs, "Peter, I need you to come down here and visit with Dave." "Oh, Dave," I said, "I'll let Peter explain to you what has just happened. I need to go upstairs to finish filling out my application to join Wycliffe."

God has NEVER let us down. In all our 45 years serving with Wycliffe, God always supplied all our needs. He IS faithful. Truly, trusting and following Him is a good life.

California

Eager to visit my mother, sister, and friends in California, we continued our journey west, camping in parks in Nebraska, Colorado, and then south in the Grand Canyon, along the way. Both Peter and I have always enjoyed traveling, seeing God's creation firsthand, and experiencing new societies and cultures.

Arriving in Santa Barbara, California, my mother generously gave us a wedding reception in her beautifully decorated home, including my wedding flowers, gardenias. Twenty-two people, who of course, hadn't been with us in Borneo for our wedding, came to celebrate with us.

Peter and I had planned from the beginning to have Scripture verses engraved on the inner side of our wedding rings, so we went to the same store where I had purchased our rings before leaving for Borneo. Peter had Ephesians 1:6–8 engraved in his ring: "Let us praise God for His glorious grace, for the free gift He gave us in His dear Son! For by the blood of Christ we are set free, that is, our sins are forgiven. How great is the grace of God, which He gave to us in such large measure!" (Good News Translation). Ruth 1:16 is engraved in my ring: "But Ruth said, 'Don't urge me to leave you or to return from following you. For where you go I will go, and where you lodge I will lodge. Your people shall be my people, and your God my God'" (English Standard Version).

We had been married in Malaysia just two months after my sister Mary had married in the US; we wore the same wedding dress. Now, together in California two years later, we had fun taking a trick picture of us standing side by side, wearing the same dress. Yes, a double exposure, using a Polaroid camera.

Mary's Name Is Written in Heaven

Those were all wonderful events, but on June 4, 1970, our excitement knew no end. Mary told us that she had accepted Jesus as her Savior and Lord. When she had visited me in 1967 in New York City while I was flying for Pan Am, I had said to her, "Mary, I really am praying that you'll come to know my Friend, Jesus. He showed me that He died for my sins, and I believe He died for yours too. The Bible is THE Book that is now the most important thing in the world to me."

We talked a lot about God's Word that day. I said, "I believe God created us. And just like manufacturers write an 'owner's manual' when they produce a new product so the buyer will know how to use it, God's given us His owner's manual, the Bible, for our lives, so we can know how He wants us to live. The Bible says that someday Jesus is coming back to this earth to take us to heaven to be with Him. Mary, I want to tell you now, before it happens, so that if you wake up someday and lots of people, including me, are gone, you'll know where we went."

God used that thought and was the faithful Hound of Heaven pursuing Mary. I felt a deep joy welling up from down inside me, knowing God had answered our prayers that Mary had given her life to Jesus. We were double sisters now—biological and spiritual.

How Many Languages?

When Peter and I visited the Wycliffe office in Santa Ana, I so clearly remember seeing a bookcase with 20 New Testaments from different languages around the world. All had been completed by Wycliffe personnel. "That's wonderful," I said. "How many languages are there that you want to work on?"

"Two thousand," our guide answered. He detailed the need of 2,000 groups of people in this world who didn't have EVEN ONE verse of Scripture in a language they could understand! We were surprised and deeply moved. Two thousand groups speaking 2,000 DIFFERENT languages? *How can that be?* I wondered, *I didn't even know there were that many languages in the world. I only speak one.*

That very day, we both felt God was saying to us, "Peter and Sue, I want YOU to translate My Word for one of those 2,000 groups of people."

But God, I thought, *that's a big job for an ordinary girl like me! I'm a nurse. I don't even fully understand my own language.*

Yes, I know, God said in my mind and heart. *But I can do it, and I want to work through you and Peter.*

The years peeled away, and I was a little girl living in Minneapolis. It was late afternoon; the sun was going down, the trees casting long shadows across the front yard of our Colfax Avenue house. I looked up at grand colors in the sky as the soft pink and then yellow and orange mixed with the vibrant blue. It was a private, personal moment with the God of the universe. I actually said out loud to myself, "Someday I'm going to do something that no one else will do." I didn't know at that time what it meant, but I remembered; and it came back to me once again that day in Wycliffe's Santa Ana office.

Five years later, when we were actually living in the jungle with the Berik people, one morning during my morning prayer time, God whispered in my thoughts, *This is the task I planned for you that I told you about those many years ago in Minneapolis.* God had loved and spoken to me even before I knew Him personally. How special is that?

Yes, God clearly showed us His will for us that day in Santa Ana. We thanked Him for having a plan for our lives, for a special task and ministry for us, proclaiming what He had done. This was something worth giving our lives to!

We applied to attend summer school in Grand Forks and had just eight days to get there and get settled into the dorm before classes started on June 15. We hightailed it out of California, stopping one night to camp in Yellowstone Park. We set up our tent, but surprise, it snowed that night. We wound up "sleeping" in the car.

During that long night, we talked about, wondered, and imagined just exactly what the coming five to 10 years would hold for us. *Lord, we don't know the details, but we know You have a plan—a plan You designed just for us in eternity past. None of it will surprise You. We wait for You to show us Your plan step-by-step. Thank You, in Jesus's Name.*

And we began our adventure of faith. What an adventure it's been! I never dreamed the half of it that snowy camping night in June 1970.

Grand Forks

June 1970 to November 1971

For I can do all things through
Christ, who strengthens me.
—Philippians 4:13, New King James Version

Our Adventure in Bible Translation Began with Linguistics

Registration day for the Summer Institute of Linguistics (SIL) at the University of North Dakota is engrained in my memory. Long tables were set up in the lobby of our dorm, where we were to fill out all our paperwork and pick up our class schedules and books. As we were making our way from table to table, Becky, one of the instructors, came up to me. "Sue, please come with me. I want to give you a little assessment to see which phonetics lab class to put you in to study the sounds of languages."

I must have looked concerned. "Don't be nervous," she said. "All you have to do is repeat some words after me." I relaxed. *That can't be too hard.*

Little did I know. We went to a small side room where it was quiet. Becky asked me to repeat 19 words after her, words spoken in various languages from all over the world. All those utterances had sounds in them that we don't have in English. I was amazed. I tried hard, not wanting to look too dumb, but knew I wasn't doing well at all.

Becky smiled, saying, "It's OK. Now here's the last thing I want you to do. Say 'hello' while you are inhaling the air INTO your lungs, instead of while the air is going out of your lungs."

I took a deep breath and, while the air went strongly OUT of my lungs, nearly shouting, said, "Hello!" I tried again, drew air in deeply, and a little more quietly said, "Hello." I had no idea how to speak while breathing IN. Dear reader, did you just try to do it? Were you successful? If so, I suggest you would have an easier time studying phonetics than I did.

Becky was gentle. "Don't worry, Sue. We'll put you in the beginner's class. By the end of the summer, you'll be able to do this and more." She gave me a pat on my shoulder.

I was thinking, *Lord, I think I'm already in over my head. Help!* I remembered that in school, my lowest grades were in English, grammar, and literature classes. I disliked poetry and Shakespeare. *Lord, wouldn't You be better off using someone who You've gifted in these things?*

Never Heard of All This Before

I'll never forget the first sentence, spoken by the first instructor, in our first SIL class in June 1970. "On my way to class this morning, I picked up two items that are both the same and different," Dr. Dick began. He held up two leaves. "You can see that these are the same; they're both leaves. And you can clearly see that they are different. One's a maple leaf; the other is an oak leaf. And that is exactly what this class, phonetics, is all about. You'll learn all that is the same regarding the sounds that can be made by the human vocal apparatus. And you'll learn to recognize how to differentiate each sound from all the others. You'll learn to hear and reproduce and write a symbol for every possible sound, so by the end of this course, you'll be able to go anywhere in the world and write down what the people are saying."

WOW! Really? I thought. "Peter, is it really possible I'll be able to learn all that? It'll be a miracle for me to succeed in this class."

I was amazed as the summer went by. God enabled, and I truly enjoyed Dr. Dick's lectures and the accompanying lab classes practicing the sounds found in languages that Becky had warned me about.

All the "single-married" students lived on the same floor in the dorm. We were newly married and without children. We enjoyed studying and learning together, sharing how God was leading each of us. In the evening, a cacophony of sounds could be heard up and down the hallway as all of us first-year phonetics students tried again and again and again to successfully pronounce sounds we had never heard before. Our tongues felt twisted like pretzels as we learned the necessary control.

Phonology, the study of the sound system of a language, was also a challenging course for me. We were taught to research which sounds in a language occur word initial, word medial, and word final; which sounds occur in pairs; and which may never occur together. Learning the distribution patterns of the sounds of the language we would be studying would enable us to develop an alphabet for people who speak unwritten languages.

My mind was continually on overload all summer as I sought to internalize all these new disciplines. *Oh Lord, I really need Your help. I'd never even heard of linguistics, phonetics, phonology, and morphology until a month ago! Please help me remember all this stuff.*

Morphology, that is analyzing grammar, is the study of the patterns of word formation in a particular language, the description of such patterns, and the study of the behavior and combination of morphemes. Now that's a mouthful! And what's a morpheme anyway? It's any of the minimal grammatical units of a language. To this day, I thank God for the excellent instructors He provided for us so Peter and I could determine which words or syllables in the language we would study in the future were nouns, verbs, adjectives, adverbs, prepositions, and so on. We were taught how to figure out where the word breaks are in a stream of speech and just where in a sentence verbs, adjectives, and prepositions are placed.

The last two weeks of the summer program were set aside for working with "informants," people who spoke languages we had never heard before. This was our opportunity to put into practice all we had learned during the summer. Peter worked with a lady who spoke Cantonese. My informant spoke the Amoy language, another Chinese dialect. It was an intense and challenging time because we were working with real live persons, not just doing a classroom exercise.

But it was also rewarding and exciting because we realized we had the skills to begin a language program overseas. God had answered my cries for help to Him. I actually understood what I had been taught, got good grades, and was qualified to become a Wycliffe-SIL translator. I learned that God doesn't call the qualified; He qualifies those He calls. He delights in making His strength apparent through our weak areas. *Thank You, Lord!*

More Than Studying

Many of the "single-married" couples—that is, young married couples without children—we lived and studied with that summer, and with whom we still maintain contact today, were also applying to join Wycliffe.

In addition to our studies, we each worked on our "doctrinal statement." One of Wycliffe's requirements for membership was to write, in our own words, and using substantiating Scripture references, our own beliefs on 18 points of Christian doctrine. A challenge to be sure but oh so worthwhile. It's a good way to "dig" into the Word and thus "be ready to give an answer to every man that asks you a reason of the hope that is in you with meekness and fear" (1 Peter 3:15). I believe all followers of Christ would do well to take on the challenge and make the time to write their own doctrinal statement.

SIL was invited to take part in some of the university functions. One activity, which celebrated cultures from around the world, was held near the end of the summer in the university's main auditorium. Peter and I got all the exercise we needed practicing for that event; we provided one number for the musical show—we danced the tinikling bamboo dance from the Philippines. Peter had learned it when he served in the Peace Corps in the Philippines and had taught it to me when we worked together at the Rehab Hospital in Minneapolis.

Culminating the summer was the opportunity for Peter to follow the Lord in baptism by immersion. The previous February, when we were in Israel, the Lord had led Peter to be baptized with a group of believers in the Mediterranean Sea, there in that land where Jesus had walked. But God overruled when a storm arose the day of the scheduled baptism celebration. The waves were just too high, and it wasn't safe to be in the water.

Peter had continued to pray about it, and God paved the way for him that summer in 1970. On Sundays, we were blessed as we worshipped with the local Brethren Assembly in Grand Forks. It was a privilege to come to know one of the elders, Wesley, and his wife. Peter talked with Brother Wesley, who had also been approached by a young dentist and his wife, who also desired to be baptized. They lived on a lake in Minnesota, and arrangements were made for a lakeside baptism service at their home one Sunday afternoon.

Accepted

We completed our linguistic courses, turned in our Doctrinal Statements, had interviews with the candidate committee, and waited. And prayed, ready to accept God's decision for our future.

On August 1, 1970, we received the following letter from Wycliffe:

Mr. and Mrs. Peter Westrum
Summer Institute of Linguistics
Grand Forks, North Dakota

Dear Peter and Susan:

It is a pleasure to inform you that at a meeting of the Board of Directors held at Grand Forks, North Dakota, on Friday, July 31, 1970, the following action was taken:

> Moved that Peter and Susan Westrum, USA, be accepted as "Members in Training" of the Wycliffe Bible Translators, Inc. They have applied as translators.

We welcome you into our Wycliffe family and trust that we may be a blessing to you, even as we expect you to be a blessing to the tribes you will be serving. As your fellow Wycliffe members, we will remember you at the Throne of Grace and trust that you will uphold your Board of Directors, other administrators, and all your fellow Wycliffe members in prayer.

Sincerely yours, in Christ,
Richard Pittman
For the Board of Directors

We also received an almost identical letter from SIL, Wycliffe's sister organization, so we were now Members in Training for both organizations. Wycliffe was involved in recruiting and vetting candidates, relating to US churches and parachurch organizations, and guiding members when in their home countries. SIL took the lead in training members who were preparing to serve minority language groups in countries all around the world, coordinating work agreements with overseas governments, acquiring members' visas, and supervising members on the field.

Settling in for the Winter

Knowing that we would again be attending SIL during the summer of 1971, and because Peter had applied to be a full-time student in the graduate school at the University of North Dakota, we elected to live in Grand Forks for the coming year. The requirements for acquiring a master's degree in linguistics included taking two summer sessions with SIL. But Peter learned that if he carried a full load of classes during the upcoming fall semester, he would only have to take one course the next summer. He could write his master's thesis on data he would gather during our first term on the field.

The last week of our summer program, even as we were working with our informants, we set out to find a place to live after we moved out of the UND dorm. We found a nice building close to the university and applied to rent one of the six one-bedroom apartments for a year. And we waited and waited.

On the last day of school, Peter was notified that he had been accepted into the graduate school. We learned that the Lord often leads just one step at a time. Sometimes He shows us the next step only after we've finished the former one. He was about to emphasize that lesson to us.

The next morning, after we had packed up, loaded the car, and cleaned our dorm room, we were still waiting for a call from our prospective landlord. As I sat in the car while Peter sat by the phone in the dorm lobby, I prayed, *Father, we need to know where to go this afternoon. Where will we live for the coming year? We trust You to provide and to lead us. I pray in Jesus's Name.*

A few minutes later, Peter came out to the car with a big smile. The landlord had called, accepting our rental application. In addition, he offered to decrease our rent if we would assume the position of being the liaison between him and all the renters in that building and also take on the job of maintaining the inside common areas and the yard. Once again, God had provided far more than we had asked for or had thought of.

We moved our things into the apartment, drove to Moorhead for an overnight visit with Peter's parents, and set out on a one-week whirlwind trip. Our first stop was along the shore of Lake Michigan where we saved our pennies by sleeping in the car. The next day, we went on to Toronto to visit our friends, Richard and Veronica, who had been attendants in our wedding and with whom we had become close friends in Sandakan. They had moved to Toronto just six months earlier, and we missed them terribly.

Together, the four of us visited magnificent Niagara Falls. And then after a tearful good-bye, we hit the road again, headed for the destination of our seven-day jaunt, our friend's home near Philadelphia. They had graciously stored our furniture for us while we were overseas. They helped us load all our belongings into a trailer hitched to the back of our car. The next morning, we were off again, heading like homing pigeons to our new home in Grand Forks. We arrived just in time for Peter to register for four fall semester courses—Language and Culture, Anthropology of Religion, Sociological Theory, and German. I was delighted that we were now in charge of the yard and flower beds; I set out immediately to brighten things up by planting yellow and gold marigolds by our front door.

I had enjoyed using my nursing skills in the SIL clinic during the summer, and when I learned that an opening for an RN to work as team leader on the 3:00 p.m. to 11:00 p.m. shift at the University of North Dakota Rehab Center had "just happened" to open up that week, I applied. It was a great position that included not only teaching patients to again become independent but also instructing the staff in rehab principles.

One young lady, Kathy, had been in a horrific accident during her senior year in high school. As I worked with her five days a week for several months, she shared her heart, her fears, and her heartaches. I told her about God's leading in my life, first in coming to know Jesus as my own Savior, the serenity I now felt in following Him, and our plans to soon leave for the mission field. God blessed our visits in a special way when Kathy, and then also her mother, turned their lives over to Jesus.

Yaufun Comes to the US

Following the practice of the Malaysian school system in encouraging promising students to continue their education abroad, Leong Yaufun—Peter's star pupil in Sandakan—pursued opportunities to study overseas after high school graduation. Peter's mother and father graciously agreed to receive him into their home in Minnesota while he continued his studies. Yaufun arrived in Los Angeles on Thanksgiving Day, 1970.

On every flight during his 36-hour journey from Malaysia, he had been served a turkey dinner. He had never tasted turkey or stuffing with gravy before, and he decided he never wanted to do so again. But, by the time we greeted him in Moorhead, Minnesota, the next day, he had recovered from the shock of not having access to Chinese food. Mom and Dad Westrum welcomed him and assisted as he registered for the last semester at the local high school. *Lord, help Yaufun adjust to life in America. Lead him, guide him, and please send the Hound of Heaven to him.*

Head Start Program

With Peter's studies finished in January 1971, he sought the Lord's will for the coming months before the summer SIL classes would begin. He applied for a teaching position with the Minnesota Migrant Head Start Program. To our surprise, he was turned down. The recruiter explained, "Mr. Westrum, you're overqualified to work as a teacher with us. We'd like to offer you employment as the director of the entire program. You would supervise the teachers—a total of 70 salaried staff members and the services for 375 children." Peter accepted and started work in mid-January 1971.

When I filled out my application to join Wycliffe, God had shown me He would provide for us, and now He had shown us again in another outstanding way, beyond our imaginations. I learned that I could truly trust Him . . . no matter what.

Called to Indonesia

In February, the Indonesian government officially requested SIL workers to serve on the islands of Southern Borneo and Celebes. Indonesia is an island nation situated off the coast of mainland Southeast Asia between the Indian and Pacific oceans. This archipelago, which lies across the equator and spans a distance equivalent to one-eighth of the earth's circumference, has more than 17,000 islands (6,000 uninhabited) and is the world's fourth most populous country. SIL contacted us and asked that we be among the first translators to go to Indonesia in response to this exciting invitation. We felt God was leading us, and we trusted Him for His perfect timing regarding our departure date.

After being accepted by Wycliffe for overseas assignment as Bible translators, under the auspices of SIL, we had begun to write our relatives and friends to share with them how God was leading us. We prayed earnestly for a supporting team of about 25 units, a unit being a couple or a single person. Our "free time" became very busy with speaking engagements as people wrote asking us to give programs, not only about our time in Malaysia and our long trip home but also about our upcoming move to Indonesia. And God began to lead people to join our team to reach just one more of the world's Bibleless people groups, with His Word in their own language. In December, one couple wrote and committed to pray for us as we moved forward in this adventure. In February, a second couple joined our team.

"The LORD gives, and the LORD takes away"
(Job 1:21b, Holman Christian Standard Bible)

In mid-February, I visited a doctor who confirmed what I had suspected since December; Peter and I were expecting our first child. God had answered the deep desire of our hearts. I had had some abnormal spotting but was doing well working at the hospital. I had one surprising side effect. Peter picked me up at work every night at 11:00 p.m., and when we got home, I was hungry—for lettuce. I would often devour a whole head before bed.

When I saw the doctor in March, he reported that my uterus had not enlarged since my last visit. But the spotting had stopped, so he said we would just watch and see what he would find in April. Two weeks later, I began having contractions and was hospitalized over the weekend. We had a program about Malaysia scheduled to do with Yaufun on April 12, Easter Monday. *Lord, we commit our days to You.*

At bedtime on Easter Sunday, the contractions began again. At 2:00 a.m., I miscarried the baby. Upon examination, the doctor explained that the baby had actually died very early in my pregnancy, but the placenta had continued to grow for three months. He cleared me to go about normal activities, so Peter and I and Yaufun went ahead with the program that evening. I clearly remember the delightful group we fellowshipped with at the church and the love and concern the ladies expressed as they prayed for God's will in our lives.

God gave us the gift and blessing of extraordinary comfort and peace. We were enabled to accept that 1971 wasn't God's time for us to have our first baby. We trusted His plan.

Further Contact with the Gideons

We were trusting God's plan for our lives; now He surprised us with an outreach that had the potential of increasing our prayer support. Mr. John from the Gideons wrote again, "Mr. Bill sent us a copy of a newsletter you and your husband sent out in November 1970. We were really pleased to read this and to learn of the wonderful way in which the Lord has been using you . . . With your permission, we would like very much to give our membership an 'update' on you and the work the Lord is doing through you and your husband . . . Your testimony has been a real blessing and encouragement to Gideons throughout the USA, and I am certain this additional information would serve to undergird you with a great amount of prayer support." *WOW, Thank You, Lord. You understand how much we need prayer if we are to accomplish the tasks You've set out for us.*

Mr. John also asked me to "include minute particulars" and photos to aid them in writing the article. I wound up sending six pages and wrote "You may use this information in any way you so desire—for His glory, for strengthening the brethren, and for furthering His Kingdom." The article appeared in the February 1972 issue of *The Gideon*, and while I never learned the names of Gideons who may have prayed for us, I am quite sure many did pray, for God just kept blessing and enabling.

Team Letters

In May 1971, we sent out our first letter to the four couples who had, by then, joined our team. We listed their names and addresses and wrote of our desire to share news about one team unit in each letter, suggesting that as the years went by, we would truly be a united team, all praying for one another.

In June, Mother and her husband Glen came to Grand Forks to visit us for two weeks. Mother was growing in her Christian walk and was now a mission enthusiast. She and Glen arrived in time to attend Yaufun's high school graduation. The following week, they accompanied Peter when he led a Head Start training program and went with us when we made a mission presentation in a church. What a fantastic change God had wrought in her life. Mother volunteered to become our team secretary. She suggested we send information to her, and she would duplicate our letters and send them out to all the team. What a marvelous, unexpected provision.

Peter's supervisor in the Head Start program also supplied our needs in a surprising way. In return for Peter continuing to lead the summer program for migrant children, Mr. Fred not only gave Peter permission to attend classes for the one course he needed to take but he covered the costs of the course AND Peter's summer tuition.

After SIL classes began the second week of their visit, Mother and Glen actually attended phonetics, morphology, and literacy classes with me. They both seemed to enjoy Friday's musical chapel, Glen especially soaking in all he heard. Two weeks after they returned to Los Angeles, Mother wrote to say that Glen had accepted Christ as his Savior. Hallelujah! We serve a great God who works to make Himself known in our hearts.

Yaufun's Name Is Also Written in Heaven

Although Yaufun had been a student at the Christian high school where Peter taught in Malaysia and had attended a Christian church while we served there, he had never come to the place of putting Christ in the center of his life. He had many questions and doubts about the Christian faith. Another deterrent was that decision to become a Christian would mean at least a partial break with his family.

However, a friend invited him to attend a summer Bible camp, and after hearing a missionary speaker, Yaufun made the decision to be a Christ follower. He spoke with the camp director and even took the next step and was baptized in the nearby lake. He immediately started reading both his Chinese and his English Bible daily. *Thank You, Father, for showing Yaufun how much You love him.*

Officially Assigned to Indonesia

After successfully completing our summer courses, on August 23, 1971 we received the following letter from Wycliffe:

> Dear Peter and Sue:
>
> At a meeting of the personnel committee of our Board of Directors held at Grand Forks, North Dakota, on August 13, 1971, the following action was taken:
>
> > MOVED that Peter and Sue Westrum, USA, be tentatively assigned to the Indonesia Advance.
>
> We trust that our Lord will continue to guide you clearly in the days ahead as you serve Him.
>
> Sincerely in Christ,
> J. S. Henderson, Corporation Secretary

Off to Mexico

Though we moved to Moorhead to live with Peter's parents as soon as SIL was over, Peter continued working for Head Start through October. Thus, we were right there and were able to join a conspiracy with Peter's siblings to plan and execute a surprise thirty-ninth wedding anniversary celebration for their mom and dad. The family portrait taken that day is still treasured by all of us.

We had jumped through all but one of Wycliffe's and SIL's required hoops to qualify for overseas service: application documents, Bible exam, personal interviews, doctrinal statement, academic training, and had begun to grow our prayer team and raise our financial support. Wycliffe leaders said, "You've done well so far. But before you leave for Indonesia, we need to train you in how to survive living in the jungle. We're sending you to Mexico's southernmost state on the Guatemalan border for three months." In mid-October, we notified our team—which now numbered 16 units:

> Next month, we will be on our way south where we
> will spend three months in jungle survival training
> in Chiapas, Mexico. This will prepare us for the rig-
> ors of life that await us in Indonesia.

A week later, we found out I was pregnant again. *Oh my, Jesus! We thank You that we know You're in control of all things.*

Mother flew to Moorhead from LA; Peter loaded our car with all we'd need at Jungle Camp, and Mother and I drove across South Dakota, Colorado, and Utah to California together. We were blessed to have this time of harmonious relationship. Peter followed by air.

After we were gone, Peter's mother, Gladys, hung the following in her kitchen, where it stayed for the next 21 years:

> O Lord God
> Who has called Peter and Sue
> Your servants, to ventures of which
> They cannot see the Ending
> By Paths as yet untrodden
> And through perils unknown;
> Give them Faith to go out with You
> Not knowing whither they go

But only that Your Hand is leading them
And Your Love and our Prayers supporting them,
Through Jesus Christ our Lord. Amen.

Many of those who ate at Gladys' table prayed that prayer for us. Surely, God would be with us—even as we left for three months in a Mexican jungle.

Jungle Survival Training

November 1971 to March 1972

Those who trust in the LORD will find new strength.
They will soar high on wings like eagles.
They will run and not grow weary.
They will walk and not faint.
                    —Isaiah 40:31, New Living Translation

I was three months along in our second pregnancy when we left the US for Jungle Camp. I didn't realize what I was in for. I'd been to summer camps as a child and had lived in a cabin and had spent my days just having fun—swimming, sailing, horseback riding, learning to shoot bows and arrows and a rifle, singing around campfires, making new friends my own age. Camp. Perhaps a bit rustic but always FUN. I knew the Mexico training camp would be somewhat different since we were being prepared for the rigors of life awaiting us in the jungles of Indonesian New Guinea, but I didn't know the half of it.

But it was part of the program to which God had led us. So when Mother and I drove away from Moorhead, we were confident of God's guidance and care. We arrived safely in California five days later and greeted Peter when his plane arrived. After visiting family and friends, we stopped by the Wycliffe office in Los Angeles and headed on to Mexico, crossing the border on November 12, 1971.

After a week of orientation in Mexico City, we drove south to the small town of Las Casas where we stored our car and, the next day, flew to Jungle Camp's Main Base deep in the jungle. It was my first experience flying in a single-engine airplane and landing on a grass airstrip. I felt excited and surprisingly had total peace for I truly believed that the safest place to be is in the center of God's will. And that's exactly where we were.

Main Base

We bonded quickly with the 54 adults and 28 children who flew into Main Base the same day we did. We were all new Wycliffe recruits, wondering what in the world we had gotten into now. I was amazed that several couples had their children with them; one couple had four children, all under the age of nine. Adults and children alike needed to be prepared for the coming unknown adventure of overseas jungle living.

Peter in our one-room mud hut

The staff was well-prepared for us and graciously helped us settle into our own one-room, mud-walled, dirt-floor, thatched-roofed hut. We were given one kerosene lamp for light and a mosquito net to hang over our bed.

We adult campers spent our days together, eating our meals in a large group dining hall and studying a couple of hours each day in the classroom. But most of our training was outdoors, challenging our skills and endurance. Special programs were held for the children.

We went on excursions, riding mules and hiking, to nearby Indian villages. Three times a week, we were off, hiking up and down the mountains. Now I have to confess, I've never been one to think walking, jogging, or hiking was fun. So there I was in the jungle being asked to participate in group hikes. Staff and campers alike soon recognized I was the slowest of them all. So what did the staff do? They put me—and Peter, bless his heart—first in line as we set off on a new trail. "Sue, you set the pace," they said. I didn't hear any groans, but soon, one by one, the other hikers would pass us, and Peter and I wound up bringing up the rear.

Hanging Between Two Trees All Night

On Friday of our first week at camp, the staff took all the campers away from Main Base to have our first overnight experience sleeping in jungle hammocks. A jungle hammock has two panels of cloth—a strong base material panel and an overhead water-resistant panel—between which there is a fine no-see-um bug mesh, which provided protection from mosquitoes, flies, and crawling insects.

We hiked a short distance from Main Base to a lovely spot near the river where we each found two strong and appropriately spaced trees from which to hang our hammocks. We hung them and searched for heavy-duty straight branches we could use as stabilizers to keep our hammocks from flopping us out onto the ground as we turned over in our sleep at night. Putting our sleeping bags inside, we carefully zipped them shut, praying that none of God's creatures had gotten in there by mistake.

Trail stew was the only item on the menu for supper, and after washing up our canteen cups that served as both plates and a drinking utensil, we settled around the fire for an evening of singing.

By 7:00 p.m., it was dark, and we were exhausted. We slowly, carefully crawled into our hammocks and lay very still, praying we could sleep in one position all night and not flop over and fall out with a scream and a thud. I fell asleep quickly to the music of jungle insects and the faint sound of Christmas carols being sung by campers who still sat around the campfire.

Peter awoke early in the morning to start our breakfast fire. High in the nearby trees, we gazed at the beauty of orchids and two large climbing split-leaf philodendrons. This experience had drawn us closer to God and to one another. We had survived this new adventure—so far.

Oh, So Much to Learn!

Main Base was located on a river where we gained stamina swimming underwater—upstream. And Peter and I went canoeing together. Does that sound romantic? Think again. The canoes, dugout mahogany tree trunks, weighed one ton each. The paddles weighed about 10 pounds each, and we paddled standing up! Imagine the strength it took for us to pull one of these "ships" upstream, against the current, and through rapids. Yes, we slept deep and well each night.

We had carpentry and mechanics classes—men and women alike gaining experience in using basic tools. We had classes in food preparation, including butchering chickens—and cows. We took hikes into the jungle, learning which foods found there were edible, how to find wood suitable to make a fire, and how to cook for ourselves.

Classroom work included the basic medical care we could expect to provide for the indigenous people and writing a research paper about a jungle challenge. I chose to investigate and write my paper entitled "Army Ants," some of God's amazing and terrifying little creatures. Thousands of these ants may parade in columns through the jungle during the day, pinning down and cutting up plants and every small creature in their path. Fascinating!

A husband and wife team from Wycliffe's counseling department in the US visited camp during our fourth week at Main Base. During group classes, they gave us pointers on how to cope with culture shock and the stresses we would face living in isolation in primitive societies. At the end of class one day, they announced, "If any of you would like to talk to one or both of us privately, feel free to come to our hut any time in the evening after supper." A couple of days later, Peter told me he had secretly gone along the private trail one evening to talk with them. He said, "I told them I needed help because my wife cries a lot. They asked me if you are pregnant. When I said yes, they told me to just hug you and let you cry. They said this will pass."

I delighted in their advice. I realized that though my tears came easily and often due to hormonal changes, I desperately wanted to do well and not fail and be an embarrassment to Peter. God was so good to provide help for me; Peter accepted their advice and just held me when I needed it. Together, we made it through.

God also provided encouragement for me through one of my campmates. I received the following note one morning: "We missed you last night at prayer meeting and hope you are feeling stronger. Isaiah 40:28 and 29: 'Have you not known? Have you not heard? The Lord is the everlasting God, the creator of the ends of the earth. He doesn't faint or grow weary. His understanding is unsearchable. He gives power to the faint and to him who has no might, He increases strength.'" I rejoiced, *Thank You, Father, for the Body of Christ and for Your Word.*

Language. Ah yes, the assignment to learn to speak the local Tzeltal language, spoken by the Tzeltal Indians who lived close to Main Base, was a very hard task for me to deal with. The staff wanted us to really understand that learning the language of the people would be our primary task once we were allocated among a group of people overseas. I cried. *Lord, I can't do this! I can't remember all those strange words. I get so confused. Help me! Please. I don't even want to try to learn this language—I'll never see these people again after Jungle Camp is over. Please give me a better attitude!* Well, God gave me the kick in the pants I needed to really try, and I passed this aspect of our training. But I'm quite sure I was at the bottom of the camper list regarding my skill in this area.

Farther, Longer, Slower

Week after week, we hiked farther and farther, longer and longer . . . four miles, then six, four hours, then five. One day, our destination was the hacienda of a wealthy leader in the area. Early in the morning while it was still cool, all 56 of us and several staff members set out, with me leading the pack as usual. As we climbed a particularly steep hill, everyone passed me and Peter as we crept along. I needed to stop frequently to rest. When we got to the top of the hill, we could look into the distance and see the valley below and the hacienda where lunch had been prepared for us. We watched as the señor and señora of the hacienda welcomed all our campmates. About a half hour later, we watched from our vantage point on the hill as they said good-bye and began their way back toward us. Peter and I quickly turned and started back toward camp. Before long, everyone passed us again, and we were the last to arrive, exhausted, back in camp that afternoon.

Our longest planned hike was 28 miles, one way. We started out on New Year's Eve, hiking halfway and camping overnight in a village. New Year's Day 1972, though moving at a slow pace, I made it the last 14 miles to Naja village where we stayed for two days with the Lacandon Indians. This particular settlement is said to be the surviving remnant of the once-great Mayan civilization. We gathered word lists and made other cultural observations during our stay and discussed the ways in which the lives of the Lacandon people are the same as, or different from, the Tzeltal Indians with whom we had become familiar at Main Base.

Oh, how I praised God and thanked the staff when it was time to go back to camp, for they had a plane come for me and a girl who had sprained her ankle. An hour later, I was back in camp, took a hot shower, and had a long nap while Peter and the other 53 campers hiked the 28 miles home.

Hurrah! We had survived and passed Main Base. I felt both relieved and concerned. Relieved it was over. Concerned, not really knowing what we'd face next.

Advance Base

Thirty-eight miles from Main Base, Jungle Camp staff would teach us, observe our responses and coping techniques, and mentor us as we learned to trust God in ever deeper ways. They would help us survive for seven weeks at Advance Base.

Because of my pregnancy and how difficult it had been for me to hike, the staff arranged for me to fly. *Oh, THANK YOU, Lord, for this wonderful gift to not have to drag myself through the jungle again.* Peter and all the other campers took two long and tiring days to trek the 38 miles.

We were given one week to build our own "champa," a 15-by-18-foot, wood-pole-frame house, and our own furniture. Peter used jungle vines to hand tie all 64 joints of the champa frame. The roof and two "walls" of our house simply consisted of four-foot-wide lengths of blue plastic. The other "walls" were nonexistent; two sides of our house were completely open to the dense jungle. We needed a table, bed frame, and two desks—each requiring 40 small bark joints. We worked together—mostly, I handed things to Peter as he needed them, and he did the work.

At Main Base, we had learned how to build a mud stove, and we were eager to get started, needing to convince ourselves it would really work—that we would actually be able to bake a cake and use a pressure cooker to keep our weekly allotment of meat safe to eat all week. Upon receiving a piece of meat or chicken, we cooked a portion to eat that day and then pressure-cooked the remainder. We left the cap on the steam escape nozzle until the next day, when we opened the cooker to remove a serving of meat for that day. We repeated the procedure daily and were so thankful for this addition to our diet.

Sue in advance base house

The mud stove was raised off the ground, was waist-high, and had a thick metal plate placed over the firebox. It was crowned with a chimney. We shouted with jubilation the first time we stoked up the fire and watched the smoke pour out of the chimney and into the clear blue sky. *Thank You, Lord, for helping us learn and remember what we learned and for giving us success in this basic need!* We were required to do all our own cooking, including collecting dry wood in that tropical rainforest.

Our weekly food supply was strictly rationed. Staples per person included two cups of rice, a pound of flour, a cup of sugar, two cups of powdered milk, three to five eggs, one small bag of macaroni, a can of pineapple, a handful of raisins, and about 15 peanuts to last us one week.

Joining with other campers once a day was a great break for us from the isolation we felt, as we shared practical sessions in trailblazing, knots and measurements, food gathering, and map making, to name a few. One week was dedicated to recognizing and solving translation problems, and another week, we learned specific survival techniques.

"Oh my, Peter! What kind of a snake is this?" I exclaimed as I looked at the 10-foot snake I had just killed by whacking it with a machete.

We looked it up in one of the picture books we had brought with us from the Main Base library and discovered it was a *nauyaca*, the most poisonous snake in Mexico. Though it was not part of our planned course, I was delighted to have the time that day to dissect it. With intense interest, I studied how God made this creepy creature.

The importance of maintaining our relationship with the Lord, of spending time with Him for daily renewal, was emphasized all through Jungle Camp Main Base and during our more isolated Advance Base living. Bible studies with other campers focused on the book of *James*. We all met for prayer on Wednesdays and for community worship on Sunday morning. Tortillas and juice represented Jesus's Body and Blood when we shared communion.

Finished

By the end of our 12 weeks at Jungle Camp, we had finished all our assignments and jumped through all the required hoops. We had passed. The next planned stage of training was for all the campers to live for three months in an Indian village, a long-term experience to put into practice all we had learned.

But God had other plans for us. It was decided that we would be exempt from the Village Living requirement. We had already lived and worked overseas; thus, we were already familiar with living in another culture. God was leading us to have our baby in Indonesia. Dr. Jim, Indonesia Branch Director, and his wife, Glady, were already set up in Jakarta, Indonesia's capital city. They had alerted the university and government officials that the promised linguists would soon arrive.

We packed up, said good-bye to the Jungle Camp staff we had come to love and treasure, and flew back to Las Casas where we picked up our car. Oh, the luxury of sitting in the soft and comfortable white leather seats of a 1966 Pontiac LeMons, in air-conditioned comfort.

I remember stopping at a restaurant for lunch as we began our drive back to the US. We met an elderly couple, tourists from the States. They were finding that traveling in Mexico was somewhat strenuous for them. Learning that I was six months pregnant, the lady remarked, "Oh my dear, you shouldn't be riding around in a car down here in your condition!"

We really chuckled. I wonder what she would have said if we had told her about our activities for the previous three months: riding mules, hiking over the mountains, paddling half-ton canoes standing up, and living in a primitive champa.

Yes, Jungle Camp was a challenge. Baby and I were both stronger and healthier for it. God brought us through, teaching us that we could trust Him to lead us, to motivate and provide for us. He proved He would be with us in all things . . . including all that was to come.

New Arrivals in Indonesia

March to June 1972

Children are a gift from the Lord;
they are a reward from Him.
—Psalm 127:3, New Living Translation

From Jungle Camp to Indonesia in Eight Weeks

Though our car was clean and in great shape when we picked it up in Las Casa after completing Jungle Camp, we ourselves needed some cleaning up. After four days, driving north almost the entire length of Mexico, we crossed the border into Texas on March 4, 1972. Continuing on the next day to Oklahoma City, we luxuriated in a wonderful motel—soaking in a tub of hot water and getting a good night's sleep in a COMFORTABLE bed. We did our laundry, threw some jungle clothes away, and I had my hair done. I didn't want to look like I just got out of the jungle when we presented a program at a church the next day.

Four days later, we were back in Moorhead, Minnesota, headquartering at Peter's parents' home again. The next five weeks were a whirlwind of activity. Oh, the delight of buying new, clean, pretty maternity clothes. Visiting and saying good-bye to relatives. Praying. Giving programs in churches. Buying supplies for life in Indonesia. Packing all our supplies in three 50-gallon metal drums. Praying. Figuring out how to ship the drums to Indonesia. Driving to Minneapolis. Selling our car to my dad for $1.00. Praying. More programs in homes and churches. More tearful good-byes.

Flying to California. Saying good-bye to my mother, her husband, and other supporters. Whew!

My sister Mary flew to Honolulu with us for a delightful four days together, following which Peter and I spent a relaxing four days in the Fiji Islands. Flying on to Sydney, Australia, the Lord worked wonders for us in enabling us to get our needed visas for Indonesia in just six days.

Jakarta to Bogor

On May 1, 1972, seven weeks before my due date with our first baby, our plane circled over that sprawling capital city of 11 million people—Jakarta, Indonesia. My nose was pressed against the window, and my heart was racing as I looked down at the red-roofed houses packed together like sardines in a can. I was thrilled at the sight of white gleaming monuments pointing high into the sky, surrounded by traffic circles filled with bumper-to-bumper cars, encircling tourists visiting the monuments on that bright, sunny day. This was to be our home until our baby was born, and God would lead us to the people group He had planned for us.

I remember the increased excitement I felt when the plane touched down. We had spent the last two years studying linguistics and learning how to live in the jungle and had dreamed of and talked about this day. *Thank You, Lord, for bringing us here at last.* As we taxied to the gate, I wondered what life would be like for us now in this exotic country to which God had called us. The plane stopped at the gate, and we could see hundreds of people on the observation deck waving a welcome—I imagined they were all waving to us. Finally, they opened the door of the plane, and as the passengers pushed and shoved to get off, we were moved along with the crowd. At last—at the door—wham! We were hit by a blast of HOT equatorial air and humidity. I was speechless. I felt like we were descending into a huge oven!

I made my bulky way down the steps, carrying my pillow; Peter brought our carry-on bags. We walked across the cement tarmac with the heat rising under our feet, as if from a radiator set on 100 degrees—I thought I could fry an egg on that cement! We moved slowly through the crowd to the receiving lounge. Immediately, we were surrounded by groups of the friends and relatives of our fellow passengers. There were no security restrictions in those days; all visitors to the airport could go straight to the gates and wander about all through the airport. All those people were enthusiastically calling out greetings and who knows what else. We couldn't understand them with our limited Indonesian vocabulary. Dozens of cabbies and porters called out, "Mister! Mama! I help you. You want taxi?" Some even grabbed at our suitcases, wanting to help us get to the taxi. I was nervous and prayed, *Lord, please keep them from running off with our things.*

To our relief as we looked around the crowd, we saw a tall Western man nearby. It was Jim, our director, his wife Glady, and their two sons. Jim said, "Welcome to Indonesia. They sent me here to be the director, but there's been no one here to direct. Now that you're here, I'm a real director, and we are now the Indonesia Advance of SIL!"

THANK YOU, LORD! The vision you gave us back in Santa Ana, California, two years ago, to send us to the country that you had planned for us in eternity past, has now come to pass.

We stayed with Jim and Glady for a couple of days in their Jakarta apartment. Jim registered our presence in the country with the police and introduced us to the appropriate personnel at the University of Indonesia, our sponsors for our language and linguistic work.

Since our baby was due to be born in less than two months, Jim and Glady felt it would be best for us to live in Bogor, a suburb 40 miles north of Jakarta, in the cooler foothills of an active volcanic cone where the heat was less oppressive. A Campus Crusade couple, who had been serving in Bogor, was leaving the city, and we would be able to assume the contract on their house. We were asked to care for a car belonging to a friend, and there was a small Red Cross Hospital nearby. God had wonderfully planned each detail for us.

The ride to Bogor from Jakarta with Jim and Glady is vivid in my mind, even today. What a glorious day! *We're really here, Lord! Thank You!* All our senses were bombarded with new and interesting and thrilling sights and events.

Oh, the colors! In the fields, rice paddies and various species of palm trees, there were so many shades of green. In the dress of the people, I saw bright and complex designs that mixed colors and patterns I'd never seen or imagined before. Many women had beautiful vividly colored head coverings. In the bright blue of the equatorial sky speckled with white fluffy clouds, I felt a deep joy within as if God were saying to me, *I brought you here, Sue, to glorify Me in this nation.*

We saw women carrying baskets, basins, and bundles on their heads, filled with food, clothing, and other household items. We experienced the traffic and drivers speeding forward wherever and whenever there was an open space on the road—the path along the side of the road—ever so close to the ditches on each side of the road. We felt the heat. We smelled the garbage and sewage in the open ditches—along with the "swamp cabbage," the leafy stalks growing in the ditches—and the exhaust belching from the diesel buses and trucks. Noises accosted our ears—horns honking continuously, loud croaking motors, cars backfiring, and a singer in the minaret of the mosque calling the faithful to prayer five times a day.

All along the road, people were selling their wares, laid out on a cloth spread out on the ground. Food. Pans. Knives. Shoes. Trinkets. Watches. Carvings. Animals. Fruit that I'd never seen before, such as the putrid-smelling durian. And then there were the carpets—beautiful exotic carpets hanging on bamboo supports. And paintings—gorgeous watercolors and oils by talented artists. The bumper-to-bumper traffic often came to a dead stop, and then we could hear the salesmen who were proudly standing there, calling us to buy, "Mister, very cheap! You buy. I give you special price."

Looking back, it's amazing to think that rather than all the sights, sounds, and smells of this alien world being frightening or repulsive or overwhelming, I reacted only with excitement, wonder, and joy. Undoubtedly, God was at work in my innermost being.

Life in Bogor

In early afternoon, we arrived at our newly rented Bogor home on Jalan Guntur (Thunder Street), *nomor empat belas* (number 14). It was a pleasant four-bedroom bungalow on a corner lot. It was large enough to accommodate three families at a time as they would be coming through from abroad, in transition to moving to their tribal locations. A beautiful yard surrounded the house, with tropical plants abounding. Indeed, it was much more than we had expected, especially considering we had just recently left our own handmade Jungle Camp "house" in Mexico.

Standing in the backyard, looking up at the top of a coconut tree one day, I remember doing my very best to speak Indonesian. Trying to display what a good student I was, I told the gardener, "Di Amerika kami tidak ada kepala!" I remember the look he gave me. I had said, "In America, we don't have any heads!" I was close though—the word for coconut is *kelapa*. I had a lot more Indonesian language study to do! The good news is that Indonesian is closely related to Malay, which we had learned to speak while living in Malaysia. In fact, Indonesian is to Malay, as American English is to British English. Speaking Indonesian helped us in our relationships with government officials, university personnel, businessmen, our neighbors, and our new friends.

Dr. Dick, Southeast Asia Area Director, wanted to keep us busy and useful right from the start. He asked us to compare the word lists he had gathered from eight languages in Kalimantan, the Indonesian part of the island of Borneo. We were to check to see how closely the languages were related so we would know which language groups would need a complete translation of the New Testament of their own.

One day, we met an American couple who had come to Indonesia as independent missionaries. They took one look at me in my very pregnant condition—due in just six more weeks—and the husband said, "Sue, you can't have a baby here! Go back to the States. Or go to Singapore! Go anywhere but don't try to have a baby here!"

But Peter and I looked around us. There were 120 million people in Indonesia, and we said, "Somebody survived having a baby here! This is where God brought us. This is where He'll take care of us." And He did.

We searched for an OB doctor and found a wonderful Chinese man. I asked, "IF I need something for pain during labor, will you give me something?"

"Yes, I will," he responded.

David's Birth

So with confidence in God's care, five weeks later when my labor started, Peter took me to the hospital.

Several hours later, when my labor pains became very strong, I said to the doctor, "I think I need help now."

"Oh, I never give anything. You can make it," he said. *OOOOOOOH! Jesus help me!* And He did.

Peter was able to be with me throughout the delivery, thus witnessing David's arrival from head to toe. But not only the doctor, nurse, and Peter were present. A few minutes before David's arrival, the delivery boy from Western Union came right into the delivery room looking for me—bringing a telegram from the US. So much for privacy! The good news in the cable was that my mother would be arriving in the next few days to help take care of the new baby.

Minutes later, on June 23, 1972, Baby David Lloyd-Palmer, named after both his grandfathers and healthy at 8 1/2 pounds, was born at the Red Cross Hospital in Bogor.

Perhaps one of the reasons David was so strong and healthy is that he went through those three months of rigorous jungle survival training with us.

His arrival wasn't without excitement though. That night, they put David in a bassinette in my room with me. I couldn't sleep—what a special, wonderful day it had been. David and I were alone for the next 12 hours. When I heard him pass his first stool and begin to fuss, I got up to change him, to talk and sing to him. *Thank You, Lord, for leading me to be a nurse so that I know how to suction and care for Baby David—and for myself.*

I knew I had to keep massaging my uterus, in spite of the pain it caused. Later, I realized something was wrong; when the nurse came in the morning, she saw that all my stitches had come out. Whoa! That set up a flurry of activity. As I was wheeled down the hallway on a stretcher, I felt a mask on my face, and when I recognized the smell of ether, I remembered having my tonsils taken out when I was in kindergarten. The anesthetic quickly took effect, and I awoke to realize the doctor had properly repaired the stitches. Peter was there when I opened my eyes that morning, and he presented me with a beautiful bouquet of orchids. We rejoiced in God's gift of our son and praised Him for honoring our faith and trust.

Later that morning, Bob and Joyce, who had arrived in Indonesia the day before, came to the hospital to meet me and Peter and Baby David. I greeted them by bursting into tears! I can't imagine what they thought they were getting into, knowing we were to be colleagues in the coming years. Bob and Joyce met Titi at the hospital that day. She was a pleasant, loving Indonesian woman who we had hired to help us with housework. She came to the hospital daily and tenderly cared for me. She sat with me for hours, gently rubbing my legs, eager to help and sooth in any way. *Thank You, Lord, for blessing me through Titi.*

Grandma Visited

Four days after David's birth, we eagerly and gratefully welcomed my brave mother to Indonesia to visit. She was so thrilled to be a grandma for the first time that she flew, by herself, outside the US for the very first time. She cleared customs without incident, even though her two suitcases held mostly Pampers, baby clothes, and toys. She was a wonderful, skilled grandma, speaking often about how her mother had cared for me when I was born 33 years earlier. Our missionary friends were so gracious to invite her to their homes for visits and meals, thus tempering the incidences of culture shock she experienced. My missionary friend held a surprise shower for Baby David. She had us all pray for him, including for his future wife! We took my mother on a couple of sightseeing excursions, including to the beautiful Bogor Botanical Gardens, and after two weeks, we saw her off at the airport. What a blessing it had been to share this special time of our lives with her.

It was now my special joy to spend time alone with Baby David, often in the middle of the night. I vividly remember one special night. The outside darkness was broken only by a soft night light in the living room. When Baby David called that he needed me, I changed him and sat nursing him in a comfortable living room chair. As I looked around the room, I consciously and deliberately memorized the scene, taking in each window and curtain, the front door, tables and chairs, pictures, lamps, rug. *Lord*, I prayed, *I want to ALWAYS remember—for the rest of my life—THIS particular night, in THIS place, THIS special time alone with this precious baby You've given me. Help me and Peter to raise him to KNOW You . . . to love and serve You.*

God answered my prayer—all through these past 44 years, especially on David's birthday, as I sit in my chair where I have my morning devotions, I remember and ponder that night and the miracle of birth and life and the growth of a child. I can no longer hold him and sing to him, but I can remember. And I think of the man that baby has become, a man who's given his life to Jesus and who seeks Him with all his heart. *Thank You, Lord, for tender, precious memories of Your love, care, leading, and gifts.*

Jayapura

July to December 1972

I will never leave you nor forsake you.
—Hebrews 13:5b, English Standard Version

While we were living in Jakarta and then in Bogor, on the island of Java, Dr. Jim was in contact with the authorities in Indonesia's Department of Education and Culture. After explaining the SIL's desire to study the languages of minority groups in Indonesia, the director became convinced that SIL linguists could help his people in practical ways using scientific and technological methods. He proposed that SIL begin work in Irian Jaya, Indonesia's easternmost province on the island of New Guinea. He explained it was believed that there were more than 250 different groups of people, each speaking a different language, on Indonesia's half of that island, second largest in the world. Linguists believed there were another 750 languages on the other half of the island, which is an independent country called Papua New Guinea (PNG).

The director put Dr. Jim in contact with the president of Universitas Cenderawasih (Bird of Paradise University), which was more commonly known as UnCen. He agreed to facilitate Dr. Jim's visit to Irian to conduct a language survey, using a helicopter to visit less accessible villages.

Dr. Jim took the day-long flight out to Irian Jaya and, upon arrival in Jayapura, Irian's capital city, met with the president of UnCen who seemed genuinely pleased to support Dr. Jim's survey. Hopping from village to village by helicopter, he collected word lists and found there were 20 languages spoken in Jayapura County. Upon presenting his findings to the university president and officials, they offered to sponsor long-term visas for SIL linguists.

This was a great answer to prayer. When Dr. Jim returned to Jakarta, he and his wife Glady met with Peter and me and our colleagues, Bob and Joyce, for a time of discussion and prayer. We all believed that God was leading both couples to move to Irian to work with the people there. *Thank You, Lord, for revealing this detail of Your plan for us.*

In 1975, an official agreement, known as Project UnCen-SIL, was signed by the university and SIL leaders. In 1980, the name was changed to the UnCen-SIL Cooperative Project.

Our Adventure: Jakarta to Biak

We two couples bought our plane tickets and two days later, on October 2, 1972, were up before 4:00 a.m. to catch a large four-engine propeller plane to Irian. We flew across the island of Java, the most densely populated area in the world, teeming with about 1,500 people per square mile and which is sprinkled with active volcanos and rice fields. As we neared the eastern coast of the island and began our journey across the water, one of the plane's engines quit. My heart skipped a beat when I looked out at the propeller that was no longer rotating. But the plane didn't change speed or altitude, and I remembered my training classes with United and Pan Am. I had learned that a four-engine plane can fly quite well—for a while—on just three engines. But I was pleased when the captain announced we would need to turn back and land at the nearest coastal airport. He wasn't taking any chances.

After inspection and repair of the engine, we boarded the plane again and departed. Once more, when we were out over the water, the plane's engine stopped again. This time, I felt annoyed for the added delay. It was midafternoon, and we were tired. I expected David would soon be getting pretty fussy. We prayed, trusting ourselves to God's keeping, and watched as the plane made another U-turn. This time, we didn't stop at the east coast airstrip; we flew directly west. When we landed at 6:00 p.m., we had been in the air most of the day. But inside the air terminal, we discovered we were right back where we had started early that very morning. We were in Jakarta.

Five days later, we four adults and Baby David set out on another all-day trip. Exhausted late that afternoon, we thanked God for bringing us to Biak, a large island off the north coast of Irian Jaya. We rejoiced upon learning there was a hotel available right there at the airport that had been a strategic airfield for the Japanese army, serving as a Pacific base of operations during World War II. To weary travelers, the hotel looked great—from the outside.

When dusk hit, we found the only light in the room was provided by a table lamp. Problem was there was no plug on the lamp cord. Since there was no phone in the room, Peter went out to the desk to ask for a replacement lamp. "Oh, sorry, sir," the clerk responded. "I help you." He came to our room and simply inserted the exposed wires from the lamp cord directly into the wall outlet. Peter thanked him for his help, and we just stood there staring at each other. Then, shrugging our shoulders, said, "Well, it works."

There were two narrow single wood-framed beds but no baby crib in our room. I made plans to make a nice place for David on the floor. But then when I went in to use the bathroom, I saw a scorpion right there on the wet floor next to the open, uncovered Indonesian *bak* (a water storage tank). I changed my plan and prayed, asking God to protect us. David slept with Peter that night.

The next morning, we were eager to be on our way. A DC-3, with its small tail wheel, was awaiting us. I remember climbing up the steeply inclined aisle to our seats and watching a mechanic out on the wing as he made a last check of the engine. It was a bit unnerving, especially for Joyce who was not a fan of flying, but we knew we were in God's will and hands, so we sat leaned back in the canvas sling seats and felt relieved when we leveled off after takeoff. After flying 30 minutes across the Pacific, we got our first view of the great island of New Guinea, where we would spend the next 20 years of our lives. Staring out the window, I was mesmerized as I watched for small villages, nestled in the thick jungle and along the rivers that fed into the ocean along the jagged north coast. *Where will we live down there, Father? Where's the place You've prepared for us? What's the name of the people group to whom You've called us?*

Settling in in Jayapura

UnCen had sent us a telegram inviting us to come to Irian to work. They assured us that they would be responsible to help us find appropriate housing. On October 3, when we landed in Jayapura, we were surprised that no one from the university was at the airport to meet us. Joyce and I and Baby David stayed at the airport while Peter and Bob went to find a place for us that night. When they returned, we were delighted to learn we would be able to stay in the Missionary Aviation Fellowship (MAF) Guesthouse right there by the airport. There was only one room available, but since we had nowhere else to go, we gratefully took it. We two couples began to learn the joys—and challenges—of togetherness.

The next morning, Peter and Bob eagerly set out to find UnCen and to report our arrival. The president's secretary was surprised to see them. "Didn't you get our telegram?" he inquired.

"Yes," they replied, "that's why we came. We arrived yesterday."

"No, no," he said. "I mean the second telegram advising you not to come just yet. You'll have to return to Jakarta."

Peter and Bob then spoke with the president who apologized for the confusion and explained that housing was not yet available for us. He graciously assigned Mr. Sam to assist Peter and Bob in searching for housing on their own. They came back to the guesthouse to explain the situation to me and Joyce. We didn't have enough money to return to Jakarta. We prayed, asking God to provide for us, and thanked Him that MAF said we could stay in their guesthouse for six days.

Following one of Mr. Sam's leads, Peter and Bob received good news at the office of a United Nations project connected with the city's only sawmill. "Yes, there's a three-bedroom cement-block house available that you can have—IF you want it." The bad news was "It hasn't been occupied for several months, and the water supply is uncertain."

Since it was the only positive answer they had received regarding housing, Peter and Bob signed the contract, thanked God for His provision, and went over to have a look at the house that would be our home for the next year. It was on a hill, had a large main sitting and dining room, a kitchen with refrigerator and electric stove, one bathroom, and a patio overlooking the sawmill and the bay. It had great potential.

I'll never forget the first time I walked into that house. For months, sawdust from the sawmill had been blowing right up the hill and into the house, covering everything: walls, floor, counters, and cupboards. Even the cobwebs in the corners and on the ceiling fans were coated with sawdust! The job of cleaning it up and getting it ready for occupancy was immense. We swept the walls and fans and dusted the kitchen cupboards and closet shelves—and moved in. MAF ladies came to our rescue and blessed us with utensils and linens.

But our situation was quite distressing for me. For nine of the first 11 days living in our new home, we had no local access to water. Peter and Bob managed to find a truck and some 55-gallon drums they could use. They fetched water for us from a stream about two miles away.

One afternoon while Peter, Bob, and Joyce were gone, I was alone with Baby David who was napping. The temperature was about 95 degrees, with 100% humidity. I was sweaty and itching from the sawdust that seemed to continually cling to my skin. Since there was no furniture on the patio, I just sat on the step in the doorway and looked out over the bay.

And cried.

I called out to God, *I'm here, God. And I'm miserable! I know You brought us here, and I'm trusting You. But it's so hard! I've not experienced anything like this before. Help me! There's no water in this house. The pipes are dry. Peter and Bob are working so hard to bring us water. But we have to ration it. It's so hot—we'd just love to rinse off with cool water more than once a day. We need water for washing dishes and David's diapers. And I really want to wash out the cupboards and get rid of all the sawdust. I know there are many missionaries who have been in worse situations than this and have suffered horrible injuries. But I'm coming to You now. This is where I'm at right now. I'm suffering. For me, this is worse than Jungle Camp. I need You here with me now. I need to feel Your grace and comfort. I need patience and Your peace and joy and Your love and assurance. You promised to always be with me. I need You NOW! Please, in Jesus's Name, help me!*

I wiped my eyes, blew my nose, and looked out over the sawmill to the beauty of the bay beyond. It was amazing. My situation hadn't changed, but my heart had. The clear-blue sky with fluffy white clouds, azure water with fishing boats moving about, the palms trees and thick tropical vegetation shining in the sun with so many different shades of green all spoke to me of God's loving care. He had heard me. The great God of the universe, my Jesus who holds all of creation together, cared about me. He answered me. And gave me His peace.

I'm here with you, He said deep in my inner being. *I'll never leave you. You can trust Me.*

I had learned that tremendous strength and healing comes from honestly crying out to God. He breathed peace into my heart and mind. I knew He would give me the needed perseverance to make it through to the unknown date in the future when unlimited water would flow through those pipes as it was designed to do. I sat there for another 20 minutes and just sang praises to God who loves me like no other. A distressing event had turned into a blessing. It's a good life, with Jesus.

Life in Jayapura

Our neighbors were wonderful. They were friendly and wanted to help us, and I think they were very curious to learn about the first Americans who had come to live in their community. We developed friendships wherever we went: in the shops and government offices, at the university and at the harbor, in church and in restaurants. We had Christian friends, Muslim friends, friends who worshiped the spirits, and friends who worshipped their ancestors. Churches, both Catholic and Protestant, and Muslim mosques were abundant in Jayapura. Since Indonesia has the world's largest Muslim population, most of the government officials followed the Muslim faith.

It was a challenge for four adults and a three-month-old baby to live together, figuring out how to get around, where to buy our food, washing our clothes by hand—AND getting them to dry in spite of daily tropical downpours. But with God's strength, we learned and adjusted.

It was strenuous for me and Joyce to get to the local market to buy fresh fruit and vegetables, fish, and meat. We needed to travel down the hill and into town by "taxi." Those vehicles were actually small minivans, designed to transport small Indonesian and Irianese people, not oversized Westerners. They packed as many people in as possible; I once counted 13 passengers, including the children and babies sitting on laps. I was always hopeful I wouldn't get stuck in the back seat, for there was no way to gracefully climb over everyone to get out. I came to have a new understanding of being "packed in like sardines."

We bought our eggs in the market—right next to where we could buy live chickens for dinner. The first morning after I had purchased "fresh" eggs the first time, I was shocked when I broke an egg and dropped the contents into a bowl to make scrambled eggs for all four of us for breakfast. A skinny little baby chick with a skimpy layer of feathers was lying there, looking right up at me. "Oh my!" I said out loud. "I don't think any of us can eat this." Three of the next five eggs I cracked were the same.

The next time we went to the market, we watched the other women and learned what we needed to do. We brought a small dipper with us when we went shopping, filled it with water at the egg stand, and dropped each egg into the water before agreeing to buy it. Good eggs sink; eggs with chicks float. I wondered how much more we had to learn.

It was a half-day tiring excursion to go to the market. The sweltering heat and humidity were sometimes overwhelming. We soon realized we truly did need to hire a house girl to help us. We simply couldn't keep up with cleaning the house—trying to get rid of the sawdust and washing the floors daily—doing the marketing, butchering the chickens, cooking, and making progress on Indonesian language study and researching the cultures.

There were many tasks for Peter and Bob to accomplish in order to set up a new SIL office in a new city. One morning, Peter went to the main Jayapura post office and arranged for a PO box and a telegram address. It was essential that we would be able to communicate with Dr. Jim in Jakarta and with the Wycliffe-SIL office and our families in the US.

We also needed a group bank account so we could receive financial transmissions from the States and make cash withdrawals. Peter went to the only bank in town that handled these services and met with the manager. Both savings and checking accounts were available, and Peter filled in the proper forms. Soon, the accounts were set up, and the manager handed Peter a box of checks and gave him instructions on how to write a check and where to sign his name. Knowing that direct deposits would be made into the account from both within the country and from overseas, Peter asked the manager, "What's the number of our account?"

The manager scratched his head, went back behind the counter, and looked into his ledger. Then, with a very serious and pleased expression, he said, "You'll be account number one."

Smiling, Peter responded, "Thank you so much for helping me today. I look forward to doing business here." He left the bank with a warm feeling knowing that at the bank, and elsewhere in Jayapura, Peter would be known by his name, rather than by a number that might be assigned to him.

Our Barrels Arrive—Yippee!

In November, Peter wrote home to our family and supporters:

> It was one of those meetings that was so providential. The well-dressed man sitting next to me on our flight from Jakarta to Jayapura was just waiting for conversation. We had a pleasant talk during most of the flight and parted company as good friends.
>
> About four weeks later, when the customs office notified us that our shipment from Jakarta

had arrived, I prepared to go to the office to clear our goods. I had been warned it would take several days to process and would probably cost a lot of money. I went in to the head person's office to explain our mission and to ask for help since this was the first time I had ever been involved in the customs office.

Who should I see as the head customs official—none other than my friend I had met on the airplane. We caught one another up on our news, and then I explained the help I needed. Without hesitation, he scribbled a note to his assistant to give me all the help I needed and promptly signed his signature on the top form.

I did have to work to get several more signatures, but overall, the procedure went smoothly, and in a couple of short days, all the goods had been cleared. God had prepared the way for me long before I needed it.

A Man from the Tor River Area

It was also providential that we were living close to the sawmill. Some of the workers were curious about the white people living on the hill and came to meet and befriend us. One of the men, Martinus, had come to Jayapura from the Tor River area looking for work. We recognized God's hand in this right away, for UnCen had been in contact with the provincial military leaders seeking their guidance as to the best place for SIL linguists to begin their research. They stated we should not be near the Irian-Papua New Guinea border, nor did they want us to go to areas where there were already several mission organizations. They had taken out a map and pointed to the ideal location for us. You guessed it—along the north coast of Irian Jaya, perhaps in the Tor River area.

We learned the Tor is a large river on the north coast of Irian, about 100 miles west of Jayapura. The mouth of the Tor empties into the Pacific Ocean near the small coastal town of Sarmi. About 300 people were living there. Martinus, a tall muscular man of about 30 years of age, was shy but friendly. He had become proficient in speaking the Indonesian language. He shared with us that his first language was Berik. On further questioning, we learned that Berik speakers lived in about 10 villages along the banks of the Tor River. We "took a word list" from Martinus by asking him to give us the Berik equivalent for each word on a list of 100 Indonesian words. There were people in town from many of the interior language groups, and we were pleased to able to get word lists from several of them.

Martinus visited us frequently. One day, he said, "Mr. Peter, I didn't know that our Berik language could be written down. Do you think my people can have books in our language someday?"

"Yes, Martinus," Peter responded. "That's why we've come to work here in Irian. We hope that people from all the language groups here will have books in their own language someday. And most importantly, we will work so that each group will have the book of God's Word."

Even though we didn't yet know to which language group God would call us, we prayed, *Thank You, Lord, for enabling us to get started learning the language and culture of the people of the Tor even while we're living here in the city.*

Hurrah! Let's Celebrate Christmas

By the end of December, we had settled into a comfortable routine, but we were a bit homesick. Peter and I and Bob and Joyce looked forward to celebrating Christmas together. At the beginning of the month, we decorated the house, baked several different types of cookies, and made plans to try to find a large chicken to roast for a special Christmas dinner together about 3:00 p.m. or 4:00 p.m. on December 25. We decided to exchange gifts after dinner.

SURPRISE! About 3:00 p.m., our Muslim friends began to arrive to wish us, "Merry Christmas." They came in groups, expecting us to be ready with American Christmas treats. We rushed to try to prepare refreshments to serve them. When the first group left, another arrived. And so it went until about 7:00 p.m. I have to admit that, at first, I was frustrated and angry. *How could they do this to us? Why would they come today, of all days? Our big dinner is ruined.* And then, *Oh Lord, forgive me for my bad attitude. These visitors are the new friends You've given us. We're not here to resist them but to serve and love on them.*

The next week, we learned why all those people had come to visit on Christmas Day. It was proper social etiquette. They came to show their friendship and desire to celebrate what was important to us, with us. Muslims and Christians living side by side, enjoying friendship; each visited the other on their special day. No one had told us, warned us. I determined right then to help new colleagues when they joined us in Irian. Years later, I wrote an orientation manual and led a planned course for new-comers, including times when they could freely and confidentially share their frustrations and struggles. I grew to really look forward to visiting our Muslim friends on *Idul Fitri*, their special day, and to them coming to visit and celebrate with us for Christmas. I even had fun preparing all the goodies and food to serve.

It was a red-letter day for us when our mail first appeared in our new PO box number 12. Hurrah! We were connected to the outside world once again. Letters from family and friends were like pieces of gold that we all treasured. Our finance statement from the Wycliffe office confirmed that our prayer and support team now totaled 40 units. *Thank You, Lord, for Your great provisions.*

Word from Yaufun was also very encouraging: "I'm still an industrial engineering student. I want to finish a bachelor's degree first, and if I can get into graduate school, I would sure like to go on! In any event, I put complete trust in the Lord to lead me, and I absolutely believe He has a wonderful plan for my life as He has shown me already."

We were settled and felt adjusted to life in Jayapura. We were ready to branch out, to the interior, to get our first look at the Irian jungles.

God's Clear Leading

January to September 1973

God will make this happen, for He
who calls you is faithful.
—1 Thessalonians 5:24, New Living Translation

Tor River Area Survey

Now that we were settled into life in Jayapura, it was time to make a more detailed survey to locate the specific group of people with whom we would work and where we would actually live. In early March 1973, Peter and Bob and our new administrator, Norm, who had come from Australia to oversee our work, made a survey of the Tor River area where the government had indicated it would be best for us to begin work.

Peter, Bob, and Norm traveled 12 days, with 12 Indonesian officials, to document all the languages spoken along the coast, the Tor River, and in neighboring villages. By taking word lists, they confirmed the presence of 13 different people groups speaking 13 different languages. Seven of those groups proved to be candidates for a Bible translation project.

It was a challenging survey. The "fun" started when they set out to travel in a large dugout canoe from Sarmi, going east on the Pacific Ocean to the mouth of the Tor River, and then continuing on up the Tor. Though experienced and instructed to unload the passengers and their supplies at a safe harbor area near the river's mouth, before navigating through the most dangerous area where the ocean's waves met the powerfully flowing river, the motorist decided to save time and not stop to unload. To his dismay, and to the horror of his passengers, six-foot-high waves crashed over the boat, overtaking it from stern to bow, filling it with salty ocean water and killing the motor. The jolting, unstable boat alternately floated and sat on the muddy floor of the sea as the ocean waves rolled in, and the force of the river pushed the water back out to sea. Fearing for their lives as they went underwater, Peter and all the men fought to keep their heads up and rolled over the sides of the nearly sunken boat. Sometimes swimming, sometimes standing in the murky sandy water when they were able to touch bottom, they alternately swam and walked to tow the boat to shore.

No lives or goods were lost, but it was a close brush with death, and of course, everything on board was a soggy heavy mess. The raw rice in the 40-pound sack was now soaking in dirty, salty, seawater. After spending a day trying to dry themselves, their food supplies, and their belongings, they continued on upriver safely and without further incident to the village of Tenwer.

Because the river was flooding when they arrived, the survey team started walking into the small village, knee-deep in water. Peter was impressed that the people were friendly; even the children were eager to help. They brought a small canoe, and two team members climbed aboard for a short wavy ride to higher ground. As Peter walked through the village, he thought, *The people here must be pretty industrious. This village is neater and generally cleaner than the others we've been in. Most of the people have their own houses raised on sturdy stilts, and many of them even have walls to protect their families from wind and rain.*

"Come Back Quickly and Live with Us!"

As Peter was walking around the village, Petrus, the village chief, came up to him, and though he could only speak haltingly in the Indonesian language, he struck up a conversation with Peter who was absolutely delighted he was able to talk with the headman. He told Petrus, "I'd like to bring my wife and baby son here to your village to live with you. We'd like to learn your language and give you God's talk in your own Berik tongue. Would the village men be able to help build a house for us to live in? And would you and your people help us learn to speak your language?"

Petrus quickly responded, "Yes, we'll help you. We'll help you learn our language. We'll build your house near mine. I'll have the men start collecting the support poles and palm branches." A number of men standing nearby nodded an enthusiastic yes. And many of them ran to get hunting arrows that they gave the surveyors as gifts.

As the group was about to leave the village, a short elderly woman, named Mama Lodia, came up to Peter. She reached up to put her arms around his waist and, through an interpreter, said, "You go now. I'll stay here. But you come back quickly. Bring your wife and baby and live with us. We'll take care of you!" WOW! What an invitation! *Thank You, God!* Peter prayed. *I can't wait to tell Sue how You're providing for us.*

Since the motorist who brought them upriver had to immediately return to Sarmi, the group's return trip to Jayapura was quite arduous. The first day, they traveled downstream by homemade raft, then transferred to a small canoe. After hiking seven hours from the mouth of the Tor to Sarmi, they finally boarded a navy boat that brought them home to Jayapura.

When Peter told me how Chief Petrus and Mama Lodia had invited us to their village, we prayed and, deep in our spirits, felt God was saying, **"This is the group of people that I planned, from eternity past, for you to serve. I want to use you to give My Word to them in their own Berik language."**

Thank You, Father, for making it perfectly clear to us exactly what You've planned. Lead and guide and direct us as we move forward.

And so it was that God revealed His plan for us. Since Chief Petrus and Mama Lodia had both invited us to live in Tenwer, we perceived that God had also ordained Tenwer as our new home. That village was the most centrally located of the 10 Berik villages, ideal for reaching out to all the Berik people.

Yes, God was with Peter on that survey. He had reported:

> Several times, but especially on the afternoon of March 10 (late at night March 9 in central US), although knee-deep in mud and drenched to the skin by a pouring-down rain, I felt the very close presence of God and was reminded that some faithful prayer supporter was making specific intercession for us before the throne of the almighty God.

And now today as I type this, 43 years later, we are still praising God for the army of prayer supporters He raised up for us as we faced new and alien adventures on that primitive island for two decades of our lives.

Sunarjo

After church in Jayapura one Sunday morning in March 1973, we went to get an icy drink at a little refreshment stand by the harbor. Sitting there in the shade, with a cool breeze blowing, we enjoyed watching the marines water-skiing in the bay. It was almost noon when Sunarjo caught our gaze as he took his turn on the water skis, gliding across the glossy waters of Jayapura Bay. He released the rope and one ski and sailed straight ahead toward us, landing at the dock. A little blond boy, our nine-month-old David, was playing in his baby stroller and caught Sunarjo's attention. Peter and I had been alternating walking David back and forth, but now we were taking a little break. Sunarjo swung himself up on the dock and came over to visit with us. Tall and muscular, with a winsome smile and friendly spirit, it was a delight to get to know him. We learned he was from the island of Java and had been stationed at the local marine base for about a year.

Sunarjo and Baby David

It wasn't long before David made it known that he was ready to walk again. He was at that stage where he couldn't make it on his own, so he needed someone to help him. He would stand in front of his helper and grab one finger of the helper's right hand and then one finger of the helper's left hand. This meant his helper had to bend forward and waddle along behind David. Fun for David, very tiring for his helper. Soon, Sunarjo took his turn—and won David's heart and ours too.

Since we wanted to increase our fluency in the Indonesian language and Sunarjo wanted to learn English, we made arrangements to meet three times a week for conversation practice. I also taught Sunarjo to "10-finger type," as he called it, using our new modern manual typewriter. As we got to know him, we learned he had been in a special force of the Indonesian Marine Corps for eight years. We enjoyed his company and pleasing personality.

Our SIL Family Grows

In early May, Peter and I and Bob and Joyce were delighted to welcome two more members of SIL to join us in Jayapura. Carol, who was from the US, and Hiroko, who hailed from Japan, teamed up to follow the Lord's leading to also give God's Word to one of the waiting people groups in Irian. We all praised God that our house had three bedrooms, and the girls moved in with us. Their room was quite small, just eight feet by eight feet in size, with a built-in closet. But we were all glad for the fellowship, and we had the opportunity to improve our communal living skills.

It was at this point that we realized we needed to work out an access system for using the bathroom. There was a main door into the bathroom unit. Inside were three rooms—a shower room, a toilet room, and a larger sink room. We made a large round cardboard chart with a movable arrow and hung it on the main door. Every time one of us entered the bathroom unit, we turned the arrow on the chart to the current occupant, indicating who else could go in at the same time—spouses together, men together, and women together. It worked perfectly for us, and we all have fond memories of those months together.

At the end of May, Bob and Joyce flew to a mission station in the Irian highlands where, on May 29, Joyce gave birth to their first baby, Daniel. We praised God with them for a safe delivery and rejoiced when they came home. We were now six adults and two babies living on the hill above the sawmill.

As we continued to spend time with Sunarjo, he began to share his spiritual journey with us. He had been searching for the truth for several years by looking into Javanese meditation, mingling with Protestants and Catholics and going to their churches, and celebrating Christmas with Christians. He said, "I never found the truth, only more and more anxieties. And the question of 'Where will I end up when I die?' kept lingering."

A couple of months later, he told Peter he would like to leave the marines and work with us full-time. Later, he told us, "I saw it as an opportunity to find the answer to my question." Peter and I were in agreement to have Sunarjo help us, so he and Peter talked with the corps commander and requested that Sunarjo be released to come live with us and assist our family. "Tell you what I'll do," the commander said to Sunarjo. "I'll give you a six-month temporary leave. If, at the end of that time, you are happy helping Mr. Peter, and he and his wife are happy having you with them, I'll give you an honorable discharge from the marine corps." What a wise man.

So, on June 14, Sunarjo moved in with us—all eight of us! Sunarjo slept on the living room couch and kept his duffle bag underneath. He shared with us that he had been raised in a Muslim family. "I never questioned my Muslim beliefs until I joined the Indonesian Marine Corps," he said. "In that rugged environment, I didn't take time to practice my religious beliefs but was left with emptiness. Every attempt to search for a true God who could take away my sins ended up as a failure. Desperately, I cried for help. I felt the weight of my sins. I'd been taught from childhood that an angel followed me, scales in hand, watching and weighing my every move and thought. Good and bad, all were tallied and calculated. On Judgment Day, I would face the judge with the two angels as witnesses. That would be the time when it would be determined which way my scale would tip. As years passed, I saw less and less hope of the good outweighing the bad. In the military, I gave up practicing my religion, but I still felt the presence of that angel and knew my chances for getting into paradise weren't good."

Other Christians Sunarjo had met had encouraged him to read the Bible. Interested, he had read it through and was drawn to its truth. However, he was still confused, not sure what to believe. "What about the pastor I know, who drank excessively and mistreated his wife?" he asked. We encouraged him to go back to the Bible for answers; we read Scripture together every morning after breakfast. Sunarjo asked, "I have one question: why must we call to Jesus like we call to God?"

Preparing to Move to Tenwer

After the survey of the Tor and God's confirmation to us that we would be working with the Berik people, we began to make preparations for the big move. It was a busy, happy, and exciting time for us as we made lists of what supplies we needed to purchase in Jayapura. Since the Berik were a hunter-gatherer society, in which the main goal of the peoples' daily work was to gather enough food for the family, there were no stores or markets in the village. Thus, we would need to buy all the sugar, flour, salt, rice, and canned goods we would need for three months—the two months of our planned visit and for an extra month in case of an unexpected delay in departure. Dear reader, imagine going to the grocery store to buy all the food your family will eat for the next three months, realizing that you'll have no refrigeration and no chance to replenish or pick up what you forget. What would you buy? And how much of each? Be aware of how you'll store each item for ants, weevils, and rats will get anything not stored in metal cans or glass jars.

Peter had made plans to again visit Tenwer to meet with Chief Petrus, letting him know that we as a family would indeed be coming to live with them. Peter decided to make it an extended stay so he could work with the Berik men who were building our house, become acquainted with the people, and get a start on learning the Berik language. Sunarjo happily accepted Peter's invitation to accompany him.

Sunarjo Responds to Jesus

Their first stop was Sarmi, where they would purchase the rest of the supplies they would need in Tenwer. In the evening, they had many hours free to talk about Jesus and God's Bible message to us all. I had been in touch with my mother, and she joined us in praying that Sunarjo would respond to Jesus's call on his life.

Sunarjo wrote the story of what happened to him on June 24:

> It was Sunday afternoon, hot and humid. After the church service, Mr. Peter and I went to eat at the small restaurant in Sarmi and then went back to our dilapidated storage house for Sunday afternoon nap. However, I was restless and only tossed my body back and forth. Finally, I gave up, grabbed the Bible, and read the Gospel of Luke. When I came to Luke chapter 2, verses 8 to 11, my heart start to pound like crazy. I finally found the answer to my lingering question.

Here it is, the angel of God saying to me that I should not be afraid because he is bringing good news. The good news is for all nations, Indonesians, Arabs, Beriks, all. And the news was the Lord and Savior had come. It's the power of the Word of God that got me. I knelt down and thanked God for Jesus Christ my Lord and Savior. Yes, I am saved . . . and from now on, anything could happen to me. I am going to heaven.

I woke Peter up, and we prayed together while rejoicing.

That afternoon, Sunarjo wrote several letters. To my mother in the US, he wrote:

It's Sunday, June 24. Mr. Peter and I are still in Sarmi getting ready to go to Tenwer. We read the Gospel together, and I repeated my questions.

I found the answers in Luke 2:8–11 and John 3:16–18. And beginning this day, Holy Ghost came in my heart, and I follow Jesus Christ our Savior. Probably soon, if I know all the Gospel, I will be baptized.

He also wrote to his parents who lived on another Indonesian island. His second oldest brother wrote back, saying, "If it's true that you've become a Christian, there's no son in our family named Sunarjo." He never saw his mother again.

On Monday, June 25, I received a cable in Jayapura from Peter and Sunarjo in Sarmi, telling me that Sunarjo had received Jesus Christ as his Lord and Savior. *Thank You, Father, for answering our prayers, for speaking to Sunarjo through Your Word. Thank You for giving him the courage to write to his parents. Give him Your grace to grow in knowing You and in witnessing to others. I ask You, in Jesus's Name.* God had clearly led Sunarjo to Himself. We, his housemates, all rejoiced to learn he was now at peace. We received him with joy into our family as an unofficially adopted son. He became David's big brother.

Two Tough Months

In spite of all the good news, July and August were extremely difficult months for me. Peter and Sunarjo made excellent progress on finishing our village house, but they were gone for a whole month. I cared for David in Jayapura and tried to keep up with teaching Peter's six English classes for him. Local officials were very keen to learn and improve their English, and Peter loved teaching it, so whenever requested, he took on another group. It was great for public relations, but I couldn't keep up.

First, I picked up a stomach bug and needed to stay home. Then morning sickness, and sometimes all-day nausea, took over. Yes, I learned I was pregnant again. The nausea was tenacious and, combined with the heat, drained my energy. I felt I was a burden to my colleagues. When Peter returned, I just burst into tears, thanking God we were together as a family again.

Looking back now, I believe satan was not pleased with the progress we were making in preparing to enter his unchallenged domain. God had also led Bob and Joyce and Carol and Hiroko to commit to working with one of the 13 people groups that had been identified during the March survey. We were all pushing our limits. Bob fell sick, then Peter, then David—each one needing bedrest to recover.

Dengue Fever

The first week of August, Peter and I were both sick, and David was very crabby because he was teething. When Peter broke out in a rash and itching, we knew he had dengue fever. We were both sick in bed on August 6, celebrating our fifth wedding anniversary by remembering happier days.

Dengue is a painful, debilitating, mosquito-borne disease caused by the dengue virus. The acute stage lasts from seven to 10 days and is characterized by high fever, severe headaches, pain behind the eyes, severe joint and muscle pain, and extreme fatigue. A skin rash, which includes severe itching of the bottom of one's feet, appears after five or more days.

In mid-August, dengue got the best of me too, with aching low-grade fever and sometimes chills. Then my fever got so high and my eye discomfort so bad I once remarked to Peter, "My eyeballs feel like they're cooking in my head like a couple of hard-boiled eggs." I became so weak that when I sat in a chair, I had to lean back with my head against the wall. The fun part was when my feet started to itch, you should have seen me laughing as I tried to scratch the very ticklish bottoms of my feet.

In addition, the nausea was relentless, and I started spotting. I was exhausted and depressed. At last, after being sick for 17 days, Dr. Jerry came to Jayapura and was able to come to our house to examine me. He found my pregnancy moving along normally and confirmed that I was at the end of suffering through the course of dengue. He prescribed medication and declared that, within a couple of weeks, I would recover from dengue and most probably would be finished with morning sickness. He cleared us to depart Jayapura and move to the village, ON CONDITION that we spend two weeks in Sarmi, resting and eating well to recover my strength.

Thank You, Father, that Dr. Jerry was able to help and advise us. Thank You for bringing us through these trying months. We trust You. We commit ourselves once again to You for whatever is in Your plan for us. We do pray for healing and safety. We so look forward to bringing Your Word to the Berik people. In Jesus's Name. Amen.

God led, guided, and enabled us to prepare for our move to live in the jungle. He healed me and restored my strength as we spent a month in Sarmi. He halted my threatened miscarriage. He brought us to Tenwer as a family and delighted us with the people's all-night song and dance welcome. Without a doubt, we knew He would guide and guard our steps as we began our first months as jungle residents.

Getting Started

September to November 1973

For You are my rock and my fortress;
and for Your name's sake You
lead me and guide me.
—Psalm 31:3, English Standard Version

As I think about it now, 44 years after the fact, I'm amazed at all that God enabled us to accomplish in just nine weeks, the first nine weeks of actually living in our native-style house in Tenwer, one of the 10 Berik villages found along the banks of the Tor River in Indonesian New Guinea.

High on our priority list was for Peter to set up our Single-Side-Band radio (SSB), enabling us to have contact with the outside world. Arrangements had been made for our office in Jayapura to check in with us every morning at 7:00 a.m., asking, "How are you today? Do you have a need or message for us?" It was comforting for us to know that the call would come daily. Yes, we knew God was with us, but we also knew someone with skin on was watching out for us and would pray for us. In addition, should it ever happen that we would have an emergency during the day, we would be able to contact one of the missionary pilots who were in the air, and help would come. The SSB was powered by a 12-volt battery that was charged by solar panels mounted on the roof of our house. Agile Berik boys, who have no trouble climbing right up the trunk of a two-story-high palm tree, helped Peter string the SSB antenna in the proper direction in the trees outside our house.

A Captive Audience

In addition to starting to potty-train David, trying to become somewhat efficient in cooking and baking bread with my two-burner kerosene stove and making curtains for our bedroom windows that very first week we were resident in the village, the people began to come and, assuming we could help, requested medical aid.

One mother brought her extremely ill, malnourished, skinny baby to me one evening. She was crying, asking for help. I had no idea what was wrong with the baby or how to help. I prayed with her, but I couldn't yet speak her language, and she couldn't understand me. The baby died the next morning. *Oh Lord, I've so much to learn! Help me quickly learn to understand the people, to be able to comfort them with caring eyes and actions and also with words. Help me know how to treat diseases I've never seen before. Reach these people with Your love. I ask You in Jesus's Name to do this. Thank You for hearing me.* I knew that God would lead and guide me as I trusted Him.

So many people came to me for medical help all throughout the day that, the third week we were in the village, I announced I would hold a clinic time at our home every morning. It was a good way to interact with the people, get to know them, and I had a captive audience to practice all the new vocabulary words and phrases I was learning.

I had brought a stack of four-by-six index cards with me to the village; I had planned to use them as a simple way to keep patient records. My first question for each patient was *Imna bosna nasa?* (What's your name?). Each person was intrigued as I took a pen and a card and made marks on it. They watched intently as I made more marks after they told me what was wrong. Since I was just learning to speak and understand the Berik language, I had to rely on my examination to determine what was needed; then I wrote it all down. I had a stethoscope and otoscope; the patients and I had fun together as I let them listen to their own heart and lungs and look in their friends' ears. Early every morning, the people came and sat patiently until our family finished breakfast and prayer time. People began coming from other villages, and each week, the number of patients increased, even as the evidence of my pregnancy increased. Baby was more and more active all the time, and I was reminded of our days in Jungle Camp as I grew bigger and bigger. Halfway through our first stay in the village, we celebrated Peter's thirty-first birthday and also the fact that God had brought baby through four and a half months—halfway to my due date.

David loved being with the Berik people, and it seemed they couldn't get enough of watching him. They loved taking him for walks and helping him balance and walk on the top rung of the waist-high bamboo fences that lined the paths. The insects loved David too; he was plagued with bites, especially on his legs. With the help of triple-antibiotic ointment and covering his legs with my long white socks, the infected bites healed quickly. For a while, I almost felt envious of David, for as all children do, he picked up the ability to speak Berik by just playing with the kids while I had to study and work hard at it. Making it more troublesome for me was the realization that David was learning to speak three languages—English, Berik, and Indonesian—all at once.

Mail Days

Excitement reigned in the village whenever we heard the MAF plane circling overhead. Children ran in all directions, and some of the women ran off into the jungle, but many men bravely stood on the main trail to watch as the plane came down to treetop level and the pilot dropped our mailbag out the window. No matter where the bag landed—on the ground or in a tree—the children eagerly retrieved it and brought it to us. What a gift it was to us that the pilots were willing to drop by every two to four weeks.

Building an Airstrip

Peter also had a natural ability to learn to speak Berik, and so he learned quickly as he worked daily with 60 Berik men for six months to carve a 1,500-foot-long airstrip out of virgin jungle. Peter knew how to lead the men because the previous summer, when Peter and Sunarjo had been in Tenwer getting our house ready for us, a missionary pilot and a construction man had also made the trip upriver to select a suitable place for an airstrip for the government. The chosen site, just a half-hour jungle-hike away from our Tenwer home, was in a flat area on a peninsula formed by a bend in the Tor River. Thus, whether taking off or landing, the pilots would have a 300-foot-wide area free of trees and other jungle growth for their approach to the strip. The pilot had explained just how to go about building a jungle strip, and Peter and Sunarjo had faithfully worked hard to complete all the necessary steps before a plane could come in for a test landing.

As the strip took shape, our hearts thrilled to the thought that we would never again have to make those dangerous and arduous ocean and river trips in order to travel from the Pacific coast to the land of the Berik people. Can you imagine, dear reader, how we felt at the end of October when Pilot Pablo flew an empty plane into the village for the test? He walked the strip, testing it for firmness, and gave Peter the last pointers for completion. Two weeks later, Pablo returned with food supplies, did his final check, and then officially opened the Berik airstrip, named Somanente. I burst into tears when the plane touched down. Sixty men had worked hard to make this happen. What a HUGE job had been accomplished in just six weeks. *Thank You, Father above, for this fantastic blessing!*

Getting to Know the Berik

As if all that wasn't enough for Peter to accomplish, he also very much enjoyed talking to families about their relatives. One of our academic goals was to discover the details of the intricate Berik kinship system. Peter is fascinated by kin relationships and loves to talk with people about who they are related to and how they address each family member. How neat this was for me—Peter learned all the Berik relational terms; I just had to learn the system he had carefully diagramed.

The Berik had not only welcomed us to live and work with them, but they actually assimilated us into their tribal family. We were given "earth names." Peter became *Nyar*. I was called *Oburi*. I liked that name much better than the Berik translation of my English name, Sue, which in Berik is spelled simply Su and means "to urinate." No other Berik woman was named *Su*. But we learned that when two people do have the same name, they have a special kin relationship, and they must call each other, and their spouses, by that kin name, *Dobot*. Berik ancestors had taught the people it wasn't wise to use their own name when speaking to someone else; if they did utter their own name—even by mistake—it was believed that their teeth would fall out.

Sunarjo's Invaluable Help

Sunarjo was kept exceedingly busy each day helping with the airstrip, building desks for us, and putting up shelves in the bedroom, kitchen, and office where we needed space for our books and the area set aside for my medical supplies. When the battery for our SSB died, Sunarjo took it, floated downriver on a raft for two days with a couple of Berik men, and then caught a boat for the four-hour ride from the mouth of the river to Sarmi to get the battery checked. Unfortunately, it wouldn't take a charge, so he needed to buy a new one. He arrived back in Tenwer with us the next week.

Our First Workshop

Though we didn't have supervisory staff with us all the time, as we had had in Jungle Camp, consultants in the disciplines of anthropology, linguistics, literacy, and translation had been assigned to guide and direct us as we progressed in our program.

To enable us to move along in our goal of learning to speak the Berik language, our director had made arrangements for Ann, a linguistic consultant, to come from PNG to hold a language learning workshop for us and two other language project teams. Our colleagues Bob and Joyce and the two single girls Carol and Hiroko had also just completed their initial two-month stay living with the people groups to whom God had called them. Since their villages were within walking distance from Sarmi, where Peter and I and Baby David had spent a month in August and September, it was decided that it would be best for us all to gather in Sarmi.

Our plan was to attend the workshop and then take a break in PNG for the holidays. Thus, we would need to close down our Tenwer home. We wrapped our foam mattresses in plastic, stood them on end on the bed frames, and packed nonperishable food items in a 55-gallon drum. We turned off the kerosene refrigerator, emptied the kerosene tank, and covered the wick with plastic. Finally, packing our language materials in boxes, we each packed a small suitcase. We were ready and so very grateful that the plane could come for us; we didn't have to make the trip downriver.

Alas, the rains came. On the scheduled day when Pilot Pablo flew overhead at about 11:00 a.m., the strip was too wet—it wasn't safe to land the plane. I was so disappointed, but Peter and the Berik men took on the challenge right away. At 2:00 p.m. that afternoon, we loaded up in two canoes, and off we went downriver, overnighting in the same village where we had spent the night two months before when Baby David was so sick. God had been so good to us healing David, getting us well established and comfortable in our village life, prompting the people to love and care for us, enabling Peter and the men to put in the airstrip, and getting us back again to where we started. Amazing. God had launched us into the work with the Berik people, which He had planned from eternity past. He gave us His peace and joy.

The next day, we again paddled all day, baking in the hot sun with no stop for lunch, arriving in a village at the mouth of the river at 4:00 p.m. Though we were quite tired by then, we were very disappointed that there was no motorized boat available to take us on to Sarmi. This meant another overnight with no food, in a very primitive setting. Ugh! *Oh Lord, help! Sustain us and protect us tonight.*

But praise God! In the morning, a suitable boat was found, and by afternoon, we were settled in Sarmi. Pablo flew Ann in from Jayapura. Bob and Joyce and Carol and Hiroko all walked to Sarmi from their villages. We were delighted to be with them to learn the challenges they had faced and how God had brought them through their first village stay. It was comforting too for us to share with them, for we knew they would understand like no one else on earth. That evening, Ann led the opening session. Our workshop goal was to review all the steps we needed on the road to fluency in speaking and writing a formerly unwritten language. We met for very profitable five days and were, by then, physically exhausted and mentally overloaded. We needed a break.

Hurrah for Vacation!

Pablo came and flew us to Jayapura. I made a flight to the highlands to see the mission doctor who would deliver our baby. We praised God that Dr. Jerry found that, at six months into my pregnancy, both baby and I were doing well; he cleared us to go to PNG for the holidays. What a gift that trip was for all four of us—for me, Peter, David, and Sunarjo. We spent time at Ukarumpa, a mission station in the highlands of PNG where it was blissfully cool—daytime temperatures were in the seventies and eighties, and the humidity was low. My tears flowed when we entered our room in the guesthouse—the smooth varnished wood floors were sparkling clean in the light that came on with just a flick of a switch. We enjoyed Western food and Christian fellowship. And I cried with joy as we met and worshipped with other Christian missionaries, using our own mother tongue English. *Lord, this must be what I'll feel in heaven when we'll worship You there someday.*

After a delightful rest, we were ready to get back to the Berik to see what adventures would next come our way.

You Gotta Learn the Language!

1973

*There are doubtless many different kinds of
languages in the world, and all have meaning.*
—1 Corinthians 14:10, Holman Christian Standard Bible

Listening. Mimicking. Repeating. Listening. Tracking. Laughing. Repeating. Crying. Praying. Listening. Studying. Praying. Trying again. Listening. Trying harder. Success!

That's what it's like to learn an unwritten language, a language that no one outside of the language group has ever before tried to learn. We were basically in a monolingual situation—there was no language that both we and the Berik people could use to speak to each other. And there were no books, teachers, or CDs with practice phrases to help us, for when we arrived in Tenwer in 1973, the Berik language had never been written down. Think of it. In all those years since the Tower of Babel, no one had ever learned to speak Berik, nor had it been written. If we were to give the Berik people the New Testament in their own language, we would need to speak Berik and reduce it to writing.

Initially, we felt quite encouraged, learning the names of things as we walked around the village, continually asking, "Ai basa?" (What's this?) "Jei basa?" (What's that?) It was fairly easy for us to memorize all the nouns that we had written down in our vocabulary notebook. Some of the people would speak slowly and give us one word at a time. This was such a relief from several eager folks who rattled on and on a mile a minute.

Grubs!

We learned the names of fruit that grew in the village—bananas, papaya, coconut, pomelo (a type of grapefruit)—and in the jungle—ferns, spinach, edible mushrooms, sugarcane, various tubers, and grubs (beetle larvae).

Ah yes, the grubs. They were a treasured delicacy for the Berik people. They found them in abundance in rotting trees in the jungle. I remember the first time a man came to our house, smiling broadly and bubbling with excitement. He opened a palm-sized banana-leaf-wrapped package to show me what he had roasted in the fire for his lunch that day. Those inch-long worms were warm, thick, tan in color, with darker brown stripes and spots, and fat oozing out all along the length of each worm. The man picked up one after another between his index finger and thumb and popped them into his mouth. Chewing with delight with his mouth open, I could see just how juicy they were. *Oh Lord, PLEASE keep him from offering me one!* And God spared me; the man ate them all by himself. Further happy news for me was that throughout all our 21 years living with the Berik people, no one ever offered me a grub for dinner. Peter was not so blessed. But then I think he has a stronger stomach than I do. God kept me from gagging one day as I watched Peter take the offered prize and chew and swallow it without a problem.

Other food was not so easy to obtain. Peter would sometimes go hunting with the men who often left the village at sunup in the morning. We would awaken to the sound of the village men calling "Aatsssss, aatsssss, aatssss!" to their dogs—up to 15 of them—who reacted by running around, jumping, howling, and barking. They too loved going out for fresh meat—birds, cassowary, tree kangaroo, large rodents, fish, and small shrimp. The men used a fishline and hook when they could acquire them but were quite clever to be able to stand in the river shallows or streams and spear a fish. They also caught crocodiles both for food and to sell their valuable skins.

How Does <u>Your</u> Gallbladder Feel?

But the real prize was bringing home a wild boar, which one of the men in our village was able to do about every three weeks. The animal would be butchered by the successful hunter's village house, and the meat distributed to all—usually each person would get a two- or three-ounce piece. Unfortunately, Berik cultural taboo required that if a young hunter killed the pig, the members of his own family and his in-laws were not permitted to partake. An indication that we had been accepted into Berik society was that the hunters always shared a piece of pork with us.

The butchering of a pig was an exciting village-wide event. It was a perfect language learning time for me as I sat watching one day, asking, "What's that?"

"What are you doing?" This was a good way to get verbs: cutting, lifting, turning, breaking. I was eager to learn words for internal body parts: lungs, heart, muscle, intestine, liver, gallbladder.

As the men were removing the pig's liver, I saw that they were VERY careful as they slowly excised the green gallbladder. "What's that?" I asked.

i (pronounced "ee"), they responded.

"*i*?" I asked.

Bunar (True), they confirmed.

Yes, the word for gallbladder in Berik is just one little letter, the letter "i." We also found other one-vowel words in Berik: *o* means dirt, *u* means excrement.

Peter recording a Berik woman's story

As the weeks passed, we recorded and transcribed stories that the people told us. We then analyzed the words, phrases, sentences, and paragraphs. We found the word *ini* popping up all over the place. We had already seen that nouns in a Berik sentence are marked with the suffix *-ni* added to the noun.

We looked through the stories we had transcribed, looking for the adjectives associated with *ini*. Sitting at my desk, digging deeper one afternoon, the light of understanding went on. I was thrilled with a major discovery about the Berik language.

Unlike English, where our heart is used as the seat of our emotions, for the Berik people, God has so designed their language and culture that the gallbladder is the seat of their emotions. When they're proud, they say their gallbladders are lifted up—in the sky. When they feel sad, they say their gallbladders have fallen. When they're happy, their gallbladders are warm. And when they take hold of Jesus, that is believe in Him, He comes and sits well in their gallbladders. I was amazed as I studied the extensive use of *i* in Berik speech.

The Gallbladder in Berik Expressions

My gallbladder is lifted up.	I'm proud.
My gallbladder is fallen.	I'm sad.
My gallbladder is warm.	I'm happy.
My gallbladder takes hold of _____.	I believe in _____.
My gallbladder doesn't hear.	I don't understand.
My gallbladder is on the ground.	I'm humble.
My gallbladder is open.	I'm receptive.
My gallbladder isn't open.	I'm lonely.
My gallbladder is pulled by both ideas.	I'm undecided.
My gallbladder is running.	I'm guilty.
I say in my gallbladder.	I think.
I don't see his gallbladder.	I don't know his opinion.
My gallbladder is strong.	I'm courageous.
My gallbladder is big toward . . .	I desire . . .
My gallbladder is hard.	I don't grant requests.
My gallbladder is heavy.	I'm concerned.
My gallbladder is one with his or hers.	I have the same desire or goal.

My gallbladder is short.	I'm impatient.
My gallbladder is tall or long.	I'm patient.
My gallbladder is weak.	I'm discouraged.

National Geographic Magazines

To help the Berik people with initial literacy skills, like learning to understand a picture, we had *National Geographic* magazines available on the porch of our house for the people to look at. Many had never seen pictures before. Until these magazines came along, adults had only seen the world in natural three dimensions. Now they had to develop the skill of recognizing nature's scenes in flat two-dimensional pictures. They were intrigued, especially as they looked at pictures of mountain scenes, oceans, animals, and gorgeous flowers that were totally out of their realm of experience.

At any time of day, there could be as many as 20 people—men, women, and children—sitting on our porch pointing, laughing, and talking. It was a perfect language learning time for us. Pointing, they would often say just one word, which we would repeat, write down, and memorize. They would exclaim and comment on what they saw, often using just short phrases, which we would try to repeat. If they laughed at us, we knew we didn't sound natural, and we would try again.

How Did Niko Get in There?

Learning a previously unwritten language that no one in the world except the speakers of that isolated group have heard before is a daunting task. By the end of the first month in the village, we had learned a lot of individual words and sentences; it was time to dig deeper. We approached the task with enthusiasm—and a tape recorder, a reel-to-reel tape recorder. When the people came to visit us, we would ask them to tell us about their hunting or fishing expeditions. And then we would request that they tell it again on the tape recorder. When we played the tape for them to hear, we were amazed as we watched their expressions. A couple of the oldest people looked afraid and moved back away from the machine. One man reached out to pick up the recorder and look under and around it. Others just stared, thinking—I imagine, *How did Niko get inside that little thing?* But after the initial shock wore off, they chattered happily, excited to hear their own voices. As we listened, we would repeat what we were hearing and then replay certain phrases and sentences over and over until we could accurately pronounce the sounds and imitate the speech rhythm.

"I Told You That Already!"

Every afternoon, we would walk around the village and practice what we already knew and continually ask questions: "Who owns it?" "What do you use it for?" "Where did you go today?" What are you eating?" We would transcribe what we learned, using phonetic symbols, and would try to internalize all the new information.

One young man, Bular, would sit with us in our office as long as we wanted and just repeat words and phrases over and over—just like our tape recorder—as we tried to isolate a sound or find other words that had the same sound at the beginning of words or in the middle or at the end of words. And Bular was willing to correct our mistakes and never seemed to tire in helping us. What a gift he was!

Petrus, the village chief, was a dear friend, always dependable, and ready to help and encourage us—except in this one area. He had helped us learn several phrases, and we practiced them often. But then one afternoon when Peter was talking to him, Peter forgot one of the phrases, and as he stumbled trying to get it right, he asked Petrus, "What was that word again?"

"Oh no," Petrus responded. "I told you that last week, and I'm NOT going to give it to you again!" Petrus was not being helpful in refusing to give a word again, but on so many other occasions, Chief Petrus was one of our best helpers.

Tracking and Tape Loops

Every day, we went to Berik homes and also walked along with the villagers wherever they went. Often, we used a technic called "tracking." Before attempting to do this, we would explain, "We really want to learn to speak your language well. So now we are going to try to repeat everything you say, as quickly and as accurately as we can—AT THE SAME TIME YOU'RE TALKING." At first, they would just look puzzled, wondering how in the world we could do that. Then we would demonstrate, using some of the Berik sentences we knew well and then also using Indonesian. The people would burst out laughing. I guess to them it was just one more funny thing about us that they had never experienced before. It was like a game.

It usually took several tries for them to understand and to be able to just keep talking, even though the speaker was hearing us say the same thing. But once they caught on, they enjoyed it too.

Magdalena, a tall thin teenage girl, agreed to give it a try. She began to tell about going to the jungle to get vegetables. As soon as I heard the first three syllables, I began to repeat what she had just said, at the same time listening for the next syllables and words she would say, tracking just a couple of syllables behind her. It was much easier for her if I spoke almost silently so she wouldn't be distracted or confused by what I was saying.

At first, it was quite difficult for us to track Berik speech because we didn't recognize even one word drowning in an ocean of speech. But this exercise trained our tongues, lips, and mouths to pronounce patterns of word formation in the Berik language, patterns that we don't have in English.

Another exercise we found helpful in learning to speak Berik, a formerly unwritten language, was to make and practice phrases and sentences using "tape loops." We often asked Bular to work with us when making our loops. He understood the procedure and what we were doing, and he got quite proficient in helping us. We would practice with him before recording and could thus make a new loop within a few minutes. Using our reel-to-reel tape recorder, we would record a sentence in English—for example, "What's your name?" Then Bular would give the sentence in Berik, "*Imna bosna nasa?*" He would pause for the length of time it took to repeat the sentence under his breath and then repeat, "*Imna bosna nasa?*" After again leaving time to repeat the question, we would stop the tape and, with a scissors, cut the recorded portion from the reel of tape, usually about 24 inches. Then we would take the two-foot length of tape and splice the two ends of the tape together, forming a continuous loop.

Removing the plastic reels from the recorder, I would thread the loop through the record or play back head, leaving the rest of the loop lying limp on the recorder. Using my index finger inside the loop, I could pull gently so the tape was no longer limp. Pressing "play" on the recorder, I could listen to whatever was recorded on the tape loop over and over, as it just went around and around, allowing me to continually hear and repeat the sentence I was trying to learn—again and again and again.

Peter got to where he could make tape loops over 50 inches in length, with several expressions on it for us to practice. We especially targeted expressions with sounds in them that we don't have in English and were difficult for us to master. As we practiced, Bular would sit and listen to us, smiling when we repeated the sentences correctly and frowning when we needed to keep practicing. Our goal was to get our pronunciation as close to that of a Berik speaker as possible.

The advantage of the tape loop over the tracking technique is that instead of having a couple of hundred new words bombarding our ears in a short amount of time, as happens with tracking, with a tape loop, the number of words and sounds are limited and controlled, and we knew the meaning of the sentences we were practicing.

Only Six Colors

One day, we received a letter through the post office from an anthropology professor who was studying colors. He wanted to learn how many color words are used by isolated people groups in the world. The professor invited us to participate. It sounded interesting, so we accepted, and a couple of months later, we received a wooden box containing 300 various-colored poker chips. We were instructed to show the chips one by one to 30 different Berik people, individually, and to write down the name each person gave to each chip. We would then learn all the Berik color words.

It was a bit tedious to do this, but it gave us a great opportunity to interact with 30 different people personally, and it was great conversational practice.

We were quite surprised to find that every pastel-colored chip we showed them was *sinsini*. In fact, we learned that the Berik language has just six color words:

sinsini—white
seseye—black
berbere—red
ibam-ibama—blue
bwelkat-bwelkata—yellow
ikikini—green

When the professor shared the results of his research, we were again surprised. Some languages in this world have just two colors: black and white. If a language group has three colors, the third will be red. In languages using four or five colors, the additional words will be either blue or green. Finally, when six colors are used, yellow will be included.

Opportunities and a variety of ways to learn abounded all through our 21 years living and working with the Berik people. Each year, we would dig deeper and deeper into getting to know the Berik and understanding their language and their culture.

Could 1974 possibly be as adventuresome for us as 1973 had been? Ah yes . . . we didn't yet know what God had planned for us.

Baby Scotty's Birth

March 1974

Children are a gift from the LORD; they
are a reward from him.
> —Psalm 127:3, New Living Translation

Unlike his brother David, who was born in a suburb of the great metropolis, Jakarta, the capital city of Indonesia, Baby Scotty was born in the isolated mountainous jungles of Irian Jaya, Indonesia's easternmost province.

Just as Baby David was "with us" all through our jungle survival training course in southern Mexico in 1972, so too our second baby Scotty was "with us" during our first eight weeks living in an isolated jungle village on the north coast of Indonesian New Guinea in 1973. Contrary to expectation, the rigors of jungle living seemed to strengthen me and both our boys.

Since it was necessary for us to be in the same location as the doctor for two weeks prior to my due date, on February 19, 1974, after our lovely PNG vacation over the holidays, Peter and I and 20-month-old David flew by single-engine mission plane to Mulia, a mission station in the cool mountains of Irian Jaya. A new hospital had been built in Mulia to serve the local Dani people and the missionaries on the island. Dr. Jerry, his wife, and mission nurse, "Corky," received us; and we settled in to the guesthouse, which stood right beside the airstrip.

The 16 days before Scotty was born was a restful time for us. We had brought some linguistic work with us, and several of the mission families invited us to their homes for meals. Most interesting was learning about the Dani people, a tribal group—about whom many books have been written—who lived on that part of the island. They invited us to take part in one of their "pig feasts." The people had just received medical checkups, and the churches were preparing candidates for baptism, so a feast was in order.

A Forty-pig Feast

It was a grand experience! The Dani men had killed about 40 pigs, and the women and children had collected vegetables for the feast. Early in the morning, we heard the shouts and cries of the Dani men echoing through the valley as they carried the pigs to the roasting grounds. They had dug a 60-foot-long trough, filled it with firewood, and piled it high with large rocks. We watched them light the fire as they jumped about, whooping and singing their own native chant. About an hour later, when the firewood had burned away, the rocks were white hot.

While the fire was burning, the men dug and prepared about 40 ovens—round pits in the earth—each one about eight feet wide and two feet deep. The women lined each pit with banana leaves and filled them, layering in all the vegetables. First, sweet potatoes. Then hot rocks. Corn on the cob. Hot rocks. Bushels of various kinds of spinach or edible jungle leaves. And finally, the pigs, which had been split in two from the neck and down the length of the belly and gutted. The pigs were carefully placed, head and hooves included, back side up on the very top, now about two feet above ground. Buckets of water were added. Hot steam arose. The men quickly covered the ovens with a two-inch-thick layer of banana leaves and large cool rocks to form a type of seal and hold it all in place. Two hours later, each pit was opened to reveal a scrumptious pork dinner.

The next Sunday, we gathered with Dani people who had hiked over the mountains from miles around to witness the baptism of 150 new Dani believers. The river had been dammed up the day before to form an area where five candidates at a time could enter the water for baptism by immersion. What a spectacular sight it was that day to be with 3,000 Dani believers as they celebrated with their new brothers and sisters in Christ, proclaiming through the ceremony and verbal testimonies that they now walked with Jesus. As we watched, we could hardly talk. I had such a big lump in my throat, and as I wiped away tears, I prayed, *Oh Lord, how long will it be until we will celebrate with new Berik believers as they also declare their faith in Jesus?*

A Walk across the Airstrip

Labor pains woke me up shortly after midnight on Thursday, March 7, 1974. I timed them, and when they became regular and stronger, I nudged Peter and said, "It's time to take a walk across the grass airstrip to the hospital. Baby's coming." Peter got up, went to the phone, and called Dr. Jerry to let him know we would soon be on our way. A friend came to the guesthouse to care for David.

Dr. Jerry got the hospital generator going and turned on all the hospital lights, forming a great beacon for us as we navigated the path through the tall grass that grew on each side of the grass runway, then down into and up and out of the required drainage ditches that were parallel to the runway, and across the runway itself. We walked slowly, and I hung on to Peter, resting my head on his chest every five minutes when we had to stop to let another contraction do its work. The walk took us about 30 minutes, so Nurse Corky had the delivery room ready by the time we got there. She was wonderful as she prepared me for delivery. She met us with a wheelchair at the door to the hospital, and when it was time to move into the delivery room, Peter was right at my side. Good thing too. I must have been quite a sight as I got up from the wheelchair, stepped up onto a stepping stool, and began to get onto the delivery table. A contraction hit. I was stuck right there. Bent over. Couldn't move another muscle. Peter hung on to me for dear life. I imagine that Dr. Jerry and Corky chuckled a bit at the tableau before them, for Peter and I laugh about it even now as we remember.

We had brought our little handheld reel-to-reel tape recorder with us to the hospital. Peter had it in his hand but got so excited he forgot to turn it on. Dr. Jerry called out, "Now, Peter!" And yes, Peter reacted instantly and caught our baby's first cry at 4:08 a.m. Baby Daniel Scott weighed in at a healthy seven pounds and eight ounces. Later that afternoon, with Corky carrying Scotty, and Peter helping me, we walked back across the runway to the guesthouse where David squealed as he met his baby brother.

Peter notified Sunarjo, who was waiting for us in Jayapura, that Scotty had arrived. Sunarjo then sent a Western Union cable to my mother in California. She later told us that as she was preparing for bed on March 7, she was so anxious, awaiting the announcement of her second grandchild's arrival that she called Western Union to instruct them to call her at once, no matter what hour of the day or night, when a cable came in for her. "Would you believe," she said, "that while I was talking to the operator, the message from Sunarjo came over the wire?" She was then able to go to bed and get a good night's sleep, rejoicing that her prayers for Scotty's safe arrival had been answered. We rejoiced as well—that Mother was experiencing a period of emotional stability.

We're a Family Now

Peter and I clearly remember attending an English worship service the next Sunday with the missionaries and visitors who were at Mulia. We both experienced the awesome feeling of being a family for the first time. We hadn't felt it when we had just one child, David. But now, with four of us in one pew—Peter helping David and I held Scotty—we felt God's special blessing and joy. We sang and praised and prayed, *Father, enable us to raise these gifts You've given us to really know and love You, to serve You. When they are grown, cause each to pray: 'My whole being follows hard after You and clings closely to You; Your right hand upholds me'* (Psalm 63:8, Amplified Bible, Classic Edition).

On March 12, when Baby Scotty was just six days old, he took his first plane ride—to Jayapura where he would spend many happy days in the years to come.

New Vistas for Sunarjo

Having waited patiently for us to return to Jayapura from the mountains, Sunarjo was excited to meet our plane at the airport. The previous month, three of us had left; now four of us were returning. Smiling broadly, Sunarjo came right over to me to see Baby Scotty who felt, to all of us, like Sunarjo's new baby brother. After helping Peter with our suitcases, he asked if he could hold the baby. It was my delight to see how gentle and tender he was, how he smiled and talked to Scotty.

The previous January, all seven of us adults and two preschoolers who were living together had moved into a different three-bedroom house. There was one small bedroom, with a desk, a freestanding wooden closet unit, and two metal-framed single beds, available for our family in that house. After placing David's playpen at the foot of those beds, the room was FULL. Arriving "home" from the airport, we looked around our room and asked one another, "So where will Scotty sleep?" We stared at our suitcase that we had placed on the desk and simultaneously said, "A suitcase would be perfect bed for Scotty!" We moved the rest of our clothes onto a shelf in the closet and tied the suitcase cover to the wall in the open position. And so it was that Scotty spent the first months of his life sleeping in a suitcase.

As soon as we were settled, Sunarjo eagerly began to share what had happened in his life while we were gone. He had become more active in a good Bible-based church there in town and had attended a new believers' class. "I'm going to be baptized," he said. "God showed me that I should make my commitment to Him public. My baptism is scheduled for March 31." This was joyous news for us, and we praised God for this evidence of Sunarjo's total commitment to His Savior.

We were surprised when he told us that while we were gone, the leaders of SIL's translation work in PNG had contacted him asking for his help. "Three of our missionary couples who are currently here in PNG have learned of the need for translators in Irian Jaya. They've been praying about it and believe God wants them to respond to this need. But they need to learn the Indonesian language. Sunarjo, will you come over here and teach them?"

Sunarjo prayed about it and felt God leading him to accept this invitation. "I'll be leaving Jayapura in May, Mr. Peter," he said. "I may be there a couple of years."

Though we thanked God for His leading in Sunarjo's life and for Sunarjo's readiness to respond to God's plan, it was a distressful time for Peter and me. Sunarjo had become a part of our family. He had shared all those previous months with us when we moved to the village for the first time and then again when we really got started in our academic work. Our plan for April and May was to prepare to return to the village again, this time for the whole summer—June, July, and August. And now we learned Sunarjo wouldn't be with us this time. *Oh Lord, be with Sunarjo as he moves from his home country to PNG. Help him adjust to the climate, the food, and a class schedule. Keep working in his heart as he grows closer to You. And lead us, Father, in the glorious adventure You've planned for us as we return to the village. We commit ourselves afresh to You today. In Jesus's Name, we ask it.*

It's a Hostile Environment

1974

Bless the LORD, o my soul . . . who
heals all your diseases.
—Psalm 103:2a–3b, English Standard Version

It's a hostile environment living at sea level on the equator in a tropical rainforest, where the temperatures range from 95 to 100 degrees most of the time, the humidity runs at about 100% but feels like 300%, and where it rains 250 inches a year. That's 21 feet of water annually! That much rain on flat terrain produces swamps. Many of God's creatures love those swamps and the heat and humidity. They crawl, fly, chirp, croak, sing, and when they're hungry, lots of them bite.

During the summer of 1974, when we were living as a family of four in the village for the first time, those creatures showed up again—and showed us how they had missed David since he left the previous November. The biting insects came after him again. One day in June, just before his second birthday, I counted 68 red itchy swollen bites on David's back and 72 on his legs. I started him on oral antibiotics. The next day, those bugs came out to try once more; our little guy had additional bites on his face and arms. *Oh Lord*, I cried. *Place your healing hand on our David. Relieve him of the pain and itching. Give me wisdom on how to help him.*

And God answered. During the following years, we were able to keep the bites and infection under control; praise God it was never that bad again.

Some microscopic creatures, including the pests we called "no-see-ums," seemed attracted to me. I felt like a victim for, once bitten, I would itch unrelentingly for weeks! I confess to not following my own advice and giving in to scratching with a vengeance, in spite of the futility of doing so. A variety of viruses also came after us, attacking our intestinal tract and giving Peter and me the chance to fight with them. We praised God for the mission doctors with whom we could consult via our SSB and for the availability of medicine for intestinal parasites, which we could buy in town.

The equatorial jungle was also hostile toward the battery of our SSB. Just as it had died during our first stay in Tenwer, so also it malfunctioned again during our second stay there. The previous summer when Sunarjo was in the village with us, he floated downriver in a very old, almost rotting canoe and went on to Sarmi to get a new battery for us. This time, we cheered when the aviation department was able to send a plane with a new battery.

As more and more rain fell, the swamps enlarged. The mosquitos loved it. Swamps breed . . . mosquitos. And mosquitos carry . . . malaria, that is, the female *Anopheles* mosquito carries malaria. Medical books declare that she bites at dusk. I'll testify that she hasn't read the books; those female mosquitoes were after us whenever we were out and about.

During the night, when we were sleeping and couldn't swat those gals, it was an absolute necessity for us to sleep under a mosquito net. Our first net was wonderful. Peter's sister, Sally, had custom-made it for us. It was large enough to form a tent, covering two single-bed kapok mattresses laid side by side, and large enough that we didn't have to be concerned about the net contacting our skin, enabling mosquitoes to bite right through the net. It had four long cloth loops, one on each corner by which we hung the net on four nails in the four corners of our bedroom. Sally had extended the height of the net so we could sit straight up under it, without having the net touch the top of our heads. Finally, Sally reinforced the bottom of the net with heavy cloth that we tucked in under the mattress all around. That special net served us well for several years, freeing us from pesky insects and letting us sleep at night.

One More Pole

And then in the late seventies, God provided an even bigger net for us; our colleague Hiroko gave us a Japanese room-sized net. It was huge: eight feet by eight feet by eight feet in size. It was made from very fine netting that kept even the vicious, invisible "no-see-um" insects out. We laid a piece of linoleum on the bark floor of our bedroom, moved our bed and two bedside tables into the room, and made plans to hang our new net. It was so big and so heavy that, rather than hanging it by tying attached cloth loops to nails in the wall, the net had three metal rings on each side of the net. We could then hang it using two straight bamboo poles, which could be put through the walls on each side of the bedroom. Sliding the rings along the poles, the net could be pulled opened and pushed closed against the wall at will.

We needed two straight bamboo poles to hang our grand new net, but we had only one. So Peter, holding up his index finger so our Berik helpers would clearly understand what he was saying, went to the helpers and said, "Hey, fellows, would you go out in the jungle and get me one more straight bamboo pole?"

"Sure." And off they went.

We thought, *How long does it take for men familiar with the jungle to get one pole? About 20 minutes?*

An hour later, they came back dragging three poles. "Thank you," Peter said, "for helping me. But why did you bring three poles? I only asked for one."

"Well, Mr. Peter," they responded, "you said 'one.'" And then holding up the index finger of their right hand while using their left hand to hold down the third, fourth, and fifth fingers of their right hand, they said, "But when we looked at your hand, we saw you really meant 'three.'"

And that's how we found out that when the Berik people gesture numbers, they count the fingers going down.

Another lesson learned. We needed to know and speak the Berik language. We needed to know Berik culture and use their gestures, facial expressions, and body language in order to communicate to them accurately. How important this would be in the coming years when sharing Gospel truths with the Berik. We thanked God for teaching this to us early in our months of language study. What if we had used our Western gesture of holding up our index finger for demonstrating number one, instead of doing it their way while telling them about ONE hope, ONE Lord, ONE God (see Ephesians 4:4–6) and ONE Savior, Jesus Christ.

What Are Your Counting Gestures?

This new revelation of Berik gestures prompted us to probe into the complete Berik counting system. A literal translation of how the Berik people express the numbers from one to 20 is, in fact, a one-two binary system:

- 1—one
- 2—two
- 3—one plus two
- 4—two plus two
- 5—one whole fist
- 6—one whole fist plus one
- 7—one whole fist plus two
- 8—one whole fist plus one plus two
- 9—one whole fist plus two plus two
- 10—two whole fists together
- 11—two whole fists together plus one on one foot
- 12—two whole fists together plus two on one foot
- 13—two whole fists together plus one plus two on one foot
- 14—two whole fists together plus two plus two on one foot
- 15—two whole fists together plus one whole foot
- 16—two whole fists together plus one whole foot plus one on the other foot
- 17—two whole fists together plus one whole foot plus two on the other foot
- 18—two whole fists together plus one whole foot plus one plus two on the other foot
- 19—two whole fists together plus one whole foot plus two plus two on the other foot
- 20—two whole fists together plus two whole feet together

Cumbersome, to say the least. In practice, in daily life and in telling stories, when communicating numbers, the Berik actually routinely only use "one" and "two." Anything more than that is simply "a lot." So what, you ask, did we do when translating the New Testament into the Berik language? Since the Indonesian language was being used by government officials and was being taught to the children in school, we used Indonesian numbers—one word per number.

Pray to Who?

Malaria. A vicious disease. It's characterized by high fever, excruciating body aches, extreme weakness, and bed-shaking chills. There are three types of malaria. Praise God none of us ever had the type that's almost always fatal. But all four of us have had the more common type known as vivax. It attacks every other day, each sequence of feeling sick one day, and well the next, gets more severe as the illness progresses, leaving its victim feeling increasingly miserable.

Baby Scotty

When Baby Scotty was six months old, he got malaria. His fever hit 105 degrees. He was lethargic and wouldn't eat. We feared for his life. *Oh Father, You gave us this beautiful baby for Your purposes. You're allowing this disease to ravage his little body. Please say Your healing words and bring him through this. Use the malaria medicine You've provided to kill the malaria parasite. We ask You in Jesus's Name to do this.*

The next day, Chief Petrus heard that Scotty was very ill, and he came to our house. Smiling broadly, he said, "I can help you, Mama Sue. Give me one of Scotty's shirts. I'll take it out to the jungle, singing as I go. I'll go to the Ninsar tree, circle it, and pray to the spirit of the tree. He'll throw down a leaf—a big one—from the top of the tree. I'll catch the leaf, wrap Scotty's shirt in it, and put it in his bed with him. And he'll get well."

"Thank you, Petrus, for caring for us and for wanting to help but tell me who is this spirit you're going to pray to?"

I was shocked when he casually answered, "satan."

"Thank you, Petrus," I said, "for loving us so much that you want to help. But, Petrus, we've already prayed to Jesus. We know that His power is far greater than the power of any spirit. We're going to trust Jesus to heal Scotty." And He did. Scotty's fever came down, and instead of the expected attack hitting Scotty two days later, he became more active, and his appetite came back.

Word spread quickly about what God had done, exhibiting His Power to the Berik people. He had also demonstrated His healing power once again to us, confirming we could trust Him, no matter what He had planned for us next.

Conquering Major Milestones

March to October 1974

*The eyes of the Lord search the whole
earth in order to strengthen those whose
hearts are fully committed to Him.*
—2 Chronicles 16:9a, New Living Translation

Village Challenges

Having become comfortably settled in to our jungle home and life, with all our needed supplies, including a wonderful four-inch foam mattress, we were able to move on to other projects. Some of the Berik men had made their way out to town, and now they asked Peter to bring some desired basic items—like salt, sugar, cooking oil, matches—into the village for them. And so our first *toko*, a small store, was established. We created jobs for men, women, and children alike to earn money to purchase these necessities. Learning the value of paper money and coins and the basic math involved in making change and also learning the cost of basic food items helped the people in relating to and dealing with outsiders who began to make their way up the river to visit and interact with the Berik people.

The availability of salt, sugar, and oil was a part of my medical program to help mothers deal with their children's intestinal illnesses. I taught them the importance of keeping their kids hydrated and how to counteract the effects of severe vomiting and diarrhea, namely replacing water, sugar,

173

and salt. The agency TALC—Teaching Aids at Low Cost—makes a special spoon available to accurately measure the correct amounts of sugar and salt to be given to a child in eight ounces of water. This green plastic spoon is about six inches long and has a cup on each end, a slightly larger cup for measuring sugar and a smaller cup for salt. I was delighted when the mothers responded and used the spoons I was able to give them.

In mid-June that summer, I found myself facing what was, for me, a major challenge. I needed to stay alone with David and Scotty in the village while Peter made a trip downriver to Sarmi for supplies and a new battery for our SSB. He was to be gone two nights. *Oh Jesus*, I prayed. *Help! It was one thing to survive overnight alone in the jungle in Mexico during training, but this is different! During Jungle Camp, the staff was nearby. Now we're out here with no backup staff—and the SSB isn't working. I'll have no way to be in contact with the outside world. And I've two children here to care for. And what about lighting the gas lantern? Who'll do that? The lantern scares me. What if it blows up? What if the mantle, that fragile silk bag that glows brightly when heated by a flame, breaks? Peter's the expert. I just enjoy the light. Please give me the right attitude. I need Your peace and wisdom.*

And God answered.

Peter patiently taught me to light the lantern, and I was able to practice several times before he left. We made arrangements for Magdalena, our house helper, to sleep in the house with me. She was capable, a hard worker, was loyal to us, and dedicated to helping me. We knew she would run to ask one of the village men to help if I ran into a big problem. I needn't worry. After all, God was with me. He hadn't let me down before. Was I expecting Him to desert me now? Of course not. As Peter and I talked about it all, God gave me that peace that passes understanding. And Peter went on his way.

While he was gone, I was able to sleep at night. God had saved me from the intense pain of isolation. I didn't encounter a major problem. I even lit that lantern and didn't break the mantle. I managed to hang that hissing thing instead of just leaving it on the table. And it didn't blow up. God had covered me with His strength.

Two Thousand Computer Punch Cards

Just one of the items we had brought with us to the village, we had acquired the cards when we took our linguistic courses in North Dakota in 1970 and 1971. We were now eager to put them to use.

A punch card is a simple piece of paper stock that can hold data, usually in the form of small punched holes. Until the midseventies, most computer access was via punched cards. Some of Wycliffe's linguistic consultants were familiar with the cards, and in the late sixties, they developed a way for field linguists to use punch cards to aid in analyzing the sound system of an unwritten language. The cards we used measured seven and a half inches by three and a half inches and had 100 small holes around the perimeter of the card.

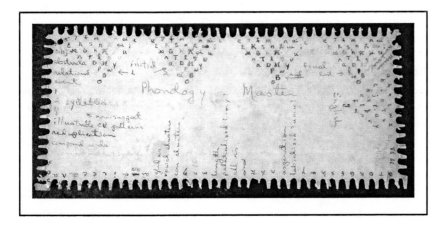

Using a special hand punch that matched the size of the holes, we punched out all 100 holes on one card and fashioned it to be the master card for phonological studies.

We assigned a value to each hole, one hole to each sound we had found in spoken Berik and other holes to represent the sounds and combinations of sounds that occurred word initial, word medial, and word final. We then wrote one Berik word on each of 300 punch cards. Placing the master card on top of one of the word cards, we punched out the sounds that occurred in that one word and the place in the word where the sound occurred.

To sift out all the words that, for example, began with the "s" sound, we took a stack of about 20 or 25 cards and put the master card on the top. Then taking a tool that looked like a long knitting needle with a handle, we put the needle through the hole marked "s" and shook the handle. All words with "s" fell onto the desk; cards without "s" hung from the needle.

This method was also a help to us in learning to speak the difficult, for us, sounds that we don't have in English. We would sit with a language helper and have him or her repeat the words with the same sound over and over with us until we pronounced it correctly.

The punch cards also were an aid in the development of a dictionary for the Berik people and in studying the fine points of Berik grammar.

Culture Studies

Since Peter is really fascinated by the study of anthropology, he spent many hours with Berik men and their sons when the boys were taken away from the Berik villages to live in a location deeper in the jungle for a period of three months. During this initiation into manhood, the older men taught the boys necessary skills in hunting, fishing, house building, disciplining their wives, some aspects of folk medicine, making and beating drums, and the men's songs. Peter learned that many of the songs sung during those all-night singing events spoke of killing, cannibalism, demons, and sexual activity. The young men were also introduced to the folklore and some musical instruments handed down from their ancestors, especially folklore that women are forbidden to hear.

One of the goals set for us by our academic supervisors was to document anthropological data about the people. During our time in the village that summer, Peter was able to type up our notes on about 75% of the required topics, such as tools, arguments, and marriage. Understanding Berik culture would enable us to translate New Testament stories and books more clearly and naturally into the Berik language.

English Classes

The opportunity for Peter to teach English while in the village was quite unexpected. When the Indonesian military established a base by the Somanente airstrip, Peter immediately reported in to them, explaining our credentials and goals for living there. The commandant quickly discovered Peter's special public relations abilities and that Peter truly enjoys spending time with new friends, getting to know them and learning about their backgrounds. We had now lived in Indonesia long enough to know that fluency in speaking English is highly valued by Indonesians and is encouraged by the government. Still, we were surprised when the commandant asked Peter to hold English classes for the soldiers in the village. Peter's classes were interactive; he has the knack for making it fun to learn conversational English. They all enjoyed their time together two or three times a week.

Our Language Exam

We believed we had made considerable progress in learning to speak Berik. And we had collected all the data we needed to write our phonemic paper, a statement of all the sounds used in the Berik language and how those sounds are placed in words and speech forms.

It was time for Ann, our linguistic consultant who had led our language learning workshop, to come again from Papua New Guinea to hold another workshop for us and our colleagues studying other languages. It was decided that it would be best for us to gather this time in the coastal village where Bob and Joyce were living and studying the Sobei language. Pilot Pablo made three shuttle flights to get our family of four from our Somanente airstrip to the beach in front of Bob and Joyce's village home. Ann flew in from town. And finally, Carol and Hiroko arrived from the coastal village where they were studying the Isirawa language.

Our workshop goal was twofold: evaluate our progress in speaking Berik and reduce the Berik language to writing.

Ann began by reviewing our data and, using the official checklist of what we were expected to know at this point in our program, checked our progress. I was both pleased and nervous when she announced we were indeed ready for our language exam, a requirement if we were to attain the status of senior members of our dual organizations, Wycliffe and SIL.

Two Berik language helpers attended the workshop with us so that Ann could administer the exam. "Sue," she said, "please explain the life cycle of the malaria mosquito to your helper, Magdalena."

GULP! *Oh my, how do I do that?* I screamed in my heart. But I tried, digging deep into my memory, using words and idioms that I had learned the Berik understood. I was nervous and sweating the whole time I talked to Magdalena. Bless her heart, she listened to me intently. And when Ann asked comprehension questions afterward, I was amazed and relieved when my brilliant helper was able to answer correctly.

I passed. Hurrah! Praise the Lord!

Then it was Peter's turn. "Peter," Ann said, "please explain traffic lights to your helper." What a challenge. Peter needed to explain to a man who had never been to town, had never seen a vehicle or lights of any kind, especially colored lights. But Peter did a great job. He also passed.

We rejoiced over this first small hurdle toward God's goal of giving His Word to the Berik people. We had begun to move on the track of fluency in speaking Berik. Ann declared we were now senior members. "Yippee!" I shouted. "Praise the Lord!"

During our lectures and discussions the next day, we learned about the necessary steps in writing a Berik-Indonesian-English dictionary, and Ann helped us set our academic goals for the rest of our first term on the field.

Reducing Berik from an Oral Language to a Written Language

Making extensive use of our punch cards, we were able to tell Ann what "phones," that is sounds, are used in the Berik language. During our three-week workshop, she led us in analyzing those sounds and in writing a descriptive research paper stating our findings.

Based on those findings, we were able to formulate a tentative Berik alphabet, with 15 consonants and seven vowels:

a, aa, b, d, e, f, g, h, i, ii, j, k, l, m, n, o, p, r, s, t, u, w, y

We were thrilled to have reached this milestone and immediately prepared the first Berik book to introduce the people to their alphabet and the fact that their language was now among the ranks of other written languages. The book, *Galgala Berikmana* (Berik Things), contained pictures of 20 Berik artifacts, articles the Berik used in everyday life: a wooden fork, a coconut ladle, a drum, a spear, and so on. We included the name of each item and a two-sentence statement, in both Berik and Indonesian, about each artifact.

When we returned to the village at the end of October, it was a delight for us to watch Berik expressions as they handled and looked at a book in their own language for the first time. Several Berik had been to town and had seen books used by educated people from outside their jungle world, books in the Indonesian and English languages. Realizing that their language was also valuable and important enough to be written gave them feelings of value and dignity.

We were ready to sprint on to conquer the next linguistic juncture.

The Good Life

October 1974 to May 1975

Yes, all the things I once thought were
so important are gone from my life.
—Philippians 3:8, The Message

Dr. Ken Pike

Ken Pike was an American linguist and anthropologist. He was the first president of SIL, the Summer Institute of Linguistics, and the originator of the linguistic theory of tagmemics. The author of more than 20 books and 200 articles, Pike was an internationally recognized scholar and was nominated for the Nobel Peace Prize 15 years in a row for his work in linguistics. He wrote, "As I developed my linguistic principles, I discovered they extended far beyond language and linguistics. They spilled over into areas like anthropology, religion, sociology and philosophy. In fact, they turned out to be general principles about human nature itself."

Ken's mission was to train and equip hundreds of linguistic students to analyze and reduce the earth's languages to writing. He led workshops in remote areas all around the world. Our SIL leadership invited him to lead our first grammar workshop, scheduling it to be held in January 1975. They felt it desirable that a facility be made available where Dr. Pike could meet with the language project teams, their language helpers, and university linguists. Because of its central location and the availability of a variety of trees that could be used to build a workshop center quickly and economically, a site was chosen at Danau Bira, a lake that was 90 minutes flying time—in single-engine aircraft—from Jayapura.

To help prepare workshop leaders, Ken arranged to conduct a consultant training workshop in PNG in early October 1974. Peter was invited to attend. Thus, after completing our phonology workshop with Ann, we flew once again across the Indonesian-PNG border to Ukarumpa, SIL's center in the mountains of PNG.

While Peter attended his classes, I was kept busy typing and getting final approval of our phonology paper . . . and caring for David and Scotty. It proved to be a challenging time. Scotty got a middle ear infection, and I came down with the flu. Peter, David, and Scotty drew our time to a close by all getting severe colds. It was actually a relief when we returned to Irian and went out to the village for another three months.

Back in Tenwer

As in previous visits, our days were super busy. During the summer, we had planted peanuts, but now we got serious about a garden. We planted corn, then lettuce and green peppers in an old rotting dugout canoe. Finally, we added cucumbers, which flourished as the vines spread out on the knee-high frame that Peter and the Berik men built for the plants. There was a dearth of flowers in the village; I made a mental note to bring seeds or plant sprouts from our Jayapura friends' gardens in the future.

We continued to learn the language, as did little David. One old Berik man commented that David was learning it faster than we were. Sigh. We worked on the dictionary and opened our little store once a week. I held clinic almost daily, except when David had the measles. When the wife of one of our language helpers went into labor, the ladies who were assisting her called me to help. It was a very difficult delivery, but God gave them a healthy baby boy. It was a stretching experience for me to meet the challenge of delivering a baby while Mama was lying on the floor on a banana leaf. I wrote up the details of what I learned about Berik beliefs and practices for addition to our book of anthropology notes.

By the end of November, we had been in Indonesia two and a half years. We had prayed and consulted with our branch director regarding when we should go on our first furlough. Considering both our needs and the needs of the branch, it was decided we should return to the US after three years on the field. It was essential that we meet face-to-face once again with our family and supporters and share with them what God had done.

We made plans to begin our furlough in May, after the upcoming Pike grammar workshop to be held at the Danau Bira workshop center, which was under construction.

As we began to prepare for Christmas, we prayed and felt ready to begin our translation work by translating the Christmas story from *Luke*, chapter 2. Matius, a Berik man who had lived in Jayapura for a short time, suggested we invite the people to gather on Christmas Day. If it hadn't been for the earthen floor, you could have heard a pin drop when Berik men, women, and children sat on the floor of one of the Berik homes and listened to Matius as he read the Christmas story to them for the very first time in their own language. *Thank You, Lord, for bringing us here to watch You work among the Berik people. Thank You for telling them of Your gift to them in the language of their hearts.*

After the New Year, we really went into high gear to collect the necessary data Dr. Pike had instructed that we would need during the workshop. We finished typing our first draft of the *Berik-Indonesian-English Dictionary*. We harvested and enjoyed our first crop of peanuts. Perhaps, we theorized, peanuts would be a good cash crop for the Berik people.

My Desk, an Operating Table

A particularly exciting medical event happened when a young boy, about 10 years old, climbed a coconut tree with a machete in hand. He wanted a drink of the refreshing coconut milk and a snack of the coconut "meat" now; he didn't want to wait for the fruit to fall from the tree of its own accord. Alas, when he saw a snake in the tree, he dropped his machete to the ground and jumped, the outside edge of his right foot landing right on the upturned machete blade.

We heard yelling and screaming as he was carried to our house. I moved our books and papers aside, making room for the boy on my desk. *Lord, I need You again. I've not sewn up a wound this deep before. Help me remember all that is needed. Thank You for Your people in the US who provided the required suture material. Thank You that I have the pain pills and antibiotics he needs. Give me a steady hand. Let this boy see and experience the power of Your love for him.*

Again, God answered. The boy's wound healed well, with no residual side effects.

Joy and Peace—In Spite Of . . .

Even before we left the US, we knew that our life in the village on the banks of the Tor River would be an extremely new and alien adventure. Not wanting to get writer's cramp by writing extremely long letters but wanting to share everything we were experiencing with our families, we purchased four small reel-to-reel tape recorders, one for each of our mothers, one for my sister, and one for us. Reel-to-reel tape recorders, popular in the early seventies, were about the size of a cassette player. Each reel measured about two inches in diameter.

So it was that one dark evening, during this last month in the village before we returned to the US for our first furlough, we were sitting in our kitchen-dining-living room at our wooden three-foot-square dining table for four in our village house. I looked around the room that I had enjoyed setting up, making it our home.

The kitchen cupboards were open shelves—dishes covered with clean diapers to keep sawdust from feasting termites and God's crawling creatures off the dishes. The sink had a piece of bamboo for a drainage pipe; the "faucet" was simply a bucket of water with a dipper. I looked up at the underside of our palm-leaf roof; there was no ceiling. I looked at the walls, the bottom one-third of which were made of palm-frond stems. We had screened the next one-third of the walls, which kept village dogs and chickens out. The final one-third above that was open to the outside. And I looked at our floor made of strips of bark. "Sue," Peter had warned me, "be sure the legs of your folding chair are balanced right on the top of the strips of bark so the legs of your chair won't fall through the half-inch cracks between the bark strips, and you won't wind up sitting on the floor!"

I carefully followed his warning and began to jabber away onto the tape recorder about the day's activities. Our gas camping lantern was hissing away overhead, and swarms of evening insects were buzzing around— dive bomber beetles circling and crashing onto the table.

Spontaneously, I said, "You know, Mom and Mary, **this is the good life**."

I was flabbergasted. I turned off the tape recorder and said to Peter, "Did you HEAR what I just said?"

"Yeah. What'd you say that for?"

Indeed, I thought. *Considering all we'd been through the past two and a half years, why did I feel and know deep in my heart and verbalize it to those closest to me that we were living the good life?*

"I can only think, Peter, that the Lord must have put this joy for living here in this primitive situation into my heart because this is the place that He wants us at this time. When I consciously or logically think about the differences between our culture at home and what we are used to and our situation here, how can I be happy? The peace in my heart is so contrary to popular beliefs in the US where marketing ads for tennis shoes, vinyl siding on your house, patio furniture, Pepsi, cigars, vacations at resorts, and so on are advertised as ways to *the good life*. The truth is I am happy and content and at peace right here. And I'm not afraid."

Peter agreed, "It's true, Sue. We <u>are</u> enjoying our busy life here, and we daily thank God for the work He's given us, for the opportunity to watch God work in Berik lives, for our good health, and for all His provisions for us."

Outfoxing Mama Mouse

In January 1975, as our fourth stay in the village was coming to an end, we once again closed our village home. We turned off the kerosene refrigerator, emptied its kerosene tank, and covered the wick with plastic. We stored food items in a 55-gallon drum and packed our language materials in boxes to take with us.

But this time, we didn't roll our foam mattresses, cover them with plastic, and stand them on end on the bed frames. Why not? Because when we returned to the village last time, after leaving them in contact with the bed, we found Mama Mouse considered those mattresses a great place to build a nice soft nest to have her babies. It wasn't easy for me to get rid of the smells—but I learned vinegar and hot sunshine could do the trick.

"Peter," I said, "there must be a way to outfox Mama Mouse." We prayed, and God gave us an idea. For each mattress, we used two long pieces of wire to keep the mattress rolled up. About three feet along the length of each wire, we tied a knot in the wire and fed the end of the wire through a hole punched in the center of a five-inch-in-diameter flat metal can lid. Finally, we tied the ends of the wires around one of the beams above the bed. Thus, the mattress was hanging free. Mice can run on overhead beams and up and down wire, but they cannot balance on the free-floating metal lid that obstructed their path.

The Pike Workshop

I had tears as I said good-bye to Magdalena and Bular, two of our faithful helpers who I had come to love. At the same time, when the plane came to fly us to Danau Bira for the Pike grammar workshop, I was excited and happy that we would soon be with family and friends in the US.

A special delight was that Sunarjo had been asked to assist with building and maintenance during the workshop. We felt blessed that we were able to live as a family in a newly built small three-bedroom cottage with running water in an inside bathroom. It felt luxurious to us.

The workshop ran for three months: February, March, and April 1975. Novice linguists from other missions and experienced and novice Indonesian linguists also joined us. Lectures were given by Ken and his wife Evie and some of the experienced linguists. Peter was appointed as the workshop coordinator; Evie Pike was Peter's consultant, and she mentored him in his consultant-in-training assignments.

I shook in my boots, and my heart skipped a beat when told that Ken was to be my consultant. *Who? Me? I'm a beginner's beginner. How can I relate to him?*

Ken had a plan. He said, "Sue, there's an area of study that needs research. I want you to investigate how the Berik language works. The title of your paper will be 'Chronological Mapping as a Useful Tool in Identifying Semantic Paragraph Groupings in Berik.'" What a mouthful. I had no idea what he was talking about. But Ken led. And I followed. Day by day, he gave me assignments; I worked with my language helpers and reported back to him each day.

The next month, in February, when the workshop was in full swing, that heartless female *Anopheles* mosquito attacked; I experienced malaria for the first time. The thermometer of my compassion for others, who had already lived through a malarial attack, went up 100%. Though I lost about four days of work, with the fever and chills and body aching, we praised God for His healing and the medication that won the battle. And I returned to my battle with linguistic research.

Then one day, halfway through the third and last month of the workshop, Ken said, "OK. We've got good information. Write it up."

"Really?" I questioned.

"Yes. Write what you understand. Then we'll work on it together."

Oh Lord, I need Your help again. I've never written a grammar paper before. I feel I'm in over my head. I'm a nurse; I don't have an affinity for this linguistic work. Please enable me to do this.

I tried. The next day, Ken reviewed my work and gave me directions on what to do next.

I tried again. The next day, I received more instructions on the details.

I tried. After Ken reviewed my third try and began to explain what was next, I burst into tears and sobbed, "I can't do anymore! I've done my best."

"Great," he said. "You're done. That's what I wanted to hear. I always push until my students admit they've done their best."

What a relief. It was over, but I felt so embarrassed at what seemed a failure to me. Then I took a deep breath and thanked God for bringing me through such a stretching experience.

A week later, the workshop came to a close. All the participants had finished their papers; Peter wrote 'A Preliminary Analysis of Berik Clause and Clause Root Types.' Everyone at the workshop center—professors, instructors, linguists, language helpers, and maintenance and construction staff—celebrated together with a special meal, formal ceremony, and a time of thanksgiving and praise to God. Together, we had proved the functionality of the workshop center; God had led, provided, healed, motivated, and established us as a group to provide His Word for the people of Irian Jaya.

Peter and I had completed our first term on the field. We turned our hearts and minds to our first furlough in the US.

Our First Furlough

May to October 1975

*Upon arriving in Antioch, they called
the church together and reported everything God had done through them.*
—Acts 14:27a, New Living Translation

FUROUGH! What an exciting thought. It was time to return to the country of our birth. A time to be with family and friends. A time to introduce them to our sons, David and Scotty. A time for David and Scotty to meet their cousins. A time of relaxation and refreshment. A time to share with loved ones and supporters about all that God had done in our lives and for the Berik people during the last three years. A time to eat a real hamburger. A time to introduce our boys to the wonders of fall colors and walking through crunchy fallen leaves. A time to get our clothes really clean. Yes, we looked forward to it all with eager anticipation.

A New Way to Get Off a Train

Being the venturesome travelers that we are, we planned a challenging trip home from Jayapura to Minnesota. Since we wanted to meet Sunarjo's family and learn more about his home island of Java, the first leg of our journey was to fly from Jayapura to Surabaya, a large city on the north-eastern coast of island. The previous month, Sunarjo had gone ahead to smooth the way for us. He met our flight from Jayapura, and the next day, we took a train to Jogjakarta, another large city in central Java.

Java, home to 145 million people, is the most densely populated place on earth, with more than 2,800 people per square mile. It's crowded. The train was FULL. But we had a pleasant trip observing the rice paddies and picturesque villages as we rolled along. Sunarjo was our guide the next day as we toured the historic sights of "Jogja."

Our train trip the following day was an entirely different story. I've never again seen anything like it. The train was so full that people were not only sitting on the laps of passengers who had seats, but they were sitting on the floor, at the feet of those in the seats, and packed like sardines sitting on the aisle floor, the full length of the car. When the train arrived at our stop, about one quarter of the people stood up to get off. They walked right on and over the people in the aisle!

"Sunarjo!" I called. "What do we do?"

"Just walk right on them, like everyone else is doing."

I couldn't believe it. But Sunarjo picked up Scotty and his diaper bag and expertly pushed his way off the train. Peter took David and another of our carry-on bags and began to try to move toward the exit. I was in a near panic; my heart felt like it would beat right out of my chest. I was afraid we wouldn't be able to get off, that the train would carry us away to someplace else. I grabbed the back of Peter's shirt and hung on for dear life, apologizing as I stepped on people. It didn't seem to faze them a bit.

We took a half-dozen steps and couldn't get any farther because another whole crowd of people were pushing to get ON the train. We were stuck. We looked out the window at Sunarjo who shouted to us, "Quickly! Pass David out the window to me and then just push your way off the train. Go fast!"

Peter forced his way between the people sitting on the floor by the nearest window and passed David and our remaining carry-ons out to Sunarjo, who had given Scotty to someone else to hold. Then Peter turned, took my hand, and we just elbowed our way through the pack of people and onto the platform. I was in tears by then, tears of relief, tears of tension released.

The crowd on the platform just smiled and welcomed us to their town. The helpful man didn't run off with Scotty, as I had feared, but gave him back to Sunarjo. He helped us get a taxi to take us a short distance to his hometown, Cilacap, on the south coast of Java. It was a tremendous relief to check into an air-conditioned hotel, with foam mattresses and our own bathroom.

We had a delightful visit with Sunarjo's family for a couple of days, following which we took an all-night bus ride, with five of us sitting in four seats, arriving at last in the capital city of Jakarta at 8:00 a.m. After a two-hour bus ride to Bogor, David's birthplace from which we had departed three years before, our colleagues welcomed us royally. They fed us breakfast; then we showered and fell exhausted into bed for a long nap. We thought things were looking up.

But that night, Scotty came down with a cold and was up, crying, almost all night. He was miserable and just clung to me for the next couple of days. I was relieved that Scotty, David, and I could just stay put, resting up from our arduous trip to regain our equilibrium. Peter and Sunarjo needed to go to Jakarta daily to get Sunarjo's Indonesia exit permit and US student visa stamped into his passport. Peter picked up our roundtrip tickets to fly on Air Siam from Jakarta to Los Angeles. After three amazing years experiencing God's leading and provision, we were ready to fly to Hong Kong, the pearl of the Orient.

Back to the US

After taking a day to go sightseeing in exotic Hong Kong, we flew to Tokyo and Honolulu on May 1, 1975, three years to the day from our arrival in Jakarta before David was born. Actually, because of the international date line, we did May 1 twice—once before and once after crossing the date line.

We were thrilled that Mother joined us in Honolulu for a couple of days. Unfortunately, following her second husband's death in February, she had begun to struggle emotionally again, and after just two days with us in Hawaii, she went back to Los Angeles under very unpleasant circumstances. We were very disappointed and prayed earnestly that our upcoming two-week visit in California with her and my sister Mary and her family would be a happier time. Mary had had her first baby, Chris, on New Year's Day in January. I was eager to hold my new nephew, and we were eager for the cousins to be together. God answered our prayers, and we did have some lovely visits and outings together, but it was like walking on eggs around my mother, wondering when anger would raise its ugly head again.

After visiting the Wycliffe office, where we were the grateful beneficiaries of a car-donation program, we set out to drive to Minnesota, making stops in the Grand Canyon, Denver, and at Mt. Rushmore in South Dakota. Since none of our Minnesota relatives had yet met David and Scotty, we were excited to the core to be with everyone again.

What a joyous visit we had in Minneapolis with Dad and Evie, Jim who was in college, and eight-year-old Nancy. We arrived in time to see my favorite tiny spring flowers, lilies of the valley, still in bloom in Dad's beautiful gardens. We kept a busy schedule visiting friends, the dentist and doctors for checkups, and the Children's Rehabilitation Center where we had met and worked together before we were married.

We were also able to spend some time with Yaufun who had become a part of the Westrum family. The past three years had been momentous for him. After finishing two years studying pre-engineering at Moorhead State University, in 1973, he had transferred to the University of Minnesota in Minneapolis as the first foreign student to be accepted into their engineering internship program. We felt proud of his success; he was scheduled to graduate in December 1975. He had also studied diligently to become a US citizen, proudly declaring the Oath of Allegiance in 1974.

After just five days, we continued on to northern Minnesota, visiting Peter's siblings and families, finally arriving at Peter's parents' home in Moorhead on June 5. They too started spoiling David and Scotty right away and loved taking care of them whenever they were needed. Peter's mother had arranged for us to present programs about our work at her church on Sunday and for the children at vacation Bible school. We were delighted to share what God had been doing in Indonesia.

Peter's parents were pleased to meet Sunarjo. But when Peter's dad, Lloyd, heard that Indonesians only had one name, he said, "Sunarjo, you can't live in America with only one name. You have to have a first name and a last name."

"Well, what should I do?" Sunarjo asked.

"You have to choose a first name. What would you like us to call you?" Lloyd asked.

"I don't know. Please choose a name for me."

"George Washington was our first president. I think you should take his name. We'll call you 'George.'" And so it was. Sunarjo signed registered for school and signed in everywhere as George Sunarjo.

Teaching at SIL

SIL, whose headquarters was in Los Angeles, ran summer courses in several locations around the US. We had attended their course in Grand Forks, North Dakota, during the summers of 1970 and 1971. With the work in Indonesia now underway, several more translation teams had been assigned to Indonesia; the decision was made to require the teams to study the Indonesian language before moving to Indonesia. Thus, it was that Peter and I were asked to teach the Indonesian course at SIL in Grand Forks from mid-June to mid-August 1975.

It was a wonderful time full of memories. David and Scotty thrived as they spent their days playing with all the children. Peter, Sunarjo, and I team taught and became good friends with the students who would soon be our colleagues in Indonesia. We made frequent weekend trips to Minneapolis and almost always gave a program about our work wherever we visited friends and relatives. Also, because of the article about my salvation in *The Gideon* in 1967 and because we had kept on sending our prayer letters to The Gideons International office, I received frequent invitations to give my testimony at the pastors appreciation dinners given by local Gideon camps. We surely enjoyed meeting with these fine men and their wives.

Invitation from The Gideons International

Unbeknownst to me, in April while Peter and I and the boys were visiting with Sunarjo and his family in Indonesia, the executive director of The Gideons International had sent a Western Union telegram to me in Indonesia, inviting me to give my salvation testimony at their upcoming international convention.

I was quite surprised by this invitation. It's true that I had been in contact with the Gideons since my first contact with them in 1967 and again in 1971, but this invitation was totally unexpected. Peter and I prayed about it and believed God wanted me to accept. Then I prayed fervently about what God would have me say in the 12 minutes, EXACTLY 12 minutes, I was given to speak at the pastors appreciation banquet. Peter and I enjoyed the trip to Denver and luxurious hotel accommodations the Gideons provided for us for the weekend in July. Peter's mother took care of the boys while we were gone.

We arrived in Denver a day early. The next morning, we were delighted to be able to share what God was doing in our lives with two youth groups, teens who were attending the convention with their parents. In the afternoon, our host took us to the banquet hall and explained the schedule and what I could expect. The program would be conducted according to a very strict schedule. Standing at the podium where I would be speaking, my host explained the three lights that would be visible to me while I spoke. The steady green light would tell me I was free to keep talking. The yellow light would tell me I better be winding down—I had two minutes left. The blinking red light signaled I must stop in one minute. A steady red light meant I had exceeded my time. *I wonder*, I said to myself, *is there a trap door that will open up and swallow me if I don't stop on time?*

As we were seated at the head table when the banquet started, I looked out at 3,400 people. *Oh my! Lord, help! I've never done anything like this before. Look at all those people. Please keep me from fainting, stuttering, going blank, and forgetting what I've planned to say. Speak for me, Lord. Glorify Yourself tonight.*

God answered my prayer. I didn't choke up or stutter as I related the four ways God had reached me: through the testimony of two individuals, the joy and friendliness of a church, prayer, and God's Word. And I finished before the red light became steady. Hallelujah!

Several Gideons came to talk with us after the banquet. Two of the men were the very ones who had placed the Gideon Bible that God had used to reach me in the Ohio hotel in 1966. *Thank You, Lord, for how You orchestrate Your plans in our lives.*

Peter Goes on a Speaking Tour

Talking about banquets, Peter was also asked to speak at a banquet—in fact, 14 of them. Wycliffe Associates (WA), an organization of volunteer lay people, was called by God to support the work of Wycliffe Bible Translators. Among other things, WA's ministry included sending short-term volunteers overseas to assist field workers, providing linens for missionaries on furlough, and raising funds for field projects. One WA fund-raising method was to sponsor complementary banquets during which attendees heard an inspirational message by a missionary and were given the opportunity to make a donation toward a specific project. Peter accepted the invitation to be a banquet tour speaker and traveled with a WA representative for three weeks, speaking in 14 cities in Kansas, Missouri, Arkansas, Oklahoma, and Texas.

While Peter was gone, the boys and I flew out to California to be with Mother and my sister Mary and her family. Meanwhile, Sunarjo began taking a course in auto mechanics at a vocational tech school in Moorhead.

Time to Go Home

Peter finished his banquet tour on October 9 and flew back to Minneapolis; the boys and I also flew to Minneapolis that day from

California. It had been a wonderful, eventful five and a half months of furlough. It was time to say good-bye and return to our second home, to our ministry with the people we had come to love, the Berik people in Indonesia.

Back in Moorhead, when we met with our church fellowship for the last time, they presented us with the marvelous gift of an outboard motor to use as we traveled up and down the Tor River, visiting Berik villages. After completing our final shopping, we packed a couple of barrels of supplies, crated the motor, and arranged for shipping to Indonesia.

On October 15, we said a tearful good-bye to Sunarjo who stayed in Moorhead, living with Peter's parents, to continue his schooling, and we began our return trip by once again driving across our awesome beautiful country, visiting relatives and supporters along the way to California. We returned our car to the Wycliffe office and, on November 1, took off across the Pacific.

First stop, Honolulu—on our way to challenges we had no idea were awaiting us.

God's Magnificent Love

November 1975

*I will tell of the LORD's unfailing love. I will
praise the LORD for all He has done.*
—Isaiah 63:7a, New Living Translation

Unexpected

Flights from Los Angeles to Honolulu are always joyful trips, even sometimes festive, for most passengers are starting out on a vacation to that
island paradise. Our flight on November 1 was no exception, for we were
rejoicing for the wonderful six months we had just had in the US and
excited for the new adventures God had planned for us during our second
term on the field. We took a taxi to our hotel on Waikiki Beach, checked
in, got settled in our hotel room, and took a short nap. David and Scotty
were still asleep when I got up.

I took the opportunity to call my mother in California and was
totally shocked by her greeting. She was angry, very angry. She blamed and
accused me and Peter for hurts she felt we had inflicted on her while we
were in the US. The hurt that I felt deep in my heart while listening to her
was like a stabbing, piercing knife. My thoughts about her were not God-
pleasing thoughts—I was overwhelmed with the same feelings of rejection
that I had struggled with through the years. I didn't know how to respond
to her tirade, "I'm glad you're gone. Don't bother to contact me again."

My heart skipped a beat, started pounding in my chest, and I burst
into tears. After my heart achieved a slower rhythm, although I was still

crying, I called Mary in California and asked what had happened. She confirmed that Mother had become upset with the behavior of a neighbor and was lashing out on several fronts. Knowing what was happening relieved some of my turbulent emotions, but I knew I had to deal with the strength of my reactions. Peter and I prayed about it, asking God to heal me and to shower His grace on Mother to release her from her agony.

On November 4, we flew to Hong Kong, arriving on November 6. Because of the international date line, we actually skipped November 5, thus making up for the day we lived twice on our flight the previous May from Asia to the US. After an overnight in Hong Kong, we went on to Singapore for a four-day visit and then spent a week in Jakarta, Indonesia, before taking the final flight of our trip back to Jayapura on November 20.

It felt like we had fallen into a whirlwind of activity and assignments, for just four days later, after doing our grocery shopping and helping our little three-year-old and one-year-old boys adapt to yet another new location, we were off again to our workshop center at Danau Bira. Our US headquarters office had sent a husband-and-wife team, Phil and Barbara, from the counseling department to lead a workshop about coping with stress on the mission field and how we can help one another. They announced that they would be available to meet individually with anyone who would like to talk with either one, or both, of them.

I signed up to talk with Barbara on Saturday afternoon. I needed help regarding the hurts and feelings I was harboring about my mother.

Healing

I told Barbara about my phone call with Mother earlier that month when I was in Honolulu. This led to talking about other times through the years when Mother had been emotionally troubled. Finally, sobbing, I told Barbara about that excruciating time 25 years before when I was 12 years old and Mother had taken me to the school in southern Minnesota "to put you away with the other bad girls so you can learn how to behave." I told Barbara that I had never before verbalized that horrible day to anyone else because the emotion was just too deep the words would stick in my throat. I simply wouldn't let myself bawl in front of someone else. *Maybe they'll think I really was that bad. Maybe they won't ever talk to me again. Maybe I'll lose my friend.*

Barbara listened with compassion, asking only a few questions. When I finished, and my tears slowed down, she said, "Sue, I want you to now, out loud, say all the things you wanted to say to your mother that day in the reception room of that school. Say out loud the things you couldn't say to her as a little girl at that time, the things you've never spoken out loud. Speak to her, as you wish you could have spoken that day. I'll just sit here with my eyes closed."

"I can't do that," I told her.

"You must get it out. You're stuck in deep-down pain because you've not acknowledged your true hurt, your anger." With that, Barbara sat there quietly with her eyes closed, hands folded. I imagined she was praying.

I was silent for what seemed like several minutes. "Go ahead, Sue. You can do this," she said.

After another long wait, I started slowly, quietly to speak. I cried with 25 years of pent-up emotion. I was angry and, for several minutes, said hurtful things. "Why do you want to get rid of me? What have I done to make you so mad at me? I try so hard to be a good girl, to do what you want. But you just keep yelling at me, telling me I'm bad. Mothers are supposed to love their children, but you're just mean to me. I can't please you, no matter what I do." Abruptly, it was over. I sat there silent and exhausted. Finally, I opened my eyes.

Barbara looked into my eyes and said, "Now, Sue, tell me what Jesus would have done if He had come through that door from the school into that reception room and had seen that little girl there, begging her mother to take her home and not leave her there."

At first, I just stared at Barbara. Then the dam broke; the truth dawned on me. Just as the 25-year-old hurt had been etched into my mind and emotions, in that moment, the healing of God's love took over, etched even deeper—forever. Crying with relief, I said, "Jesus would have opened His arms wide and looked with compassion into the girl's young, weeping, and terrified eyes and heart. He would have gone to that little girl and held her tight and hugged her. He would have said, 'I love you. I want you. I'll care for you.'"

"Yes," Barbara said. "You've known and believed in God's love since you accepted the fact that Jesus died for you back in 1966. But now you've experienced Him in the depths of your soul. Let's pray and thank Him for His love and for meeting you today."

And we prayed. I felt peace, where before deep down I had felt turmoil. Before I felt rejected; now I felt accepted. Before I felt unlovable; now I felt loved. Before I felt discarded; now I felt valuable. Before I felt anger and hate; now I felt compassion and sympathy for all Mother had suffered. Amazing love. I was free of a 25-year burden.

Even today, I smile when I remember that day in 1975. I remember Jesus with His arms open wide. I remember what a relief it was to know that I am loved. Sometimes, even now, when someone does something that feels hurtful to me, my heart will skip a beat, triggered by the hurt of abandonment that cut so deep when I was a child. And then I remember to just whisper, "Jesus." Though past memories, with the accompanying hurt feeling can pop up, Jesus's healing touch is there again. Always there.

Twenty-two Months in Administration

November 1975 to September 1977

Base your happiness on your hope in Christ.
When trials come endure them patiently,
steadfastly maintain the habit of prayer.
—Romans 12:12, J. B. Phillips New Testament

With the glow of God's love filling my heart, Peter and I completed the coping-with-stress seminar, and we attended a goal planning workshop. We laid out our strategy for meeting our linguistic, anthropology, literacy, and translation goals for the coming four years. This planning was designed to help keep us focused on tasks that would support finishing the translation of the Berik New Testament. A research study had shown that if two translators attempted to accomplish all the good and important things that could be done, it would take 250 years to do so. We couldn't do it all.

Emergency Flight

Our colleagues Bob and Joyce had been unable to join us at Danau Bira for the workshops. Their six-month-old baby son, Timmy, had needed emergency abdominal surgery in Jayapura the very day the rest of us flew to Danau Bira. When Peter and I returned to Jayapura after the workshops, we were stunned to learn that Baby Timmy was near death. The doctors recommended taking him to Australia by emergency flight the next day.

197

Peter and Bob worked around the clock with the government offices to get the necessary paperwork completed for an early morning departure. Joyce went home from the hospital to pack suitcases for herself, Bob, their two-year-old son, Danny, and Timmy. I worked with the hospital to prepare the medical supplies that would be necessary for the trip.

Before dawn the next morning, we piled into a station wagon to take the one-hour drive from the hospital to the airport. Timmy had an IV running. I held him on my lap and held the IV bottle up with my right arm and hand—outside the window! It had proved impossible to get the bottle high enough inside the car to keep the IV flowing. What a relief when, once in the plane, I was able to hang the bottle and ensure the life-giving fluid ran into Timmy properly. I waited with Bob and Joyce at the airport in Papua New Guinea until they were able to board a Qantas Airline flight to take them to Australia.

I flew back to Indonesia and joined in the prayer vigil that had been set up for Timmy and his family. A week later, we praised God and rejoiced with Bob and Joyce that Timmy had survived further surgery and was doing well.

Non-Berik Project Assignment

Along with our leaders, Peter and I had recognized the need for programs and organization for our fledgling group; Peter was assigned to administer the work for at least the coming year. In the end, he filled this position for 22 months. My assignment was to help in any way that I could and do whatever else was assigned to me. My first task was to write and run an orientation course for all the new members coming to join the SIL advance in Indonesia. The years of 1976 and 1977 turned out to be very difficult and challenging for us.

It all started when pinkeye struck. What a miserable infection, especially for a child who naturally wants to rub his eye all the time to try to get rid of the itching. David was the first to come down with it. Then I took my turn and had red, weeping, matted, irritated eyes and blurred vision; and finally, little Scotty got it too. We praised God that Peter was spared.

Earthquake!

Up until this point, the Indonesian government hadn't given SIL permission to begin an aviation program in the country. And then in June

1976, a 7.1-magnitude earthquake convulsed the mountains of Irian. Combined with the following landslides when six villages simply disappeared into the valleys thousands of feet below, 5,000–9,000 people were missing and were assumed dead.

Peter was part of SIL's response to aid in disaster relief by bringing in planes and pilots to fly supplies to the people who had survived but whose farmland was gone. It was a massive effort that the government rewarded by allowing SIL to begin an aviation program to serve not only our own members living in isolated areas in this province but also government officials and our sponsoring university staff at Bird of Paradise University. The Helio Courier, a short-take-off-and-landing (STOL) plane that had already made dozens of flights to the mountains, was given to the university and dedicated for use in Irian.

He Did WHAT with His Mother?

A couple of months later, when the program was well established and the number of flights for disaster relief had diminished, the president of the university asked Peter to join him on a trip to Wamena, a mountain town in the Baliem Valley, in the heart of the Dani area. The Grand Valley Dani people were first seen from an airplane in 1938. Their earth-oven method of cooking, their unusual type of dress—or, better stated, undress—and their Stone Age culture soon began to attract tourists. Brochures advertised trekking in the highlands with people from the Stone Age. Peter and the president decided to visit Wamena's major attraction, a mummy.

They had not been prepared for what they saw. A Dani man had smoked his mother. Truly. After his mother died, some 10 years before, the man had placed her in a squatting position on a chair, her head hanging forward, her knees near her temples, her feet close to her buttocks, and her arms outside her legs with her hands by her feet. She was blackened like a brick of charcoal by the smoke of the fire over which she had been preserved. Even her skin had been retained. Amazing. A tremendous attraction. A definite sight to see for anyone dropping by the Baliem Valley.

Challenging and Diverse

My life living in Jayapura was challenging and diverse, including caring for David and Scotty, continuing the orientation program for new members, coordinating Indonesian language classes for many of us, heading up our newly instituted literacy department, and attending monthly meetings with the Indonesian ladies' club. This group was basically for Indonesian women, wives of civic and government leaders, but they invited some of us Western women to join them. Peter and I became good friends with the family of the director of the local immigration department. Our two families—they also had two children—simply enjoyed being together in each other's homes. The director's wife, Ati, taught me how to sew, and I gave her piano lessons. Sometimes we all just sat and ate popcorn while watching a movie together.

When the government and mission doctors planned a three-day medical-nursing seminar to be held in the highlands, I was one of the first to sign up. I was eager to meet and get to know my colleagues from other missions, and attending the seminar would help to prepare me for the medical situations I would face when Peter and I and our boys returned to our village location.

Formerly, the doctors had set up schedules whereby nurses could call one of them on the SSB radio frequency to ask for advice about a patient in need. Now the doctors invited nurses, who were ministering in villages where no other medical help was available, to come and together study the tropical medicine challenges we faced day by day. We learned physical assessment and diagnostic techniques. The frosting on the cake was that our US state nursing boards would recognize the course and grant us continuing education credits so we could maintain our US nursing licenses. God is soooo good.

Guesthouse Managers

The summer of 1976, Peter and I were assigned to be the first managers of a group guesthouse, which was being built on the university campus. Peter isn't a carpenter, but he was able to work with the builders who were ready to begin the finish work. In the fall, our job was to make the place livable. Buying or having furniture built for the guest rooms. Making curtains and bedspreads. Setting up the kitchen and group areas. Establishing management procedures. Decorating. Organizing landscaping plans, including a flaming hibiscus hedge we could enjoy when looking out our window. Finding, hiring, and training workers and cooks. Talk about a challenge! But God knew what I needed. We found a cook who had had previous experience cooking Western food. Since I wasn't skilled using a treadle-type sewing machine, I praised God for Ati who had taught me the basics.

The guesthouse included a manager's apartment; we moved in the day after Christmas. It was imperative that we quickly get settled in our own space, for on Monday, January 3, we were to welcome a full house of 17 guests from Jakarta, Papua New Guinea, Australia, and Holland to take part in the Third International Linguistic Conference.

Peter had a major challenge to deal with; the electricity for the guesthouse had not yet been connected. *Lord, please help me know what to do so we can care for our guests,* he prayed. And God showed him a way. He requested help from the men's dormitory next door. They helped Peter run an extension cord out the window of a side room in their building and across the tree limbs into our guesthouse. Flexibility—the name of the game.

Bali

After several months working non-stop with increasing pressure, we realized we needed a break, a real rest, away from and out of reach of all our responsibilities. We chose to go to the vacation island of Bali. After three nights at the beautiful Bali Beach Hotel and then four nights at the Respati Inn in a little cottage of our own on the beach, we finally felt relaxed. It was then that we realized how exhausted and tired we had been. It had taken us a whole week to unwind. We played games, built castles in the sand, chased the ocean waves, and went for sailboat rides. We toured and became acquainted with Balinese culture and dances. We went bowling and played miniature golf.

The second week of our vacation, we moved across the island to Kuta Beach. It was there, in the pool of the Legion Beach Hotel, that David and Scotty learned to swim. Peter took the four of us on a rented motorcycle for rides around town and past tranquil irrigated rice fields.

When we arrived back in Jayapura after three weeks, our colleagues, who had taken over the guesthouse responsibilities while we were gone, met us at the airport. Handing us the guesthouse keys, they said, "Welcome back. The guesthouse is full." And so we jumped right back into the frying pan, praising God that we were rested and ready for the tasks ahead.

Guess What Scotty Just Did

It was a quiet, restful Easter Sunday afternoon at the guesthouse. I had just gotten up from a nap when Andrea, the seven-year-old daughter of a fellow SIL member, came into our apartment. She had been playing and was obviously very excited about something. "Guess what Scotty just did," she said.

"I don't know. What?"

"Well, I asked him if he had asked Jesus into his heart. He said, 'No, not yet.' So I said, 'Well, what are you waiting for? Why don't you pray right now?' And he did!"

"Yes, I did," three-year-old Scotty added, with just as much excitement. "I told Jesus I'm sorry for being naughty. I asked Him to live in my heart."

He was so excited that he was going to be with Jesus in heaven forever, and he couldn't wait to share his decision with us. *Thank You, Father, for even using a child to reach my son. What a special Easter!*

Acting Director

When it was necessary for the director of our branch to be in the US for five months, Peter was appointed to be acting director of our now-established work. With 34 SIL members working in the country, his responsibilities increased greatly. Seven language teams were involved in seven different translation projects. He made arrangements to rent a building near the university for the branch to use for an office, and he supervised the needed renovations and painting.

Peter had the use of our SIL group vehicle. One afternoon, a young man from an isolated village in the interior of the island stopped by our home. He was looking for a job; Peter invited him to help wash the van and offered to pay him for his work. Peter put up the windows on the car, got out a hose, and demonstrated how to spray the outside of the car with water from the hose. He showed the man, who had never seen a car before he came to town, how to wash the car with a rag from a bucket of soapy water and rinse it again with water from the hose. The man happily set about his new task. Greatly relieved to be free for more pressing duties, Peter left.

When he returned about 20 minutes later, he was shocked to see the man hosing down the inside of the car. "I finished the outside," he said.

Such is the type of culture clashes we've experienced through the years as our experience and expectations collided with people from Stone Age cultures. Some things are almost completely irrelevant to people who have grown up in environments totally different than city life with which we are more familiar.

Busy, Busy, Busy

Civic and business leaders asked Peter to hold conversational English classes for them. He enjoyed this very much, and was good at it, I might add. When he took on the role and title of acting director, he was required to do extensive traveling, so I filled in for him when he was gone. He was often called away from our little apartment in the evening for meetings or government events. We were both on overload. We didn't have time for each other. We were tired and irritable.

Though I didn't acknowledge it at the time, the fact was that I wasn't making enough time every morning to read my Bible and to pray, to gain the equilibrium of God's perspective, peace, and joy that I needed. I remembered the admonition from Philippians 4:8: "Fix your thoughts on what is true and good and right. Think about things that are pure and lovely, and dwell on the fine, good things in others. Think about all you can praise God for and be glad about" (Living Bible). But too often, I quickly forgot. It had become easy for me to think about what Peter needed to do, instead of how God wanted to change me. I needed to reinstate a habit of prayer. Easy to know in my head. Much more difficult to do.

In mid-August, relief from our myriad of duties was in sight, for as of September 17, we would be able to return to our village work; we would be released from the load of our administrative duties. We turned over our guesthouse responsibilities and moved into a house in town. Though it was quite a mouthful for three-year-old Scotty, he loved to tell people in his little singsong voice, "We live in the *Jalan Gerilyawan* [Gerilyawan Street] house." With the help of one of our colleagues who had just taken on the role of primary school teacher for our SIL children, we got David started in kindergarten. I canned chicken and ground beef and pickles to take to the village. Peter made a three-day visit to Tenwer to let the people know we were coming back and to get the house ready for us. When we made a tape recording for our families to let them know this exciting turn of events, Scotty contributed, "We're packing up!"

Peter and I felt somewhat rejuvenated and more united, as we turned our minds once again to our ministry with the Berik people. We wondered, "How quickly would we remember the Berik vocabulary we had learned two and a half years before? Would the Berik children remember David and Scotty? Would the people be as eager as they were before to learn to read and write and to help us with translation?" We'd soon find out.

Digging Deeper

September 1977 to April 1978

And whatever you do, in word or deed, do
everything in the name of the Lord Jesus, giv-
ing thanks to God the Father through Him.
                    —Colossians 3:17, English Standard Version

Back in Our Village Home

At the end of August 1977, Peter checked with the aviation department and learned that the Berik airstrip in Somanente was being used by the government officials who were now living there in that village. The airstrip had fulfilled a great need; government personnel and the Berik people had maintained the strip in good condition. WOW! Praise God! Maintaining a grass strip in an equatorial rainforest is no easy task.

During Peter's three-day visit in September, he let the Berik people know that we truly hadn't forgotten them, and our whole family was coming to live with them again. He hiked 30 minutes on the well-used jungle trail to visit Tenwer and check on our village house to see what repairs were needed. Considering it had a palm-leaf roof, palm-frond walls, and a bark floor, the house was in surprisingly good condition. God had preserved our residence for us. Many of the Berik men eagerly volunteered to fix what was necessary, including reinforcing the leaky roof, before the boys and I arrived.

On the seventeenth of the month, our family flew back to the land of the Berik, where we had left our hearts two and a half years before. A great crowd of about 100 Berik people, from two or three villages, had gathered at the airstrip to welcome us. They jumped up and down, smiling and exclaiming greetings. Their gallbladders (hearts) were warm (happy) indeed. We felt like celebrities. Men, women, and children helped the pilot unload the plane and told Peter they would porter all our stuff on the long winding jungle path to our Tenwer house. What a joyous day it was.

Many of the children remembered David and Scotty and were surprised at how tall they were. As we listened to the people excitedly babbling away to one another about us and all our supplies, we understood the topics of their conversation but not the details. We knew we had our work cut out for us to get back to the fluency we had had in early 1975.

Medical Challenges

The day after we returned to the village, a young girl with a severely infected tropical ulcer—measuring about three inches by two inches and more than a half inch deep—on her right foot was carried to our home. She hadn't walked for weeks. Our hearts cried for the extreme pain she was suffering. I treated her medically. Then Peter got out one of David's Bible story picture books and, in simple halting Berik, translated stories about how Jesus had healed sick people. He told her that Jesus had raised a widow's son from the dead. He said that Jesus could also bring her "dead" foot back to life. The girl listened intently and seemed to understand. Peter prayed for her. At first, her friends had to carry her to our house for a daily dressing change, but two weeks later, she walked to our house. God was revealing Himself and His power to the Berik people.

The next weekend, I was called to help deliver a baby. The mother was lying on a banana leaf, on the bark floor of her hut. Actually, the baby girl came easily. Then I watched in horror as one of the Berik women cut the cord with a dirty rusty knife. *Oh Lord,* I prayed, *help me teach the women here about sanitation and disease prevention.* The baby seemed to do well . . . for a few days. And then she passed away. It was emotionally traumatic for me, but the people seemed to just accept it.

One day, standing on the river's edge—in the same area where children played, dishes and vegies were washed and which was used as a bathroom—I was stunned to silence as I saw a Berik woman squat in the shallow part of the river to deliver her baby. Later, as we dug deeper into our study of the Berik culture, especially when our language helper's newborn son also died, we learned that the Berik people don't name their children for several months after birth because they know the child may not live. As I researched the health and medical needs of the people during the following years, I found that the mortality rate for Berik children under the age of five was about 20%.

Preparing to Read

If you had visited the living room of our 1,000-square-foot house at this time, you would have found it full of people of all ages. Some would be putting puzzles together, some looking at picture books—especially the *National Geographic* magazines and children's books that we kept there for them—and some would be coloring. Our five-year-old David loved to sit there with them and chatter away, using English and new Berik words he heard about both familiar and new images.

Puzzles, magazines, and coloring were not just great ways to pass the time; they were all, in fact, part of our prereading program, preparing the people for a full-scale literacy campaign. David and his friends and their parents spent hours playing with a colorful blue-and-red plastic Tupperware Shape-O toy, a hollow ball with 10 holes of various shapes—circle, square, star, cross, pentagon, and so on. The challenge was to take each of 10 yellow plastic shapes and insert them into the matching holes in the ball. This toy was an exercise in visual discrimination, helping nonreaders become oriented to the idea of "same" and "different," essential in recognizing letters.

We also demonstrated the usefulness of reading—the ability to gain the same meaning from written material, which could be obtained from the same material given orally—by hanging a blackboard on the wall of our porch. Some days, we listed the items for sale in our toko. We noted the days and times when the clinic would be open and when the plane was scheduled to come again. When someone came to the house asking, "When's the plane coming?" I would answer, "It's written right there on the board."

And when they responded, "But, Mama Sue, I can't read that," I'd say, "Oh, I'm sorry to hear that. Be sure you plan to come to the reading classes when they start." Usually, the person would smile and promise to do so.

Kindergarten

Doug, a pilot, and his wife, Marilyn, a teacher, had arrived in Indonesia in early 1977. They were assigned to live at Danau Bira, our branch workshop center, which had been built in time for the 1975 Pike workshop we had attended just before our furlough. After getting settled in their house, Marilyn got right to work preparing curriculum for seven-year-old Andrea and three five-year-old boys—David, Dirk, and Dale—to start school. The boys were eager and very ready to start kindergarten together. Marilyn provided lesson plans and all the school materials I needed to teach David in the village. Thus, each day, I taught David the same things in the village that Marilyn was teaching Dirk and Dale at Danau Bira. David's teacher called us weekly on the SSB radio to talk over any problems we had. Whenever we went to Danau Bira, David joined the other three kids in the school classroom. It was a fabulous system for which we thanked God.

David Wanted to Be Sure

The most exciting event during our first three months back in the village with the Berik people happened on a Sunday in October when our family was having a singing and worship time together. We were talking about the fact that Scotty knew the date when he prayed to Jesus, asking Him to forgive him and promising to follow Him always. David said, "I don't know the exact date that I prayed to Jesus."

We asked him, "Would you like to have an exact date to celebrate every year?"

"Yes, I want to have a date too. I want to remember when I knew for sure I'll live in heaven with Jesus forever."

We listened as David prayed, right there in the living room of our Tenwer house, saying he was sorry for his sins and asking Jesus to forgive him. Then he prayed Jesus would come to live in his heart and always be with him.

"Dear Jesus, we thank You that our David has responded to Your love. We pray that he'll grow to be a strong man of God who would seek Your will for his life, a man who will follow You, no matter where You lead him."

Daily Clinic

Besides teaching David every morning when we were in the village, I held a clinic in our home for those needing medical help. It worked well for me as clinic time was also an enjoyable study time for me. I had a captive audience. Before I gave a pill or a shot to each person, I would just sit on the clinic side of the porch with them and talk and practice pronouncing all my new Berik vocabulary words and phrases. It was a major encouragement to me that, within one month of living with the Berik again, I had gained the ground I had lost by being away from the village for more than two years and was making progress once again in learning to understand and speak Berik.

"What's your name?" I asked each patient. One day, when I couldn't find the man's card in my clinic patient-record box, I inquired, "Have you come before to get medicine?" When he said, "Yes," I looked again. Then, feeling frustrated, I whispered, "*Jesus, help me.*" Immediately, I got the idea—ask him what his name was the last time he came to the clinic. Voila! He had changed his name. I learned to change my initial question to "What was your name the last time you were here?"

Many of the small children were severely malnourished; they had very thin arms and legs, huge potbellies, and pale-red hair. Adults and children alike suffered from infected sores and cuts; babies often had crusty infected head lesions. A common Berik practice was to make small cuts in the skin with a piece of broken glass over the painful area of the body. They did this to let the "bad blood" out. This probably did help when the problem was a large boil, but without soap or any kind of cleansing, cuts on essentially normal skin soon became grossly infected.

Realizing the people could be greatly assisted by better hygiene and an understanding of nutrition, I made plans to initiate one-on-one instruction for mothers regarding hygiene, and before long, I developed picture flip charts to use along with demonstrations on bathing babies and children. Peter and I began to bring soap into the area. Peter's mother in Minnesota was a tremendous help, for she visited neighboring motels, requesting to have the little leftover bars of soap that were normally thrown away. The motel owners were delighted to know that these useless soap pieces would help people in faraway Asia. Friends helped Peter's mother cover shipping costs to send boxes to us through the post office. Since they were sent by sea, most packages took about five months to reach us. We were surprised a couple of years later when the Berik people said they preferred the medicine soap from America. "They're much better than those big bars from Jayapura," they said.

Fire—A Fundamental Berik Need

I was fascinated with the Berik people's creativity and ability to build a fire whenever they needed it—rain or shine.

Hot coals were always available in a Berik home. Firewood was always on hand under the house. I used to watch with amazement as a Berik woman would place small sticks of firewood in a circle like the spokes of a wheel, put some hot coals in the middle of the pile, and blow. Poof, just like that, she'd have a flame burning and shortly a fire as big as she needed to roast something. She would leave the wood in a circle, keeping the fire going by simply pushing the "spokes" toward the center at regular intervals.

One day, we watched several Berik boys start a fire from scratch. "We'll show you how our ancestors did it," they said. A couple of them tore a very dry piece of *niwu*, a clothlike article made from a reed, into small shreds and mixed in bits of cold, crushed, burnt wood. One young man split one end of a yard-long piece of wood and forced a small piece of wood into the crack to keep the two sides of the split wood apart. He placed the wood on top of the shredded cloth. Another boy prepared a one yard long piece of dry jungle vine, attached a wood handle on each end, and put the vine under the split wood and on top of the cloth. Two guys stepped on either end of the split wood.

Then one of the fellows grabbed the handles on the vine and created friction by rapidly pulling the vine up and down on alternating sides. Within three seconds, there was smoke. He continued the rubbing action until the vine broke; then quickly, he bent down and blew on the cloth and cinders. And there it was—a tiny flame. The boys took turns blowing and laying very small pieces of slivered wood on top. With more blowing, the size of the flames increased. As they added slightly bigger pieces of wood and kept blowing, they soon had a small fire.

Satisfied, they picked up the whole pile and put it in a neighbor's fireplace. Laughing and whopping, off they went—proud as can be.

That may be a fun activity for a group of teenagers, but Berik men wouldn't often go through all that trouble to get a fire started. Usually, a Berik man would carry his own fire-making tool, a *tatabanik*—I call it "Berik matches"—with him when he left the village. A *tatabanik* is a 12-inch piece of bamboo with a cork in one end. Inside, the man kept a broken piece of china pottery and some very dry fuzz—that is, cotton-like shavings taken from the bark of a softwood tree. To light a fire, the man would simply place some of the fuzz on top of the pottery and strike the sharp edge of the pottery along the length of the bamboo. Amazingly, there would be a spark, and the fuzz would begin to smolder. Placing the smoldering lump with dry twigs and blowing on it all produced the fire. Ingenious. Though most of the Berik had never seen paper or pen or books or schools before we came along, we were continually impressed by their creativity and intelligence in practical matters.

Figuring out the Grammar of the Berik Language

Every afternoon, Peter and I worked on digging deeper and deeper into understanding the Berik language and how it works . . . the study of linguistics, the scientific analysis of the structure of language. We found that God had created a fantastically complex language.

- We learned that Berik adjectives follow the nouns. A big house in Berik is *jina unggwandusa*—literally translated, "house big."
- Berik sentence structure is like German in that the verb is at the end of the sentence: "Peter went to the jungle" in Berik is *Peter jei onap sofwa*—literally translated, "Peter he jungle to went."
- That sentence demonstrates another interesting point. Locative prepositions, in this case "to," are noted simply by the letter "p" attached to the noun *ona*—"jungle," thus forming *onap*—literally "jungle to."

Truly, it surprised me that I found these linguistic discoveries fascinating. God had placed that interest in my heart, AFTER I said yes to His call and leading to do language and translation work. I was learning more about our awesome God, how He equips us to do, and enjoy, what He calls us to do. *Oh Father, thank You for making this work interesting to me. Please now, I ask You, make speaking Berik second nature for me, just as it is for all these little Berik children who speak this language fluently.*

Christmas in Tenwer Village

It had been three years since we had been in the village for Christmas, and we looked forward to being with the Berik again at this festive time of year. But we were sad that, as far as we knew, no Berik person yet understood what Christmas was all about. Nevertheless, we were excited to be in Tenwer as a family. Peter worked with a language helper to revise the *Luke* 2 Christmas story that he had translated in 1974 and which we had read with the Berik people at Christmas that year.

We set up a small nativity set on a table in our living room, clearly visible to everyone who visited us and to the people who were constantly standing on the porch of our home, looking in to see what was going on. We decorated with red and green crepe-paper streamers and played Christmas music on our boom box. And we read the Berik Christmas story over and over with the people whenever we were sitting around visiting. In our hearts, we prayed, *Oh Lord, how long will it be until You bring a break-through among the Berik people? When will You make Yourself known to one of these dear Berik friends?*

When a huge wooden crate arrived in the village, it seemed like a Christmas gift for us and for the Berik too. It contained the 10-horsepower outboard motor that our church in Minnesota had given us the last time we were with them at the end of our furlough. It had finally made its way all the way to Tenwer. Men, women, and children all gathered around Peter as he opened the crate. Everyone wanted to see how it worked and wanted a ride in a canoe that they didn't have to paddle. During the next week, Peter and some of the Berik set to work constructing a mount on the back of a large dugout canoe. News of this new arrival spread like wildfire to all the villages up and down the Tor River. That motor served us well for the next 20 years.

Helicopter Survey

The year of 1978 started with even more excitement. Just as it was imperative that we learn to speak Berik well, it was essential that we knew, with certainty, the boundaries of the Berik language area. When our SIL aviation department acquired a helicopter, Peter put in a request to survey the entire region by air, with plans to land in every village he and the pilot would see.

When Pilot Doug flew in to Tenwer, the people were startled by the huge metal bird hovering over their village with a roaring noise, before nestling down on the sandy bank of the river nearby. Many people were so frightened they hid behind trees, but after the monster was quiet, they came near to get a closer look. Word about this most unusual bird spread quickly to the villages up and down the river so that when Peter and Pilot Doug arrived in the other villages, the people greeted them with much excitement and festivity.

For three days in January, Peter and Pilot Doug hopped from village to village along the Tor River, pleased to be initiating contact with village leaders. At each stop, Peter talked with the people and took a word list, thus finding the border between the Berik and two neighboring language groups. Taking word lists was one of our branch linguistic goals since lists, from all language groups on the island, would enable senior linguists to have the necessary data for comparative studies to better define language groups and migration patterns.

House Building and Workshops

As we advanced in our Berik project work, it became clear that we would need two residences—one in the Berik area and one at SIL's Danau Bira Workshop Center. We listed the differences of our work in each place:

Berik Village—Tenwer	Workshop Center at Danau Bira
intensive language learning	intensive language analysis
intensive ministry to Berik needs	fellowship with and ministry to other missionaries
collect language data	attend workshops with consultants to write government-required research papers
translate Scripture with Berik speakers	check translated Scripture for accuracy
teach the Berik to read and write	write the needed primers and Berik books
live in a Beriklike house	be refreshed with a more substantial house with electricity four hours a day
	attend group meetings and workshops

At the end of January, we closed up the Tenwer house and went to Danau Bira so we could be there, helping in our free time when our colleague, Larry, and his Dani construction crew built our center house for us. The Dani people at Danau Bira were Christian families who had come as missionaries from their native highland area in Irian to aid in the outreach to other indigenous groups.

Magdalena and Bular

While our house was being built, we once again enjoyed living in the same Danau Bira cottage where we had stayed for the Pike workshop in 1975. Our dear helpers, Magdalena and Bular, went to Danau Bira with us. They enjoyed living there in the helpers' quarters where they could have their own cookhouses. One day, Bular said to me, "We don't get sick when we're at Danau Bira."

"Why do you think that is, Bular?" I asked.

"We eat three times a day. We have lots of fish and bananas and papaya and coconut and spinach," he answered. I was thrilled Bular had internalized what I had been teaching about nutrition.

A myriad of tasks kept us occupied day after day; the weeks seemed to fly by. SIL leaders had made arrangements for a semantics workshop to be held at Danau Bira in February. We were prepared with hundreds of manual punch cards filled with grammar data and pages of charts regarding Berik verbs. We were very grateful for the help we received in analyzing all the material. Initiating plans to begin translating a booklet, *Life of Christ*, we worked our way through studying a foundational book regarding translation, *Translating the Word of God* by Beekman.

I canned ground beef and chicken to take back to the village with us. We got caught up once again on our letter writing. We planted a hibiscus hedge in front of our new house. And finally, we prepared a couple of Berik picture books about fish and trees to take back to Tenwer so we could begin to check the receptivity of people for the Berik alphabet we had developed.

It had been another incredibly busy time. We thanked God for giving us the strength and stamina we needed. We rejoiced in April when we had a picnic sitting on the floor of our new center home when the electricity was functional, and on May 8, we slept there for the first time. The next week, Bular and Magdalena went back to Tenwer, and we followed two days later. We had missed our Berik friends and were eager to live in the village with them again. We looked forward to advancing our literacy program and beginning translation in earnest.

Would this be the time God would establish His church among the Berik?

A Typical Moving Day

1978 and 1979

The LORD keeps watch over you as you
come and go, both now and forever.
                    —Psalm 121:8, New Living Translation

Returning to the village after an absence of any length of time was always an adventure. Moving from Danau Bira to the village meant getting up before the sun, doing our final packing, making bag breakfasts and bag lunches for each of us, and taking a 20-minute boat ride to the airstrip. While the pilot loaded the plane, we had time to eat our breakfast in the hanger. After boarding the plane, the pilot would taxi to the end of the airstrip at the top of the hill, where, perched like a bird, we'd wait and watch—engine running—for the sun to come up. Truly, the view from the plane on those days was glorious, like God shining His blessings down on us.

As soon as it was bright enough, the pilot would take off, and we'd soar over the lake and across the jungle, the pilot praising God he got an early start on his upcoming long flying day. We ourselves were always delighted to fly early in the morning because we could count on a smooth ride. Flying midday, when the sun was mercilessly beating down on the jungle, we knew we were in for a bumpy trip as the small single-engine plane would bounce over gravity waves in the sky.

Since we had no way to let the Berik know the exact day and time of our arrival, at the end of the 30-minute flight from Danau Bira, the pilot would often circle the village and tip his wings, announcing our imminent landing. The people knew they should run to the grassy airstrip to clear it of all activity, especially dogs, playing children, and grazing chickens and pigs.

Once on the ground, the pilot unloaded the plane as we greeted everyone who came to welcome us. The people carried all our boxes, including our three-month supply of food, to our house. David and Scotty each carried their own backpacks. I picked up my own personal bag, and we followed the parade to our house while Peter went to the government office to officially report our arrival.

Our boys are in the upper left corner of the picture

Prepping the House for Occupancy

We each had our own settling in jobs. After Peter and I checked the house for snakes, centipedes, and scorpions, the boys, just four and six years old, swept the floor and cobwebs off the walls, dusted their bed frames, and helped me get the hanging mattresses down. They also liked spraying Raid at the walls, especially in the bedrooms, to chase the roaches away. Roaches loved living in the dark spaces between the concave palm-frond stems of which the walls were made. After unpacking their own clothes and toys, they ran out to play with their village friends, who were happy to share their homemade toys—mouth harps, balls formed by weaving strips of palm leaves, small hand-carved drums—and group games.

Peter's first task was to set up the SSB radio, connecting it to a freshly charged 12-volt car battery. Teenage Berik boys were always available to help string the antennae from one palm tree to another in the yard outside the office side of our house. I loved watching them shinny up the trunks of the trees—with bare feet. Their one aid in climbing like that was a length of jungle vine tied around their ankles. As they pulled themselves up with their hands and then brought their feet up, with the soles of their feet on either side of the trunk, the piece of vine pulled tightly against the bark providing the needed grip so their feet wouldn't slide back down.

Next, Peter assembled our Katadyn water filter system. We were always sure to bring in a one-day supply of fresh drinking water, but it was imperative to get the filter going so we'd have more pure water by suppertime.

His third major task, hopefully finished before lunch, was to clean and light the kerosene refrigerator. It only took about a half hour to clean the wick and adjust the flame to the correct height, but the rest of the day, Peter needed to frequently check the flame and make adjustments to make sure the coils in the back of the fridge were heating properly. I remember chuckling as I'd ask Peter, "Is the fridge hot yet?"

My job was to get our beds made and the mosquito nets hung over the beds. To this day, remembering acceptable village sleeping arrangements, I thank God for a clean, dry, bug-free place to sleep. Next, Magdalena and I got started on the kitchen, washing all the dishes, silverware, and pots and pans that I had stored in barrels and on shelves in our storeroom. On arrival day, Magdalena and I would unpack the boxes of canned goods we'd just brought in and place the cans on the storeroom shelves. We kept packages of noodles and other perishables that weren't in cans or glass jars in a 55-gallon drum with a locking lid, where the mice and roaches couldn't enjoy them. I had learned that mice can quite easily eat through Tupperware containers when they're hungry.

After lunch and a nap, if we'd not been called to help in a village emergency, we would complete our kitchen work and get ready for cooking supper. Peter needed to unlock the drum of kerosene, fill the two lanterns, and replace the mantels if needed. Darkness fell quickly, like blackout curtains or window shades, between 5:45 p.m. and 6:00 p.m. We had put in a freshwater well across the path from our house. About 5:15 p.m., with the village children also splashing in the clear water, I'd give David and Scotty their baths. Fresh and clean, the boys would run to watch and help Peter light the lanterns before 5:40 p.m. It was a great bonding time for a father and his sons.

Bringing the Day to a Close

Right after supper, with the lanterns glowing, Peter would unpack his accordion from one of the barrels and sit down in the living room. The minute he started to play, the Berik would come running to enjoy the evening with us.

By 8:00 p.m., Peter and I were more than ready for a shower and a good night's rest. Taking a shower was a production all its own. We had hung a metal bucket that had a round rose-head nozzle in the bottom in the corner of the bathroom. We heated a kettle full of water on the two-burner kerosene stove and used the boiling water to take the chill off the cold well water. We needed only one bucket of water for both of us.

Emergency stitches

One particular moving day in May 1978 had gone very smoothly for us, but the next day held a surprise all its own. The steps in the front of our house were set on a firm foundation—two rock-solid bags of cement supported the base of the stair stringers. As four-year-old Scotty attempted to run down those front stairs, he missed a step and fell, his head landing right on the cement. I had actually been in the process of unpacking all my medical supplies when I heard his cries. Peter also heard him, and we both ran to him and found him lying on the ground at the foot of the stairs by one of those cement boulders. I gave him a chewable aspirin, and Peter held him until his sobbing eased as I prepared to care for the wound. We laid him on my desk where the outside light was brightest, and Peter stayed with him, comforting him while I put in several stitches.

Thank You, Father, I prayed. *Thank You for preparing me for times like this. Thank You for preparing me with the needed skills and suture materials to stitch Scotty's two-inch cut. Thank You that he's had his tetanus shot and that the cut isn't very deep. Thank You for being with us no matter where we are, no matter the circumstance.*

My main concern for the next 24 hours was that Scotty might have a concussion. I watched his pupils carefully and, the next day, praised God there were no complications; Scotty was up and about again—but not ready to run down those stairs!

Yes, except for the undesirable event of my son needing stitches, this was truly a typical, satisfying, routine day for us. And the time for which we had been praying for six long years, the time God had planned for the Berik people from eternity past, was about to begin.

God Reveals Himself
to Essau and Aksamina

May 1978

For God so loved the world, that He gave
His only Son, that whoever believes in Him
should not perish but have eternal life.
            —John 3:16, English Standard Version

Essau

Essau was a remarkable man. He was average in height—for a Berik man—about five feet eight inches, very muscular and strong. He was healthy, not thin like many Berik people, and had very black hair, not pale or reddish like those who were malnourished. One of the first Berik men to offer to help us, we found Essau was friendly, outgoing, and a hard worker. He had made friends with David the first time we were in the village back in 1973. When Peter and I walked jungle paths to visit other villages, Essau would guide us and carry David in a baby carrier on his back. While Peter and I often had to walk carefully on the trails, watching our steps, Essau was sure-footed as he stepped, barefooted, on twigs and stones and twisted tree roots. I remember watching his very large feet, with callused soles, as he led the way on both dry trails and through the mud. His toes seemed to spread out and grasp the jungle floor. I felt safe with him leading; he clearly knew his way around the incredibly dense rainforest all around us.

Essau was industrious and intelligent. He had learned to speak the Indonesian language and to read and write by going as far as third grade at a school on the coast. He was eager to learn more and to learn about the world outside the village area.

In the early seventies, an evangelist had traveled up the Tor River, visiting all the villages and calling the people to gather for church. He told them they needed to become Christians by being baptized and taking Bible names and discarding the earth names they were using. We had been quite surprised during our first stay in the village when some of the people told us their names: Abraham and his wife, Sarah, Filemon, Isak, Essau, James, Peter, Adam, and so on. It was during that time that Essau was baptized and adopted his Bible name. Unfortunately, this visiting preacher only stayed a short time in each village and didn't teach the people about the Bible or Jesus before or after his visit. Thus, the Berik had no foundation about what it meant to be a Christian.

But, though Essau didn't know it, God had His hand on him; he wanted to learn more. When he made his way out of the village all the way to Jayapura, he met people from other language groups, and he saw buildings called churches. Being inquisitive by nature, he visited some of the churches and asked detailed questions.

Back in the village, since Essau was a leader, often organizing the Berik for community activities, it was natural for him to call the people to gather. "We need to have church and learn about God," he told them. God was pursuing Essau and making use of the skills He had implanted in his personality. While we were gone in 1976 and 1977, a group, with Essau leading, had started to meet in Tenwer on Sundays. Upon our return, we attended the meetings and listened to his teaching. We felt he had a heart for God and was seeking Him.

Aksamina

Aksamina, Essau's wife, was the only Berik woman who had some knowledge of reading and writing before we began to live with the Berik. She was taller than most Berik women and was healthy and strong. She was extroverted, very opinionated, and not very easily swayed to someone else's point of view. She was a live wire—people were not surprised when she got involved in other people's business or was found in the middle of some village dispute. She worked hard and cared for her children and her husband.

Our Plan Needed Changing

We had made a plan and set goals for the progress of our work. But God had other plans. Through the following months and years, we realized that God had called us to have the privilege of being there to watch Him carry out His eternal plan for the Berik people, who, we learned, had been cannibals up until the sixties. God had brought them out of that practice, and now He blessed us by allowing us to be a part of His plan for the Berik.

We had planned to wait until we were fluent in speaking Berik, not only regarding the activities of daily living but also in things pertaining to the people's understanding of the spirit world. We were working diligently to progress quickly, but we weren't yet able to discuss spiritual matters in depth. But when we listened to the details of what Essau was teaching on Sundays, mixing and confusing Old Testament stories with New Testament doctrines, we knew God wanted us to adjust our thinking. Peter began to work with Essau daily one-on-one. Using Christian books and tracts in the Indonesian language, they discussed the topics in Berik, as much as Peter was able, supplementing with Indonesian. When they began to translate stories about Jesus into Berik, we thanked God for answering Peter's prayer to initiate translation work.

The Truth of His Love

God had waited 1,978 years to start His church among the Berik people. He didn't want to wait any longer.

Late one night, though Aksamina and their four children were asleep on their palm-leaf mats under a mosquito net, Essau was wide awake. He had worked with Peter that day translating some Scripture passages, and now he couldn't stop thinking about Jesus and the stories about Him. He crawled out from under his mosquito net and lit the small lantern he had made—a glass jar filled with kerosene and with a cloth wick. He sat there in his little hut, with its bark floor and palm-frond roof, pondering things he and Peter had talked about that day.

In that quiet remote setting, in the middle of an isolated equatorial jungle, the Spirit of the great God of the universe came upon Essau, an insignificant man of the jungle, and revealed to him the depth of meaning of the Bible verse 1 *John* 2:2: "Christ Himself is the means by which our sins are forgiven, and not our sins only, but also the sins of all men" (Today's English Version).

Essau got so excited! He woke Aksamina up. "Aksamina! Listen! God just told me Jesus died for ME! We've heard Jesus died for the sins of all the people in the world, but God just showed me He died for ME! Aksamina He died for YOU!"

Essau and Aksamina hear God's call

And God also revealed the truth of His love to Aksamina. Together, husband and wife broke down and wept. They remembered their sins and wept tears of remorse. Then their tears changed to tears of joy for what Jesus had done for them. They thanked Jesus for loving and dying for them, took hold of (believed in) Jesus, and turned their lives over to Him.

It was a miracle of love and grace. The Creator of the universe reached out and touched the innermost depths of their spirits, the spirit of Essau, who had been seeking Him and Aksamina's spirit, the independent one who had her own opinions. God sought them both, and they knew He was real and wanted them for Himself. What a contrast to their ancestral beliefs in the spirits of the jungle in whom they had believed and had worked to appease.

For the first time in the history of the universe, two Berik names were written in God's Book of Life (Luke 10:20). And all heaven rejoiced! God had acted. Angels rejoiced. The good life had begun for Essau and Aksamina.

Breakthrough

The next morning, they came running to our house. "Praise God! Praise God!" they shouted. "We've taken hold of Jesus. He's sitting in our gallbladders now. Our gallbladders are so warm." Those words, freely translated from the Berik, mean "We believe in Jesus. He lives in our hearts now. We are so happy." They told us the full story of how God had spoken to them and changed them from the inside. Our gallbladders too swelled with joy, and we praised God with them and had a time of prayer together.

Berik listening to Essau's testimony

And immediately that day, they went out and began telling all the villagers they met about God's great personal love. Many heard and believed. The Berik church was born. What a grand breakthrough God had accomplished—Berik people were telling other Berik people, in their own language, about God's love for them. With power, God had established His church among the Berik people.

Revenge, the Norm

About midnight two months later, as Essau lay sleeping, he was awakened by a man running toward his hut and calling his name, "Essau, Essau, come quickly. Your older brother has been beaten by five men with clubs. He's badly hurt and unconscious."

Essau jumped up from his woven mat on the floor, grabbed his club, and was about to leave his house, when he stopped. *No. I can't go in anger. Jesus is with me now. But I need some ointment and bandages. I know. Mr. Peter will help.* Leaving the club behind, he ran through the village to our home.

Peter was fast asleep under the mosquito net in our Tenwer village house, when he heard a loud cough at the door. Coughing, not knocking, was the accepted Berik way for someone to announce his or her presence and desire to talk with you in your home. Then Peter heard Essau's urgent call, "Mr. Peter, can you help me?"

Peter quickly arose and opened the door. He could tell something was terribly wrong. Essau was very upset; his usual smile and the sparkle in his eyes were gone.

"I just got word from a village downstream. Five men have beaten up Oref, my older brother. He's badly cut and is lying unconscious on the floor of his hut. He needs my help. Can you give me some ointment and gauze bandages to take with me?"

"Yes, of course," Peter said. "I'll get what you need right away."

While he was preparing the needed items, Peter could hear the men of the village gathering outside the house, and he understood what was happening. Revenge, returning evil for evil, wound for wound, was the cultural norm for the Berik people. The men—carrying their spears, heavy clubs, bows, and long arrows—were waiting for Essau so they could accompany him to Oref's village to retaliate the beating of a kinsman.

As Peter was handing the medical supplies to Essau, Essau said, "My friends and relatives want to go with me to help me get revenge on the men who injured my brother."

"And what about you, Essau?" Peter asked. "Do you feel the same way toward those men?"

"I know what the village elders teach—that wound for wound must be given to anyone who injures a friend or family member. But since I took hold of Jesus and He's sitting in my gallbladder, I need to show His love to others, even to my enemies. Those men outside can't go with me . . . only Jesus will go with me."

"It could be very dangerous," Peter cautioned. "Let me go with you too."

"No," Essau insisted. "I must go alone. I know it's dangerous, but I think this is a test God's giving me. Before I go, will you pray with me that Jesus will show me what to do and say in my brother's village?"

Looking into Essau's eyes, Peter could see Essau was sincere and was truly trusting in God's protection and power. Even as Jesus was crowned with God's power when He was tempted in the wilderness, Essau realized that God would give him His power in this time of testing.

"Oh Father in heaven," Peter prayed, "You called Essau to be the first Berik man to testify to his kinsmen of Your great love. Please protect him as he goes to his brother. Make him aware of Your presence every step of his way tonight. I thank You for hearing me. I pray in Jesus's powerful Name. Amen."

Meanwhile, the men outside were shouting, "Come on, Essau! We're ready to help. Whatever they've done to your brother, we'll give them in return."

Essau went to the door of our house and faced the crowd, men in the front, women and children standing all around watching. Essau raised his hand, quieting them, and said, "My fathers, my uncles, my brothers, you must stay here and not go with me tonight. You see, I've taken hold of Jesus, and I know that His love and power are far greater than anything we've ever known. He's going with me."

Well, those men were surprised. Some questioned, "What? We've never heard anything like this! Won't we get in on a fight tonight?" Though they were quite disappointed, they honored Essau's request and disbanded, leaving Essau to go without them.

Guided by the light of a full moon, he made the 20-minute walk on well-worn paths toward his brother's village. We don't know all that Essau was thinking as he made that distressing trip through the jungle. Perhaps he remembered the verses from *Matthew* 6 that he and Peter had been discussing. Verse 14 says, "If you forgive those who sin against you, your heavenly Father will forgive you" (New Living Translation). We do know that Essau prayed, as he hurried along, that God would fill him with love for Oref's abusers.

Reaching the village and seeing no one, he went straight to his brother's small one-room thatched hut and found him unconscious, just as he'd been told. A smoldering fire in one corner of the room, tended by Oref's wife, provided the only light. Tears welled up in Essau's eyes as he examined his brother and found that his jaw was broken, and there were several severe wounds on his head and arms.

Essau washed the wounds, removing some of the dried blood, applied antibiotic salve, and carefully covered the gashes with gauze and taped them in place. As he worked, he could hear people milling about in front of Oref's house. *Oh Jesus, help me now as I go outside to them!*

He told his sister-in-law to call him if Oref began to stir. As he slowly went down the notched log that formed the stairway of the house, he looked all around at the crowd, the women and children staring at him from behind and from the sidelines. The men were carrying their clubs and spears, bows and arrows, and the five who had attacked his brother were right in front. They were absolutely astonished that Essau had no weapon. They asked one another, "Where are Essau's friends? Why is he alone? Don't we get a good fight tonight?" It seemed that everyone was holding their breath, waiting to see what Essau would do.

As he walked toward the assailants and began to lift his right hand, which had been down by his side, the five men ducked in order to dodge the fist blows they expected from Essau.

Forgiveness, Not Revenge

They were dumbfounded when instead of a fist, Essau reached out with an open hand and grasped the hand of each of the five in turn, saying, "Thank you for bringing this trial into my life. Now I can show you that Jesus's love is far greater than anything we've ever known. I forgive you."

"We don't understand," they responded. "What are you saying? This isn't what our ancestors taught us."

"You're right," Essau replied. "Our ancestors taught us we must get revenge. God's book says that it's not good to repay evil for evil. Even though I feel great pain because of what you did to Oref, God's giving me His power to love you. In the past, I didn't live a good life, but since I took hold of Jesus, He's changed me. Now I want you to know Jesus too."

These words hit the men harder than if Essau had struck each of them with the clubs they had used on his brother. They could hardly believe what they were hearing. No one had ever acted like this before. Essau's attitude of love and forgiveness was overwhelming. One of the attackers threw his club aside and fell to the ground as if some giant hand had knocked him down. With tears streaming down his face, he sobbed, "Our ancestors taught us wrong." Another man said, "I want to take hold of Jesus too." Still another said, "I see that Jesus's way is better than the way we've been living. I want to follow Jesus's way."

The next morning, the other two men also went to Essau expressing their repentance and decision to follow Jesus. All five men grew in faith and determination to, like Essau, tell others about Jesus. Three of the men are some of the leaders in the Berik church in that village today. Oref recovered from his injuries and also asked Jesus to sit in his gallbladder.

When Essau returned to Tenwer, a couple of days after the miracle demonstration of God's love and power, he came directly to our home. "God's showing His power to more and more people," he said. "It's just amazing what He's doing!" And Essau told us the whole story. God had worked mightily through Essau, the first Berik man He had chosen to be His own. He had revealed the truth of 1 *Peter* 3:9, "Don't repay evil for evil. Don't retaliate with insults when people insult you. Instead, pay them back with a blessing. That is what God has called you to do, and He will grant you His blessing." God had motivated Essau and given him the strength to live that truth, even though it meant going against almost everything he'd previously been taught. Amazing grace.

As the years have passed, I've often referred to Essau as "God's Moses to the Berik people."

The Church Grows

May and June 1978

They praised God. They were
respected by all the people.
Every day the Lord added to their group
those who were being saved.
—Acts 2:47, New International Reader's Version

Fetishes

The dictionary describes a fetish as an object that is believed to have magical powers. Many isolated people groups around the world make use of fetishes as part of their religious practices. The Berik people were such a group, and Niko, one of our language helpers, adhered to such beliefs. As a child, he had been taught to fear the spirits that roam the jungle and to protect himself by appeasing those spirits through the use of fetishes.

When an evangelist visited the Berik area, proclaiming the people should become Christians, teenage Niko had listened intently and was one of those who had been baptized and had taken a Bible name. Niko chose Nicodemus and became known by the shortened form, Niko.

The morning that Essau and Aksamina first gave testimony to their Berik neighbors that God had shown them Jesus had died for them personally and they had taken hold of Jesus, Niko was there—again listening intently.

And God spoke to Niko. He acknowledged his sins and also took hold of Jesus. I love this Berik concept of "taking hold of" in the spiritual sense, for it doesn't simply mean to take something and put it down some-where else. It means to take it with a tight grip, determined to never let it go. I actually learned that Niko was a new believer in Jesus when I went by his house a few days later. He was sitting on a little stool in front of a fire by his house. I watched as he put a pig's tail, some balls of hair, and a couple of unusually shaped stones into the fire. His small cloth bag that he always carried with him was lying on the ground by his feet.

"Niko, what are you doing?" I asked.

"I'm burning these fetishes," he stated. "When I took hold of Jesus and He forgave my sins, I asked Him to sit in my gallbladder. I know He doesn't want me to use these to pray to the spirits anymore."

Oh, thank You, Lord. You've done it again. You revealed Yourself to Niko. He's showing us all that his hope and faith are now only in Jesus and not in those items of magic in which he used to place his trust. Thank You for allowing me to be here to watch You at work in Berik gallbladders.

Maria's Knife

The afternoon calm was suddenly interrupted by the loud unnerving sound of a woman wailing her heart out. Knowing something tragic had happened, perhaps someone had just passed away, Peter and I ran out of our front door, down the steps and past our neighbors' homes, following the distress call. We found Maria, Chief Petrus's wife, sobbing on her front porch. "Maria, what's happened?" we exclaimed.

"My knife is gone! Sem lost it in a nearby creek. How could he do that?"

Knowing that owning just ONE small paring knife was as much of a treasure for a Berik woman as it would be for a Western woman to own a valuable diamond necklace, we realized how tragic this was for Maria. Her ONLY knife was gone. Our hearts hurt for her.

We learned that Maria's younger son, Sem, had taken the knife and had gone down to the creek. He had been warned to be very careful with the knife, but he had accidently dropped it in the oozy mud on the bottom of the stream. Actually, even though the stream was perhaps only two feet deep, there was a bit of a current. The knife was nowhere to be found. Little Sem's cries pierced the air as he shouted, "Help! Come help me! Mama's knife has fallen into the water. I can't find it!"

Sem's older brother, Eliaser, heard Sem's cries and ran to him as he stood there in tears, vigorously searching the now-churning muddy water near the bank of the stream. Both boys searched and searched, bending over in the water, carefully pushing their hands into the mud, feeling for the knife. They walked back and forth, hoping to touch it with their toes. It was all to no avail. When they went home and told Mama Maria the sad news that her knife was gone, she began to wail.

The two boys returned to the creek, again hunting for the knife. By now, many of the villagers had gathered on the bank and were watching the frantic quest. Some were undoubtedly concerned for the punishment Sem would soon receive.

Suddenly, Eliaser, who had only recently taken hold of Jesus, stopped, stood straight up, and said, "We'll pray about this." And so, turning toward the crowd, lifting his face toward heaven, in his own Berik language, he prayed, "Father God, we have no power. You have all the power. Please help us to find Mama's precious knife. In Jesus's Name, we pray." It was a very simple prayer to God, given from a heart of newfound faith. That was all.

The boys continued looking, and as they were about to give up and go home, Sem's toe felt something cool and sharp under the water. Ever so carefully, he reached down, into the muck, and picked up Mama's prized lost knife!

The crowd erupted in cheers. The boys wept tears of joy, thanking God for hearing and so wonderfully answering Eliaser's prayer. "God listened to me," he said. "I know He hears me and will answer me. This is what I've learned about the Lord Jesus."

Maria had a very warm gallbladder (was very happy). She forgave Sem, admonishing him to be more careful in the future. For the next couple of days, she listened to the substantiating testimonies of her neighbors, who had witnessed the event, and then she too asked Jesus to forgive her sins, and she took hold of Him.

God had once again revealed His power and strengthened the faith of the new believers and, as a result, drew more Berik to faith. He had shown the Berik that He cares about the things that are important to them. God was about the business of growing His church.

We Need to Tell Others!

In November 1978, about six months after God worked His miracles in Essau's and Aksamina's gallbladders and then throughout Tenwer and nearby villages, several of the young Berik men came to Peter and said, "We need to bring the Good News about Jesus to our friends in the upriver villages."

WOW, Lord, You really are on the move!

Peter met with the believers to pray and discuss the logistics of the trip to the isolated, remote Berik villages. It was decided that Peter and eight Berik believers would go together using our dugout canoe with the motor. The boys and I would stay in Tenwer with the other believers, and we would pray for the group while they were gone.

Peter tells the story of this, the first Berik missionary journey:

The Tor River was at flood level. We knew that maneuvering the motorized canoe upstream would be much easier than paddling. Small chunks of wood and logs were floating in the water, and just as we rounded one bend in the river, a large white heron gracefully flew fairly low, right over us, heading upstream with us. We watched the bird land on a floating piece of debris in the swollen river and begin its ride downstream, perched on its own little raft. Closer and closer, it floated toward us as our motorized canoe continued upriver.

I thought for sure the noise of the motor would scare that beautiful bird away, but no, it floated directly past us—we could almost reach out and touch it. It was not afraid. The Berik men laughed and pointed as the stately bird passed by us.

When it was less than 20 feet past our canoe, it again flew upstream, landed on a small log, and, drifting downstream, alight on its own little vessel, passed our canoe a second time, and drifted on downstream in the flooded river. What an unusual sight. We laughed and pointed and commented how strange for a timid big bird like this to come so close to our motorized canoe. One Berik man verbalized what was going through all our minds—surely, God is going to lead and bless and prosper this first missionary journey.

Shortly after our experience with the beautiful white heron, we arrived at our first stop. The whole village was in an uproar—a time of mourning and grief. One of the villagers had died that morning, and preparations were being made for burial of the body. We went and wept with the people who were weeping.

One of our Berik missionaries quickly surveyed the situation and decided to read Scripture and pray for the family and villagers before the burial. I can still hear the speaker's opening words, from the *Gospel of John*: "Let not your hearts be troubled." And with a captive audience, he gave a complete message of the Person and work of Jesus, the One who gives life, eternal life. Several responded by putting their faith in Jesus.

After the burial, we continued our journey upriver. After stopping in one more village, we went as far as we could by canoe and then continued on foot following the shallow river to three more villages. In each place, we read Scripture, including portions of the Berik booklet *Life of Christ* Essau and I had prepared before this trip. We preached and prayed in Berik and sang newly translated Berik hymns. Our whole team was well received, and the people pleaded with us to come back soon and tell them more about Jesus and His Word. After two days, we headed back downstream, retracing our route on foot. The alternating rocky and muddy shores of the river made hiking difficult.

When we returned to our canoe, we boarded and headed for home. We were tired. Nothing spectacular happened until we were only about three bends in the river from our village home. There on the left riverbank, stretched out yet curled among the branches of a large tree, was a huge snake—the body about the size of a man's thigh, perhaps 20 feet long. Its midsection was distended, evidence of having eaten some large jungle animal. The Berik men were frightened. The motorist teased us by steering closer to the tree for a better look. Two of the men shouted and screamed; one threatened to jump overboard if we didn't turn away. But we passed by unharmed, our fright fading into the distance. One of the evangelists commented, however, saying that satan, symbolized by the snake, was alive and well. Though the Lord had given us the white bird to signify blessing on our way upstream, so too He had given us a message to remember that satan still has control over many areas here, and we need to always be ready to tell God's Word to people around us.

Celebrations

June through December 1978

I will praise the name of God with a song;
I will magnify Him with thanksgiving.
　　　　　　　　—Psalm 69:30, English Standard Version

A midst all the excitement of the growing Berik church, we continued on with renewed enthusiasm. Peter and Essau worked daily translating verses from *Matthew* and *Luke*, desiring to have a mimeographed booklet, *Life of Christ*, ready before Christmas. Berik people talked to Essau and Aksamina almost daily, and by the end of June, 24 Berik men and women had taken hold of Jesus. God was on the move. We rejoiced. *Thank You, Father, for allowing us to be here to watch You work in Berik gallbladders and lives.*

God was also on the move in Sunarjo's life. We were surprised and delighted in June when we received a letter from him saying that God was leading him to join Wycliffe. He was applying to be a translator and would be starting his studies at the University of North Dakota that month. *Thank You, Lord, for this wonderful news!* We wondered what the extent of God's plans for Sunarjo would entail.

I Want You to Move

One morning, the county commissioner—the man holding government authority over all the villages in Berikland and who lived right by the airstrip—called for Peter to visit him in his office. "I want you to build a house here in Somanente; I want you to live near me," he said. "It takes a

233

runner 30 minutes to get to Tenwer from here when I need to get hold of you. That's too long; when the rains are heavy, it takes even longer. You can dig a new freshwater well by your new house here. Come on, let's take a walk and go choose a site for you."

And so it was that the same year we had built a house at the Danau Bira workshop center, we also wound up building a new dwelling near the Berik airstrip in the developing area the government called Somanente. Three or four times a week, Peter hiked through the jungle to check in with the commissioner and to review the progress the Berik men were making as they built the new house for us. It would be similar to our Tenwer house, being built on stilts with the walls made from the same jungle materials that the Berik people used for their homes. But it was larger and had corrugated aluminum roofing over the office-storage-kitchen half of the house. We designed a 1,000-square-foot floor plan to accommodate our larger family and the increasing number of gatherings and meetings happening in our living room. David and Scotty would each have their own room. And because more and more Berik people were coming for medical help and to work on literacy books with me, we laid out my enlarged office and clinic space by the living room on the end of the house opposite the bedrooms.

The government had begun to build houses for their officials and were sawing timber for the floors and walls. Peter arranged to have nice flat planks for the floor of our new house. I was pleased when I visited the house and half the floor was in; for just like the Tenwer house with the bark floor, there were also small cracks between the planks in our new home. Thus, I'd still be able to "wash" the floor by splashing dippers of water all about and then sweeping the dust and dirt through the cracks to the ground below. And the planks were a delight, for we no longer had to carefully balance the feet of our chairs on a strip of bark before sitting down.

Even with all the details involved with our pending move, we continued on full steam in several areas. We finally completed the goal we had set of working through all the details suggested in the 40 lessons of our language learner's guidebook. My medical load continued to increase, with more women asking for help delivering their babies. We began work on our prereading program by developing picture books for the people. Two-dimensional drawings of things familiar in Berik life would assist the people when they learned to recognize differences between letters on a page. Though most Berik people hadn't set pencil to paper before we got there, I was amazed that several men were able to draw very detailed pictures—even showing distinct differences in the scales of the variety of fish they caught in the rivers and streams. We sent the first Berik picture book entitled *Fish* off to the printshop. Along with the picture of a different fish on each page, this book had just two words accompanying each picture—the Berik and the Indonesian name of the fish.

Government officials began to make frequent use of SIL's aviation program. A bright spot for us each week was that the pilots always remembered us and brought our mail—and sometimes fresh vegetables. Hurrah!

Spending three weeks at the Danau Bira workshop center was a time of progress and provision. Peter worked with a consultant, checking the accuracy and naturalness of his translation of some Jesus stories he and Essau had completed. I worked on writing a linguistic paper about Berik verbs and checking our ideas for more books for the Berik. Our time at the center culminated with all Wycliffe personnel assigned to Indonesia, including 20 new members who had joined us during the previous 12 months, gathering for a retreat and fellowship.

Celebrating in Sabah

"Please come visit us. It's been 10 years since you and Sue were married here in Sandakan. We'd like to help you make it a special anniversary celebration, and we're eager to meet your children. Come, celebrate here, meet your old friends, and see all that God has done here in 10 years." What a delight it was to receive such an invitation from FahLin, a friend who had become the principal of the school where Peter had taught for three years. We prayed and felt God leading us to accept and to take David and Scotty to see and learn about Sabah, the Malaysian province on the island of Borneo, where Peter and I began our life together in 1968.

A group of our old friends met us at the airport and received us like royalty, and our trip down memory lane began. As we got off the plane and I saw everyone standing there by the fence, I could visualize the group that had welcomed me and Peter's mother upon our arrival in 1968. After greeting each one, many began to share with us their memories of that day and the following 15 months when we lived and worked with them.

They had provided a room for us in a hotel and gave us a schedule of celebrations they had planned for us with church leaders, teachers, and students, many of whom had become civic leaders. One day, about 60% of Peter's former homeroom class gathered in the classroom where they had started each day together 10 years before. The students sat at their same desks, and Peter called the roll just as he had done hundreds of times in the past.

Peter preached in church on Sunday, sharing what God had done in and through us in Indonesia in the work of Bible translation. We were thrilled to learn about how God was continuing the work with the Kadazan people who lived at Mile 86, so named because it was the eighty-sixth mile on the planned national highway that would run straight through the interior of Sabah. To our surprise, two years earlier, in 1976, the highway had been completed. Residents, businessmen, and even tourists were now driving on the 206-mile-long paved road from Sandakan to KK, that is Kota Kinabalu, Sabah's capital city. When Mr. Lee, a wealthy businessman, offered to let us use one of his cars to make the trip, we jumped at the chance.

"Thank You, Father," we prayed, "for the chance for the four of us to be alone for four days in this beautiful land." As Peter drove the comfortable air-conditioned car, so different from the clanking old Land Rover we had used in 1968, David and Scotty got an earful of what the drive had been like for us back then. First stop—the Mile 86 mission station. We hadn't been able to let the people know in advance that we were coming, but we were pleased to see the buildings were still intact and being used by the church volunteers who continued to make weekly ministry visits. As we walked about the mission complex there on a hill, looking down onto the swiftly flowing Labuk River, some of the people who hadn't gone to their gardens that day came to greet us and shared their current news. As gracious hosts, they provided a beverage for us—fresh coconut milk that we drank straight from the coconuts they broke open for us. This was accompanied by a tasty breadfruit.

Continuing on up and down the mountainous drive, we were amazed to pass through about 100 miles of palm oil plantations, an area that in 1968 had been thick jungle. We contrasted the 206-mile drive to KK, which only took us four and a half hours traveling at 50 miles per hour on a paved road, with our past 86-mile trips to Mile 86 that also took us four and a half hours, at 20 to 25 miles per hour on a grassy dirt road.

After staying two days in KK, enjoying the beach and parks, we started back to Sandakan and made an overnight stop in Mt. Kinabalu National Park. At an elevation of 13,438 feet, the sometimes-snow-covered mountain is the highest peak in Southeast Asia. Building family memories, we rented a log cabin, hiked mountain trails, found some famous bug-eating pitcher plants, and sat in front of a dancing fire in the fireplace that night, making s'mores before falling happily into bed.

Celebrating a Lesson Learned

Rested and ready to dig into all aspects of our village work, we said good-bye to our Sabah friends and flew back to Jayapura. Allowing two days to stock up on supplies for the coming months in Berikland, on a bright and sunny, and thus HOT, Tuesday morning, we endured a bumpy flight to Somanente. A severe headache made the duties of opening up our house a challenge for Peter, but he got it all done and got some sleep— before the fever and chills of malaria attacked the next day.

I was delayed in getting ready to start David in first grade and in setting up my desk. But on Friday when I sat down to get my files out of my wonderful wooden two-drawer filing cabinet that I had had a carpenter make for me, I was shocked to find that termites had made the drawers their home. The hungry beasts had eaten straight through all the files and documents stored therein. I sat down on my red folding chair, pulled up a big box to use as a wastebasket, and began to go through the files one by one, page by page.

Now these were the days before computers and copy machines lightened our load. I had typed all those documents on a manual typewriter, making copies with carbon paper. As I found dozens of pages totally destroyed, I started to cry. *Oh Lord, how long will it take me to replicate my work? Help me figure out what I need to do now.*

At that moment, Essau walked in. "Mama Sue," he exclaimed, "what's wrong?"

"Oh, Essau," I cried as I wiped the tears away. "It's so hard to live in the jungle!"

With a puzzled look on his face, he simply asked, "Why?"

I was stunned. I felt like slugging him for not understanding. Why didn't he know it was hard for us to move in and out of village life? Why didn't he realize it was tough trying to function with Peter lying sick in bed? Why didn't he understand how much work I had put into those pieces of paper and how valuable they were?

And then it hit me. The truth was I was in culture shock because I brought expectations with me from my US culture, namely that a hardwood, well-made Western-style filing cabinet would surely keep my valuable papers safe and secure until I returned. After all, I knew how to triumph over creatures in the US, and I had learned how to keep ants and roaches out of my kitchen cupboard in Borneo. Why shouldn't my brilliant idea of having a solid two-drawer unit keep unwanted pests out of my papers in my present house?

And then God gently brought thoughts from Essau's perspective to my mind. The jungle was his home. It's where he was comfortable and could function with confidence. When he came and went from the village, he simply picked up one net bag and walked off with it hanging over his shoulder. Periodic sickness was a normal part of life; just lie down until you get over it. And he didn't have any paper that needed protection.

Oh Lord, forgive me for my angry, pity-party thoughts. Thank You for teaching me to see life here in the jungle from Essau's point of view. Please keep teaching me so You can use my life and example to reach the Berik people.

Celebrating Our New Somanente House

By the end of September, our new house was ready for us. Unlike the floor of the Tenwer house that was somewhat "bouncy" and that was quickly disintegrating because of termites, our new abode was solid and sturdy.

The week before our scheduled move, Peter worked daily with the men to finish up. On Sunday, he suffered another bad headache, and on Tuesday, two weeks after his last attack and the day we moved from Tenwer to the new Somanente house, the fever and chills of malaria attacked again. It took him most of the week to recover. This time, I gave him several medicines, following a regime we call "an eradication treatment." Peter responded well, and he didn't have another relapse.

We were able to settle in to our house, which we had all to ourselves, at first. The creatures hadn't had time to move in yet.

We immediately became aware of several advantages to living in Somanente. Wide open space, for one. The trees in and around Tenwer were tall, and the jungle was thick, forming a dark canopy over us. We hadn't realized how enclosed we had felt in Tenwer. Building the airstrip mandated removal of the trees for the strip itself, of course, but it was also necessary to take down the trees for the approaches at both ends of the strip. From almost everywhere in Somanente, we could look up and see an expanse of the dome of heaven. I reveled in the beauty of the sunrises waking us in the morning and the sunsets when we strolled through the village at dusk. In my heart, I sang praise to God thinking of Psalm 19:1,

"The heavens proclaim the glory of God, and the sky above proclaims His handiwork."

Also, while the county commissioner's helper could run from Somanente to Tenwer in just 30 minutes, it took me about an hour one way. I was pleased that I no longer had to make that frequent hike. I was now able to easily meet the planes when they came in; it was a treat to have the chance to speak English to someone other than my family. When the commissioner granted us the use of the new primary school building for our upcoming literacy and tutor training courses, we realized that God had orchestrated our move.

Finally, while living in Tenwer, I had been pondering how I could get more exercise. Now that we lived near the airstrip, I asked the group buyer in town to buy a bicycle for me and to have the pilot bring it on his next flight. What excitement that stirred up in the village—the people had never seen a bike before. They eagerly lined up on the side of the airstrip and watched as I rode back and forth on the grassy path down the middle of the strip just before sundown each afternoon. It wasn't long though until the teenagers learned to ride as well.

A Short Break

Leadership meetings; working with consultants on anthropology, literacy, and translation projects; and attending the annual nursing seminar were all necessary activities that took us away from the village for the month of October. David and Scotty became very adept at packing their things and adjusting to all our various moves. Having their own rooms, in both our village and Danau Bira houses, was a tremendous help to them as they knew exactly where they were going and what it would be like there. Even when we needed to be in town, the boys adjusted easily since we had also lived in the guesthouse there for a period of time.

The day after we arrived back in Somanente, my medical ministry started again with a bang. Forty patients were sitting and waiting on our front porch when we finished breakfast that morning. I had designed a medicine cupboard, with narrow shelves inside and on the doors so that all my medicines could be easily arranged and accessed. The carpenters in town had built it for me; the pilot had flown it in, and Peter had seen to it that it was hung in the new house before we moved in. Thus, I had stocked it up before we left the village, and upon our return, I could simply open the doors and get to work with the patients. Truly, God had led us to prepare in advance. *Thank You, Lord, that all was in place and ready before I faced all these patients today. Lead me clearly in how to best help each one who has come.*

Fire!

We knew we had entered satan's domain when we went to live in uncharted territory on the Tor River. We found out once again how unhappy he was with our presence.

One bright, sunny day there in our jungle home, I decided to wash a thick pink three-foot oval throw rug . . . by hand! I liked that rug. We had had it in our apartment in the States and now kept it on the floor by our village bed. I'd never washed it in the jungle but decided, "Today's the day."

Boy was it heavy when soaking wet! I got one of the village girls to help me twist it in an effort to wring it out. We hung it over the fence in the front yard in the hot sun. But then when the sun went down, I brought it in and threw it over a chair in the kitchen to drip there during the night. Since the humidity was 90% and it rained every day, I guessed the rug would take several days to dry.

Now I'm the kind of person who just doesn't want to become fully awake in the middle of the night. If I do waken, I just lie there keeping my eyes closed tight, or maybe I just peek a little with one eye. That's what happened that night. I woke up and lay there just squeezing my eyes shut. *I wonder why I woke up. Is something the matter?*

I peeked. Since there was no ceiling in the house, I saw the underside of the corrugated aluminum roof over our bedroom.

Hmmm. That's funny. The roof is a yellow goldish-red color. Odd. We don't have any electricity . . . no lights. The kerosene lanterns are off. Is there someone walking by outside with a flashlight? Oh, go to sleep! I couldn't relax. Opening both eyes, I saw a flickering. I nudged Peter. "Look at the roof."

"Hmmm. That's funny," he said.

The head of our bed was against a wall that had an opening or window in it. Standing on the bed, with my head pushing up against the mosquito net and looking past the kerosene lantern hanging there in the window, I looked into the living room and at the wall on the other side of the room. Our kerosene refrigerator was in the kitchen—on the other side of that wall. I could see that it was on fire. *Thank You, Lord, for waking me up!*

We ran to the kitchen. Though the flames were flaring up, Peter, with great presence of mind and confident assurance, pulled the kerosene tank out from under the fridge. I grabbed that rug that was hanging there, and Peter threw it over the tank, thus smothering the flames. Using water from the three buckets under the kitchen sink, we doused the flames on the wall. The fire went out.

We thought and talked about the whole event. "Why did I wash that rug this morning? Why did I throw it over the kitchen chair, instead of on some other chair in another room?

It was clear and obvious to us; God knew our need before we did, and He had led and protected us. The boys had slept soundly in the other room. We were comforted by God's promise in Psalm 91:15: "I will be with you in trouble." He's not promised that we won't have trouble, but He promises to be with us IN trouble. God cares. It's a good life—with Him.

We later found out that the 55-gallon drum of kerosene that had been sent to us from town for use in our lanterns and in the fridge was accidently mixed with gasoline. The fridge could have exploded. We were ever so grateful that we didn't lose the house, our language materials, or all the medicines for the people that were in the fridge.

Yes, We Had Much to Celebrate

Yes, we had much to celebrate and thank God for during this short six-month period of time. Though satan would have been delighted to discourage us—perhaps he was wishing we'd quit and go back to the States—God's underlying peace was with us all the way . . . even when Peter and then Scotty and then I got malaria . . . in learning about my own ethnocentrism . . . leading us to plan ahead for Berik medical needs . . . through the danger of fire . . . despite the difficulties of travel to remote villages.

Even heaven was celebrating. By December, just six months after God revealed Himself to Essau and Aksamina, approximately 200 Berik men and women had taken hold of Jesus and were learning to follow Him.

Finishing Our Second Term

January through July 1979

*Whatever I have, wherever I am, I
can make it through anything in the
One who makes me who I am.*
—Philippians 4:13, The Message

Hectic Months

We were coming up on the end of our second term in Indonesia; it had been a very busy three and a half years. We had established goals in each of the four academic disciplines—anthropology, linguistics, literacy, and translation—which are essential to completing a translation program. And now, in January, with our August departure for furlough looming before of us, we determined to push to complete as many of our goals as we possibly could. This meant we would need to move back and forth frequently between our village life in Somanente and our workshop center activities at Danau Bira. We praised God that David was doing well in first grade, with Scotty watching over his shoulder, and both boys were able to easily adjust to each shift in location.

Phones in the Jungle?

With the rapid growth of the Berik church spurring us on, we felt an added urgency to work on the preparatory assignments for our literacy program that our literacy consultant had given us. What good would it be to give the people the New Testament in their language if they couldn't read it? Bible translation GIVES the Book to the people; literacy enables the people to USE the Book.

Before we could begin to write primers to teach the Berik to read and write, we needed to determine how to spell Berik words. But first, I needed to count the Berik "phones." "Phones in the jungle?" you ask. In the linguistic world, a phone is an unanalyzed sound of a language. I needed to count all the different sounds we had found in all the stories we had recorded. We would then look for "minimal pairs" and other features of Berik to analyze the Berik sound system. We learned that the Berik words for "my" and "mouth" were a "minimal pair." The Berik word for "my" has the /a/ sound as found in English "father." The word for "mouth" has the /a/ sound as found in English "apple." They are distinct phones that need to be written differently because when reducing a language to writing, the phonetician always uses a different symbol for each sound. When I reviewed my work with a consultant at Danau Bira, we decided to use "a" for the /a/ sound in "father" and "aa" for the /a/ sound in "apple." Thus, for the Berik, we write *aarem arem*, "mouth my."

Surprisingly, I found I enjoyed this research. The characteristic God had given me to delight in symmetry and order served me well in this part of our work. Examining two or three pages of each of the different styles of writing and speaking we had collected, I laboriously counted each sound on each page. After two weeks of this tedious work, I had a list of all the sounds in the Berik language, starting with those most frequently used and ending with the least used. I found that /t/ and /n/ were the most common consonants in Berik, and /a/ was the most common vowel. I looked forward to drafting the primer lessons for the Berik literacy course.

Other literacy work, completed before we left on furlough, included working on a *Conversation Book*, producing another picture book, *Birds*, and aiding the Berik to create two books—*Animals* and *Tools*—with pictures and short explanatory text. During the literacy workshop, we had learned it's essential that the first books available for newly literate people be about topics with which they are all familiar. *Tools* included a statement of how each item was used. *Animals* contained men's hunting stories. Since one of our goals was to bridge the indigenous people to familiarity with their national language, Indonesian, all the books were printed with the Indonesian translation of the Berik texts side by side with the Berik.

Preparing the *Conversation Book* for the printshop was an arduous task. This book, which we sent to the printers in May, consisted of 90 simple conversations written by our language helpers regarding common everyday interests in their lives: food, working, animals, and so on. I typed those 90 Berik conversations in the center of each nine-by-seven-and-a-half-inch page, with the Indonesian translation on the left and the English translation on the right. Two paragraphs in the book's preface state:

When we began our study of Berik in 1973, it was an unwritten language. Having done a preliminary analysis of the sound and grammar systems, we have begun to prepare reading materials for the Berik people. These are being produced in diglot—Berik and Indonesian—to enable the people to more easily make the transition to reading and speaking Indonesian, the national language.

Since 1976, a number of government, church, and university workers and teachers have come to live and work among the Berik people. This book has been written to aid non-Berik speakers in their study of the Berik language and in their efforts to communicate with the Berik. It will also aid Berik speakers in their study of the Indonesian language.

After the preface, we inserted 12 pages entitled, "Brief Summary of Berik Pronunciation and Grammar." Truly, it was a short academic sketch of all we'd learned so far about the Berik language in the areas of phonetics, phonology, and morphology—those three courses of which I'd never heard when we were introduced to Wycliffe and SIL in 1970. The Lord had brought me a long, long way.

The book also included 10 conversational fluency drills and a 10-page thesaurus. Desiring the remote people groups of Indonesia to become familiar with the national language, Indonesian, our government sponsors were especially pleased with this book—so pleased that they paid to have it reprinted in 1984.

The Berik were also delighted with the book because they experienced pride in seeing their language written side by side with their national language and an international language. Though our intent was never to teach the Berik people to speak English, Essau used the book for that purpose. One morning when we were in the village, he came to our house and, pointing to a man sitting on our porch, asked in English, "What's his name?" I was surprised. "Essau, where did you learn that?" I asked. He held up his copy of the *Conversation Book*. He was an amazing man.

How to Fight a Crocodile

With over 250 inches of rainfall a year, the swollen Tor River flowed swiftly by our village. It was filled with sediment—and sometimes crocodiles. The villagers were usually cautious when they bathed in the river, but one day when a young Berik man named Isaskar finished work, he went to an isolated place in the river to take a refreshing bath. He was up to his waist in the murky water and couldn't see below the surface. As he splashed about, a large 15-foot powerful crocodile was slowly making its way along the muddy bottom of the river toward Isaskar.

Suddenly, without warning, the vicious beast lunged forward, sank its nail-sharp teeth into Isaskar's right leg, pulled him off balance to the bottom of the river, and began the death roll. But Isaskar had astonishing presence of mind. Though filled with fear and nearing the limits of holding his breath underwater but desiring to escape the vicelike grip the crocodile's jaws had on his leg, he placed both his hands on his right thigh and slowly moved them down, past his knee, until he touched the snout of the vicious brute.

He continued creeping his hands up the closed mouth of the crocodile to its eye sockets. Then with all the strength he could muster, he jabbed his pointer fingers like little daggers directly and powerfully into the bulging eyes of the beast. Even in this life-or-death situation, he knew which buttons to push! With almost instantaneous reflex, the jaws of the croc released their grasp on Isaskar's leg, and he bobbed to the surface of the water. Gasping for breath, he swam for shore, dragged himself out of the water, and lay down on the bank. His leg was bleeding profusely, but he was free from what had seemed to be certain death. He shouted for villagers to help, and they carried him home. After two months, his leg healed; God had spared Isaskar's life. Grateful to be alive, he later took hold of Jesus and became one of our language helpers.

Preparing for Furlough

Remembering our first furlough and all the programs we had been asked to present to civic groups and in churches and thinking about the challenge it had been to work up new presentations, we were thrilled when we received news that SIL was providing a furlough workshop—led by Bill, a colleague from Australia—for us in February at Danau Bira. The workshop was wonderful. Bill was a personable man who had already led furlough workshops for several SIL branches. He was a great teacher—leading by demonstration and then critiquing us as we practiced. Bill's foundational message to us was that we were going home to minister to ALL—family, friends, pastors, churches, relatives, whoever. He taught us to present programs using transparencies with an overhead projector. We learned to make use of a dozen or more transparencies from each of 10 different programs, such as *Barriers to Communication, How We Do It Out There, and Wouldn't It Be Easier to Teach them English?*" He emphasized that we should be free to mix transparencies as needed to fit the needs of the group to whom we'd be speaking.

Showing slides was also popular back in the seventies and eighties, so Bill also led us in writing a script of the story we wanted to share about our work. We made plans to take the pictures to illustrate our story when we returned to the village. By the end of the workshop, we felt prepared and ready to present programs during our upcoming year in the US.

We stayed on at Danau Bira after the workshop so Peter could have a consultant check of the translation of 33 passages from the Gospels of *Matthew* and *Luke*, which he and Essau had translated. The booklet, a kind of mini-New Testament, presented the life of Christ from His birth all the way through His sacrificial death and joyous resurrection. After making the necessary corrections and preparing the 83-page photo-ready copy, we sent it off to our SIL printshop, which was now fully functional in Jayapura.

Finally, it was time to ready our Danau Bira house for colleagues who would live there while we were gone. We packed our stuff in three 55-gallon drums, sealed them tight to keep all the critters out, and stored the drums under the house. We prayed that the family who would live there for a year would be blessed with what God had provided for us.

Second Missionary Journey

The hot equatorial sun was shining brightly the morning of April 4, 1979, as a large group of villagers gathered with the second Berik missionary team on the banks of the Tor River. They prayed for God to again be with them as they traveled to the most remote Berik villages. They asked God to protect and use them at each stop on their journey. The purposes of the trip were:

1. to challenge more Berik men, women, and children to trust Jesus as their Savior,
2. to encourage and instruct the believers, and
3. to train Berik missionaries.

No beautiful white bird accompanied the team as they had experienced on the first missionary trip. But Peter reported:

Most of the way, we did follow a lovely moving veil of water made by the point of the right outrigger as it skimmed the surface of the river. I gazed at the cascading veil for over an hour, thinking about the precious fountain of living water we have in Christ and also pondering His eternal promises, such as the everlasting life He's given us and the fact that people from all nations will be gathered around God's heavenly throne someday.

As they neared the first village and the canoe brushed up against the weeds along the riverbank, they heard the mournful sound of the death wail. An older man had died just hours earlier. The missionary team wept with the grieving family and then helped to make a coffin, using the deceased's small canoe.

Meanwhile, Essau prepared for the team's first meeting, a burial service. Peter related:

I found him a little later in a state of sheer joy as he shared with me verses that the Lord had given him from *John* 14, *Acts* 2, and 1 *Corinthians* 5. Essau was able to read these verses from his Indonesian Bible, but he preached in Berik. He said, "My gallbladder is so warm to know that I'll be able to preach to these people at this time of sadness for them." During the service at noon, Essau led in singing Berik hymns, not translations of Western hymns but those that the new believers themselves had written.

That afternoon, most of the children and young people played games while the adults watched and laughed. This was in stark contrast to Berik ancestral ways in which the relatives of the deceased would run around the village, wailing, killing the decedent's animals, cutting down his fruit trees, and then destroying his house.

In the evening, the people gathered in the largest house in the village. Only a fraction of the crowd could sit inside on the floor; most of the missionary team sat outside with the rest of the people. Several of the believers prayed, and Essau preached about Jesus's sacrifice for sin and that He was the only way to heaven. Five people took hold of Jesus for the first time, and over 30 believers indicated they wanted to reconfirm their trust in Christ.

After a time of prayer and singing a hymn, the meeting ended, but the people didn't want to leave. They stayed until late into the night asking questions, and since most of the upriver villagers couldn't read, the team read Scripture verses to them.

The team had a short prayer meeting the next morning and went on to another village where, the team reported, "the response to the message was almost nil." It was so obvious that God had worked in the people's minds and hearts in the first village before the team's arrival. But in the second village, they were planting the first seeds. After the second meeting, the team promised to visit them again at a later date and went back to the previous village where they had a good meeting on the value of prayer. They sang and again shared late into the night and returned to Somanente the next morning, praising God for what He had done and praying for what He would be doing in all the villages.

Easter in Bora-Bora

Yes, we made plans to be in Bora-Bora for Easter—no, not the islands of Bora Bora in the South Pacific Ocean but a very remote Berik village near the headwaters of the Tor River. During our helicopter survey early in 1978, Peter and I had "dropped in" on the people living in each of the 10 Berik villages. Peter had visited the upriver villages again on the first Berik missionary journey, and he had promised the people that he would return with me and our boys. In Bora-Bora, Peter had walked the length of a 200-yard flat grassy area and had asked aviation if it would be possible for a Helio Courier to land—AND take off—from there. We had decided that an overland trip by dugout canoe and hiking would be too arduous for our five- and six-year-old sons.

When the pilot said, "Yes, I think our single-engine STOL (Short Take Off and Landing) planes can handle that," we cheered with delight.

On Thursday, April 12, 1979, at 2:00 p.m., Pilot Doug flew two seven-minute flights to get us from our Somanente airstrip to the Bora-Bora strip. Amazing!

The people welcomed us with smiles and cheers, jumping up and down with their bows and arrows. Carrying our boxes and bags, they escorted us to a villager's one-room hut that they had emptied out for our use. We thanked them profusely, left our things inside, and took a walk around the village with the crowd that followed us everywhere as we greeted and shook hands with everyone.

Returning to our weekend home before 5:00 p.m. so we could get our mosquito net hung before dark, we four were ready to work together to get set up. David said he wanted to spray the roach spray on the walls and floor where we'd place our air mattresses and hang the net. He gave the can a good shake and started to spray.

Within seconds, I couldn't believe my eyes, and I exclaimed, "David, STOP!" Hundreds of roaches were pouring out of the palm-frond-stem walls and were running in all directions around the small 10-by-10-foot room.

We all stood there hunched over in the low-roofed hut, our mouths hanging open. We watched. And the roaches, with no more spray bothering them, went away—either outside or back into the walls. We decided we'd just have to live with them. *Father, please we'd really like it if You'd keep those creatures in their homes and away from us. Help us to not think about them. Enable us to go about our planned activities. And thank You, Jesus, that roaches don't bite.*

We put a tarp on the bark floor, laid our air mattresses on it, and made up our cozy family bed with a couple of sheets and hung the net, careful to tuck the bottom of the net under the edges of the tarp all around. After dinner and an evening of visiting with the people—David and Scotty played with the village kids—we returned to our hut and gave a quick check for creatures. Seeing nothing moving, we crawled into our together bed. God was so good—He provided the sleep we needed. We curled up together each of the four nights we were there and slept well.

We hiked to other villages, one on Friday and another on Saturday. As Peter and the Berik missionary team had done on the first missionary journey and on recent visits to two Berik villages closer to Somanente, Peter led in a time of singing, reading Scripture, and sharing the Gospel.

On Easter Sunday, Scotty's second spiritual birthday, we worshiped with the villagers of Bora-Bora. Were we decked out in our finest clothes? No. The people themselves wore little more than loin cloths. Did we have a fancy Easter dinner? No. But the villagers lovingly and generously kept a fire going at all times near our hut. We were able to cook a simple meal of rice or noodles and canned vegetables and fruit whenever we wanted without the challenge of getting our own wood and starting the fire. And we praised God—for meeting our needs, for protecting us, and for giving us peace and joy in the most primitive setting we, as a family, had ever encountered. He enabled us to make it through that four-day visit.

On Easter Monday, Pilot Doug returned to fly us home to Somanente. Since the grassy "airstrip" was so short, he still needed to make two trips, but the flight load was much lighter. We had given away the gifts we had brought with us, and though we had eaten up all our food, I think we all weighed less. It takes a great deal of energy to live under those conditions.

Back in Somanente, Peter kept busy writing a linguistic paper about Berik grammar and collecting the data he needed to write his master's thesis on furlough. I was super occupied with medical work, teaching David, and drafting primer lessons.

And we scheduled our workday to include photo shoots. We needed them for our furlough slide program and to fulfill one of the anthropology goals our sponsor, Bird of Paradise University, had requested. They wanted us to document the Berik way of life with pictures of their housing, food, dress—or lack thereof—tools, care of animals, and celebrations.

Back to Admin

Since we were so close to leaving the country on furlough, our director was sorry to ask it of us, but he called us to fill in for him in town for a month while he was out of country. So we packed up again and moved into a house in an area of Jayapura where none of us with SIL had lived before. Oh my, what a challenge that dwelling turned out to be. The house was in a bit of a valley and had no door or windows on the back side of the house, so there was no cross ventilation. The electricity was off much of the time; thus, our fans were useless. The plumbing was bad. And to top it off, it was almost impossible to keep the place clean. Even trying to sweep the cement floor was an exercise in frustration, for the cement was only one-quarter-inch thick; just moving the broom gently across the floor would dislodge bits of cement and the underlying sand. I thanked God we would only have to stay there a month.

In spite of our living conditions, I was able to continue work on our get-done-before-furlough list. I developed all the pictures we had taken documenting Berik culture and put them together in a report that Peter presented to the president of the university.

Another SIL couple had enrolled their child in an Indonesian kindergarten class, and they suggested Scotty attend with their son. Though it was for only a short time, it was a good experience for Scotty, who had an outgoing personality and was comfortable speaking Indonesian.

First Berik Baptism and Communion Services and Scripture Distribution

All this moving back and forth was taking a toll on us. We were very, very tired. But God had plans for our encouragement. Just at that time,

God sent several Bible school students from Jayapura to share their faith and to hold Gospel meetings in our area. More and more Berik men and women became Christians.

News of the exponential growth of the Berik church spread among our colleagues living in Jayapura and to the churches where they worshipped. As a result, an evangelical church assigned an Indonesian evangelist to begin work in the Berik area. What a blessing Mr. Jon was to us all. Essau often joined him when he met with new Berik believers. Mr. Jon was amazed to learn that the new believers had given up smoking. No one had told them to do so—the Holy Spirit Himself had worked in their gallbladders.

Mr. Jon and Essau discussed God's command to be baptized, making a public declaration of faith in Jesus and a commitment to live for Him. We were overjoyed when we returned to Somanente in the middle of June. Essau and a group of men came to let us know they wanted to be baptized. Petrus, our village chief, was among them. He was the very one who, two years earlier, had offered to pray to satan for little Scotty to be healed of malaria. Can you begin to imagine, dear reader, what joy filled my heart when I heard Petrus say, "Mama Sue, I've taken hold of Jesus. He's sitting in my gallbladder now. Can I get baptized?"

First baptism group

On June 26, 1979, just one year after Essau and Aksamina had taken hold of Jesus, Mr. Jon baptized them and 75 other Berik men and women—our dear helpers Magdalena and Bular among them—from several of the Berik villages. Even as Jesus was crowned with resurrected life when He was baptized in the Jordan River, so had each these new followers of Jesus received the promise of resurrected life as they were baptized in the Tor River. And I believe the angels in heaven sang along as God was praised with our songs of worship.

First communion service

The next day, with many who had yet to take hold of Jesus watching, all the believers met under a large spreading tree and, using sago cakes—the Berik equivalent of bread—and water, we celebrated the Lord's Supper together for the first time. Truly, I cannot describe the peace we felt and how our hearts overflowed with thanks to God for allowing us to see God work out His plan, made in eternity past, to draw the Berik into His Kingdom.

Our colleagues in the Jayapura printshop had really put themselves to work quickly. They got the *Life of Christ* booklet printed, collated, and boxed in record time so that the pilots could bring this first Berik Scripture book out to the village to us in time for the communion service. The Berik who could read eagerly received their copies and began reading to others.

The next week, the missionary team made a three-day missionary journey. Mr. Jon went along and helped to lead the meetings and assisted in the distribution of the Scripture books to those who could read.

It seemed there was no end to the exhilarating events that God kept bringing into the lives of the Berik people. The people of Tenwer, the first village where we had lived among the Berik, built a church building. The number of Tenwer believers desiring to worship together was more than any villager's home could survive. We attended their dedication service and, the next Sunday, joined them for worship and the Lord's Supper in their new building.

Back to Danau Bira

With all these wonderful things going on, we had very mixed emotions about going on furlough. We were very much looking forward to seeing our families again and to sharing with our supporters all that God was doing. At the same time, saying good-bye to our Berik friends and the growing Berik church was so sad. But we knew God was at work and would keep them in His love.

Once again, we closed up our village home. This time, we packed all our dishes and books tightly in 55-gallon drums to protect them from all of God's hungry insects, creepy crawlies, and rodents. I washed everything and loaded the drums only when the day was hot and dry, never when it was raining. There were challenges to be sure—Peter spent two days in bed with the flu, and David had malaria again—but God was good; they recuperated quickly, and we were able to meet our deadline, aviation's scheduled pickup date.

At Danau Bira, we took part in another goal planning seminar and laid out all our yearly and monthly goals for our next term, July 1980 to July 1984. These plans were an aid to the administration in scheduling the consultants who would come to Indonesia from other countries.

Following the seminar, we joined all our SIL Indonesia colleagues for our annual branch conference. Peter led the business sessions; I was secretary for the meetings. We started by praising God for all He had done over the past eight years to develop our branch:

- language research begun in over 16 languages
- more than 80 adults working with the goal of providing Scripture for all language groups in Indonesia
- ministering on two islands: Irian Jaya and Celebes
- developing of a center for workshops and seminars

We had arranged for mission doctors to be with us to do routine physicals. A couple of other nurses and I gave immunizations. David finished first grade with his class.

The fellowship, worship, and recreation times together were upbuilding and refreshing. By the time conference was over and we had said good-bye to everyone, we were ready for our second furlough, ready to return to our Antioch (Acts 14:27) to share all that God had done in our lives and in Berik gallbladders. He had:

- settled us among the Berik people in the Tor River area
- enabled us to learn to speak the Berik language, formulate an alphabet, produce books of Berik stories, and translate and publish Scripture portions from *Matthew* and *Luke*
- raised up a body of believers
- given us a team of His people to pray and encourage us in the tasks He designed for us in eternity past.

We were on a magnificent adventure. It was a good life.

Our Second Furlough

August 1979 through July 1980

I will tell of the LORD's unfailing love. I will
praise Him for all he has done for us.
—Isaiah 63:7a, Good News Translation

Having adjusted to perpetual summer while living on the equator for four years, we were eager to return to Minnesota, a land of changing seasons, hot showers, and FRESH eggs. Peter and I had fun sharing with our boys, now six and eight years old, all the new things they would see and do on furlough. Since they were only one and three years old when we were in the US on our first furlough, we realized all the people, places, and activities would be new and strange to them this time. We wanted them to happily anticipate all the changes they would experience. We also realized we would go through "reverse culture shock"—our US lifestyle, standards, and ministry would be in stark contrast to our simple life among the Berik on the Tor River. Peter and I knew we needed a break from third-world and cross-cultural living.

We thought we had prepared David and Scotty for how long it would take us to travel to the States and for all the various flights and airplanes on which we'd travel. But even Peter and I didn't realize all that was ahead.

An Adventure Getting from Danau Bira to Los Angeles

Bright and early on July 31, 1979, we boarded our SIL single-engine Helio Courier aircraft and took off from the Danau Bira airstrip. As we flew over the lake, we looked down at our home there at the workshop center and thought of all the wonderful days we had spent there with our colleagues—swimming in the lake, fellowshipping, getting the boys started in school, attending seminars and conferences. *Thank You, Lord, for blessing us so greatly during our second term in Indonesia.*

And then my time of reverie was brought to a halt as the jungle and hills below us faded away, and we flew into an immense gray cloud system. Seeing nothing but the wings of the plane, we lost all sense of orientation. I watched the instrument panel and could see that the pilot increased altitude. I saw him turn first one way, then another, and finally observed we were making a 300-degree turn. I didn't have earphones, so I couldn't hear what he was saying on the radio, but after several minutes, he took off his headset and turned to tell Peter and me that we'd have to go back to Danau Bira. He was sorry, but the clouds were just too thick and too high. He had confirmed with ground control that the cloud coverage was extensive over the whole area of our route to Biak, the large island just off the north coast of Irian Jaya.

The consequences of not making it to Biak that day were that we lost all our confirmed flight reservations all the way to the US. There was nothing that could be done. There was no way to communicate with airports or airlines from that isolated interior location to let them know why we would be missing our planes. We just prayed, *Father, we thank You that we know You're in control. This is no surprise to You. We trust You to get us through—in Your time.* On the ground at the center, we were free to have a fun game night.

August 1 dawned bright and sunny, so we flew to Biak with no delay. The airline authorities understood the weather problem from the day before and put us on standby for a flight to Jakarta. We cheered when, after all the other passengers were boarded, the ground agent called our names and we were given the last four seats on the plane. Arriving in Jakarta, we explained our situation to the personnel of our next airline; to our delight, we were given seats to go on to Singapore. *Thank You, God, for providing for us—just as we've come to expect that You'll do.*

In Singapore, when asking for a flight to continue on to Hong Kong, we encountered another surprise. We would have to stay there at least overnight, for a massive typhoon was, at that very moment, discharging its fury on that city. The light of understanding flashed on for us as we realized why God had changed our plans to fly when we thought best. He knew about that typhoon long before it happened, and He had put His plan in place to protect us.

The next day was sunny with fluffy white clouds in the beautiful blue sky as we flew to Hong Kong. Even on approach for landing, we could see the devastation wrought by the storm the previous day: streets flooded, trees down, boats in the harbor damaged. Amazingly, we were told that our flight was the first to land after the airport was opened. Then we learned several lives had been lost.

Though our suitcases didn't arrive with us, we felt so grateful that God had delayed our arrival and then provided seats for us to go on to Taipei the following day, where our luggage caught up with us. Incredibly, space was available for us to go on to Tokyo and Honolulu without further incident. Two days of rest and playing on picturesque Waikiki Beach revived us for our last flight—to Los Angeles—on August 6, our eleventh wedding anniversary. Mary and her family, including four-year-old Chris and two-year-old Chad, met us at the airport. It was a grand week as the four cousins got to know one another and enjoyed spending an entire day together at Sea World. Wonderful family memories are made of such times as that.

Seattle was our last stop before going on to Minnesota. My mother had married again; she and her new husband were living in the mountains in a delightful place west of Seattle. We enjoyed staying with them for a week, but I made the mistake of starting us on the medication required to eradicate malaria from our systems. The side effects of the three needed drugs left the boys feeling crabby, probably from the same symptoms Peter and I were experiencing—nausea, loss of appetite, heartburn, and cramping stomachs. Ugh!

Hurrah! Home in Minnesota

The last flight of our long halfway-around-the-world trip took us to Minneapolis. What a blessing it was to be with Dad, Evie, and Nancy, who was now 12 years old. We had been quite disappointed that we weren't able to be with them when my brother, Jim, married his sweetheart, Pam, in July. But we had a delightful time in August looking at their wedding pictures and sharing our Indonesia slides with the whole family.

The Minnesota State Fair, one of my favorite fall events, was in full swing the week we arrived. Nancy and I took David and Scotty to the fair one long fun-filled day, and then Evie and I also spent an indulgent day at the fair, just enjoying being together again. Dad helped us find a used car and got us lined up with insurance, so on August 28, we were ready to be on our way to Moorhead, Peter's childhood home, in time for Scotty to start kindergarten and David to start second grade in the public school. This was a new experience for them—to be with 24 other kids of their own age every day for school.

We had wondered what housing God would provide for us. To our delight, the college across the street from Mom and Dad Westrum's home had just acquired a house two blocks away, and it was available for us to rent. YIPPEE—we had a two-story, three-bedroom home, with a big back-yard exhibiting magnificent lilac bushes, and a detached garage for the whole school year. The first floor had a large kitchen, dining room, and living room; we bought a washer and dryer at a thrift store for use in the dark and dank basement. No need to wash clothes—or rugs—by hand. It doesn't get better than that.

We had happy reunions in Moorhead with Yaufun and Sunarjo. The latter had just moved to Moorhead from Grand Forks where he had attended SIL to take the same linguistics courses we had taken seven years earlier at the University of North Dakota. We were amazed that he was able to pull As when studying in his third language. During our furlough year, he was a junior at Moorhead State University, working on his Bachelor of Science in Industrial Technology with a Certificate in Engineering. Yaufun was living in Minneapolis with friends and came up to Moorhead to see us. He was very excited to share with us that in April, God had worked through numerous obstacles, and he had been granted an immigration visa. Both Sunarjo and Yaufun were willing and able to help us on moving day in Moorhead. It was a big job moving furniture people were loaning us for the year and other items we purchased from a thrift store. Mom and Dad Westrum had stored our boxes of dishes, books, and clothes in a sec-ond-floor closet of their home. What a blessing when those two strong young men whisked all that stuff to our new abode too.

So Much to Learn

And now we needed a phone. Our previous experiences with Ma Bell had been that she provided telephones for those who connected up to her service. When I made the call to initiate service, I pictured the black rota-ry-dial phones with which we were familiar. "When will you deliver our phone?" I asked the clerk.

"We don't provide phones. You'll have to buy your own," she responded. "Really. I've not heard of that before. Where do I buy a phone?" I questioned.

I was actually surprised when she said, "At the telephone store." Oh my, so much to learn. Peter and I decided to go together.

Peter relates his visceral feelings upon encountering what he found there:

I was not prepared for what awaited me. Row upon row of different-colored telephones. I needed to decide between rotary and touch tone. Some were wall phones; some were table models. There was a choice of many different colors and costs! But all I wanted was a regular black rotary inexpensive telephone. It was not to be. I felt my frustration level rising. Back in Indonesia in the village, we didn't even have a phone. And in town, they still used the crank system to get an operator. I wasn't feeling good at all. I had adjusted to a much simpler style of life and found greater difficulty adjusting back to our home culture. Too much to choose from when so many around the world had nothing at all. I excused myself and went outside, leaving the task of buying a new phone to Sue, who seemed to be enjoying it.

Once we were settled, Peter connected with his advisor at the University of North Dakota, settling his plans for writing his master's thesis. He was required to make the one-and-a-half-hour drive from Moorhead to Grand Forks every two weeks. Throughout our whole furlough, he diligently kept at it, analyzing the linguistics data he had collected in Indonesia, thus completing his research, turning in his assignments, and writing his thesis, "A Grammatical Sketch of Berik." I felt so very proud of him in July when he passed his oral exam to earn his master's degree in linguistics.

For a time, I basked in the fun of being a US housewife, unpacking all those boxes and just nesting like a mama bird in my home. It seemed like Christmas as I unwrapped kitchen supplies, clothes, and decorations, some of which were wedding gifts we hadn't used in nine years. Once everything was in place and the boxes disposed of, I again followed my passion for nursing and registered to take a weekly nursing course to meet Minnesota's continuing education requirements so I could keep my RN license active.

But Peter and I had more than linguistics and nursing—and telephones—to learn about. We had to learn new phrases that had become a part of the local English-speaking culture while we were gone. One day, I sent Peter to the store for groceries. At the checkout counter, the clerk said to Peter, "Paper or plastic?"

"Excuse me. Please repeat your question," he requested. Speaking slowly and a little louder, and sounding annoyed, she asked, "Paper or plastic?"

Peter couldn't figure out what she meant but thought about it a while and then, smiling, answered, "Things that begin with the letter 'p.'"

"Sir, just answer the question. Do you want your groceries in a paper bag or in a plastic bag?"

"Well, what do you use?" he asked.

"Plastic."

"OK. I'll take plastic."

When Peter got home and related this encounter with me, I laughed so hard my sides hurt! Plastic bags weren't in use in Minnesota grocery stores when we left, but I thought Peter was clever to remember *Pyramid*, the TV game show that had been popular before we first left the States.

What Is It That You Do?

We were hardly settled in our home when we began to receive requests to give programs to civic groups and churches to tell God's people about our experiences, what God was doing in Indonesia, and explain the work of Bible translation. It had been quite a challenge for us to work up presentations during our first furlough. Knowing we were prepared this time, we confidently thanked each one who contacted us for being interested and for their invitations.

One day, at home in Moorhead, the phone rang. I picked it up. "Good morning. This is Sue."

"What IS it that you do?" the voice on the other end asked.

"Well. I'd be happy to tell you. With whom am I speaking?" I responded.

"This is Pastor Dale from the Lutheran Church in Peaceville. We've never had a mission program at our church, but I think God wants me to have one this year. So I called three of my pastor friends to ask them what they do regarding mission presentations and what advice they had for me. I was quite surprised when all three said, 'Get hold of Peter and Sue Westrum and have them give a program at your church.' So I repeat, what is it that you do?"

"Thank you for calling and asking, Pastor. Peter and I would be delighted to meet with you and show you how we can plan a presentation together that will meet the needs of your congregation. When would it be convenient for us to come to your church to discuss it?"

And so it went. I can truly report that we enjoyed each of the 60 programs we gave that year during our furlough. One church flew us to Kansas City to take part in their four-day mission conference. God even arranged that the general public would be better informed about missions—we were contacted by the local newspaper on several occasions and were pleased that the articles were well written and accurate, not altering what we shared in the interviews. One reporter writing "Why furlough?" explained our exhaustion after the pressures of jungle living and thus our need to be refreshed by being with our family and in our home culture.

David and Scotty liked being involved when we gave programs. We always had a display table with Berik artifacts—a pounder, a comb, a basket, spatula, etc. The boys would stand there with us and explain to people what each item was and how it was used. One night, a well-dressed Scandinavian lady said to David, "Say something to us in the Berik language."

He looked at her carefully and said, "You don't have the right face."

Thankfully, she was delighted; Peter and I substituted and had a short conversation in Berik for her listening pleasure.

In between programs and school and church activities, our family enjoyed the crispy fall leaves that carpeted our backyard. We'd rake the leaves into piles forming a big circle with an X in the middle, and then play fox and goose, chasing one another until we fell laughing and buried one another in the biggest leaf pile in the corner of the yard. As much as we liked fall, David and Scotty kept asking, "Is it winter yet?" They had never before seen snow and were eagerly waiting for the weather to turn cold. And I admit that because it had been nine years since Peter and I had experienced winter, we were also looking forward to the beauty of the first snowfall when every twig on the trees would have a hat of snow and the winter wonderland would sparkle like diamonds in the sun.

When the first flakes floated through the sky, David and Scotty were ecstatic. My mother's heart thrilled to watch my sons squeal in delight as they experienced new pleasures. When I told them the snow would pile up so high that we'd have to shovel it off the sidewalk, they thought it would be great fun to help with that job. Little did they know how much work it would be. But Daddy always made it a fun bonding time together and usually had a rollicking snowball fight before they were done.

Sometimes, when the consistency of the snow was just right, we'd all get out there and build a five-foot-tall frosty snowman that had one hand on his hip and the other raised waving a greeting. The boys didn't seem to mind wearing all the necessary winter clothing, including face masks when the temperatures were below zero. It took us a good 15 minutes in the mornings to get them all dressed to go out to wait for the school bus.

Malaria Strikes Over and Over Again

I well remember the school nurse's phone call one morning in October. "Mrs. Westrum, I need you to come and get Scotty. He's not feeling well at all and has a fever."

"I'll be right there," I said.

Scotty was indeed quite sick. I immediately recognized it as malaria and thanked God that the doctors in Indonesia had given me the medicine and instructions I needed to treat my young son. I started his week-long course of treatment right away.

Imagine my surprise when David got off the school bus that afternoon looking sad and droopy. "David, what's wrong?" I asked.

"Mommy, I don't feel good. I'm real hot," he replied.

Yes, he also had malaria. And then nine days later, again the following January, and also in July, Peter found himself under attack from that vicious disease. The fact is that once malaria invades a person's body, an attack can pop up at any time.

I escaped—until April. Then it was my turn; I was in for a very tough week. The day before Easter, the attacks began with general body aching. I felt fine on Easter Sunday, but on Easter Monday when I was sitting at my desk feeling well, I was suddenly attacked again. Within an hour, I was down in bed with body aches, feeling cold, and had a temperature of 100 degrees Fahrenheit. It's called an attack because the reversal from feeling good to being miserable happens so quickly. After about four hours, the attack was over, my temperature came down, the chills stopped, and I was able to eat. Tuesday, I was a bit weak but had no pain or fever.

Wednesday was an entirely different story; I was brutally attacked again. It's hard to describe what it's like to be burning up with fever but, at the same time, feeling as cold as a block of ice in the deep freeze. I put on my long winter underwear and flannel nightgown and curled up under an electric blanket turned on high. It didn't help—I just lay there shaking. I put on my winter coat and curled up between a warm blanket and the electric blanket. I felt so wretched that Peter took me in to the clinic to have a blood test done. We wanted to be sure I wasn't suffering from the worst fatal type of the disease. Praise God the test confirmed that I had vivax malaria, the milder usually nonfatal type. I had no attack on Thursday, and as the medicines took effect, the Friday attack was mild and thankfully the final round. *Thank You, Father, for enabling me to cope, for the availability of a lab that could run the test, for the medicine, and for Your healing power.*

Good-bye to Dad

We buried my dad on November 15, the day before my fortieth birthday. The year before, in 1978 while we were in Indonesia, I had received a fortieth birthday card from my dad. He wrote, "Forty, Sue. That was a birthday that had a big impact on me. Thirty wasn't hard. Fifty wasn't hard. Even 60 was easy for me to face. But that 40 made me feel old. So happy fortieth, Sue. I hope you have a great day."

I wrote back and told him he was a year early. I had just turned 39. When his response letter reached me a month later, he apologized for making me older than I was. "Next year, when you're home here in Minnesota, we'll celebrate together," he penned.

I was really looking forward to that time with him. But it wasn't to be. Dad had been out in his front yard raking leaves when he collapsed on November 3. A neighbor saw him lying there unconscious and called 911. Evie notified me, and I went to Minneapolis to be with her, Jim, and Nancy. Dad never recovered consciousness but hung in there until November 12.

Understanding that the sense of hearing is the last to fail when a person is dying, I remember sitting at Dad's bedside talking to him, telling him I loved him, and sharing my remembrances of our special times together through the years. I thanked him for all he had done for me, for loving me. And I prayed that he would spend eternity with Jesus. "Daddy," I said, "I think you can hear me, even though you can't respond. We've talked about Jesus in the past, about how much He loved us that He died for us so we can spend eternity with Him in heaven. You read the book by Josh McDowell, *Evidence That Demands a Verdict*, and you heard me pray just now. Daddy, if you haven't already done it, I beg you to think about Jesus now. Thank Him for dying for you. Give yourself to Him. It's not too late. Tell Him you want to live with Him forever." I never got a response from Dad, but I know that Jesus responded to any prayer that Dad prayed.

Peter brought David and Scotty down from Moorhead to gather with the family and for the funeral on November 15. We spent a quiet day at home on the sixteenth. We celebrated my fortieth just one way—Jim took a picture of me holding one big fat red candle. The huge hole and ache in my heart spoke of how much I missed Dad.

Months before all this, Peter and I had accepted an invitation from the pastor of Dad and Evie's church to present a series of programs at their church on Sunday, November 18, with follow-up messages on the nineteenth and twentieth. Peter preached at all three services Sunday morning; I did a program in Sunday school, and we gave the transparency presentation *"How We Do It Out There"* on Sunday evening. That made a total of five programs that day—the most we did in one day all furlough. It was a special gift we could share in that way the week after Dad's passing.

Christmas in "Minne-snow-ta"

For several months, we had made plans for Christmas, and then in December 1979, our plans came to fruition. Mary and her family all left sunny California and came to "Minne-snow-ta," as Mary called it, to play in the snow and celebrate Christmas with us. And play we did—inside and out.

I drove down to Minneapolis to meet them when they flew in to spend a few days with Evie and Nancy and to visit other friends. The timing of their trip was perfect—we were able to attend Nancy's Christmas dance recital. And we had lots of time for games.

Then we were off to Moorhead where the snow was abundant. We built snowmen, lay down and made angels in the snow, and, though wobbling and falling down a lot, enjoyed ice-skating. Coming inside, cold and tired, Peter's mother treated us to hot apple cider and cookies. Because Mary and her family needed to return to California on the twenty-fourth, Peter's mom and dad, Yaufun, and Sunarjo all joined us on the twenty-third for a big Christmas celebration together at our house. I loved cooking a traditional meal for everyone in my own kitchen. What delightful memories we all have, especially of the four young cousins being together.

A Normal Housewife

One reason this furlough was so very special was because I felt like a normal American housewife. With the exception of giving programs and fighting malaria, I was simply involved in all the things that occupied the lives of my housewife friends; I had my own kitchen, laundry, and yard. Our boys went to school, took swimming lessons, and David took a Yamaha music class. Like every housewife, I took care of them through colds, earaches, and the flu and to the doctor and dentist for checkups. I remember sitting in the waiting room at the pediatric dentist office while they had their very first dental exams. When finished, the dentist came out to see me. "You don't give your kids candy, do you?" he asked. I told him I really tried to keep those snacks to a bare minimum. I thanked God the boys had had a pleasant experience and rejoiced to see their big smiles due to the dentist's praise that they had been brushing their teeth just as they should.

Scotty and David had chores, played outside with their friends, and went bike riding and bowling. In the winter, we added sledding and trying to ski on the snowy hills in the city park with neighborhood kids and families. We visited relatives in their homes and on farms where the boys could pet the lambs and pigs and try to milk a cow. We went to the zoo, to the circus, and on a family camping trip—with tents—to the state park and walked across the Mississippi. We even spent a week in Grand Forks, and while Peter worked with his advisor on his master's requirements, we lived in the university dorm, as we had done on our first furlough.

David and Scotty stayed with Grandma and Grandpa Westrum when Peter and I went to Hershey Park, Pennsylvania, to attend a *Basic Youths Conflicts* seminar, following which we traveled to Washington DC to be with Peter's sister Gloria and her family. While there, we were also able to go to the Indonesian embassy to arrange for our visas to return to Indonesia for another four years. At another time, Peter stayed with the boys while I went to California for two weeks to be with Mother and Mary.

We enjoyed it immensely when friends and relatives came to be with us, such as when Nancy came for an eight-day visit and Evie joined us for Easter. We treasured being at the family reunions, with fun at the lake and playing croquet, so our sons would have time with their aunts and uncles and cousins, and they could get to know our boys.

All this activity wore me out! Yes, we wanted David and Scotty to experience life in their home country and state, so we were intentional in including as much as we could. We even made it a point to travel short trips by bus and by train. But a major result of all this was that I came to understand and appreciate the load carried by the American housewife—NOT an easy job but a ministry of love.

One of the most wonderful aspects of living in our US home, one that brought me peace and rest and that was so very different from our jungle home, was that I knew we all had a warm, clean, dry, bug-free bed welcoming us—every night.

Ministries

The women of our church were so wonderful. They asked us for ideas of what the Berik people needed and proceeded to gather items to mail to Indonesia. They had those wonderful ladies' parties where they sewed clothes, especially for the children. During our last two months in Moorhead, the church had packing parties, preparing boxes for mailing. Peter's mother also continued with her ministry of sending clothes for the Berik. She kept track of the dates she mailed each box. In fact, she sent a box every two weeks for 20 years! The ladies at her church would slip her cash on Sunday to help pay the postage.

Urbana, one of the largest student mission conferences in the world, was first held in Toronto, Canada in 1946 with a gathering of 575 students from 151 schools. Sponsored by Inter-Varsity Christian Fellowship, two years later, the conference moved to the University of Illinois at Urbana-Champaign with 1,331 students from 254 schools attending. When we arrived in the US for our furlough, we learned that the next conference, which is held every three years, was scheduled for the upcoming week between Christmas and New Year. Peter and I realized it would be good for us to learn more about missions and other mission organizations, so we registered to attend as students. Peter was assigned to the men's dorm; I was with the women. It was indeed a remarkable experience to be with 18,000 college students singing and praising God and seeking His will for their lives.

All through the year, Essau sent us a copy of the monthly *Berik Newssheet*, which we had initiated while we were living in the village. We were so very pleased that he was faithful to write the news articles in Berik, translate them into Indonesian, type up a stencil in both languages, and then run off copies on a duplicating machine the Lord provided just before we left. Some of the topics he wrote about included Indonesian Independence Day celebrations on August 17, a death from snakebite, church celebrations, a new government officer visiting the Tor area, and a Berik missionary team visit to upriver villages.

Going Home—Again

In order to have time to purchase and pack our needed supplies and gifts for our friends in Indonesia and to have time to make good-bye visits before leaving the US, in June—after just 10 months in the US—we moved out of our rented house and into the home of Peter's parents. The boys sold lemonade and Kool-Aid from a little stand in our front yard as we had a moving sale.

David, Scotty, and I flew to LA on July 4 and stayed with Mary and her family, not only enjoying being with them but also with time to visit Mother who flew down from Seattle. Mary also went all out to give us great days of rest and play at Raging Waters, Disneyland, and Knott's Berry Farm. After Peter took his master's oral exam, he had some final days with his mother and father, and with Yaufun, before flying to California to join us on the fourteenth.

Three days later, we flew to Honolulu for a four-day rest stop. We had made it a guideline and tradition for our family to spend time alone and visit cities in other countries both upon leaving Indonesia, before arrival in the US, and then again on our return trip after leaving the US and before arrival in Indonesia. After four days in Honolulu, we skipped a day crossing the international date line, spent three days in Tokyo—even going to Mt. Fuji by bullet train—and finally to Taipei for five days. It was a good thing we took that long, for once again, Peter was down with malaria for three days. It was quite disappointing that the malaria eradication treatments we had all taken hadn't done their job.

August 1 was a very long day as our flight landed in Hong Kong, Kuala Lumpur, and Singapore before finally bringing us to Jakarta. Meetings with our administrators, visiting friends, and doing necessary shopping kept us busy until our final return flight to Jayapura on August 13.

We were home again—in our second home. We were rested and ready for whatever the Lord had for us as we began our third term.

I Want to Learn to Read

August 1980 to June 1982

Seek and read from the Book of the LORD.
                    —Isaiah 34:16a, English Standard Version

Constantly unpacking, settling in, packing, moving, and unpacking again. Researching. Treating patients. Teaching David and Scotty. Attending workshops. Entertaining guests. Training interns. Enjoying overseas visitors. Writing, checking, revising, typing stencils, proofing, revising, and printing books.

Like a runner in a marathon, we jumped into our third term of ministry in Indonesia and the all-consuming activities related above. Having arrived in Jayapura, we quickly shopped for our food and the office supplies we would need to set up housekeeping once again in the Berik village of Somanente and at Danau Bira, our workshop center. While we were in Jakarta the previous week, Peter had submitted flight requests for our move to the interior. As soon as we had all our *barang* (stuff) packed in boxes, Peter brought it all to the SIL aviation hangar where he also checked the details of our upcoming flights.

We went first to Danau Bira and opened our house, which—except for God's creatures—had been unoccupied for a couple of months. David and Scotty were a great help as we cleaned the house and unpacked our things, including all that we had stored in 55-gallon drums before furlough. We had one week together as a family to get settled before the boys started school on September 1. Two days later, Peter flew to Somanente where he opened our village house, which—except for an army of God's creatures—had been unoccupied for a year. I got busy canning chicken and ground beef to add to our village-life food staples.

My big pressure-cooker canner, which held seven quart-sized or 20 pint-sized jars, was such a blessing. It allowed us to have more than canned Spam, corned beef, and mackerel in our village diet. I had shipped the canner, along with canning jars and lids, from the US. It was imperative for me to grind the grisly beef with my KitchenAid mixer-grinder because it had metal gears. I had learned the hard way that other grinders were useless in that setting. Their plastic gears broke under the stress of the well-conditioned meat available to us.

A week later, when David and Scotty were well-settled in school and felt comfortable relating to their teacher, Aunt Marilyn (as the children called her), Scotty and I joined Peter in Somanente while David stayed with his friend's family at Danau Bira. He did well for a week but then got really lonesome for us, so we decided not to do that again.

When away from Danau Bira, I took over teaching Scotty daily, using lessons Marilyn had prepared for me. What a marvelous system this was for us. Marilyn chose the curriculum, provided all the materials I needed, had an SSB conference with us once a week, corrected and graded Scotty's papers, and was responsible for report cards and permanent records.

Kori

On June 15, 1958, a baby boy had been born to Silas and Miriam, a young Berik couple who lived in the village of Tenwer on the Tor River in Irian Jaya. They gave their baby two names, one traditional, Kado, and another, Kornilius, which was later shortened to Kori. He would grow up to be one of the most enthusiastic promoters of our upcoming reading and writing classes.

Since each Berik village was occupied by two related clans, Kori was related to most of the people in Tenwer. His father was responsible for hunting game in the extended area surrounding the village. His mother went to the jungle or to her garden daily to get vegetables for the family meal. Kori learned much from her as a little boy when he accompanied her on her jungle excursions. Twice a week, they started out together early in the morning when the sun first came up and walked an hour or two deep into the jungle to get sago, the dietetic basis for most of the coastal people on the island of New Guinea.

sago palm in bloom

Sago

For the Berik, who are very resourceful people indeed, the most important jungle item is a tree, the sago palm tree.

The duty of Kori's dad was to precede his wife to the jungle a day or two before she planned to go for this essential need. Silas could identify a ripened tree by the very large brown leafless blossom reaching high into the sky above the palm branches. He would fell the tree and split the bark off the top of the resulting log lying on the ground. When Kori and his mom, Miriam, arrived at the site, she would first use her machete to cut down a large banana leaf and place it on the ground nearby where Kori could sit and watch her or play with stones he had gathered.

Miriam would then cut down a suitable branch to lie across the palm log to sit on. Using a *jok* (sago pounder), she'd work hard until the sun was high overhead, pounding out the pith of the log. Each time I watched a Berik woman pounding sago, I was amazed, and I would almost hold my breath in nervous fear, for the women sat with their feet inside the log, using them to push the resulting shavings out of the way as they continually pounded, and sang, as they worked.

Kori would help his mom gather the shavings into large leaf baskets, some as much as 15 gallons in size, and carry them to the river's edge. Using the broad base of a sago palm frond as a trough, the end of which was covered with a straining cloth made from a jungle leaf, Miriam would then set up an intricate structure to wash the shavings with river water. The water flowed into a leaf basket on the ground where an edible sediment, which is 100% starch, collected.

At the end of the day, when the sun was moving toward the horizon, with Kori trailing behind her, Miriam would trek back to the village carrying that very heavy—perhaps 20 pounds—dripping basket that rested on her back hanging from a forehead strap. For supper, Miriam used a wooden spatula to mix some of the sago starch with boiling water to form a thick pudding. Sago pudding—not potatoes, bread, or rice—is the staple food for the Berik people. Though void of taste and nutrition, that pudding, eaten with various kinds of jungle spinach, filled the family's empty, growling stomachs. The sediment produced by one day's hard work would feed their family twice a day for two or three days.

It's not only the pith and the base of the sago palm frond that is vital to the Berik people. Since there was no bread in Berik society, the sago sediment was used during communion services. Heating, and thus drying, a cup or two of the sediment in a metal pan over a fire formed irregularly shaped thumb-nail-size crumb-cake pieces to represent Jesus's Body.

The Berik also used the narrow stem of the palm frond to form the walls of their homes. Hundreds of stems placed upright, side by side, formed a beautiful walnut-colored corrugated wall. The palm leaves sewn together made long leafy shingles for the roof. The narrow stiff spine of the stem of each palm leaf was removed, and 100 or more tied together formed a very efficient broom to sweep the house or yard. And finally, empty sago logs were left to rot, and flies would lay their eggs therein—in time producing grubs, a squiggly protein-rich delicacy.

The Death Wail

Kori had one older brother who taught Kori many of their cultural ways, and they enjoyed playing together as children. More children were added to Kori's family. And then suddenly Silas, their father, died.

"I'll never forget that evening," Kori told us when we came to know him as a teenager. "Just before dark, nearly all the people of the village squeezed into our small hut and wailed the death of my father. Some people said a curse had been put on him by an unknown enemy upriver. Others said an evil spirit was angry with him. We wailed and sang sad songs for a long time. By midnight, most of us children had fallen asleep, and by daybreak, everyone was exhausted. Very early the next day, they buried my dad in the ground, in the village cemetery."

I remember the first time I heard the death wail. My heart skipped a beat, and I felt a deep sorrow in the pit of my stomach, for the wail is raised by the family immediately upon the death of their loved one. The exceedingly loud and prolonged moan announces to all in the village that a death has occurred. All the relatives of the deceased quickly make their way to the house and join in the ritual wail, thus demonstrating their sorrow. Most family members continue this mournful keening even while the male relatives construct the coffin and prepare the body for burial. The women find the best and most valuable piece of cloth available to the family in which to wrap the body. Because of the heat and lack of embalming, they work exceedingly fast and hard so the burial can take place before dark.

Kori Became a Man

Kori never had a chance to go to school. And now without a father around the house, and since his brother had married, Kori was obligated to do much of the work for the family. He was kept busy repairing the roof of their hut and hunting wild boar in the jungle with his bow and arrows. Lean and skinny dogs, which were quite valuable in sniffing out game when he went hunting, always eagerly accompanied Kori, impatient for even a tidbit to eat.

Kori was soon able to do everything required of a Berik man in a hunter-gatherer society: chop down trees, build a house, hunt for meat, plant, and maintain a garden. But when looking at the blackboard on the porch of our house or at the signboards by the county commissioner's office at the airstrip, he realized there was one thing he couldn't do. He couldn't read. As a teenager, he had been one of those sitting on our front porch looking at *National Geographic* magazine pictures and testing his skill with the Shape-O toy.

He thought about the weekly Berik newssheet that Peter and I had started to distribute in an effort to stimulate an interest in reading. Kori, young, intelligent, and curious, was enticed.

Then one Sunday in church when Essau was preaching, he read from God's book. "How do you know that what I'm saying is really in this book?" he asked. "If you learn to read, God can speak to you through His book any time—not just on Sundays or at church meetings. You can find out for yourself what God and His Son, Jesus, are like. You won't need someone else to tell you."

Kori felt challenged and told us, "It seemed like Essau was talking directly to me, as if he knows what I've been thinking about lately. Right then, I said yes in my gallbladder and determined to learn to read at the first opportunity."

Essau had further reported that a reading course was being planned, would begin very soon, and that 10 people would be invited to attend the Tenwer class. Kori wondered, "Will I be chosen?"

Preparations

Essau had a heart for his own people. He could read and write and knew well the advantages of these skills. Thus, he was on board with us, taking a prominent role in priming the literacy pump, challenging his relatives and neighbors, and building their enthusiasm for what was coming.

The Berik had been classified as a preliterate people group. Since there were no books or paper or pencils available in their society, no Berik child had ever sat on Grandma's lap to look at pictures or to listen as she read stories to them. They had never colored a picture or seen a picture of themselves or of their house or pet animal. Without these kinds of preparation, the Berik people weren't ready psychologically or physically to learn to read and write. They lacked desire and motivation and fine motor skills.

Realizing this, from our first week living in the village with the people, we had been actively pursuing stage one of our literacy program:

- Providing incentives—such as putting up signs; writing instructions on medicine-bottle labels; making paper, crayons, and the Tupperware Shape-O toy available on our front porch; and frequently pointing out the advantages of being able to read and write.
- Preparing to begin a literacy campaign—such as developing the Berik alphabet, distributing a weekly newssheet in the Berik and Indonesian languages typed side by side, and planning the total program. We guided some of the Berik to actually write and draw the pictures to make books about fish, birds, and animals that are familiar to them and about tools they use daily. We also completed a sociolinguistic study that looked at factors on both the national and local level regarding geographical, linguistic, educational, sociological, and political considerations.

We were ready for the next step—writing the primers we would need to teach the reading course.

Primer Construction Workshop

Our academic leadership team had arranged for Vera, our branch literacy consultant, to conduct a three-month workshop at Danau Bira for the language teams who were ready for this step in their programs. Ramona, a senior literacy consultant who worked in Papua New Guinea, came for part of the course to assist. When we told Kori that we would be gone from the village for a while to write the needed books for the reading course, he was very pleased and began to spread the news to others in the village.

With that kind of grassroots enthusiasm already building, we eagerly completed the assignments we'd been given to prepare for the workshop, and in January 1981, we moved back to Danau Bira, raring to go.

During the first two weeks of the workshop, Vera and Ramona lectured and steered us in outlining a five-book primer series. "The first book you'll write will be a prereader," Vera explained the morning of the first day. "You'll choose pictures regarding topics of importance to the people and designs that are interesting and familiar, things that will entice them to scrutinize and talk about the details they see. You'll present designs, shapes, and letters in varying sizes and degrees of difficulty and challenge them to match things that are the same and distinguish those that are different. You'll also introduce numbers and vowels, in both word-initial and word-final positions. And finally, you'll develop several pages in which the students will be requested to verbalize the name of the item in a picture and choose the symbol for the sound at the beginning or end of the word."

That's a huge task, I thought. *It'll take the whole workshop to accomplish all that!*

Little did I realize what we were in for. That afternoon, Ramona took the stage. "In the next three books of your primer series, you'll teach your students to read each letter and the most common grammatical units—such as in, at, but, and the—found in the language of the group you're working with. You'll teach them in the order of the frequency found in your phoneme count."

Oh, good. We've got that list right here. This will be easier than the first book. I was so naïve.

"We are teaching you to use an eclectic method of primer construction," Ramona continued. "It follows the principle of introducing one new element at a time, controlling vocabulary to match only that which the students have already been taught, and teaching grammatical elements as whole units. You'll introduce each chapter with a keyword that is easily pictured to illustrate the new letter to be taught. You'll follow with drills, helping students to recognize the syllables making up the keyword and also the new letter or sound in other words. With each lesson, you'll prepare a short story—always looking for emotive topics—which will contain only words and units already deposited in your bank of taught words. You'll need to keep a detailed chart showing the lesson in which you introduced each letter and unit, AND the lessons in which you've reviewed each letter and unit four more times. Finally, at the end of each lesson, you'll work with your students for 10 or more minutes to practice writing on their own individual blackboards and to learn to write the new letter or unit presented in that lesson."

Heavens! How can we possibly do all that in three months? I groaned.

The next day, Vera shocked us by presenting information about the fifth and final book of our series. It would be a 12-lesson reader, in which new words would be introduced, followed by a short story, again using only words and units that had already been presented in the series. Each lesson would end with a series of questions that the student would be expected to read and answer by printing the correct answer to each question. Any student able to hand in *Book Five* with legible answers, at least 60% of which were correct, would pass the course and receive a graduation certificate.

Amazing! What a goal. Thank You, Lord, for providing Vera and Ramona to teach and guide us. I admit we felt overwhelmed by the time the two weeks of lectures were over. Writing a primer series for a formerly illiterate people group would be a massive undertaking! But Vera and Ramona assured us we were ready and could do it.

Getting to Work

On Monday of the third week, two Berik men, Essau and Sowenso, joined us at the lakeside workshop center. Sowenso, a short and thin man, was a new believer who had joined the Berik missionary team on its second journey. Though he was a beginning reader, he was a willing worker. Realizing the importance of literacy, he was committed to working with us so his people could read and write.

After Peter explained to the men that he would be working with them to choose appropriate words, draw pictures, and write 77 stories, Essau and Sowenso took to the task like ducks to water. They were excited and jumped right in to decide on pictures, a picture story, and common Berik designs for lesson one in *Book One*, the prereader. Lively discussions ensued as their ideas centered around village friends and events.

My job was to be the keeper of the chart, letting the men know which letters, words, and grammatical units they needed to repeat in their story each day and, of course, which new letter or unit would be introduced. Our punch cards were once again an invaluable aid in choosing the keywords for introducing new letters. I loved it. I thrived on all the detail, patterns, order, and record keeping. In eternity past, when God chose and designed me and decided His plans for me, He included gifting me for this task. What an awesome thought!

After laboring through all the pictures needed for *Book One*, Peter and the men tackled the first lesson in *Book Two*, writing the first story in the series in which they could use only the grammatical unit we had taught in the prereader and the letters t, n, a, and e. When they finished, the men were literally jumping with excitement and came running to me in the other room to show me their story: "*tane je natan. je tini*" (child he natan. he went.) We had planned that the use of capital letters would be introduced in *Book Four*.

After Ramona left, Vera worked with us all daily as we progressed story by story, lesson by lesson, review by review, and edit by edit. To our amazement, we were all happy to keep our noses to the grindstone and were encouraged by slow and steady progress. David and Scotty loved being in school with their friends and swimming in the lake each afternoon. Each Sunday evening, about 15 of our co-workers gathered in our home with us for "Singspiration," an evening of singing worship and praise songs to God who had brought us together in this beautiful place to serve Him. We were blessed to have a spinet piano that had been flown—hanging by a chain from a helicopter—to Danau Bira the previous year. All those who had instruments brought them along for a joyous time together. Before everyone arrived, the boys and I would often make donuts or popcorn balls to serve. Essau and Sowenso smiled and took part in as many of the activities as they could with us. They were like a part of our family.

One Sunday night, after all the singers had gone home, Essau asked, "Mr. Peter, now that we're finished writing all the stories for the books, what work will we do?"

"Now we must make 50 books to take back to the village with us," Peter responded. "Mama Sue will type stencils, and I will make copies using a machine in the office. Then we'll lay out all the pages for one book at a time, on the big table in our house. We'll walk around the table picking up one page at a time and staple the book together. We'll all go around and around until we have all 50 copies ready for our students in Tenwer and Somanente."

The guys were amazed. They had never seen stencils or a mimeograph machine and couldn't imagine what Peter meant by walking around the table together. But, being eager learners, they seemed to have fun helping Peter and me, and David and Scotty, complete the job. Essau's and Sowenso's families were thrilled when the men returned to their village homes and told their families of all their experiences making books at Danau Bira.

Trial Literacy Classes

Before we could print the whole primer series in the printshop in Jayapura, it was imperative that we test our work by actually teaching two trial classes to adults. From January through April 1982, Peter, assisted by Musa, ran a class for 10 students in the village of Tenwer. Sowenso and I taught 10 men and women in Somanente. Our plan was that Musa and Sowenso would be full tutors in the future when we conducted a full literacy campaign in all 10 Berik villages up and down the Tor River.

Each day was an adventure. We never knew who, or what, would come to class, which was held in the village church building. Dogs came with their masters. Mothers brought their babies, hanging in a sling around their breasts. Chickens jumped over the partition placed in the doorway to keep the pigs out. Occasionally, the partition would be forgotten, or knocked down, and I'd be surprised by snorting or oinking right behind me as I wrote on the big class blackboard. Birds flew in the window openings, right past the people standing outside looking in. Toddlers played on the dirt floor at their mothers' feet. But surprisingly, it was basically quiet during class—everyone being interested in what we were all doing. Something very new had come to town.

Since the village chiefs knew the abilities and interests of everyone in their village, it was up to them to choose who would take part in the very first reading classes. Kori had prayed about it, deeply desiring to be included. He was beaming with excitement when he came running to our house one day, saying, "Mr. Peter. Mama Sue. I was chosen! I get to learn to read! God answered my prayers."

Our next-door neighbor, a woman named Dorsi, was also excited about the class. She hadn't impressed us as one desiring, or able, to learn. She had a newborn baby and a two-year-old constantly at her side. We had secretly hoped that she wouldn't be one of those chosen to attend the first classes. And she wasn't. We breathed a sigh of relief. But Dorsi had other intentions.

When Peter opened class at 7:00 a.m. on Monday of the first week, Dorsi was there, baby at her breast and a toddler tugging on her dress, as she sat in the group with Kori and the other nine students. Peter was surprised. "Mama Dorsi, why did you come to class today?" Peter asked.

"I want to learn to read," she simply and clearly replied. And so Peter allowed her to stay. To his astonishment, she came again the second day and every day thereafter. Later, she even brought her husband too.

A picture of a hand was on the cover of *Book One*. Since many of the students hadn't handled books before, they didn't know how to hold a book, didn't know which side was up or down or right or left. We taught them, "Put your hand on top of the picture of the hand. Then move your hand to the right and open the book from that side." As Peter and I led our classes, working our way through *Book One*, our students became more enthusiastic as they were successful in matching and distinguishing different shapes. Writing practice was a lively time as they realized they could actually copy what I had written on my big blackboard. I thrived as I shared their joy of discovery.

News of the fun of the classes spread, and more adults came to sit in. One lady, Dita, diligently came daily to Peter's class. By the time we were finishing *Book Two*, most of the students—including Dorsi—had caught on and could, for example, recognize the letter "o," say and write "o," and give a word that starts with "o." Dita could repeat all the letters or sounds as Peter taught them, but to produce an "o" sound when looking at the letter "o," Dita never got it. Peter told me, "I think somehow she believes that by just being present and sitting on the bench, the skill of reading will just be absorbed into her being."

But Dorsi was different. Though she had a large family to feed and a house and garden to take care of, she had faithfully applied herself and was one of the first in the class to catch on. Actually, to our amazement, Dorsi turned out to be the best student in the class, quickly learning the skills of both reading and writing. She overcame all obstacles to becoming literate because she had a desire to do so, even though neither we, nor the local leaders, had recognized her potential.

We ran the two trial classes from 7:00 a.m. to 9:00 a.m., Monday through Friday. Besides actually teaching, we had set two exceedingly ambitious goals: revise the five primers and draft the teachers' guides each day as we moved along. When we got home after class, Peter and I would meet, discuss any problems we had encountered while teaching, evaluate and revise the primer lesson for that day. After lunch and a rest during the hottest portion of the day, we worked on the text of the teachers' guide to accompany the day's lesson. Since we had decided on the presentation format of the guides' lessons during the workshop the previous year, it remained for us to write the text that the Indonesian teachers or Berik tutors could use to present and teach each aspect of the lesson. As we worked together each day, we drafted the text in English. Later, since the published guides would be printed in diglot—with the Berik and Indonesian on each page side by side—we translated everything into both Indonesian and Berik. All the correct answers to the exercises were given, as well as diagrams of all the writing drills. It was tedious, exacting, sometime frustrating, time-consuming, satisfying, and rewarding work.

God provided encouragements along the way. One day when Kori and Peter were returning home by canoe from Tenwer to Somanente, Kori's eyes lit up as he exclaimed, "Mr. Peter, I get it now! I just pronounce the sounds of the letters I see in syllables or words or in a sentence. I listen to the sounds of the words—and they have meaning. When I put them together in a sentence, I communicate an idea."

"Yes," Peter added, "just pronounce the sounds of the letters you see and understand what you say—and you are reading. That's what reading is, Kori. Praise God that He's helped you to learn." Kori could hardly wait to read the next story.

Not Only Teaching

As we revised the primers, they needed to be prepared for submission to the printshop; the mimeographed test copies were designed to self-destruct. By April, three of the books were out of our hands and given to our skilled and dedicated printshop colleagues. We continued to work on other Berik books: beginning work on a thesaurus to be published in three languages—Berik, Indonesian, and English; and a revision of the bird book. I was also pleased to work with other translators on their literacy programs.

During the opening two weeks of the test classes in Berikland, and also at other times when our assignment required us to be in locations other than the village or Danau Bira, David and Scotty stayed with friends' families at the Danau Bira center. Whenever the boys were in the village with us, Peter taught David fourth grade while Scotty and I did second-grade work. Every evening, the boys and I would ride the length of the airstrip and back home on our bikes. Often, the people would stand on the side of the strip waving as we raced by, and soon some of the Berik boys wanted to learn to ride too. Before supper, David and Scotty took a refreshing bath by the well, but I opted for a bucket shower inside our home.

We thanked God for enabling our sons to be marvelously flexible and content during these four incredibly busy months testing and revising the primers and writing the teachers' guides. We came to realize that one of the greatest blessings of being on a foreign field is the extra prayer that goes up for one's children. One of the boys' cousins wrote, "I pray for David and

Scotty every night. I pray they will grow in wisdom, increasing in favor with God and men." Knowing they were thus being prayed for was a treasured gift to us.

So were the prayers of our new prayer partners—one of the pilots, John, and his wife, Irene. Our branch leadership had decided to encourage our support personnel to pair up with a translation team. John and Irene contacted us, and God richly blessed us through their partnership all the rest of our years working in the Berik program. We had SSB radio contact with them regularly, shared our joys and concerns, and prayed for one another. John sometimes piloted Somanente flights, and on one occasion, he brought Irene and their daughters, Tanya and Danielle, to Somanente to spend several days with us. The love, concern, and prayers of their whole family helped to sustain us as we labored.

In April 1982, we celebrated the closing of our trial literacy course. Berik people from several villages came to see if it was true that their friends and relatives really could make sense of those mystifying marks on paper. Kori and a young Tenwer woman read, in both Berik and Indonesian, to all those who were gathered. What a deep joy it was for us to see pride and happiness on the faces of our friends for whom the world of reading had just opened up.

The county commissioner and the principal of the government primary school led a graduation ceremony during which certificates and reading books were given to all those who had participated in and successfully completed the course.

Essau had watched all that was going on throughout the course. His dream, that his own people—living in an isolated jungle, on the banks of the winding, muddy Tor River—would soon be literate and able to read God's Word for themselves, was coming to pass. We shared his dream. We knew God would continue to take us through all that He had planned. But there was still much to be done. And we were soon to learn the additional plans God had for us.

Danau Bira

August 1980 to October 1981

. . . whatever you do, do it all for the glory of God.
—1 Corinthians 10:31b, New Living Translation

Danau Bira, a lake 90 minutes by air west of Jayapura, is a beautiful sanctuary of peaceful and natural beauty, created by God when an earthquake caused a landslide resulting in the natural damming of a river some 200 years ago. The lake, which lies at an elevation of 1,243 feet, is surrounded by lush rolling hills in multiple shades of green and sporting massive ironwood trees. Though most of the trees and underlying jungle growth left standing when the lake formed had long since rotted and disappeared, the branchless trunks of the ironwood trees remained standing in the middle of the lake, a stark witness to the devastation wrought by the earthquake.

Peter's introduction to Danau Bira occurred in 1973 when he accompanied our Asia area director and Larry, fellow SIL member, on a visit to the lake to search for a suitable place to build a workshop center to serve SIL language project personnel. Larry and his wife, Jeanne, had been assigned to Indonesia to head up the building of a workshop center. A visionary, skilled leader, and experienced builder, Larry was well qualified for the job.

Crocodiles

Besides being involved with the scouting out of a building site, Peter took linguistic word lists from the nearly naked Bauzi people who lived in villages near the lake. One evening, an Indonesian-speaking Bauzi man extended an invitation to the SIL men, saying, "Go get your flashlights, and I'll take you out on the lake tonight to search for crocodiles." Once in the canoe, their host said, "Hold your flashlight directly at eye level and then scan the shoreline as we slowly move along."

A short time later, the guide, sitting in the bow of the canoe, cried out, "*Di sana!*" (Over there!) When the beams of all the flashlights converged on the area to which he had pointed, they saw all that was visible, in the black of night, of that notorious creature—two shining crocodile eyes. As the canoe edged slowly and quietly toward those sparkling red spheres, the guide whispered, "Steaaady." Then gliding within reaching distance of the small croc, they heard a splash and were startled as the guide's arm struck out with lightning speed at the neck of the little creature and pulled it, squirming and twisting, out of the water and into the canoe.

The adventurers continued their search in the dark and saw about 20 more pairs of red shining eyes. When they heard the deep, noisy bellowing of some of the larger crocs, they were careful to keep their distance and move on. Peter later learned that the crocodiles inhabiting fresh water lakes are quite tame and are actually more beneficial than dangerous. The indigenous people capture the larger specimens, enjoy them for supper, and sell the valued crocodile skins for a good profit. In contrast, the saltwater crocodiles found along ocean beaches have been known to pull paddlers right out of their canoes—to have them for supper.

Building the Center

In 1974, two additional couples joined Larry and Jean in the huge job of carving space out of the thick jungle to build a workshop center—in time for the Dr. Pike linguistic workshop that was to be held in February, March, and April of 1975. With Jeanne's expertise in design and organization, one gal's skills as a nurse, the other woman's willing support wherever needed, and the manpower of indigenous Christian workers who had come from the Irian highlands, the men built a large guesthouse-dining-meeting-hall building—in just three and a half months. The three couples had lived in one-room bark houses during this construction period. They were my heroes. I stand amazed at their sacrifice and ability to cope, survive, and be productive in such an isolated setting. They felled trees, floated them on the lake to the building site, and sawed all the lumber by pitsaw, a large saw with handles at each end, used in a vertical position by two people, one standing on a platform above the timber to be cut, the other in a pit below it. In the ensuing months and years, they built a sawmill, clinic, primary school, large meeting hall with a library, study cubicles, administration building, two cabins, a dozen homes, and an aviation hangar. *Thank You, Lord, for Your servants who You called, equipped, and enabled to provide a center for reaching out to the Bibleless peoples of Irian.*

The Christian workers were from the Dani tribe, the largest group of indigenous people in Irian Jaya. They were first discovered living in Irian's Baliem Valley and were evangelized in the fifties. By the seventies, many desired to use newly acquired skills to reach out as missionaries in their own right. Thus, several families, having heard about the lake and warmer climate, hiked approximately 90 miles from the highland mountains to the Danau Bira area. There they lived side by side with the Bauzi people who lived in three villages near the lake and in the surrounding area. The Bauzi were first described by anthropologists in the sixties. Bauzi men had a distinctive "dress"—jungle vines wrapped around the waist, from the navel to the top of the thighs, from which they hung a loin cloth over the anterior portion of their bodies.

To the delight of the Bauzi and Dani families living at Danau Bira, and to visiting language project helpers, one of our SIL pilots had the foresight to stock the lake with tilapia fish, which rapidly increased in size and population. Tilapia was one of the reasons our Berik language helpers were always elated when we asked them to go to Danau Bira with us. Though we invited them to eat with us, they declined and requested that we provide a cookhouse for them where they could cook their food their own way. Most days, they had filleted tilapia drying on the aluminum roof of the cookhouse to take back to the village with them for their families to enjoy. In later years, the Bauzis and Danis were able to supply tilapia to restaurants in Jayapura.

A Beehive of Activity

Danau Bira was a lively and growing hub of activity, always buzzing with workshop participants, language helpers from various indigenous groups, visitors, conferences, and fellowship activities. Following that first workshop in 1975, Peter and I also attended most of the workshops that were offered and received on-the-job training in all our academic disciplines—anthropology, linguistics, literacy, and translation. There were also workshops in stress management, goal planning, furlough preparation, and so on.

Our lives, both at Danau Bira and in Somanente, also mirrored a beehive. From the time we got off the plane, arriving back in Irian in August 1980, we hit the ground running and never slowed down. Every cycle of moves between the workshop center and the village—requiring us to clean, unpack, and settle in and then a short time later to reverse the process—was exhausting. Upon settling each time in Somanente village, I taught Scotty first grade, ran the clinic, worked on assignments to prepare for our first intensive workshop about translation principles, and hosted a university student who was doing her seven-week internship during her senior year of language study.

After completing the translation workshop in October, Peter began studying to translate the *Gospel of Mark*, and I took on the goal of translating the first 20 stories of an abridgement of *Genesis*. Some of the Berik people had questioned us, "Did Cain kill Able, or did Able kill Cain? We don't understand what we've heard." To provide the Berik with further background information, we also began to translate a template book, *How the Jews Lived*. The Berik people couldn't imagine flat-roofed houses, grapevines, or camels. This book, which we published in 1981, was a great help to them as they learned more of Jewish life and culture.

During village clinic hours, our house was always abuzz with activity as patients sat in large groups on our porch chattering about pictures and puzzles. Peter felt a need to get out of the house to better concentrate, so he built a little study house along the dirt path about two blocks away. Every Friday afternoon, several of the men, who had been on the missionary journey and were getting involved in translation, met with Peter. They studied recently translated passages together, defined the key verses, and developed a theme for a message. On Saturday, the men fanned out to other villages, prepared to lead and teach during a time of worship on Sunday. A visit by two men from our Minnesota church to get a first-person look at our work, both in the village and at Danau Bira, was an encouragement. We knew the reports they brought back to the congregation would greatly increase the prayers being offered for us.

In mid-December, even though I was sick in bed with the flu for three days and Scotty had a bout with infection, I finished my goal of translating and checking 20 *Genesis* stories and started working on a health book, *Flies Are Your Enemy*. Peter made overnight visits to other villages. Together, we celebrated Christmas with the Berik in Somanente and in Tenwer, our first village home. Using a generator and slide projector, we wowed the people by showing slides of village life and scenes from around the world. Back at

Danau Bira, January through March, 1981, we attended the three-month primer-writing workshop.

I wonder now, as I write, how did we survive such a whirlwind life. Truly only by God's grace.

Assigned to Danau Bira Administration

It was with mixed feelings that we accepted our director's request for Peter to assume the responsibilities of Danau Bira administrator for six months, April through September 1981. Having just written the Berik primer series, we were on a roll in the Berik program, looking forward to going back to our village life in Berikland to run the trial reading and writing classes. On the other hand, the assignment offered a promise of some stability and family togetherness.

David and Scotty loved living at Danau Bira, exploring the jungle in and around the center's homes and buildings, swimming every afternoon in the lake, and often board skiing. One of the dads living at the center had attached one end of a sturdy rope to a motorized dugout canoe and the other end to a board, which measured three by five feet in size. Either a child or an adult could stand on the board and, while hanging on to a second rope attached to the board and shouting with delight, could be pulled along on the surface of the water as one of the dads piloted the canoe around the lake. The dad, of course, had to be especially careful to avoid the tips of the tree stumps hiding just below the surface.

There was one tree in the lake that the boys called "the diving-board tree." That lone tree with leafless branches remained standing in the lake, swimming distance away from the center dock. Someone had added a board to the branches high in the tree. The children loved diving into the water. I tried it once and said, "No more! That weightless feeling in the pit of my stomach, as I flew through the air, is not for me."

Opening a Pringles Can

We were intentional in doing things as a family. We loved to go for rides in our motorized dugout canoe and explore the bays and inlets of streams that drained into the lake. One beautiful Sunday afternoon, we packed a picnic lunch and took a ride up the river that feeds the lake. About a half hour upriver, we noticed two Bauzi huts in a little clearing to the right of our canoe. One hut had some people sitting in it around a fire. The other hut was empty. It looked like a rain shower was going to pass through, so we decided to try and go ashore. The people seemed friendly, but we couldn't speak Bauzi, and they didn't know Indonesian, Berik, or English.

Going ashore, up a muddy 15-foot embankment, from our little dug-out was no easy task! David jumped out on to the bank first and sank knee-deep in oozing mud. Scotty followed but, being a little lighter, didn't sink so deep. I didn't want to follow their act, so I just sat there in the canoe, holding two-year-old Gracie (who we were taking care of for three weeks while her parents were in Australia) on my lap.

Peter said, "We've got some boards here in the canoe with us. I think I can place them on the bank, and we can step on them so we don't sink too deeply into the mud." He had to crawl, with the boards in hand, past Gracie and me, our picnic basket, and thermos so he could place the short planks appropriately on the bank of the river. He gingerly got out of the canoe, stepped carefully onto the planks, and only sank down to the soles of his tennis shoes. Taking Gracie from me, and giving me a helping hand, as the canoe wobbled under me and I exclaimed over and over to go slowly and be careful, Peter carefully pulled me, almost crawling, up the bank. After several minutes of struggle, we reached safety on the solid grassy ground above. The Bauzi family stood watching the whole time and enjoying a good laugh on how inept and clumsy we were. With just one or two quick leaps from their canoe, they would have been up the bank in seconds.

Feeling humiliated, we went straight to the unoccupied hut and put little Gracie up on the platform with our food basket. The people watched us intently. We gave thanks for the food and started to eat. We had brought sandwiches, a ziplock bag of roasted peanuts, and a can of Pringles with us. Knowing Bauzi people were familiar with peanuts, we wanted to share some with them. But their shelter was separated from ours by a little ravine and that knee-deep oozing mud. So we emptied the Pringles out onto a plate, put some peanuts inside the Pringles can, closed the top with the tight-sealing plastic cover, and, the contents rattling inside, tossed the cylinder across to our new Bauzi friends.

They smiled and ran to pick up the red container. They jiggled the can and played with it—but how to open it? They had never seen anything like it before. We motioned to remove the plastic cover, and the headman turned the cover round and round and tried to pull it off. No luck. After throwing the canister in the air, turning it over and over with more shaking and jiggling, we could see their growing frustration and held back on our impulse to chuckle at their inability to accomplish, which was to us so simple a task. They really wanted those peanuts. Finally, a small child had a try. Very carefully, holding the can upside down over a little piece of cloth, he peeled back one side of the cover, and the peanuts dropped out. We rejoiced, laughing and smiling with them, and watched the peanuts quickly disappear.

They threw the can back to us. We loaded it with a sandwich and threw it back. No trouble opening it up this time. Surprisingly, they loved the sandwich and pitched the can back for more. We sent over more peanuts. Soon, with the mud giving him no trouble at all, the headman leaped over to our side of the ravine. Without understanding a word of each other's speech, friendship between the members of two extremely different cultures had been established. What a delightful experience for us all.

David and Scotty walking to school in the morning

Not All Fun and Games

Life, of course, wasn't all fun and games. David and Scotty went to school daily with three other children and had their chores to do in the afternoon before going out to play. They were actually in the Danau Bira school program for two full school years, fall 1980 through spring 1982. They also began the practice of Bible memory work.

For Peter and me, the work treadmill never stopped. Peter was kept extremely busy relating to government officials, which sometimes required him to travel overnight to other government posts. Other responsibilities included administering the office, handling correspondence, overseeing the completion of a preschool building, and putting in a new higher dock. The deck of the first dock, which when built was elevated six feet above the surface of the lake, was sometimes three feet underwater after a prolonged rain. Since Peter was also on the EC, that is, the Executive Committee, advising our branch director, he was required to attend the one-week-long meetings wherever they were held.

I was asked to assume the role of Branch Nurse, ministering to the medical needs of Bauzis and Danis alike at the center. Larry and the men had put up a two-room clinic building. It was up to me to make it usable. I thrived on the tasks: sanding, varnishing, cleaning, organizing, stocking medicine shelves, establishing inventory, and treating patients daily. Since trichinosis is a risk when eating pork, whenever our members attended a local Dani feast in which a pig would be roasted in a pit, one of my duties was to examine the liver of the pig, looking for trichinosis nodules, to be sure the animal wasn't infected.

Medical and Literacy Helicopter Survey

One of our goals in the area of anthropological studies of the Berik culture was to do selective research on the topic of our own choice. I chose to dig into the Berik understanding of health. Peter studied deviant Berik behavior. Since we also needed to evaluate the receptivity of the Berik people to our planned upcoming literacy campaign in June 1981, we requested the use of our SIL helicopter for four days, during which time we would visit all 10 Berik villages along the Tor River to collect the necessary data. We invited Sangga, the government medical officer who was now residing in Somanente, to accompany us, both for his help and to enable him to assess the needs of the Berik for himself.

Oh, how I enjoyed this work. I first became interested in this research when I realized that some Berik people would die without ever having asked for help. Others, with seemingly minor complaints, would urgently request immediate aid. When I ran basic laboratory tests, the results were often far from generally accepted medical "norms." The question arose, "What's normal for the Berik people? What do the Berik people regard as normal, as healthy, as sick?"

Pilot Jim entered into the survey with enthusiasm, helping whenever he could. After he landed the helicopter in each village, and the excitement of the villagers calmed down from seeing a huge metal bird for the first time, we greeted the headman. We entreated his help in having the people divide themselves into two groups, healthy and sick. Sangga examined and treated the sick while I worked with those who had declared themselves to be healthy. I worked with five men and five women in each village, including one child, a baby, and two persons described as "old." I recorded my findings on each person regarding the following: sex, approximate age, height, weight, temperature, pulse, respiration, blood pressure, hemoglobin, white blood count, urinalysis, hair, ears, throat-mouth-teeth condition, lungs, chest, and abdomen.

One of my most surprising findings was the very low hemoglobin readings. The average Berik hemoglobin I found on this survey was 10 grams, with the range being between nine to 13 grams for men and three and a half to 11 and a half grams for women. In *A Medical Laboratory for Developing Countries* (1973: section 7.4), the normal hemoglobin is given as 14 to 18 grams for men and 12 to 16 for women. According to this value system, all the healthy Berik examined were found to be anemic. I attribute this condition to be due to the high prevalence of debilitating malaria. For me, it was a fascinating study to be sure and one that was a tremendous aid to me as I treated patients—both the sick and the healthy. My research paper was published, in both English and Indonesian, in a university periodical in February 1983.

While Sangga and I cared for the medical needs of the people, Peter canvassed both men and women in each of the 10 villages, closely interviewing those who claimed to be able to at least hold a book. He wrote down the names of 450 adults who indicated a desire to attend classes to learn to read and write in Berik—sometime in the future. We were astonished and thrilled that God was preparing the way for readers to be ready to read the Scripture for themselves—someday—when God enabled us to finish translating the Berik New Testament. We had received word from Somanente that 60 more Berik men and women had taken hold of Jesus and had been baptized the month before. We prayed, *Oh Lord, thank You for calling these special people to a saving knowledge of Jesus. Please keep us healthy and able to keep progressing to complete the task before us—in Your time.*

The First Spiritual Life Conference

There were now 120 adults and about 50 children, from nine countries, serving with SIL on three different islands in Indonesia. Our leadership was well aware of our need for unity, fellowship, and spiritual refreshment. In July 1981, Peter was a co-coordinator for our first spiritual life conference. We gathered at Danau Bira for one week. The restful schedule included time for singing and worship, prayer, quiet reflection, messages brought by an excellent speaker from another mission, and group Bible study. The Scriptures we studied provided more fodder for the weekly ladies Bible study that we held year-round at Danau Bira. Vacation Bible study activities were provided for the children. We all felt that the week was so very profitable for everyone that we voted to make it an annual event.

The next week, we extended our time together to attend business meetings, have more time for fellowship, practice skits for what turned out to be a hilarious skit night, and to conduct a water sports day. The sportsmen among us led races of all types for all age groups, complete with ceremonies for first-, second-, and third-place ribbon winners. There were swimming races. Inner-tube races. Canoe races, with and without paddles. Nine-year-old David's swimming skills had so improved that he was in the group that swam the half mile across the lake. Peter had followed along in one of the canoes, watching over the safety of the swimmers. A couple of years later, when Scotty was a little older, he joined the ranks of the "half-mile swimmers."

Our Sunday evening Singspiration times were delightful and so very meaningful as we praised God and shared in an informal setting. On Sunday mornings, and during some of our other group worship times, many of us, on a variety of musical instruments, formed an amateur symphony orchestra, raising a joyful noise to the God of glory, thanking Him for bringing us to the ends of the earth to serve Him.

Completing Our Danau Bira Assignment

Many wonderful activities continued to fill our last two months on assignment at Danau Bira. Even though I worked daily in the clinic, treating everyone who had a medical need, I very much enjoyed having time to give piano lessons to our boys and other children living at the center. Since we always had two Berik speakers with us at the lake, I was able to continue translating *Flies Are Your Enemy*, and I cheered when the checking of the *How the Jews Lived* book was finished and was sent off to the printer.

Our afternoon boat rides on the lake provided a respite, for which we were very grateful, from our continual pace, as if on a treadmill. Often when we were out for a canoe ride, one of us would say, "I wonder how deep the lake is." One day, Peter responded, "Well, let's measure it and find out." It was a grand family adventure. We acquired and taped together some large pieces of grid paper and, using an aviation map, traced the shape of the lake on the paper. We made a plan for where we would measure the lake's depth, our special interest being to try to locate the original and lowest path of the river through the now-flooded lake. Peter devised a 50-foot-long rope with a rock at one end, and off we went to one of our chosen spots where we lowered the weight and were thus able to determine the depth at that point by the feel of the weight settling on the bottom of the lake. Some spots were surprisingly shallow, only about four feet, but we found many depths between 25 and 35 feet. I enjoyed our family expeditions as much as the boys. We all felt the satisfaction of success when we connected the dots noting the deepest measurements on our chart. We believed that we had indeed found the pathway of the river that had flowed through the valley, before a natural dam had caused the formation of a wide lake, our Danau Bira.

Our lives at the lake were so busy and hectic that I don't even remember how Cuddles, our family dog, became a part of our family. That friendly black-and-white mutt was just there. And when she had five pups, the boys were thrilled and accepted the responsibility of caring for them.

Danau Bira had truly become a home for us. We all anticipated many more happy times there in future years and to the upcoming year, 1982, being a fulfilling year of ministry in the Berik program—or so we thought.

Ups and Downs

October 1981 through December 1982

Look to the LORD and His strength;
seek His face always.
—Psalm 105:4, New International Version

What's a Computer?

"We're pleased to announce that the setup of our branch computer department is complete. The next time you're in Jayapura, plan on spending time with Marvin, the department manager, to become familiar with the services now available to you." So read the memo we had received from the director's office. "What's a computer?" I asked Peter. "I wonder how it can help us?"

"Well," he responded, "I need to attend the executive committee meetings the week after our assignment here at Danau Bira is finished. Let's plan to go to town together and see this new machine that's come into our world."

And so it was that in October 1981, we found ourselves staring at a computer for the first time. "You'll be able to type Berik Scripture and storybooks without using carbon paper," Marvin told us. "Let me show you what a computer can do." I'll never forget sitting next to Marvin as I watched his demonstration of how a computer could ease our workload. I stared, my mouth hanging open, as I learned how the computer could find—and correct—spelling errors for me, enable me to move sentences or whole paragraphs around within a document or, with one stroke, replace all occurrences of a word with another more desirable word. Fascinating. Amazing! I was thrilled. Peter and I signed up to come in regularly to learn more, and we made plans to type, not only our Scripture and storybooks but all our data, including our 5,000-word Berik dictionary. I was really 100% sold on computers when Marvin proved his claim that, without retyping all those dictionary entries, I would be able to alphabetize the dictionary according to the Berik words or the Indonesian words or the English words. I became quite proficient in using, what was at that time, the state-of-the-art program, MS-DOS.

Marvin told us that Wycliffe USA had researched and found a personal computer that was appropriate for translators to use on the field. We bought one. It was a Sharp PC-5000. It had an eight-line screen and, because there was no internal hard drive, came with an external drive that used three-and-a-half-inch "floppy" discs. I never did figure out why they called them that, for they weren't floppy at all but were stiff. Later, we had five-and-one-four-inch discs that were indeed floppy. But whatever, I relished learning as much as I could and praised God. *Thank You, Lord, for sending us help and equipment to aid in doing the work that You've called us to do.*

Continual Moving

And then it began—each of us engrossed in our own responsibilities, continually moving back and forth between Jayapura, Somanente, and Danau Bira. Sometimes Peter and I moved together, helping each other in all the activities of a typical moving day—packing and closing in one place, then opening and unpacking in the next place. Many times, we were on our own, as it was at the end of October 1981. Peter left Jayapura to spend a week in Somanente, gathering the final data needed for an upcoming anthropology workshop while David and Scotty went to Danau Bira—staying with friends and going to school—and I stayed in Jayapura.

I spent my days in the computer office, first typing on the group desktop computer, then, later when our laptop was ready, learning to be proficient in using it. Marvin taught me to copy my data and stressed the importance of having backups of my work both at home and on our group equipment.

When Peter returned to Jayapura, he eagerly reported, "Sue, it's true. The Berik church is thriving. Believers are gathering on Sundays for worship. Some believers pray, some read Scripture, some preach the Word; they all sing together in Berik. God has established a functioning indigenous church along the banks of the Tor River."

Thank You, Lord, for bringing us here to watch You work in Berik gall-bladders and lives.

After attending a finance seminar, we joined our boys at Danau Bira and jumped right into a six-week anthropology workshop. By the end of that time, we had written up our publishable papers and—"HURRAH!"—had completed all our required anthropology goals. My paper, *Berik Concepts of Health*, and Peter's paper, *An Update on Berik Social Organization*, were published in 1983, along with the papers of the other 10 workshop participants, in an ethnographic studies manual, *Gods, Heroes, Kinsmen*.

We decided to stay on at Danau Bira, after the anthropology workshop, for the group Christmas celebrations, which were held in mid-December. The number of students at the Danau Bira school had swelled, as had the number of willing and creative mothers who had painted beautiful children's-story murals on the nursery building walls and spent time coaching the kids in presenting programs to the growing Danau Bira community. I can still picture David in all his regal garments as he sat as King Herod on his throne and Scotty as he solemnly came in as one of the wise men in the Christmas pageant.

A group of about 30 of our colleagues joined to form a choir. In the evenings, many walked around the center singing Christmas carols at various homes. It was a special treat for me to accompany them on the piano during three choir performances that concluded with singing the "Hallelujah Chorus."

Celebrating 10 Years

Just after we finished running the trial literacy classes during the months of January through April 1982 to test and revise the Berik primer series, on May 1, we celebrated the tenth anniversary of our arrival in Indonesia. We reflected on what an amazing 10 years it had been. David, Scotty, and Sunarjo had been added to our family. God had led us to minister to the Berik people, had called hundreds of the Berik to Himself, and was growing His church in the Tor River area. And God had enabled us to learn to speak the Berik language and to write and test a series of primers, looking forward to the day when the Berik would read the New Testament for themselves in their own language. It had been a good life. We rejoiced in God's goodness and blessing.

In mid-May, we went to Jayapura to begin typing the primers and teachers' guides into the computer, preparing them for printing at the printshop. It was hard to believe, but by that time, we were at the halfway point in our third term on the field. We made exciting plans for June— to celebrate the past 10 years, David's tenth birthday, and Sunarjo's wedding . . . in Switzerland.

Jubilee in the Alps

After we left Moorhead in 1980, George Sunarjo completed his studies at both Moorhead State University and North Dakota State University, graduating in the spring of 1981 with a Bachelor of Science degree in Industrial Technology and a Certificate in Engineering. He had done exceedingly well and had enjoyed interacting and studying with other foreign students, including Doris, a lovely young lady from Switzerland. The spark of their friendship burst into love, and in the fall, Sunarjo accepted an invitation to visit Doris and her family in the Swiss Alps. In September, he got a job and began studying German with Berlitz. It wasn't long before the couple perceived their love had become an eternal flame and were engaged on Christmas Day. Sunarjo's letter inviting us, his adopted parents, to be his only family members present at his wedding to Doris was enticing. We prayed extensively about making the trip and became convinced that God was leading them and us and that we should be with them in person as God joined them together at their church wedding celebration.

We left Irian the first week of June and spent several days in Singapore, giving David and Scotty ample time at the zoo and a water park. Desiring to enhance their education in geography and history, during six days in Rome, we introduced the boys to historical Christian sites and other famous places, including the catacombs, colosseum, and Sistine Chapel.

Ah, the Alps. God's magnificent Alps! The majesty of the mountains, ablaze with tiny exquisite alpine flowers, can't be imagined. We were grateful to experience them. And the strawberries. A friend had given the bridal couple a gift of taking all of us out to their strawberry farm to pick as many strawberries as we wanted. They didn't specify that we had to take home everything we picked. So there we knelt, popping the biggest strawberries I've ever seen—one into the tray, one in the mouth. What grand memories we have, not only of that day but about all our experiences learning about Swiss culture. Hearing the cows with bells around their necks, ringing their way down the mountains. Listening to Doris's brother yodel and blow an alpine horn. Riding a cable car up a glacier to walk inside a carved-out ice palace. Staying in a Swiss chalet and dressing in traditional Swiss dress.

On June 25, 1982, all of Doris's extended family, friends, and the children from Doris's primary school class attended the wedding in festive dress. Many of the older boys carried a wooden crossbar with elegant, joyful cow bells hanging from each end. The children formed an arch of flowers as Mr. and Mrs. George Sunarjo exited the church. The day concluded with a wonderful dinner, accompanied by a live band.

Unexpected Request

Reversing our route to return to Indonesia, we flew from Zurich to Rome, straight on to Singapore, back to Jakarta, and on to Jayapura. We were all looking forward to getting back to work at Danau Bira. Our cycle of packing-moving-unpacking was about to begin again. The boys and I went back to Danau Bira while Peter flew to Somanente to get Magdalena to bring her to help us at Danau Bira.

I have to admit I did enjoy working daily in the Danau Bira clinic and participating in the nursing seminars each year. The doctors were happy to deliver missionary staff babies at the stations where they worked but required that each mission provide their own nurse to accompany expectant mothers the week before their due date, during delivery, and the week following, until mother and baby were ready to go home. I was delighted to serve our SIL members in this way. One day when I was caring for a mom and her newborn, I was shocked when the doctor told me that Irene, our prayer partner, had been severely burned in an accident with a kerosene stove in her home in Jayapura. She was on the plane coming to the medical station for care. *Thank You, Father, for allowing me to be here to help Irene. Thank You for the training and experience in caring for burn patients that You provided for me back in Minnesota. You plan everything well, for our good and for those You've placed in our lives.* Everyone in SIL Indonesia prayed earnestly for Irene. She recovered well, but it was a long, slow, and painful process.

At the end of July, we were dismayed when Dick, our branch director, requested a meeting with us. He explained the branch need and asked Peter to take on the role of associate director of the branch for one year—August 1982 through July 1983. "Dick," we replied, "we need to take a couple of days to pray about this, asking God to confirm that this is His plan for us." Dick agreed.

Oh Lord. What's happening now? We were planning to start running our full Berik literacy campaign, starting in January, as soon as the primers and teachers' guides came off the printshop press. So many Berik people are excited and waiting. It seemed to us that the time is now for them. But we know that those of us who were the first to come to start the SIL work in Indonesia need to take our turn in administration. And we don't want our will. We still want to know Your plan for us. Please show us clearly if moving to Jayapura for a year is what You want. We ask You in Jesus's Name.

God confirmed that Dick's request was indeed right for us. The first week of August, Peter was flat out busy as the coordinator for the annual spiritual emphasis conference, followed by business meetings. There was no time on skit night, August 6, to celebrate our fourteenth wedding anniversary. Water sports day and traditional Dani feast followed. Then we did the pack-and-close-up act again and moved to town, not fully unpacking because it was necessary to stay temporarily with friends. David and Scotty wanted the new experience of being with other missionary kids at the mission school, Sentani International School (SIS), so on August 10, they moved into one of the mission dormitories. Their classes in fifth and third grades began the next day. PHEW! Another two-week whirlwind came to an end.

Then shockingly, I received a letter from my mother telling me she was so unhappy she had decided to commit suicide. I did manage to get in touch with Mary who was ministering to her, and we prayed earnestly for God to strengthen them both and to give Mother the peace she was seeking and needed so badly.

A New Life for the Boys

David and Scotty adjusted well to life with the other 100 students at SIS. They liked their teachers, even though David said, "My teacher is pretty hard on us; we have a lot of homework." He learned lifelong study skills that year. The boys really appreciated all the nonacademic school activities: gym, band, roller-skating on Friday nights in the gym, and the school swimming pool. About three weeks into the school year, Peter and I were able to settle into a house being vacated by one of our colleagues and were delighted to have the boys home for the weekends. Living in the dorm went well for both boys, but after a couple of weeks, Scotty began to ask to live at home. We consulted with the dorm parents, and they agreed that he really needed to be with us. So in October, he moved home and daily rode to school and back in a chartered taxi with other SIS students who lived near us.

Full Steam Ahead

Peter and I jumped aboard our assignments, full steam ahead. In a letter to our supporters in September 1982, Peter wrote:

> Here we are bringing the Good News of Jesus to the Berik, and there you are supporting us in this ministry and helping to fulfill that great promise given to Abraham that all the peoples of the world would be blessed. How we thank God as we see, in these latter times, the Gospel literally going into all the uttermost parts of the earth. How we thank God for you who are involved in this Great Commission.
>
> We've had many new members coming to the field recently, and the work here continues to expand. God has shown Sue and me that we are needed in the work of administration for 12 months. We're in the position of receiving new members, orienting them to life in Indonesia, setting up language courses for them, and helping to oversee the work of translation in about 10 other projects. We appreciate your continued prayers.
>
> During the coming year, our living in the Tor area will be limited. Nevertheless, the work of Scripture translation continues forward with four Berik men getting their translation feet wet by drafting passages in four New Testament books. I plan to visit them in the village next month, and our whole family will spend part of December with the Berik people in the Tor River area.

Peter's duties included mountains of correspondence and frequent traveling to assist other translators and to accompany university personnel to multiple destinations. In my roles as branch nurse and chairman of the literacy committee, I was also sometimes called on to be away from home. Sometimes I'd go one way and Peter another.

I allowed myself to become immersed in all the tasks that presented themselves to me—all good things to do. Every morning for four hours, I chipped away at the massive task of typing the teachers' guides into the computer. I wrote an orientation manual for our new members and held classes for them. On Monday, Tuesday, and Thursday afternoons, I worked in the finance office. We entertained a lot, hosting a Thanksgiving Day celebration at our house.

All the moving and immersion in our separate responsibilities took its toll on us. We had no time for each other. We were on overload. It had been suggested that Peter could do the required PR (public relations) work in the mornings and Berik translation work in the afternoons. That simply doesn't work. Too many times, he would receive a notice at 11:00 a.m. that he needed to be at this or that government meeting at 3:00 p.m. or 6:00 p.m. I had begun to let my daily devotional time slide. My pressing duties and schedule often took precedence over reading my Bible and talking to God. I skimped and often skipped making time for spiritual refreshment. The result? I became irritable and demanding with Peter. He was tired and, it seemed to me, withdrawn from me.

And then God provided help for us. Phil and Barbara, Wycliffe counselors from the US, came once again to conduct a two-week seminar, "Handling Stress." Experienced Wycliffe leadership already understood the pitfalls of field life and had arranged the seminar many months earlier. The group sessions were very helpful for all of us, and Peter and I were able to have time to talk privately with Phil and Barbara to come to grips with things we needed to work out between us. I had alone time with Barbara, and Peter had personal times with Phil. God was working His refining process in us. We thanked Him for meeting us in a meaningful way to become more pleasing to Him and to each other.

In mid-December, we flew to Somanente to celebrate Jesus's birth with our Berik friends. The day after Christmas, we hiked to Tenwer and overnighted with Magdalena and Bular in their very small house. Peter had prepared a special program for the 400 people who gathered that night. He had brought a generator and slide projector to the village with us and showed a program, *A Journey into Bethlehem*. The people were enthralled, watching with exclamations and animated chattering about all they saw. It was a wonderful way to close a challenging year.

Thank You, Lord, for this splendid way to remember Your great gift of Jesus to the Berik people. We're ready for whatever surprise You have for us in 1983.

Finishing Our Third Term

1983 through June 1984

And we know that God causes everything to work
together for the good of those who love God and
are called according to His purpose for them.
　　　　　　　—Romans 8:28, New Living Translation

God Allowed—and Protected

1983 started with a bang. David and Scotty were exposed to chicken pox. Scotty spent a week in bed with the flu, and I had my first experience with a food allergy. We were living in a rented house, next door to a wonderful Indonesian family. "We've more mangos on our trees than we can possibly eat. Please feel free to help yourselves," Mrs. Tan said.

"Thank you so much," I responded. "Peter will enjoy them a lot. But, I'm sad to say, I think I'm allergic to mangos."

"It's true that people react to many types of mangos, but one of our trees has a type of mango that doesn't cause allergies. You'll be able to eat those."

"Oh, thank you, Mrs. Tan. I'll surely look forward to enjoying them."

Then the day came that the fruit was ready to be enjoyed, and Mrs. Tan brought several mangos to our house. I cautiously ate one small piece and waited 24 hours. Nothing happened. I ate three small pieces and waited another 24 hours. Nothing. "Yeah," I said to Peter, "you see, it helps to follow the knowledge of the people who have lived here all their lives." I ate half of one mango for lunch and rejoiced at bedtime that I was hive free.

Peter got up before me the next morning while I slept in. Entering the bedroom an hour later, he said, "Good morning, Sue. Why don't you open your eyes?"

"They ARE open," I responded in agony. My face had swelled up like a balloon, my eyes swollen shut. The itching of my cheeks and forehead was intense. I took antihistamine pills, which promptly put me to sleep. I had to use great discipline to not continually scratch whenever I was awake. Realizing that a breathing allergy of the same severity I was experiencing could be fatal, I prayed, *Thank You, Lord, that You protected me and the hives didn't affect my respiratory tract. I'm still here to continue our work with the Berik people.* I concluded that Mrs. Tan's experience with mango allergy was limited to those of Indonesian ancestry. I've not dared to touch another mango since.

Preserved Again

Though Peter and I had been doing well in working on, and looking to God for, growth in our relationship, we wound up getting on the treadmill again. We still had the same responsibilities. Vera, the senior branch literacy consultant, and I led a literacy planning workshop for several other translation teams—a part of my training to become a senior literacy consultant. I made a village visit to consult with one of our teams about their literacy work; Peter made trips to Somanente to consult with the Berik people.

In the midst of all this, we needed to move to another house, which had a lovely ceramic-tile floor. We set up bricks and boards to form a bookcase in the living room. One afternoon as I was busily cleaning and settling in, enjoying being barefoot on the newly washed floor, I placed our tapedeck "boom box" on the top shelf and plugged it in to the 220-vault outlet. After bringing the boxes of books designated for those shelves into the room, I decided to first dust the shelves with a damp rag, thus removing delinquent sawdust. I drew the rag across the top shelf and picked up the boom box extension cord. Enclosing the cord in the damp rag, which I held in my right hand, I pulled on the cord with my left hand. The next thing I remember, I was lying on my back on the floor, with my knees pulled up close to my chest. When I opened my eyes, Scotty was standing over me and said, "Mommy, why are you lying on the floor?"

Oh, thank You, Jesus, that the kick from the electric shock was great enough to force me to let go of that extension cord. Thank You for preserving my life today. I was able to get up but needed to rest and sleep the remainder of the day.

I had learned my lesson—the hard way. Upon examination, we found that the wires of the extension cord had been exposed by a hungry rodent.

Grateful to have survived both events, I finished the school year well and continued chipping away at the tedious job of typing the teachers' guides into the computer. I had four piano students while David and Scotty took piano lessons with a more experienced teacher. They also joined the school band—David studying the french horn and Scotty the trumpet. Peter and I savored the May piano and band recitals, proudly watching our sons play in both events, and in many track and field day competitions. The older children delighted the whole mission community with a performance of *Ants'hillvania*.

Another Year?

In June, our director returned from overseas sooner than expected—and threw us another curve ball. He asked Peter to extend his commitment and continue on as the associate director for one more year, this time living at Danau Bira and taking charge of all the work at the workshop center, including all the translation teams who based out of there. We again prayed extensively about this and felt the Lord would have us go ahead. However, we also felt God's leading to submit an official letter to the director and Executive Committee requesting that, after our next furlough, we be permitted to do a five-year term 100% free of administrative work, allowing us to concentrate only on the Berik translation program. At the end of that five-year term, David would graduate from high school, and we felt the Lord wanted us to be in the US during his college years. The cry of our hearts was the certainty we felt that God wanted us to keep pressing on in the Berik project until the Berik people celebrated the dedication of their own Berik New Testament.

The directorate agreed to our request, indicating it was—in fact—their desire for at least one team to soon complete a translation program. So, at the end of May when school was out, David and Scotty went to Danau Bira to stay with friends while Peter and I moved to the group guesthouse—and cleaned, closed, and moved out of our Jayapura house. I preceded Peter to Danau Bira, did the clean-open-unpack act again, getting our Danau Bira home ready for Peter's arrival on June 23, David's eleventh birthday. The next day, Peter made an allocation trip by helicopter with the husband of a young translation family who had chosen the language group and location where they believed God was leading them to work. Peter's job was to confirm the suitability of the housing and water supply in the village where they wanted to live. Everything went smoothly until it was time to leave—the helicopter wouldn't start. The pilot and his passengers were forced to stay overnight. The following day, a rescue team came with a new battery, and Peter was able to come home, exceedingly grateful for the teamwork of all our colleagues in the rescue effort. Life was often full of surprises and the unexpected.

Family Visitors

Desiring to see our work firsthand for several months, Mary, her husband, eight-year-old Chris, and five-year-old Chad had been planning a five-and-a-half-week trip to visit us in Indonesia. Their plans coming to fruition, we met them in Jayapura on July 4. It was like Christmas when they unpacked their bags, bringing all the goodies we had on our wish list. After four days visiting our favorite places in town, including a day at Base G, one of General MacArthur's Pacific beaches during World War II, all eight of us flew to Somanente for 11 days. Mary, a nurse, was an invaluable help to me in the clinic daily. And when Scotty fell and broke his arm while swinging like a monkey from jungle vines hanging temptingly from three-story-high trees, Mary was there to help me set Scotty's arm. I was so grateful I had the necessary casting supplies in the village.

"What projects do you have for me, Susie?" she asked.

"Oh, Mary, it would be a really big help to me if you would brighten up our home by making curtains for us."

"Would love to do that," she responded.

I gave her a measuring tape, the curtain material I had purchased, and my sewing kit that was a large Tupperware cake keeper. She measured the living room windows and got set up on the kitchen table, ready to cut the needed panels to the correct length. She took the Tupperware cover off and let out a squeal. I raced in from the other room in time to see Mama Mouse jump off the table and scamper across the kitchen floor, with two little baby mice still hanging on to her nipples. We heard a chorus of squealing. And there, nestled in my sewing kit, we saw three more tiny baby mice, their eyes closed tight, loudly protesting Mama's quick departure. Recovering from the shock, Mary volunteered to take on the task of cleaning out the container and all the sewing supplies. Mama must have been living in there for quite a while.

Heaven Rejoiced Over the Witch Doctor

The highlight of Mary's family time in the village was the day another 32 Berik believers, including Yoab, the man who for many years had been the active tribal witch doctor, were baptized. On many occasions, we had watched him dance and gesture while singing incantations against the evil spirits that plagued the people. We were aware that he, and some of the new believers, were mixing their traditional practices of appeasing the spirits with their new Christian practices. We had prayed earnestly for God to reach into their gallbladders (hearts). And then one day, Yoab came to our home and announced, "I took hold of Jesus. I want to be baptized." All heaven rejoiced with us that day, and we felt honored and blessed to be there to observe God's transforming power at work as He changed Yoab's mind, and gallbladder, and actions. Yoab turned from appeasing the spirits to praising his Savior. WOW! *Thank You, Lord. You did it again!*

Since Mary's husband had been a chaplain, the Berik church leaders asked him to administer baptism. He diligently memorized the appropriate words in Berik, and taking his place with the baptized church leaders, standing waist-deep in the flowing Tor River, he baptized 32 new believers. David and Scotty and their cousins had also expressed a desire to be baptized in the Tor with the Berik. Mary and I sealed Scotty's casted arm with plastic and rejoiced as we watched our boys publicly declare Jesus as Savior. The next day, we all joined in worship and celebrating the Lord's Supper together.

Surprise at Danau Bira

Mary and her husband had timed their visit to coincide with our annual spiritual emphasis and business conferences. Servants at heart, they came not only to experience our lives but eager to volunteer and serve in any way they could for the duration of their three-week stay at Danau Bira. Mary and I had the pleasure of working together in the clinic, assisting the vising doctor. We also ran the clinic for the Bauzi and Dani people who came for help.

August 6, our fifteenth wedding anniversary, was so much better that year. Conference was over. We were able to set aside time for our traditional anniversary celebration activities: listening to our taped recordings from past years, looking at our wedding pictures, and taking our annual picture. Mary was busy cooking a chicken dinner for us, when half an hour before we were to sit down, a Dani man came to our door asking for help with his injured brother. We spent the next half hour sewing up a bad wound on his leg. Later, having finished our wonderful dinner, someone else came to the door. *Oh no! What's happening now?* I thought. And just then, five couples walked in to have a surprise party for us. They had prepared a *This Is Your Life* time where they reenacted scenes from our courtship and married life. We still have the greeting card they had made, using clippings out of magazines. *Thank You, Lord, for friends who are so gracious to shower love on us.*

The Most Extraordinary Event—Ever—at Danau Bira

Living at Danau Bira while David and Scotty were at school in town, our lives settled into our new normal. Carrying on our administrative and nursing responsibilities. Typing the teachers' guides. Traveling frequently. Visiting the Berik in the village and the boys in Jayapura. Attending and helping with workshops.

For four weeks in November and December 1983, I took part in a writers' workshop. Two Berik men, Gijon and Sowenso, came to the lake and learned to write and type their stories about both new experiences and Berik myths. Using the silk-screen method of duplicating pages, they gained skill in printing their small booklets. They also had sewing classes, made bread pans and bread, and even built an oven in which to bake their bread.

On Sunday morning, December 11, I received an early morning phone call from Vera, our workshop coordinator, who was eight months' pregnant. Her husband and two-year-old son were in Jayapura. "Sue, I need your help. I'm having contractions."

"Can you walk down the hill to the clinic, Vera?"

"No. What can we do?" she asked quickly.

"Don't worry, I'll get a couple of men to come to get you."

Peter grabbed one of the other men at the center and went to the guesthouse to get Vera. With their hands grasping each other's wrists, they formed a seat with their forearms and carried Vera to the clinic. After examining her, I blithely said, "Don't worry, Vera. At eight months, your baby is big enough to not have a problem and small enough that you'll have no problem. But I'm going to go to the radio and see if I can get hold of your doctor to see if we can stop your labor."

I ran to the Danau Bira office building that housed the center SSB. I prayed on the run, *Please, Lord, help me on this Sunday morning to get through to Dr. Ken.* God answered my prayer, and I reported Vera's condition to the doctor. "Ken, what can I do to stop Vera's labor?" I wrote down his orders. He said he'd stand by, and I returned to the clinic. When I got there, I found that Vera's water had broken; I knew there was no stopping her labor now.

While I prepared for the delivery, my dear friend, Joyce, appeared at the clinic door. "What can I do to help?"

"Please, Joyce, go to the phone and call everyone at the center and ask them to pray for Vera—and for me! And ask Larry to turn the generator on. I need power and lights in here."

Excitedly shaking her head saying, "Yes," she ran off down the path.

Back at Vera's side, I found she was close to delivery. In fact, a few minutes later, she was holding her little girl. I put my hand on Vera's tummy and was shocked. "Vera," I said, "your work isn't done yet." Puzzled, she just stared at me. The month before, the doctor had told her that even though she looked quite large, he had found only one heartbeat. "There's another baby in there, Vera. You're having twins."

Just then, Joyce again appeared at the door. "Everyone's praying. What can I do now?" I didn't tell her what I had just learned. I simply said, "Go back and call everyone again. Tell them Vera's had a baby girl and that I need them to keep praying."

"Praise God!" Joyce said, her eyes popping out of her head. And off she ran again.

While tending to Vera, shortly I saw two tiny little feet, crossed at the ankles. *Oh Lord, a breach birth. Help us and this second little one NOW!* And to Vera, I said, "You're doing great. Next baby's coming."

Vera was holding both her babies when Joyce came back again. "Everyone's excited and praying. Now what can I do?"

"Joyce, go back to the phones again. Tell them all we have two baby girls in the clinic. Ask them to keep praying." I thought she'd faint. But she recovered quickly, and off she went.

I immediately went to the clinic phone and called the home of another nurse at the center who was having lunch with yet another nurse. They had not had OB experience and had asked to bow out of an obstetric event. "Girls," I said, "I need you now in the clinic. I've got Vera and TWO babies here to take care of." And so God had provided a nurse for each patient. Joyce not only called everyone but managed to get through to Daddy Jim in town. The pilots flew him, and big brother Jonathan, out to Danau Bira the next day.

With Vera stable, and the babies being cared for, I went to the SSB and called Dr. Ken. "Ken, I really need you again. Vera's had two baby girls, weighing about four pounds each. What do I do with two preemies here at Danau Bira where it'll be cool tonight, about 65 degrees?" Ken reviewed what needed to be done. I called a meeting of all the ladies at the center, and we set up a roster to be with Vera and the babies all night. Ken instructed us to bundle the little ones with hot water bottles, refilling them every hour.

Most people at the center gathered at 7:00 p.m. for our usual Sunday night Singspiration. What a glorious time of praise and worship and thanksgiving and prayer it was. God had once again revealed His love and power and care and peace and joy to us all. It's a good life.

Closing Our Third Term

Jim, Vera, and their family returned to their home in Jayapura. David and Scotty's school let out for Christmas break, and they came home to Danau Bira for Christmas. On December 28, we all went to Somanente for a week. Another pilot, Rex, his wife, Judy, and their three children—Jeff, Mark, and Lisa—joined us for five days. We celebrated the arrival of 1984 with Berik believers in a church service that started at 8:00 p.m. on December 31 and concluded about 12:30 a.m. on January 1.

January through May 1984, I continued to plug away at typing the three teachers' guides. It was then that I realized God had planned our assignment in administration to provide the time for us to complete the massive job of preparing all the necessary books for our full literacy campaign. It had taken a lot longer than I had hoped or expected.

The day finally arrived when I finished typing all 93 lessons in the teachers' guides—in both the Berik and Indonesian languages—and had a computer printout in hand. Essau came to town from the village and lived with us while he and I worked together daily. We read every word of the Berik lessons on all 788 pages of the guides, making corrections as we went along. Then Sowenso traded places with Essau, and Peter and Sowenso did a second check while I sat with an Indonesian teacher who was available to us because we were living in town, not in the village. We read—out loud—and corrected the Indonesian text of every lesson. When the three guides were out of our hands and our printshop colleagues said they would take it from there, we all heaved a big sigh of relief—and had a party. Soon, the Berik would be able to read their own books and stories and, as was our constant dream, read the New Testament—in Berik, their own treasured language.

At the end of June, the boys especially enjoyed two final weeks at Danau Bira before leaving and returning to the US for a one-year furlough. Peter and I went through all our "stuff"—sorting, discarding, washing, cleaning, packing, selling, and sometimes just giving things away. Saying good-bye to our friends and colleagues, our family flew to Somanente for a final two weeks with our Berik friends.

The house we had put up in 1978 had been deteriorating. The wooden support posts were rotting or being eaten; more and more creatures were taking up residence, and with the increase in our village ministries, the house was no longer serving our growing needs. Earlier in the year, Peter had begun working with the Berik men as they built another house for us, right next door to the one that was falling down. This time, they used ironwood posts and corrugated aluminum roofing over the entire house. We enlarged my office-clinic area, and the new floor plan included a much larger living room to accommodate all our Berik, government, and military visitors. After supper in the evening, as soon as Peter started to play a lively tune on his accordion, 20 to 30 people would join us. As we repeated the sort-discard-wash-pack-give-away process once again, we moved into the new house. The Berik were delighted to take down the old house, carrying away and using all that they thought was redeemable.

When the plane came for us, it was again a sweet and sour emotional time for me—sour to say good-bye for a year, sweet to think of being with family and friends in the US once again. Upon picking up our mail in Jayapura, we learned that God had paved the way for us in the US. Two letters brought the news that a car was being provided and a house was available for rent near the school David and Scotty would be attending. *Thank You, Lord, for caring and providing these important basic needs. And thank You for letting us know now before we begin to travel.*

Our third term had been exhilarating, challenging, difficult, overwhelming, fun, demanding, disappointing, adventuresome, disturbing, exhausting, and celebratory. We needed a break, further help in our marriage, and refreshment. In July, we were READY to leave for our third furlough and to be loved on by family and supporters whose prayers had seen us through these four years.

How would God act and provide to renew and rejuvenate us?

Our Third Furlough

July 1984 through July 1985

Go home to your own [family and relatives
and friends] *and bring back word to them
of how much the Lord has done for you.*
—Mark 5:19b, Amplified Bible, Classic Edition

The Trip Home—R and R and Discovery

As we took off from the Jayapura airport on July 13 and flew along the Irian Jaya coastline, I looked down at the Tor River as we passed over it and, in the distance, in my mind and heart, could visualize the Berik villages and our friends going about their daily activities. *Oh God, be with them while we're gone. Draw the believers into a deeper relationship with You. Lead them in continuing to reach out to those who have yet to take hold of You. Bring us back to them, I pray. Please continue to use us to bring Your Word to them in the language of their gallbladders. I ask You in Jesus's Name to do this. Amen.*

After a business stop in Jakarta, we flew on to Hong Kong for a couple of days of R and R. Valuing "discovery through experience," we were intentional in planning our stops and activities in other cities and cultures every time we traveled halfway around the world. Besides taking in fun and famous places, like Victoria Peak, Ocean Park and Water World, we took David and Scotty on a one-day guided tour into the People's Republic of China. The contrast between mainland China and Hong Kong was striking—we wondered what the differences would be after Britain's 99-year lease on Hong Kong expired in 1997.

July 23, 1984, was a very long day. Since we crossed the date line, we lived the day twice. Our plane took off from the Hong Kong airport at 9:30 a.m. We had a two-hour stop in Tokyo and flew straight on to Honolulu, where, at 9:30 a.m. on July 23, we were walking down the street on our way to a restaurant for breakfast. A fun benefit of international travel. Adding to the boys' education, we toured Pearl Harbor, a pineapple factory, and went snorkeling in the crystal-clear waters near Waikiki Beach.

Our first stop in Continental US was in Santa Barbara, California, for a visit with my mother. After a pleasant stay, we moved on to the Los Angeles area to stay with Mary and her family. Always eager to have the cousins spend time together, we all enjoyed excursions to Disneyland and Raging Waters. The four boys also then spent a week at a Christian camp while I went back to Santa Barbara for a time alone with Mother. She was eager to share the challenges she had been experiencing. Peter and the boys joined us for the weekend before we flew, at last, to Minneapolis, which was to be our home for the year.

In One Day—A School, House, Job, and Car

It felt so strange to me that Dad wasn't with Evie when she met us at the Minneapolis airport and took us home to be with her and 16-year-old Nancy until we could settle in our own place. Even though it had been four and a half years since Dad passed away, my heart was looking for him. Whenever I went into the living room, I expected him to be sitting there, in *his* chair reading a book. One of the heartaches, and realities, of life and of passing time.

The next day, August 14, 1984, was a red-letter day for all four of us. Evie took us to Meadow Creek Christian School where David and Scotty had an interview with Mr. John, the principal. My heart was singing as I observed how he treated the boys, asking questions and interacting with them. After explaining the school's rules, he asked them, "Will you abide by these requirements?" I was so proud of them as they respectfully answered and then smiled ear to ear when Mr. John announced that they were officially accepted as students in the fifth and seventh grades.

After saying good-bye to Mr. John, we all piled into Evie's car, and she took us directly to the house that Mr. John had found for us, just one and a half miles away from the school. The landlord was expecting us, and we excitedly made all the necessary arrangements to rent his lovely three-bed-room home for the coming 11 months. Stopping for a fast-food lunch on the way, we made our way to the home of a Wycliffe representative with whom we would be working 20 hours a week during our furlough. He had made arrangements for a car for our furlough use. After signing the papers, we said a tired but happy good-bye and followed Evie home. What an amazing day it had been. Within eight hours, we had completed arrange-ments, not only for the boys' school but also for our house, job, and car.

Reconnecting with Family

Now that we had wheels, we were eager to connect with Peter's par-ents in Moorhead and to move our stored belongings from their home to our rental home in Minneapolis. Arriving in Moorhead, Peter honked the horn over and over in greeting as we drove down the street to Mom and Dad Westrum's home. They rushed out their front door with open arms, and we enjoyed a delightful week with them. They had been in contact with George and Doris in Switzerland and shared the news that Benji, their first child, had been born on July 26, when we were in Honolulu. *Thank You, Lord, for Benji, a blessed addition to our family.*

The annual Westrum family reunion was held the next weekend at the lakeside cottage of Peter's brother, Rod, and his wife, Char, on one of Minnesota's beautiful lakes. We were pleased that their children and Peter's sister, Gloria, and her family were able to come from Washington DC to be with us all.

Two weekends later, we celebrated my sister Nancy's seventeenth birthday with Evie, my brother, Jim, and his wife, Pam. How blessed we were to spend time with all these loved ones, right at the beginning of our furlough year. *Thank You, Lord, for family, with whom we feel connected and loved and for these wonderful furloughs when we can be together.* All through-out the following months of our furlough, we were able to be with them all again to celebrate birthdays and holidays, special events, and many other casual times as well. Family—the glue that holds society together.

Yaufun and His Family

We were also eager to connect with Yaufun, his wife, and 10-month-old son. The years of our third term in Indonesia had also been momentous years for Yaufun. In November 1979, he had met Sharon Hsiao, a lovely woman from Taiwan, who was visiting her sister in Minneapolis at that time. In 1981, on his way to visit his family in Malaysia, Yaufun made a stop in Taiwan to see Sharon. On January 15, 1981, they were married in a civil ceremony by a Taiwanese judge, fulfilling the requirement of needing a marriage certificate in order to apply for a visa for Sharon to join Yaufun in the US. The lovebirds' church wedding was in Minneapolis on August 29, 1981. They became active in the Twin Cities Chinese Christian Church, especially with the youth fellowship. Another of their outreaches involved ministering to Taiwanese women suffering from homesickness and relational issues. It was my special joy to hold Baby Nathan for the first time and to get together with them often throughout the year.

Meeting Students on Twenty-two College Campuses

On August 27, we got up early and packed up the remaining items we had at Evie's home. She served us a hearty breakfast and stood in the yard waving as we set out, taking David and Scotty to their new school. We then made a beeline to our new home to prepare a place for the boys to come home to after school. We knew that the unavoidable stresses of travel would be relieved in the security of being HOME. Although all our things from Moorhead were there in the house, as were the bikes Grandma Evie had given the boys, there was a lot of work to do to get settled. We set up our bed and bunk beds, which friends had loaned us for the boys, so we could sleep at home that night. After school, David and Scotty were delighted to get their personal treasures put away just where they wanted them in their own room. At dinner that night, Scotty announced, "Starting now, my name is Scott." We smiled at this evidence of his growing up. Before falling into bed, Peter set up my desk, which was part of a large bookcase unit in our living room, and organized the third bedroom for his office.

Our Wycliffe furlough assignment was under the direction of Wycliffe's national recruitment office. We were given a list of 22 colleges, both Christian and secular, in the twin cities of Minneapolis and St. Paul, and were instructed to make as many contacts with those colleges and their students as we could creatively figure out and manage during our furlough year. We started out making phone calls to set up appointments to give mission presentations in appropriate classes, using the overhead projector transparency programs we had used during our last furlough, missionary films, and slide programs. Once we got started on the various campuses, we weren't able to keep up with all the invitations we received to return or speak to other groups. It seemed that the students had hundreds of questions about our life in the jungle, how God led, and how we had survived it all. We emphasized the need for support personnel, especially administrators, for we had spent 46% of our time during our second term and 63% of our last term in administrative roles. Since we were in contact with our colleagues in Irian, we could share with the students that there had been another Berik baptism celebration in the village, and it was now estimated that 20% of the Berik people were baptized believers.

What we enjoyed the most was meeting with students one-on-one or in small groups, getting to know them personally, testifying to God's love and grace in a foreign country, and challenging these wonderful young people to move forward as God was leading them. We were NOT out to get every student to join Wycliffe. No. We encouraged them to discover God's will. And then DO IT. I remember telling students, "If God doesn't want you in Wycliffe, we don't either."

Making New Friends

We became an active part of Meadow Creek Church, very much enjoying entering into the life of the congregation, sharing in various Sunday school classes and programs, and especially making new friends and developing deep friendships, some of which we still enjoy as I write today. The number of programs we were invited to give at Meadow Creek, and in other places, increased.

An article in the *Minneapolis Star and Tribune* newspaper lent veracity to our ministry. The newspaper reporter wrote a wonderfully accurate article about our work with the Berik, in which they highlighted the complexity of Berik verbs:

"We actually found in Berik verbs, such as 'give,' you have to mark the number of items you are giving," said Sue. "You have to mark how big the items are . . . whether the person you are giving them to is male or female and . . . the hour of the day—whether it's daylight or dark out. Also, with the verb 'to give,' you have to tell about the distance (how far away the action is occurring)."

"People say they're such primitive people (that) they must do things very simply," said Sue. "It's not true. God has given them a beautiful complex language, which they understand and use perfectly."

The article went on to promote the fiftieth anniversary celebration of Wycliffe to be held the following weekend in Minneapolis. Six thousand invitations had been distributed. We were thrilled to be able to attend and talk with the visitors about the needs of the Bibleless and unlettered peoples of this world. When taking part in a weekend missionary conference in Pine City, Minnesota, we were blessed with royal hospitality and became close friends with our host and hostess.

JAARS

When funds were provided for us by several couples who knew our financial situation and wanted us to visit them in Washington DC, we fulfilled a dream we had had to introduce David and Scott to our nation's capital. We flew to DC, again staying with Gloria and Lowell and their four children. Day after day, they escorted us to all the famous tourist sights and also cared for us royally the whole week we were with them.

We had also dreamed of visiting Waxhaw, North Carolina, a small town that lies just 12 miles south of the Charlotte city limits and which was the location of JAARS (Jungle Aviation and Radio Service), one of Wycliffe's sister organizations. Gloria generously loaned us her car, enabling us to visit the JAARS Center for one week.

For the whole length of our 21 years laboring on the Berik project, the dedicated, skilled, and giving JAARS personnel serving in Indonesia ministered to us. The pilots flew us in and out of Somanente hundreds of times. The mechanics kept the planes safe and in the air. Communications experts not only repaired our SSB but our electrical appliances as well. All the men's wives helped in ways too numerous to list. JAARS personnel—true servants at heart. I remember one day when Pilot Tom brought supplies into Somanente for us. He detected that Peter was troubled by something. Right then and there, even though he had other stops to make that day, he invited Peter to share. They sat together on a log, under the shade of the palm trees while Peter poured out his heart to Tom, and he prayed for Peter. How did we live, survive, manage to work, and even thrive in the jungle for so many years? Through the prayers of God's people, not only in the US but also right there on the field through the loving ministry of His servants called to support the village work.

Though Peter had had a severe malaria attack while on our trip to the east coast, he recovered in time to welcome Mary and her family when they arrived in mid-December. Our two families delighted in celebrating Christmas together—three times. Our first gathering was with my side of the family at my brother's home in Minneapolis. Evie and Nancy also joined us. Jim's wife, Pam, a deluxe hostess, was a busy gal caring for their three-year-old Tiffany and year-old Tony. I marveled at the passage of time as I remembered Jim as a one-year-old cutie. The only damper on our time together was that David had malaria again and thus wasn't very peppy.

We spent Christmas week in northern Minnesota for a traditional Swedish meatball Christmas Eve celebration with Mom and Dad Westrum. Christmas Day found us all with Peter's sister, Sally, her husband, Bill, and their children, who were home from college, for a turkey dinner with all the trimmings. And finally, almost at the Canadian border, we delighted in being with Peter's cousin, Rachel, and husband, John, on their farm for a day in the snow, even speeding over their fields on snowmobiles. In cahoots with Jim, we then returned to Minneapolis and threw a surprise birthday party for Evie on January 3. Yes, having our families together had truly been a blessed memory-building time.

Mother

I had felt deep gratitude to Mary and her husband when they treated me to a trip to California the previous October so I could spend several days alone with Mother in her home. It turned out that she was going through a period of deep distress, angry about many things. Try as I did to listen well, console, answer her questions, and share Scripture and Jesus with her, she only became more upset. I spent much time in prayer for us both. Unable to get much sleep, it was a most difficult and unpleasant time for me. When Mary came back to get me, I told her I just wouldn't be able to spend a prolonged time alone with Mother again. Mary had had similar experiences. She understood.

To our dismay, things only got worse as 1985 progressed. Mother phoned me frequently and talked for 45 minutes to an hour, venting her anger and repeating the same wretched stories over and over about hurts she'd endured throughout her life, beginning with the seven years she was in an orphanage between the ages of three and 10 and including wrongful things I had done, starting in primary school. She would be especially infuriated if I wasn't home to take her call. I struggled to know what to say or do. Mary and other female friends experienced the same struggle with her many phone calls. We all prayed diligently for God to release her from this bondage.

Help Needed

The first half of our furlough had been incredibly busy. We had been on the go continually. Traveling. Settling in. Unpacking. Making college contacts and routine doctor and dentist visits. Preparing and giving programs. Moving from home to home. Recovering from each bout with malaria. Ministering. Delighting in new and old friends and family. Enjoying concerts and the St. Paul Winter Carnival. Building snowmen and driving snowmobiles. Praying for Mother and the stresses resulting from the hours I spent dealing with her current mental anguish.

The result? Peter and I again had no time for each other. I agonized over times we snapped at each other. I nagged about what I wanted. I had a critical spirit—finding fault with Peter when I thought he didn't measure up to my standards. I stubbornly believed my view was correct. Peter did the same. God had sent Phil and Barbara to help us when we were in Indonesia. Things were now once again in such a state that I said to Peter, "I think we need to pull back on our plans to return to Indonesia this summer, unless we get help to improve our relationship." It was heartbreaking for me to say this because I was so sure God wanted us to finish the Berik translation program.

In the midst of our relationship struggles, we received more stressful news. The previous October, our support had started to drop; by January 1985, it was down to 20% of the quota Wycliffe had set for us. When Wycliffe notified us that unless our support level increased to 100%, we wouldn't be allowed to return to Indonesia; things seemed bleak indeed. But we asked each other, "In whom do we trust?"

We prayed. And God gave us a godly man, Dr. Will, to counsel with us. We took some baseline tests, such as a personality inventory. We confirmed that our family backgrounds and expectations were very different. I realized I needed to learn to work on changes in me, in my heart, and attitude. I needed to let go of some of my self-centered expectations, let go of demanding that Peter do things MY way. I felt God say to me, "Sue, stop being upset if Peter doesn't do things your way—if he doesn't want what you want." We confirmed that we were committed to God, to our marriage vows, and to God's leading in our lives. Would we respond to God's work in our hearts? Would He continue to use us to give the Berik people His Word in their own language?

We talked with Dr. Will about principles of sharing and listening. These foundations laid, Dr. Will gave us one of the most helpful pieces of advice I've heard: "Make a daily appointment with each other. Put it on your calendars. When invited to be involved in something at that time, politely decline. Quality time with each other must be your priority." We really heard Dr. Will. We followed his advice. We MADE time for each other, not allowing the outside world to intrude. We went for rides in the car to pretty areas of town. We had leisurely lunches together, instead of while on the run. We sat, facing each other, and just talked, about our dreams and expectations, about both fun and difficult topics. We spent private, alone-time together. Most importantly, we would choose something the other wanted and just do it together. The whole point was that we did these things alone, focusing on each other, not on our various ministries and responsibilities. And God blessed. It was remarkable how we quieted down and got our priorities right. We were able to attend well to keeping our new resolves during the rest of our furlough.

Looking back today, I believe satan was continually working on us to take advantage of our busyness. I believe he didn't want us to return to Indonesia, that he tried to distract and divide us.

Winding Down

It was hard to believe, but suddenly, it was May, and the school year was coming to a close.

We took an active part in Meadow Creek Church's annual mission conference. I was invited to be the speaker for the women's luncheon. I felt humbled and was very nervous about it. It's a whole different ball game to speak in front of your friends than it is to relate to strangers. *God, I need You to be the one speaking to these ladies. Please put Your words in my mouth!* And God answered. When it was over, I realized I had actually enjoyed sharing.

We had applied and, now in May, were accepted as members of the church, and at the end of the month, the congregation voted to take us on as one of their missionaries. Our relationship with the church continued until our retirement from active Wycliffe service in 2015. God was faithful.

The Pine City church invited us back and added us to the list of their missionaries. Individuals also started to come on board, committing to monthly financial support. Wayne was one such man. He had been supporting a Wycliffe missionary from his church in Missouri. When that person was no longer able to serve with Wycliffe, Wayne instructed Wycliffe to give his gifts "to the one with greatest need." Wycliffe gave him our names, and Wayne joined our team of supporters. Wayne became a dear and close friend. God works in wondrous ways. By the time school was out, Wycliffe notified us that our support was at 100%, and we were permitted to return to the field.

At David and Scott's school awards banquet, we sat with David's close friend, Bryan, and his family. Both boys were called up front multiple times to accept awards. We felt quite proud of David in making the A honor roll and for receiving a seventh-grade medallion for Christian character.

It was time to pack up again. It seemed we were getting used to it, that it took less time and energy this time. We returned all the furniture that had been loaned to us, loaded our things, including my piano that I purchased when I graduated from nursing school, into a U-Haul and went back to Moorhead to once again store things in "our" little front bedroom at the home of Peter's parents. We drove all the way to John and Rachel's farm to say good-bye to them and our friends at their church who had now also committed to pray for us, and while in northern Minnesota, we were also able to make one last visit with long-term, very close friends, Ben and Brenda. After day-after-day good-byes in Moorhead with each family who had become so dear to us, and again attending the annual Westrum family reunion, we were on our way again . . . to Minneapolis, where we stayed with Evie and repeated that difficult good-bye time with our friends and relatives there. Continual times of smiling—while saying, "Thank you" and "Please write often"—and at the same time crying inside is exhausting. And then, when at last I said good-bye to Evie and Nancy, I couldn't stop the tears flowing.

Our last stop, before crossing the Pacific Ocean once again, was in Los Angeles for a final visit with Mary and to give the cousins several final days together—for five years. Yes, we planned to return to Indonesia for a five-year term, believing we could finish the translation of the Berik New Testament during that time. Mother's severe episode of mental torture was somewhat relieved, and we had some pleasant times with her. She opted out of coming to the airport to see us off, but we did get through on the phone before leaving Honolulu, which was the first stop on our return trip. Knowing we would not be in the US again for five years, we had a very special anniversary celebration—a Hawaiian luau on the beach at Waikiki, complete with beautiful and fragrant flower leis and, of course, Hawaiian dancers. The master of ceremonies opened the show with prayer, dedicating the festivities to the Lord and closing in Jesus's Name. How special was that at a public presentation on a public beach?

On the next segment of our journey, I wrote a letter to a dear friend, who represented the encouragement given by several friends as we left them behind:

We're on the plane, a Boeing 747 that holds 400 people, flying across the ocean from Honolulu to Tokyo and then to Seoul, Korea . . . When we get there, we will have been traveling for 17 1/2 hours.

I've thought of you so often since we left, and it's been difficult for me. One day at my sister's home, I finally had a good cry (which I didn't do the day we said good-bye), and that was good for me. You've been so good to us, and we do appreciate it so very much. Thank you again for your many kindnesses and love and support. I'm comforted by your encouragement that we have the same heavenly Father looking over us. And we all will look forward to the day that we'll be together again—here or in our heavenly home someday. We'll continue to look forward to your letters regularly and continue to treasure your prayers for us as we work toward the goal of completing the New Testament in the Berik language. There's much to do, so we'll need to choose our priorities each day and work diligently at translating if we are to finish by June 1990 when David finishes high school.

I was again experiencing the bittersweetness of another major transition. Though challenging, and sometimes tedious, the next five years would bring deep satisfaction and joy as we climbed to the zenith of the program to which God had called us 15 years earlier. God's strength had carried us through so much. And now we could only look to Him. All that lay before us seemed impossible.

Our Plans—Interrupted

August 1985 through April 1986

*For the mountains may depart and
the hills be removed, but My stead-
fast love shall not depart from you.*
—Isaiah 54:10a, English Standard Version

Choosing to introduce David and Scott to another Asian country on our way back to Indonesia after furlough, we flew directly from Honolulu to Seoul, Korea. Traveling 17 and a half hours across the international date line, we skipped the night of Wednesday, August 10. Talk about exhausted! We slept 11 hours before setting out for our first excursion to a Korean folk village. When selecting a church to attend on Sunday, we asked the boys, "How would you like to attend the world's largest Christian church? The sermon will be given in Korean, but they have headphones for people who don't speak that language. We'd be able to hear the simultaneous translation of the sermon into English as the pastor preaches." We agreed it would be a new and unique experience. Sunday morning, as we sat in the balcony of that large church and looked around us, we saw that hundreds of people from a dozen or more countries were using headphones, each hearing the sermon in their own language. We were reminded of the day of Pentecost when thousands of people heard the apostles speaking in their own tongues.

We flew on to Hong Kong, and after a day at Water World, we were pleased to be over jet lag, finding we could once again easily stay awake during the day and sleep at night. Touring the Aberdeen Harbor float-ing village, where an estimated 6,000 people live on approximately 600 Chinese junks, was an educational experience for all four of us. "These boat people," our guide told us, "are born, live their entire lives, and die here, without ever leaving their village on the water."

One week after we arrived back in Irian—on August 5, 1985—David and Scott eagerly moved into their dorm at school with their friends and got started in eighth and sixth grades. Peter and I flew to our workshop center at Danau Bira, where Peter was once again a co-coordinator for our annual branch conference, business meetings, and our Berik project planning seminar. *Thank You, Father, for our leadership who so diligently keeps us focused and moving forward toward our goals. And thank You for the weekly tape recordings we can look forward to receiving from our sons.*

Berik Literacy Campaign Begins—At Last

Eight Berik reading books, five primers, and three teachers' guides had been prepared during our previous term and were waiting to be put to use. (The guides were written in both Berik and Indonesian, thus enabling Indonesian teachers assigned to the Berik area the ability to teach Berik speakers to read and write. In the absence of Indonesian teachers, we taught Berik tutors to use the guides.) Finally in September 1985, with a promise from the administration to not interrupt our Berik assignment for the next five years, we had a green light to dive into Phase One of our long-planned Berik literacy campaign. A massive job, it loomed overwhelmingly in front of us—seeming impossible.

Peter made the necessary arrangements with the county commissioner, and word was sent out to all 10 Berik villages:

It's time to start the reading and writing classes for Berik villagers. The two men your village chief and Mr. Peter chose to lead the class in your village should come to Somanente on Monday next week for the tutors' training course that will last two weeks.

We wondered, *Will all those potential tutors, who were so eager to be involved when we ran the test classes, still be committed? How many will show up on Monday?*

We needn't have been concerned. 22 men, including three non-Berik government workers, and one woman—Essau's wife, Aksamina—arrived on Sunday afternoon, enthusiastically announcing to everyone that they were there to become tutors for the literacy course. The next morning, the commissioner led an opening ceremony, and the eight-month campaign was off to a great start. We held classes for four hours every morning, training these "cream of the crop" Berik to use the first volume of the three teachers' guides, by which they would lead their students through *Primer One*. They practiced reading and printing and made their own visual aids.

Excitement for reading and writing spread to all the villages as the tutors' course progressed. On October 3, SIL aviation made three flights to Somanente, bringing in officials from the Department of Education and Culture, the government regency office, and our own SIL leaders. With great pomp and celebration, 13 classes, for 159 students in eight villages, were officially started. Another 100 Berik men and women attended the ceremony, begging to be listed as students the next year.

A week later, Peter and I scrambled down the muddy bank of the Tor River and climbed into our 15-foot-long dugout canoe. Essau, our literacy campaign coordinator, a commissioner's representative, and a police department representative were already in the canoe waiting for us. We quickly got underway, going two hours downriver to two Berik villages to observe the four literacy classes in those villages.

When I arrived in the first village, the students were busily getting settled in their places on backless wooden benches in the church where classes were held. The benches were made by sinking three posts in a row into the earthen floor and, using jungle vine, tying a board across the top of the posts. The doors and windows were simply openings in the walls, with no glass or screens. There was no ceiling, only corrugated aluminum roofing, which during a thunderstorm drowned out all other sound that might have been in the room. Such a building was an open invitation for ALL to come to class— people, children, chickens, dogs, pigs, birds! The tutor's questions might be answered by a cackle, oink, or the inquisitive stare of a hornbill bird.

One of the tutors had a watch, and precisely at 8:00 a.m., he gave the nod for one of the students to "beat the bomb," a bomb shell left over from World War II, which was serving as the school bell. Assessing the scene before me, I counted 22 adult male and female students, eight children, three babies, two dogs, one piglet, and a chicken present.

What a thrill it was to be there that morning! I witnessed one of the things we'd been working toward for the previous five years: Berik men teaching Berik adults to read and write the Berik language, using the Berik primers and teachers' guides we had written. The enthusiasm and eagerness to learn that permeated that simple building was catching. It was a tremendous answer to our prayers and those of our team of prayer warriors in the US.

After class, I tested each student to ascertain each one's actual reading knowledge. Twenty of the 22 adults in the class were absolute beginners. But Maria was able to slowly read 85% of the short story I gave her. She already understood that symbols on paper represent sounds, and she knew many of the sounds so she could form words.

Excited, I said, "Maria, that's wonderful! You already know how to read. Why do you want to come to class?" My heart skipped a beat when she responded, "Oh, Mama Sue, I want to know how to read MY language!" *Thank You, Lord, for Maria, for giving her and the other Berik people a desire to learn to read their own language so that You might speak to them, in Berik, about Your son, Jesus.*

Health and Supplies

During Phase One, we had visited and evaluated all the classes in the eight Tor River area villages. After working through *Primer One*, we announced a one-week break. A couple of the tutors had found it too difficult to keep up, so replacements were found. In early November, we ran the Phase Two course. Though we had made announcements ahead of time, the tutors were surprised when we opened the class on Monday morning. "Now that you're familiar with how to use your teachers' guide, and you know your students' abilities, during this two-week course, we're going to do more than prepare you to facilitate the reading and writing classes. We've added two more ways in which you can help the people in your villages: health and supplies." It was a great encouragement to us when every tutor broke into a big smile. We knew they were receptive and would promote these new community development plans in their villages.

By the end of the Phase Two tutors' class, each tutor was ready to begin an under-fives health program in their village—weighing the youngsters, making and using flip charts about health and nutrition, and teaching mothers how to feed their children so they'd gain weight.

In addition, having made all the preparations in advance, we were able to assist each tutor in setting up a small *toko* (store) in their village. It was necessary to spend several hours having them practice making change and becoming comfortable handling money.

Moving Toward Our Goal

Yes, we were excited that all these activities with the tutors were moving us on toward reaching our literacy goals. And we were thrilled that after three weeks' work on the airstrip, it was in tip-top shape again. Peter was elated that since his first office had been taken over by the jungle—there were termite nests everywhere and vines growing over, around, and under the whole building—he had a new office built with ironwood posts, an office that would resist termites' sharp teeth. This new office was designed to be large enough to be used by university students and church interns who might come to stay with us to try out and study village life. Evidence that we were settled in for the long haul was given by the cucumbers and peppers in our new garden that were blooming and the beans and watermelon vines that were also doing well.

But we were most deeply satisfied and encouraged by reaching our first milestone in the area of our primary reason for being with the Berik in the first place: translating the New Testament into their heart language. One morning, Peter told me, "Sue, I'm so glad that even though we were kept extremely busy in administration during our last term in Indonesia, Essau and I were able to translate the first six chapters of the *Gospel of Mark* before we left on furlough. I've been praying about it, and I feel God wants me to set a goal of translating the remaining 10 chapters by April. Let's pray about which of our translation assistants will be available."

"WOW, Peter, that's great!" I responded. "I know you've already been studying the next chapters using the *Interlinear Greek New Testament* and Beekman's book, *Translating the Word of God*. What books on *Mark* do you have?"

"I've been digging into Wycliffe's *Exegetical Helps on Mark* and *A Translator's Handbook on the Gospel of Mark* that was put out by the United Bible Societies. It's fabulous that we have so many aids available."

"It sure is. Well, I'll try to protect you from interruptions while you translate. I'm ready to start working on the 'back translation' of chapters one to six. And I'll look forward to getting the next chapters after you draft each one." A back translation is an essential element in the Scripture translation process. Peter and Essau had drafted the first chapter of *Mark*, so I sat with a different Berik person, and we read the chapter in Berik and talked about what it said and meant. Then, without reading any version of the *Gospel of Mark*, and without referring to any commentaries or translation helps, we translated the chapter, story by story, back into English, writing down only the meaning we found in Peter's draft.

Peter's task was then to take the English back translation and compare it with the Scripture, looking for omissions, extraneous thoughts, and any areas where the meaning shown in the back translation wasn't clear. Going back to the translation desk, he'd then make the needed revisions.

After working all through September, October, and November, translating and revising the *Gospel of Mark*, the book was ready to be checked by a consultant. Kori had progressed quickly in his reading abilities and was thrilled to be included in checking the first Berik Scripture book. March 11, 1986—the day Kori, Peter, and the consultant completed checking all 16 chapters of *Mark*—was a day to celebrate. *Thank You, Father, for bringing us to this milestone. We trust You to carry us through to the end.*

Christmas and David's "Sneak"

A picnic at Pickle Falls on Mt. Cyclops—the 7,000-foot mountain towering over David and Scott's school—was just one of the fun activities in which we were involved with our boys in December 1985. We took part in and/or attended every school event: the band concert, the seventh-and-eighth-grade banquet, the dorm party, the evening of adult roller-skating, the school Christmas program. It was important that the kids spend time with their families in the interior villages, so a five-week break was scheduled over the Christmas-New Year holiday.

Our family went to Somanente for Christmas week. Since we were still very much a part of the lives of the villagers in Tenwer, the first hamlet where we lived in Berikland, we spent Christmas evening and overnight there. After the joyous Christmas church service with the believers, we strolled along the path under a star-studded sky to a newly built thatched-roofed hut and snuggled down to sleep on the bark floor, happy indeed for an air mattress. In the morning, we visited each of the 12 Tenwer homes, shook hands with everyone, and rendered blessings for the year—1986. Scott and I rode in a dugout canoe to return to Somanente while Peter and David walked the trail, with mud oozing up past their ankles.

We were at Danau Bira for New Year's Day and for David's "eighth-grade sneak" in March. Each year, the time and place for the sneak was kept secret from the eighth graders. On Friday afternoon, they were called out of class and told to pack their swimsuits and clothes for four days in a cooler place. The 11 classmates boarded the planes, not knowing their destination but were delighted when they landed at Danau Bira. Some of the kids hadn't been there before but had heard great stories of all the water sports available. Cookouts and skit nights filled out their busy schedule.

Blessings and Difficulties

Oh no—computer problems! My friendship with my computer came to an abrupt halt just before Christmas. I had a lovely little room where I could work on the second floor of our SIL office building when we were in town. It had louvered windows, and the wood floor and the plywood walls and ceiling were varnished. Before I left the building on Friday afternoon, I swept the floor, checked for spiders and their webs, and shut the windows tight. To my surprise, when I returned Monday morning, ants had invaded the room. I was able to trace their route on the outside walls of the building up to the second floor from the ground below. Those pesky creatures had squeezed in through the windows and set up their mega city inside my computer. Our colleagues in the computer department tried to blow them out—to no avail. Evidently, the acid from so many little bodies and legs destroyed the memory board. We wound up having to send the board to the States and didn't get it back until May.

But I had plenty to keep me busy and was able to work on a group computer. While Peter had been diligently progressing in translating *Acts of the Apostles*, I worked on the back translation. Two ministries took me on trips to the highlands. The biennial medical-nursing seminar gave a needed boost to my nursing skills, and I was elected chairman for the 1988 seminar. And it was satisfying and rewarding for me to be able to serve as a literacy consultant for a missionary from another mission.

But most of our time was once again spent in the village. We ran Phase Three of the tutors' course, presenting *Primer Three* and *Teachers' Guide Three* to them. Unfortunately, we could only run the course for tutors from two villages.

A difficult situation of unrest had developed in the villages near the headwaters of the Tor, and the tutors thought it best to not travel downriver for class. The three non-Berik teachers felt concerned for their safety and chose to move out of the area. Needing to protect the people, the government's appropriate response to the unrest was to station a small military contingent in Somanente as a deterrent against the troublemakers. Many of these friendly soldiers visited us in our home, and Peter enjoyed responding to their request to hold English classes for them. However, in February and March 1986, military helicopters made increasingly frequent flights to our village, raising the number of personnel stationed there.

We praised the Lord that we were able to live in the village and continue our ministry. God was actively at work in Berik gallbladders. The church continued to grow numerically, and by the end of April, a total of 220 Berik believers had been baptized, publicly declaring they had taken hold of Jesus.

Unexpectedly, at 1:15 p.m. on May 1, 1986, our lives and plans changed drastically. *Oh Lord, what's Your plan? What's happening? Where are we going? When will we be back? Be with our Berik friends and all that love You. Hold them tightly in Your keeping. We ask You, in Jesus's Name, to be with us all. Amen.*

Evacuation

May 1, 1986

I know the plans that I have for you, declares
Yahweh. They are plans for peace and not disas-
ter, plans to give you a future filled with hope.
                    —Jeremiah 29:11, Names of God Bible

*F*ather, we know You want the Berik people to have Your Word in the language that best speaks to their hearts. When, Lord? How can it happen if
we're not even in the village?

As the number of soldiers in Somanente increased in February and
March 1986, some of the Berik people shared with Peter that they were
frightened. In early April, the military helicopters were often making daily
visits, bringing in more equipment and personnel. In fact, a full battalion
was now living in their compound near the airstrip.

We asked ourselves, "What if we have to leave the village quickly?
What IF we have to evacuate?" We knew of recent incidents in other Asian
countries when our colleagues had had to do just that. We committed ourselves to God's powerful hands and prayed about what, if anything, WE
should do. We felt God's leading to be prepared.

Peter said, "Let's make a list of the essential nonreplaceable items in
our house, the things we really don't want to lose." Our list was, of course,
mostly made up of our language, literacy, and translation materials that
we had been working on, items of which there were no backups stored
elsewhere.

Examining our list, we saw that everything could fit in two cardboard boxes—one for me and one for Peter to carry, if ever necessary. So we

divided the list, agreeing that should we determine we had to leave, or if we were asked to leave quickly, we would each pack our box, tie it shut, pick it up, and go. We chose two sturdy boxes that we knew wouldn't be too heavy for us to carry ourselves, put the boxes on the bed frame in Scott's bedroom, cut two appropriate lengths of string and laid them by the boxes, and put a list of planned contents in each box.

On Thursday, May 1, the fourteenth anniversary of our arrival in Indonesia, at 10:40 a.m., I was in the middle-school building by the airstrip, teaching a Phase Three session of the tutors' training course. Mr. Jon, a Christian worker from town who was functioning as our literacy supervisor, was assisting me. Suddenly, a representative of the commissioner's office and two military officers entered the classroom and approached me. Speaking softly, they said, "You and Mr. Peter, Mr. Jon, and Ms. Yennie need to leave. The helicopter will be back in 30 minutes. You all need to be on it." They turned and left.

I faced the room full of tutors, with whom Peter and I were so close and whose faces revealed shock and dismay and fear. I shared what I had been told. "Stay close to Jesus," I said. "Trust Him. Pray that Mr. Peter and I will be able to return soon. We will be praying for you."

I quickly picked up all my teaching materials, left the building, and jumped on my bike that was leaning against a palm tree right outside the door of the schoolroom. As I leaned forward on my bike, racing down the length of the airstrip on the grassless path in the center of that jungle runway, I imagined I looked like Dorothy's vision of Ms. Gulch riding her bike on a path in the *Wizard of Oz*. The millions of thoughts running through my head kept pace with my frantic race to Peter's office where he and Ms. Yennie, a university intern, were working. *It's happening. Lord, You prepared us. Thank You. Will Peter believe me? Will we be able to pack those two boxes in the 25 minutes that are left? Will we be able to say good-bye to our friends? Where are they taking us? Will we see the boys? Can we get word to the outside world before we go?*

Though out of breath when I arrived at the office eight minutes later, I managed to speak calmly. Peter believed me. Peter and I and Ms. Yennie prayed for peace and to be able to quickly and quietly remember to take care of all that we needed to do. Peter said, "Yennie, pack your things and meet us at our house. Sue, let's get right home. Quickly pack up your box. Before I pack mine, I'll use the SSB in your office at home, see if I can get hold of a pilot who may be in the air, and ask him to notify our SIL office in town about what's happening."

At 10:55 a.m., Peter called on the SSB, "This is Peter in Somanente. Does anyone copy me?" God provided. A pilot answered immediately, "Go ahead, Peter. I copy."

"This is Peter Westrum. My wife and I, Mr. Jon, and Ms. Yennie were just told we'll be evacuated from here by military helicopter in 15 minutes. We don't know our destination. Please notify SIL. I'm going to shut down this radio now and pack it away. Thanks for your help."

"Roger, copy that. I'll notify SIL. Praying for you, brother."

Wondering why I had left class and rushed home so quickly, Berik people had begun to gather at our house. Peter turned off the SSB and began to disconnect it from the battery and antennae. A Berik boy shimmied up the palm tree and took the antennae down. Peter rolled it up carefully and placed it with the radio in my 50-gallon medical-supply drum that was right there in my office.

By then, following the list in my box, I had finished packing and tying it up. I was ready to go. Noting we had 10 minutes left, as Peter was packing his box, I greeted Magdalena who had come to be with us. I opened the fridge door and instructed her to take all the food and distribute it to the villagers. As we were doing this and Peter finished packing his box, Ms. Yennie arrived at our house, and we heard the helicopter come—and leave again. We looked at each other and said, "I guess we have more time."

Bular

Bular, Magdalena's husband and the man who was always available whenever we needed him, appeared by my side, eager as always to help. He never had excuses or something else to do if we sent for him to help with language work or a physical task needing attention. He was the one in our early years who would sit with us and repeat words over and over, like the tape recorder, if we asked. Even late in the evenings, when we needed something, Peter could stand on our front porch and call out, "Buuu-lar! Buuu-lar!" Within minutes, Bular would come running. Dear Bular, there he was with us. I told him what had happened in the classroom and that we had to leave, but we would do everything we could to come back soon.

Then we heard some activity outside. We saw about eight soldiers surrounding our home, standing with their backs toward the house and holding their rifles pointing into jungle in the back and toward the path in the front of the house. Evidently, they had reason to believe some of the troublemakers were in the area. Bular started to cry, at first just tears, and then between sobs, he said, "I'll never see you again." We went to him. As Peter held him, trying to comfort him, my heart broke; my eyes filled with tears. Peter shared with him that since he had taken hold of (believed in) Jesus, and Jesus was sitting well in his gallbladder (living in his heart), Jesus would always be with him. Peter urged him to keep trusting and praying to Jesus. Through his tears, Bular nodded and managed a weak smile.

When a group of six armed soldiers arrived, stating they would accompany Ms. Yennie and us to the airstrip, we said good-bye to everyone who had gathered in our living room. Bular stayed in the kitchen, not wanting to watch us leave. The soldiers surrounded us—two in front of us, one on each side, and two following us as we walked the equivalent of three or four city blocks to the commissioner's office. Mr. Jon was there, waiting. The four of us were not permitted further contact with the people while we waited for the helicopter to return. We just sat there not talking, each of us withdrawn into our own world. We realized the government was taking all means available to them to protect us from any harm. We were not, of course, privy to any intelligence they had.

Meanwhile, Out in Town

The pilot had been successful in alerting our Irian director in the SIL office in Jayapura. Amazingly, he was on the phone right then at 11:00 a.m., talking with our branch director in Jakarta, who had called to receive prayer requests for a prayer meeting that was about to take place in Jakarta. Is there any wonder I have no doubt that God answers our prayers even before we ask?

The two men prayed on the phone together and then discussed contingency plans. They had no way of knowing if the threat to evacuate us was legitimate or bogus. There was, after all, increased unorthodox activity on the island, and crisis management personnel had recently been dealing with the abduction and even death of mission personnel in another country.

Having been told that we'd be on a helicopter leaving Somanente about 11:15 a.m. and knowing that it was about a 45-minute flight to Jayapura, when we were not on the next military helicopter that landed at the Jayapura airport at 12:00 noon, contingency plans were put into effect. The principal at David and Scott's school, their teachers, and the dorm parents were alerted. Plans were made to care for our boys if we never showed up. Aviation personnel were put on standby at the airport, watching both military helicopters and private aircraft as they arrived.

Back in Somanente

The helicopter came back at 1:00 p.m. We were stunned as we watched the huge double doors of that massive helicopter open while the enormous blades were still spinning *whap-whap-whap-whap* at what seemed like full speed. A dozen soldiers somersaulted out of the open door and onto the ground and laid belly down, surrounding that noisy machine with their rifles ready and pointing away from the chopper.

As soon as they were on the ground, the soldiers guarding us shouted, "Hurry! Come now. Get in the helicopter!" About four dozen soldiers formed a corridor for us and our six guardians to walk through to get from the commissioner's office to the windy beast. Soldiers standing just inside the doors took our hands, pulled us inside, and motioned for us to sit down. They immediately closed those large doors while I looked around to see where we were supposed to sit. There was nothing but boxes and crates inside. I didn't see any windows. I sat on a crate near the door, as did Peter, Ms. Yennie, Mr. Jon, and several soldiers. It was too noisy to converse.

As the noise increased and I felt the helicopter lift off the ground, I closed my eyes. And prayed. *Father, You promised to always be with us. You've never let us down. I believe You're here now, on this helicopter with us. I trust You. I give myself to You again now. We don't know where we're going or what's going to happen next. We don't know if we'll ever be in the village again, or if we'll see the Berik people again. Father, protect them. Keep the rebels away from them. Give Bular and Magdalena and all our friends and the believers Your peace, that peace that passes understanding.*

Lord, You've given us everything we are and have and own. It's really all Yours. You gave us our wonderful house in Somanente. I give it back to You. I give You our living room furniture and the lanterns that are hanging there now between the living room and my office, between the living room and our kitchen. I give You our dishes and silverware and the pots and pans, the refrigerator, the stove, and all the kerosene that keeps them and the lanterns running. I give you the table and chairs, all the food left in the pantry, and the water filter from Switzerland. I give You all the medicines and medical equipment, my books, and the battery for our SSB.

It's all from You, given to us to help in our work here. If we're not coming back, I pray the people will get good use out of it all. If Your plan is for us to come back again, preserve what You want for us and help us replace whatever gets put to use elsewhere. Lord Jesus, I give you all our clothes, bedding, mattresses, and mosquito nets. Perhaps there's someone who needs them worse than we do.

Everything, Lord. It's all Yours in the first place. I release any claim I've made on it all. Thank You for the firm assurance I have that You're in control. Show us Your plan for what's coming next. I accept whatever it is. I look forward to learning what You've got up Your sleeve now. I smiled at my audacity in thinking or praying something like that. *Thank You for hearing me.*

Landing Excitement

My time of thinking and prayer must have taken about 40 minutes, for suddenly, it was 2:00 p.m., and we were landing. The motion of the copter stopped; the pilot turned off the engine. It was quiet. One of the soldiers opened the big double doors and smiled at us. Immediately, one of our SIL pilots stuck his head in the doorway and said to the soldier, "We'll take them." Then calling out to us, "Hurry, get out. Quick, come right away." I was puzzled by the urgency with which he spoke. We each picked up our one box or suitcase, and looking out, saw one of our SIL aviation trucks stopped next to the door. There were four or five of our aviation colleagues standing ready to help us and to put our things into the truck and quickly drive away to the SIL hangar. We found out later that there had been concern that we would be taken away and held for interrogation somewhere. But no one stopped us. We were released, free to go into the arms of our colleagues. *Thank You, Lord!*

The aviation personnel peppered us with questions and expressed their relief that we had arrived safely back in town. One of the pilots gave us a quick explanation of the concern and prayer that had been generated on our behalf. Then they took us up to the school where we were reunited with David and Scott, who were surprised to see us earlier than expected. They weren't aware of all the excitement that had been going on during the past several hours. Housing was provided for us in one of the mission guesthouses on the hill where the school was located. *Thank You, Father, for taking care of us—again.*

Weren't You Just Terrified?

On Sunday when we met with our colleagues, missionaries from other missions, and most of the students from the school, we were united for a wonderful time of worship and praise. There was an air of excitement, with many thanking God for our safety. I myself was surprised with my answer when one lady came up to me and asked, "Weren't you just terrified on Thursday when you were evacuated?" I just looked at her and sincerely thought, reaching deep into my heart for the answer. "No," I finally said, "I was never afraid. I realize now, thinking about it, that God gave me a wonderful gift—His perfect peace. It never occurred to me to be afraid." Truly, I had felt safe in God's keeping the whole day and was somewhat perplexed by all the excitement.

Was that strange? Or was I just experiencing the normal Christian life? Philippians 4:7 (English Standard Version) says, "And the peace of God, which surpasses all understanding, will guard your hearts and your minds in Christ Jesus." What an amazing God we know and serve, a God who brings His Word to life in the adventures of life He gives us.

Father, show us Your plan now. Show us Your purpose in having us evacuated from Berikland just when the literacy campaign was flourishing and the first book of Scripture was approved to go to press. Show us how You'll bring good out of all this.

One Thousand in Ten

April 1986 to April 1987

But Jesus looked at them and said,
"With man this is impossible, but with
God all things are possible."
—Matthew 19:26, New International Version

Yes, we were evacuated—taken away from the focal area of our ministry, 14 years to the day after we first stepped onto Indonesian soil, but God was in control. The evacuation was:

- unexpected, but we weren't unprepared,
- leaving for the unknown, but we weren't frightened,
- something to write home about, not an everyday event,
- serious, not a time for loud talking and joking,
- an interruption in our plans, but not in God's,
- a trial, an opportunity to show our confidence in God's guidance and protection.

We experienced the truth of Philippians 4:7. The peace that we felt as we left the Tor area—not knowing where we were going or what was going to happen to us, wondering if our house and everything in it would be destroyed—was supernatural.

The timing of our unscheduled helicopter flight to Jayapura delightfully put us back with our boys a few days earlier than expected. End-of-the-school-year celebrations were in the air. We felt so proud of Scott as he played both a duet and a solo in his piano recital. Our buttons burst as we listened to David play a solo on his french horn and join the 11 eighth graders who played a special number during the annual school band concert. Peter and I enjoyed the graduates' banquet and all-day picnic-waterskiing events, our chance to fellowship with the other missionary parents.

In April, when the consultant checks on the *Gospel of Mark* in Berik were completed and Peter had made the needed revisions, I was thrilled to type the corrections into the computer. Those computer floppy discs had been number one on our list of items to take with us when we were evacuated. On Monday, May 5, we brought the discs to the printshop, and in June, we held the published book of *Mark* in our hands for the first time. *Oh Lord, this is so very special. We're trusting You for the day when we and our Berik brothers and sisters will hold and hug and dedicate the whole Berik New Testament to You. Keep us going, Father. Enable us as we dream about that coming day. We ask You, in Jesus's Name.* All our SIL colleagues rejoiced and praised God with us, at our Sunday evening group meeting, for the completion of *Mark's Gospel.*

David Goes to High School in PNG

There was no English-speaking high school in Irian Jaya. However, our SIL colleagues across the border in Papua New Guinea (PNG) provided a fine high school education for English-speaking students. David and his friend, Jeff, were eligible for admission. Together with Jeff's parents, Rex and Judy, we decided to travel at the end of June to take our sons to PNG and get them settled in their new environment. We took vacation time to make this trip, toured a gold mine and coffee plantation, and had time to become familiar with the school, David's teachers, and the lifestyle at Ukarumpa, the highlands center where the high school was located. Leaving David behind in another country when we returned to Irian was a new stress to face. But David and Jeff seemed ready for their new adventure, and we consoled ourselves with the knowledge that the boys would come home for two weeks in September.

Thermometers

Scott settled into his life at school in Jayapura, and Peter and I began a concentrated period of time translating at Danau Bira. Peter continued his work on *Acts of the Apostles*, and I got started on the *Gospel of Matthew*. One of the interesting discoveries Peter made when he was translating the

Gospel of Mark, and which he confirmed as he worked on *Acts,* was that there was no single word in Berik to express many common Biblical words and key terms, such as "believe," "grace," "forgive," "prophet," "pastor." One day when Peter and Essau were translating *Mark* 2:15b (English Standard Version) "many tax collectors and sinners were reclining with Jesus and His disciples," they were challenged as they searched for one Berik word for the one word "disciple."

"Mr. Peter," Essau explained, "we must say *'angtane Yesus aa jei ne tikwebaatinnenerem.'*" As we learned more about the Berik language, we realized that that was indeed the correct way to express the meaning of "disciple" in Berik. The literal translation is "a person who follows Jesus."

Realizing that translation would be a time-consuming task as we searched for accurate equivalents and knowing we needed frequent encouragement to keep us going, we decided to make "progress thermometers." Since the books we were working on were quite long, I got started right away making two thermometers, one for *Acts,* which has 1,007 verses, and one for *Matthew,* which totals 1,076 verses. Taking eight-and-a-half-by-11-inch pieces of paper, I drew a large thermometer in the center of each page. I colored the bulb on the bottom red and calibrated the column above with 100-verse segments. Each time we drafted another 100 verses, we'd color the segment red. We set a goal of each translating 10 verses a day for a total of 100 verses a week. We took the thermometers with us and hung them on the wall wherever we were working—in the village, at Danau Bira, or in Jayapura. As the months went by, our colleagues began to join us in watching the columns turn red.

Several of our pilots were based at Danau Bira and were a major encouragement to us when we were there. Every morning, Peter and I would sit in our red canvas hanging chairs on the front porch of our Danau Bira house and have a sharing and prayer time together. Whenever a pilot would see us sitting there as he walked along the path on the way to the hangar in the morning to get started for the day, he would call out, "Praying for you each to make 10 verses today." When we saw him at the end of the day, he would ask, "How many verses did you translate today?" *Thank You, Father, for our faithful colleagues who consistently minister accountability and encouragement to us. Thank You for the sacrifices they are making to enable Your Word to be made available for the people of this province.*

What's the Word for "Go" in Berik?

Just ask a Berik person who speaks both Berik and Indonesian, "What's the word for 'go' in Berik?" and he or she will give it to you. Simple, right? Not.

"Go." A simple verb. Necessary. Used daily. Useful. Peter learned how to say, "I'm going to Abraham's house" (*Ai Abrahamem jinap tini*). Easy. No problem. I memorized it, and then when I left our house, I said to the Berik people sitting in our living room, "*Ai Essaum jinap tini*" (I'm going to Essau's house).

"*Wowo* (No)," they said. "*Ai Essaum jinap jafna*," they corrected. Surprise. The verb changed. What's going on?

I went back in the house and told Peter what had happened. Together, we went to the living room and inserted village names in the sentence. We tried, "I'm going to Duncan." "*Ai Duncanwer tini*," they responded. How about "I'm going to Winimasi." The correct form: "*Ai Winamasiwer jafna*."

"OK," I said to Peter, "let's try, 'I'm going to Safrom.'" Answer: "*Ai Safromwer aulna*." Amazing. Three different ways to say a simple "go." "Peter, how can we possibly know which word to use? We've a mystery on our hands."

Magdalena solved it for us when we were next by the lake at Danau Bira. I wanted her to go to the guesthouse to get something for me. So I said, in Berik, "Please to the guesthouse for me *go*." Berik verbs are expressed at the end of Berik sentences, so I paused and waited for her to tell me which verb to use.

She looked puzzled and then asked, "Which way does the water go?" I explained that the lake was fed by a river from the west, and the outlet was at the east end of the lake. Puzzle solved. After only a few minutes of discussion with this brilliant girl, we learned that:

- *tini* is used when going in a downstream direction.
- *jafna* is used for going upstream.
- *aulna* is used when crossing a small stream on your way to your destination.
- *artini* is used when crossing a river and mountains on the way.
- *sofwa* is used in a general way.
- *gwina* is when you are going a very long distance.

Oh Lord, I need You to help me master this language You created. Help me remember all this! Help me to make the correct choice whenever I translate a verse with the word "go" in it.

Learning how to use the six Berik verbs for "go" was, of course, helpful for Peter as he translated *Acts*. In November, he finished the translation and initial checks with Berik people who hadn't been involved in drafting it. In December, he worked with two Berik helpers to complete a check of the book by our colleague, Bob, who was by that time trained as a translation consultant. Hurrah! Two of the 27 New Testament books were ready for the people.

"HIS" School

In the fall of 1986, SIL signed a new five-year contract with the Indonesian government. With one voice, we all praised God that we would be able to continue our work for the coming five years. This agreement also provided the way for SIL to move ahead with plans to build and oversee a Christian English-curriculum high school for our children in Jayapura. It was projected that the school, situated on a 12-and-a-half-acre campus, would open in August 1987 with 45 students, including our David. This was especially good news for the 30 translation teams who were now ministering to 30 different people groups in Irian. Our children, including Scott, would never need to go out of country to school. The school, which was named HIS (Hillcrest International School), would serve international students from all the missions serving in Indonesia. Known as TCKs (third culture kids), the children of international families are unique. They develop a world view that blends their parents' culture with the culture where they live, creating a distinctive third culture.

Be Sure It Sounds Like Berik!

Magdalena and Bular were living with us at Danau Bira that fall of 1986. Magdalena and I worked together to translate *Matthew*, drafting one segment, about 10 verses each day. One of our major goals was to ensure that our translated verses sounded like Berik. It's essential that each translated verse not only be accurate but it must be faithful to the structure or grammar of the receptor language.

For example, consider *Matthew* 9:22 from the International Children's Bible: "Jesus turned and saw the woman." By translating the verse, word by word, following English grammar, this would be the result:

Jesus	turned	and	saw	the	woman.
Yesus	*irfwena*	*x*	*domola*	*x*	*wini.*

The problem is that "*Yesus irfwena domola wini*" is very bad Berik; the meaning would not be understood by Berik speakers. Berik has no equivalent word for "and" and "the," and it has its own rules. The natural grammatically faithful translation of *Matthew* 9:22 in Berik is: "*Yesus ga irfwena, jei wini jeiserem ga jes domola.*" Consider the outcome when translating that sentence back into English, word by word, following Berik grammar:

Yesus	*ga*	*irfwena*	*Jei*	*wini*	*jeiserem*	*ga*	*jes*	*domola.*
Jesus	x	stood	He	woman	that	x	her	saw.

"Jesus stood, he woman that her saw." Berik has an obligatory story marker, "ga," which we don't have in English. An interesting particle, Peter actually wrote a linguistic paper about its function and use in the Berik language. The Berik sentence also displays mandatory pronouns—one referring to Jesus and one to the woman—and the verb is at the end of the sentence. Finally, notice that though Berik has no word for "the," it's necessary to use "that" to specify the woman. And so Magdalena and I labored on day after day, and God gave me an ever-increasing understanding of Berik grammar.

Life was good at Danau Bira. All our translation helpers loved it—loved the change of scene, the lake, and plentiful fish to eat. But it was tiring for each Berik person who came to help us, so we had each pair stay just a month at a time. When Magdalena and Bular went home, Niko and Sekarias replaced them. I was thus able to check the draft passages of *Matthew* and, in November with yet another pair of helpers, was able to complete a consultant check of 10 more chapters of *Matthew*.

Because of continued military buildup in the Tor River area, even as the end of the year approached, we were not permitted to return to live with the Berik people or to celebrate Christmas with them in the village. However, we continued to experience God's perfect peace, and we praised God that the pilots were permitted to fly in and out of Somanente and the Berik people were allowed to leave and return, enabling them to help us away from the language area. How awesome is that? We learned that the literacy classes had continued in two Berik villages, those closest to the mouth of the Tor River and farthest from the headwaters where the unrest had begun.

Peter and I also relished the fellowship with other English speakers we could have when at Danau Bira, such as Sunday group worship times and Saturday game and movie nights—one special memory being when one of our colleagues acquired the whole movie series, *Roots*, for our enjoyment. To the delight of the indigenous people living at the center, we provided popcorn for the crowd each week. I relaxed by playing the piano in the afternoons and, during two music nights, enjoyed accompanying another translator as he played his clarinet.

Distressing Letter

On Thanksgiving Day, Mother wrote an angry, distressing letter to me. I received it in mid-December, the day that David and Scott arrived at Danau Bira for their Christmas break. Mother was suffering from severe depression again and vented her anger toward me. I was quite disturbed by it and just couldn't bring myself to respond while the boys were home. I didn't want to interrupt my precious time with them to spend the hours I felt I would need to write to Mother. At the end of January 1987, when I was in town seeing David off to school again in PNG, I phoned her and was able to express our love and concern. In the coming months, Mary, her husband, Peter, and I prayed and discussed the situation. God gave us peace for me to make a trip to LA to be with her in the fall. During the summer, we presented our plan to her and thanked God that she was recovering from the extreme episode and was receptive to have me visit, even offering to cover the costs of my air ticket. *I thank You, Lord, for Your every provision!* The three weeks we had together in September were pleasant, our relationship basically restored—once again.

Christmas Break

Because the Ukarumpa school year in PNG ran from January through December, David had a six-week break for Christmas. Peter and I went to Jayapura to take part in one week of Christmas activities at Scott's school—including his piano recital—and to meet David who arrived in time to attend the band concert of which he had been a part the previous year. Then we were off to Danau Bira together for five weeks. Our whole family delighted in having Magdalena and Bular and our new prayer partners with us. They all joined in much of the fun designed to refresh us after the previous intensive months. A scavenger hunt. Baking and exchanging cookies.

A treasure hunt. A Dani feast. Times of worship and singing. A center-wide party on December 31.

In January, Scott and David received their special Christmas gift from us—I went with them to visit Mulia, the mission station where Scott was born. Since many of their school friends were familiar with Mulia, and were at home in various other mission stations in the mountains, our sons were very eager to also experience highland life.

Your List, My List

Though the boys were on vacation for much of January 1987, we were not. We needed to spend at least parts of each day moving ahead in translation. Peter worked on polishing *Acts*—making the revisions that were found to be needed during the consultant checks. I continued on drafting *Matthew*.

One day during our lunch break, after David and Scott had returned to school, Peter said, "Sue, I've been thinking about the advice our consultant gave us that we're ready to take on the challenge of translating some of the Apostle Paul's letters." Smiling, he said, "I've made a list." There followed a pregnant pause.

"So you've made a list." Peter was silent. "What's on your list?" I prompted.

"Well, I've divided all the books of the New Testament into two lists, one for you, one for me." As Peter handed me "my" list, he added, "Are you willing to take the responsibility to translate and bring to completion all the books on your list?"

As I read "my" list—*Matthew, Luke, 1* and *2 Corinthians, Galatians, Ephesians, Philippians, Colossians, 1* and *2 Timothy, Titus, Philemon, 2 Peter, 2* and *3 John*—God spoke to me in His still small voice, *I've prepared you for this, Sue. This is the assignment I have for you.* Wow.

"Yes, Peter," I responded, "I think God does want me, depending on Him and with His guidance, to do this."

Peter showed me his list—*Mark, John, Acts, Romans, 1* and *2 Thessalonians, Hebrews, James, 1 Peter, Jude,* and *Revelation.*

And so, we began a new stage in our translation program. Peter started to study and prepare to translate *2 Thessalonians.* In February with a grin on my face, I said to Peter, "I'm ready to get going on the letters too. I'm going to do a whole book next weekend."

"OK. I get it," he said. "You're going to do all 25 verses of *Philemon.*"

"Yup." And so it was that from Thursday, February 27, to Monday, March 2, I got my feet wet delving into the Apostle Paul's way of writing.

I felt like we were on a roll. In fact, we were. We had the time, an excellent situation at Danau Bira, Berik helpers coming and going, encouraging colleagues, and most importantly God's motivating Spirit and enabling. We got into a routine of studying, translating, typing, checking, revising, typing, doing and typing the back translations for each other. This meant working on several books, each at a different stage in the process, all at the same time. It was exciting, sometimes tedious, sometimes frustrating, exhausting, wonderful, and deeply satisfying.

In March 1987, we sent the following cable (a wireless message, forerunner to the Internet) to our supporters in the US:

> PRAISE THE LORD PERMISSION GIVEN BY MILITARY OFFICIALS FOR US TO RETURN TO LANGUAGE AREA PETER OVERNIGHTED IN VILLAGE MARCH 4 AND SUE STOPPED THERE ONE HOUR MARCH 5 PRAY FOR WISDOM IN PLANNING AND REESTABLISHING RELATIONSHIPS AND PROGRAMS WITH BERIK PEOPLE PRAISE GOD FOR MUCH PROGRESS IN TRANSLATION WHILE AWAY FROM VILLAGE

After 10 months away, we were able to go back to Somanente. We never doubted God's timing or plan. Our disappointment in being evacuated from the Tor River area was God's appointment for us and His plan to give the Berik His Word. God had led and enabled us and had given us stamina and endurance. We kept our thermometers up-to-date and daily recorded how many verses we had each drafted. To our surprise, just before Easter in mid-April, we noted that in the 10 weeks since the first of February when Peter started working on *2 Thessalonians*, with the help of several different Berik assistants, we had drafted 1,036 verses, including *Matthew* chapters 21 through 28 and 10 New Testaments letters: *Philemon, 1* and *2 Thessalonians, 1* and *2 Timothy, Titus, James*, and *1, 2,* and *3 John*. Whoa! **"One thousand in Ten."** That's one-eighth of the New Testament! Through God's provisions, we had been kept completely safe; Berik language and translation helpers had been able to leave home to be with us, and for the first time, we had drafted more than 1,000 verses in 10 weeks.

After all the years of preparation and detours, God had brought us to this milestone of finishing the draft of another Gospel and of 10 New Testament letters. *Matthew,* and the 10 letters that we planned to publish in one book were in various stages of preconsultant checks and revisions. *Thank You, Father, for the great things You are doing! We thank You in Jesus's Name.*

We began to plan for five- and 10-week periods of time during which our goal would be to again translate 500 or 1,000 verses. We calculated we could then complete the draft of the Berik New Testament within the next three years. A challenging goal to be sure. We found translation to be stretching, frustrating, requiring perseverance, and that it was also tremendously satisfying and rewarding. We asked our colleagues to pray with us about this and to keep holding us accountable. Often, we did make our goal of each translating 10 verses a day. But sometimes we didn't make it because initial translation is only half the job. Checking and revising, typing and proofreading take just as long. And there are always interruptions. People need help. Administrative work. Sickness.

One afternoon at Danau Bira, I was relaxing down by the lake, and one of our colleagues expressed doubts as to whether we could finish the New Testament by the time our oldest son finished high school. She said, "Do you REALLY think you can do it?"

A couple of weeks later, one of our consultants said, "It's impossible; you can't do it in that length of time. Maybe you should change the order in which you're translating the New Testament books, in case you can't finish. Do the books that they need the most first; maybe do two of the Gospels last."

How discouraging. But he was right. It was impossible for us. But not for God, for His Word says, "With man this is impossible, but not with God; all things are possible with God" (*Mark* 10:27, New International Version).

We eagerly looked forward to how He would do it.

Finish the Task!

May 1987 through 1988

We pray that you'll have the strength to
stick it out over the long haul—not the grim
strength of gritting your teeth, but the glo-
ry-strength God gives. It's strength that endures
the unendurable and spills over into joy.
—Colossians 1:11, The Message

Peter's overnight stay in Somanente enabled precious time for him to visit with our friends, catch up on their news, and to assure the Berik people that we would be returning to live with them once again. During the hour I had in the village the next day, with a crowd of people following me and children scampering ahead and behind us, I was able to walk the length of the path where our house was located and greet the people in each residence. It was a delightful reunion. Peter and I were elated to see that our house and most of our supplies were in good shape; thus, we wouldn't be delayed by having to rebuild or repair anything. In mid-March, we spent 10 days together in the village, and though we weren't permitted to travel to the other villages, our Berik friends and tutors came to Somanente to see us and to report that the literacy classes had continued in two downriver villages. *Thank You, God, for these leaders who have carried on without us. We realize that they are responding directly to Your call on their lives.*

At the end of May, Scott finished his seventh-grade school year, and at the same time, we were delighted to have Burt, a friend from the States, come for a visit. We were all disappointed that his request to visit Somanente with us was not granted, so we made alternate plans. Peter and

Scott, and two of Scott's school friends, went to Somanente while Burt and I went on to Danau Bira where he jumped right in helping me run and understand how to use a couple of computer programs I was struggling with. It was a tremendous help to us that he also typed the needed revisions we had made to prepare *Acts* for the printshop.

UNS Checks

I worked daily on getting ready to do two UNS (uninitiated native speaker) checks of the *Gospel of Matthew* that I had finished drafting in April. Uninitiated speakers are those who have not yet read or heard the Berik translation of the verses to be checked. To prepare for the UNS checks, I needed to write comprehension questions on the passage. For example, questions regarding the story of Herod having John the Baptist killed in *Matthew* 14:3–12 might include: "Why did Herod have John the Baptist arrested?" "Why was Herod afraid to kill John?" and "Why did Herod give the order to kill John?"

When sitting with an uninitiated language helper, I would first read the entire story out loud, then ask the questions, and evaluate the helper's response—listening for misconceptions and any confusing elements. If the native speaker asked me a question instead of answering mine, I knew something was missing.

One of our colleagues had a shocking response to her question, "Why did Herodias's daughter ask for the head of John the Baptist on a plate?"

"Why, to eat it, of course" was the response. "Why else would she want it on a plate?"

All problems that are found must be corrected and the passage retyped and reprinted, before doing the second UNS check. If the back translation of a passage has already been completed, it must also be revised. All of this work can be tedious and frustrating, but knowing how essential it is to producing an accurate translation, we were able to keep plugging along day after day, month after month, always looking forward with eager anticipation to arriving at the finish line.

First Berik Scripture Dedication

On May 31, in Somanente, village church leaders and Peter held a long-delayed dedication and distribution service for the *Gospel of Mark* and the *Genesis* booklet. Peter wrote our supporters about the event:

Invitations had been sent out to the church congregations up and down the Tor River. By 9:00 a.m., believers and guests crowded into the largest building in the village to join in a combined worship service and to witness the dedication of the first two books of the Bible translated into the Berik language—the *Gospel of Mark* and stories from *Genesis* chapters 1 to 11. Attendance at the service went beyond our expectations as those who couldn't fit inside the church building leaned in through the windows to sing hymns, pray, and hear God's Word preached. Several chorus groups participated.

After the service, we went outside and had another more informal service. Our main translation helper, Essau, was not able to attend the ceremony but sent a tape-recorded message challenging his fellow Berik friends to continue in their reading and writing classes and to be sure to get a copy of *Mark* and the *Genesis* portions.

Thank You, Father, for our faithful supporters who are making it possible for us to serve here to give the Berik people Your Word in their own language, for the many language helpers who have faithfully worked with us, and for the computer programmers and printshop staff who published the books. We are so very grateful for the team You've raised up to reach the Berik people with Your Word.

The literacy tutors coordinated selling the books for a nominal fee. We had learned that the people hold greater esteem for the things for which they pay. The 50 copies they had brought to the outside service quickly sold out; 30 more were sold at the tutors' homes later that day—for a total of 80 books eagerly grasped by the Berik on the first day. God had placed a desire for His Word in the hearts of the Berik people. WOW! The tutors planned to make the books available to their students as they finished their literacy classes.

When David's one-year stint at school in PNG came to a close in June, Peter, Scott, and I joined him for school activities, celebrated his fifteenth birthday, thanked his house parents and teachers, and helped David pack his things to move back to Irian with us. We were proud of his accomplishments and his ranking sixth out of his class of 43. It was a joy for our family to be able to spend two weeks together in the village in July, observing the continuing friendships our sons had with their village friends who, of course, had also become teenagers. Sundays in the village were very special days for us as we met with Berik believers, singing Berik hymns together, and worshipping our God as some of the men led in prayer, some read Scripture, and some preached the Word.

The Enemy's Attempts to Derail Progress

Exponential progress in translation, our return to residence in the village, and the growth and vitality of the Berik church were all thorns in the enemy's plans. The first attack came in May when I suffered a severe back strain that really slowed me down for a week. Then the first week of June, as we were getting ready to make our trip to PNG to get David, I came down with shingles, the blisters decorating the right side of my face, and the severe headaches which, in the end required codeine to control, knocked me into bed. I strongly believe that our colleagues' diligent prayers for my healing resulted in the duration and intensity of the disease decreasing by 60%. Using a generous amount of makeup and a wide-brimmed sun hat, we were able to camouflage the blisters and scabs when I crossed the border on our trip from Irian to PNG. *Thank You, Jesus, that the disease didn't attack my eye!*

I wasn't the only one suffering from headaches. Peter was also diagnosed with migraines, and we thanked God when an effective medication was available to help him. Then in early August, just before school started, David came down with a severe boil in his groin, which necessitated flying him to Mulia, the medical mission station in the mountains where Scott was born, for minor surgery.

As God thwarted these attacks and we recovered, we were reminded of our first canoe trip up the Tor River when satan tried to distract and discourage us. *Thank You, Father, for continuing to motivate us, heal us, and for giving us strength and stamina in this land where You've placed us.*

After David's surgery, I went to town with him to handle the necessary twice-a-day dressing changes so he wouldn't have to miss any classes. He was excited to be attending his tenth grade at HIS (Hillcrest International School), the brand-new Irian high school, starting out with 28 students. In a letter to our partners in the US, David wrote: "We pray that HIS will truly be His, the Lord's school."

Scott was eager to start his eighth-grade year, looking forward to all the special activities planned for his graduating class and to being able to join David at HIS in the fall of 1988.

The Millstone Challenge

Though we moved around quite a lot throughout the summer, we were still able to continue working on the final revisions of the *Gospel of Matthew* and on the checks and back translations of the 10 letters, preparing those missives from the Apostle Paul for upcoming consultant checks.

At the beginning of August, I was ready to start studying to translate the *Gospel of Luke*. I found it was an advantage to work on the third of the three synoptic Gospels—*Matthew, Mark,* and *Luke*—for I could see the vocabulary we had used in the parallel passages we had already translated. Actually, it was not only an advantage but absolutely essential that we ensure consistency between identical verses and at the same time maintain each author's distinctive style. I praised God for a book by Swanson, *The Horizontal Line—Synopsis of the Gospels,* and that I was able to work diligently with little interruption on *Luke,* right through to finishing the draft of all 1,151 verses in November. Combined with *Acts,* which was also written by Dr. Luke, that's one-quarter of the New Testament. Yippee!

Words. Words. Words. Challenges. Challenges. Challenges. Many verses in the Bible can be used as examples to point out the many challenges encountered when translating the meaning of words from one language to another. In October, when working on chapter 17 of *Luke,* I again came upon the story about the millstone that we had already worked on in *Mark* 9:2 and *Matthew* 18:6: "It would be better for him if a millstone were hung around his neck and he were cast into the sea than that he should cause one of these little ones to sin" (*Luke* 17:2, English Standard Version).

For a group of people living in a remote equatorial jungle, whose way of life was completely different from the Jewish society in which Jesus lived, this one sentence presented at least four translation challenges:

1. "would be better"—There are no English-like comparatives in the Berik language. To communicate comparison in Berik, it was necessary to make two statements and add the word "very" to the second statement: "Niko runs fast. But Frank runs very fast."

2. "millstone"—The Berik had no concept of growing, harvesting, or grinding wheat, thus no

idea of what a millstone was nor the weight of one and the consequence of hanging it around one's neck.

3. "cast into the sea"—Since most Berik were only familiar with the river, they had no knowledge of a sea, and we needed to make it clear that a person thrown into the sea would drown and not just get wet and come ashore again.

4. "one of these little ones"—Who are the "little ones" referred to by Dr. Luke?

Truly, Peter and I were dependent on the Holy Spirit to lead and illumine our understanding, not only of the meaning of the Scripture being translated but also of Berik ways of expression to be sure the meaning of the original Scriptures was conveyed. For us, translating the Word of God was a challenging, satisfying, enlightening, tedious, exacting, frustrating, energizing, exhausting, revealing, and growing experience.

Throughout the fall months, we were able to spend several weeks in Somanente and were allowed to visit the other villages to meet with the tutors and to test the students who had finished the literacy course. We were pleased to see that the *Thesaurus*, which we first worked on in 1984 and which was published and distributed in 1986 was actually being used by the people. Seeing their language given equal status with Indonesian and English in that book really added to the Berik people's sense of dignity and worth.

By the end of the year, we had spent many weeks living both in the village and at Danau Bira, forging ahead with all stages of translation: drafting, checking, revising, doing back translations, revising, having a consultant check the books, revising, and preparing the text for printing. *Acts* came off the press in November. We looked forward to being with the Berik in the village for the Christmas dedication service the villagers were planning for the book of *Acts*. We needed two flights to get all four of us, our own baggage, and all the needed literacy and celebration supplies to the village for the holidays. We again had opportunities to meet with the tutors and to test their students. It thrilled our hearts to see the enthusiasm of not only the new readers but many of the villagers in three different villages as we joined with them to dedicate the book, *Acts of the Apostles*, to God.

Taking time to review all the progress thermometers, we were surprised in December to find that we had reached the halfway mark—4,000 verses drafted. We were halfway but very much aware of the detailed work still awaiting us. *Thank You, Father, for the miracles and good progress You've brought to pass these two years. Thank You that the Berik people now have the* Gospel of Mark *and* Acts of the Apostles *in hand. Thank You that Matthew and the 10 letters are moving along. We entrust the coming years, and all that still needs to be done, to You.*

Surprises

When the boys went back to school in January, we headed off to Danau Bira, attending a translation workshop where we learned to use good consultant skills. With all the Scripture several translation teams needed to have checked before printing, it would be necessary for us all to be able to check one another's translated materials. Astonishingly, we were able to finish all the consultant checks of the 10 letters so we could begin to prepare them for printing.

With this good news and progress, I wasn't prepared for satan's next tactic. Unable to derail us physically, he came after my thoughts. One day during the workshop, after Marge, our consultant, had lectured on a myriad of details that we should know and understand about the Berik language in order to do accurate, clear, and natural translation, satan came along whispering, *You'll never know all that. When the consultant looks at your work, she'll see how inadequate you are and send you home—a failure!*

I cried out to God, *Lord, I can't do this! You've given me more than I can handle. Could I stay and just serve in the medical work?* My Father was gentle with me. After a couple of days, I got up the nerve to tell Marge what I was experiencing and thinking. She assured me that she and the other consultants were there to teach and guide and to check our work to ensure a solid accurate final text. *Oh, thank You Lord, that we're not alone, that our translation projects are truly a team effort.*

Not long after that when we were in the village, Peter spread the word that he would be available to help the Berik people write Berik hymns. Surprise! On the appointed day, 75 men showed up! They didn't just translate hymns from Indonesian, they wrote their own new songs of worship in the Berik language. Needing to duplicate the words of their compositions, we held several sessions a week teaching many to type stencils and use the silk-screen method of duplication. Lots of fun—and often a big mess. How happy we were that we had brought a large supply of stencils, paper, and ink with us to the village.

When we began to find boxes and plastic containers chewed open, and we heard the scampering of little feet at night, we knew we had a new war to wage—against rats and mice in our house. But we were prepared—with three mouse traps and three rat traps. Before bed each night, Peter would set the traps. Sometimes before we were even asleep, we'd hear one or more traps go off. When we'd hear a couple more go off in the middle of the night, Peter would get up and reset the traps. In the morning, he would take the dead creatures out onto our front porch and call out the names of the village children who were waiting, hoping to be summoned to receive a morning treat. One by one, they'd race to Peter, as if rushing for a candy bar. Each recipient would run home, singe the hair off the treasured titbit of protein in the ever-glowing family fire, and roast the delicacy for himself and often for four others—each child receiving a small portion.

In April, after just one month away, we went back to Danau Bira and were shocked when we opened the front door of our house. It was already inhabited—by hundreds of cockroaches! The whole house seemed alive as those three-to-four-inch-long creatures scurried every which way as we walked in. After I sprayed roach spray all around the house, I counted 392 of the now-dead pests. *Thank You, Lord, that we had plenty of potent spray available.* We had fumigated our home. The next day, I was shocked when our neighbors called, "Sue, what did you do in your house yesterday? We've been invaded by hundreds of roaches this morning!"

"Oh no," I responded, "I guess those are the critters that successfully outran my spray can. Have you enough spray to triumph over them?"

Celebrating Our Twentieth Anniversary

The end-of-the-school-year activities in May were a yearly highlight for most mission families serving in Irian. It was a time for members of all the various missions to network and enjoy fellowship with many we only saw once a year. We attended all the sports and academic events at both David and Scott's schools, including Scott's eighth-grade graduation banquet, band concert—in which he played a trumpet solo—and, of course, his graduation exercises. David was elected president of the student council for the coming year and was pretty excited when he got his motorcycle license.

Borneo was drawing us like a magnet. It had been 20 years since we were married in that exotic land. We had returned for our tenth wedding anniversary when the boys were just six and four years old, and it was only through pictures that they were able to remember much about it. Now, at

16 and 14, we reasoned that a visit to that third largest island in the world would be more meaningful to them. Thus, we again happily accepted an invitation from our friends, the Lee family, to visit them. The highlight of our trip was observing the continuing enthusiasm of the church for evangelistic outreach in the interior. They had extended their ministry into 10 villages. We were able to visit mission stations at Mile 10, Mile 86, and Mile 93 along the national highway and also tour the national Orangutan Sanctuary.

Sefnad

In the fall of 1988 when David and Scott were busy once again in high school, we brought four Berik language helpers with us to Danau Bira to work on translating *Luke* and *Revelation* and also to take part in a writers' workshop. Each helper was trained to write stories in their own language. Two learned typing skills, and all four learned to illustrate their stories. The four melded their work into a small storybook, doing the typing and duplicating themselves.

One of the four, Sefnad, was a soft-spoken young man of slight stature, who had firmly taken hold of Jesus when God had first moved mightily among the Berik. He first worked with us as a translation helper in 1986 when we were doing the checks on *Acts*. We soon realized he was intelligent, an excellent language helper, quickly learning translation principles and procedures. During the workshop, we made extensive use of the tape recorder, and one day, Sefnad recorded a prayer. After translating it into English, we shared it with our prayer partners in the US:

O Great Father God,

I say thank You for giving today to us. Now I'm starting to work with Mama Sue. God, thank You for this work. Sometimes we don't know how to do it. So give us Your power so that we can accomplish Your work. We want to translate *Luke* today. Mama Sue and I want to write it down good. We don't always know how to write it good, this very good news of Yours, so give us Your power.

Great Father God, I don't forget what type of a person I am. Yes, I'm weak. Today I ask You to tell me which work I should do, continue the translation work or go to teacher training school in Jayapura. Please help me to decide. I believe that You called Mama Sue and Mr. Peter here to write down Your words. I believe You asked me to help them. Now help me to decide which work I should continue to do. God, whichever work You say to do, I will follow.

Oh God, help Mr. Peter and Mama Sue also to write Your words down well. Mr. Peter is working with Sostenes translating in *Revelation*. They need Your strength. We want our Berik people to be able to read Your good Word.

In Your Son Jesus's Name, I ask again for strength and power for us all as we write Your words down. I'm finished with this letter. In Jesus's Name, I pray. Amen.

Wayne

Our work during this time was greatly assisted by a supporter from the US whom we had never met before he came to Indonesia to help us. Wayne had spent 31 years in the US Air Force working in radio and teletype. After retiring, he worked part-time as a legal secretary; he was an expert typist. His skillful and loving help shaved off hours of time for us as he "mushed" Berik and English Scripture—that is typing a Berik verse with the English equivalent directly below each word—a painstakingly tedious job. He took his work seriously, getting up early in the morning for a time of prayer and breakfast, going to the Danau Bira computer office promptly at 8:00 a.m. to work until noon, when he took a break for lunch and a short rest. He worked another four hours every afternoon and delighted us in the evenings with his lovely Autoharp music. He was there during our annual branch conference, selflessly helping in the nursery. We chuckled at his description of the croaking of the frogs that serenaded us in the evenings, "When a lot of them got going, it sounded like a great choral society with a case of mass hiccups."

Concluding the Berik Literacy Campaign

In November 1988, having continued to diligently teach their students in the villages that were unaffected by the incidents of unrest two years earlier, the Berik literacy tutors called on us to do the final testing of those who had completed all five Berik primers. We estimated that since 1982, 40 to 50 Berik people had completed the course. About half of these had moved out of the area or had already received completion certificates as each course finished during the past six years. The tutors decided it was time to hold a ceremony bringing the entire Berik literacy campaign to a close. We agreed. Two planeloads of officials flew in from Jayapura. President Agus of our sponsoring agency, Bird of Paradise University, gave a heartrending presentation congratulating the students and challenging them to continue on to further perfect their reading and writing skills. He shared his own testimony of growing up in a small Irian village and progressing to his current leadership role. He signed the students' certificates of completion, which were awarded to 21 students by the officials present.

Aksamina's Commands

Shortly after we took up residence in the Tor River area, Aksamina's husband Essau began to work assisting the local governmental district officer. When the area designation was upgraded to county status, it didn't take long for the new county commissioner to notice Essau's leadership skills and to offer him a job in his Somanente office. In the early eighties, Essau was occasionally sent to Jayapura on assignment for a month or two. Then in the mid-eighties, he was asked to move his family to town for a year.

Life was tough for the family in town, and Aksamina became sick. Moving back to the village, near her family and her gardens, she soon recovered and was able to be one of the 24 tutors—the only woman—to successfully complete the literacy tutors' training course and to lead her own reading and writing class. Back in town the next year, she fell ill again, recovering quickly after returning to the village.

And then in October 1988, Aksamina was severely stricken. A month later, she was so sick that Essau had to take her to the hospital. On November 10 when Aksamina was lying on a high hospital bed, so different than the little woven mat on a bark floor that she was used to at home, she saw her family and friends standing around her, praying. She sat up, and pulling her thighs close to her chest with her arms around her legs and resting her chin on her knees, she called her family to her one by one.

To her daughter, Dorlina, she said, "Dorlina, Jesus sits well in your gallbladder. You follow Him!"

To her son, Frans, she said, "Frans, obey your dad and help him!"

And raising her head, looking straight into her husband Essau's eyes, she said, "Essau, finish the task! Don't stop! I want you to keep working with Mr. Peter and Mama Sue to finish translating God's Word into our Berik language. Essau, our people NEED God's Word in OUR language!"

And she died. She died!

Though there wasn't room for me on the plane, aviation was able to provide space for Peter to fly from Somanente the next day to attend Aksamina's funeral in town. I sent a letter to Essau with Peter, who submitted a request for an excused absence for David and Scott so they could also attend Aksamina's funeral.

Ten days later, we received a letter from Essau:

"Thank you, Mama Sue, for your letter that you wrote to me about my wife, Aksamina. I read *1 Peter* 5:10 from God's Word that you gave me. It's very true. Oh, Mama Sue, now my gallbladder is very warm. I say like this Aksa has gone ahead to heaven. In not a long time, she'll come back again with Jesus. She said like this to me just before she died, that I must not stop doing God's work. I must work with you and Mr. Peter to finish God's work He gave us. She said our people need God's Word in our Berik language.

Oh, Mama Sue, my children have started back to school. Don't forget to pray to God for us so He'll give His strength daily to me and to my children. Oh, Mama Sue, this letter is finished here. We'll meet again. From me, Essau."

God had taken one of His own to be with Him. We were all cognizant of Aksamina's death wish. We were more determined than ever to forge ahead, in God's will, strength, and power.

Joys and Challenges

1989 through March 1990

Consider it a sheer gift, friends, when tests
and challenges come at you from all sides.
— James 1:2, The Message

Ten New Testament Letters Dedicated

We were elated in January when our colleagues in the printshop notified us that the third Berik Scripture book, *Ten New Testament Letters* (*Philemon, 1* and *2 Thessalonians, 1* and *2 Timothy, Titus, James*, and *1, 2,* and *3 John*), was ready for distribution to the Berik people. They had previously celebrated receiving the *Gospel of Mark*, a book of *Genesis* stories, and *Acts of the Apostles*. And now they set out to plan a large-scale ceremony, inviting government, military, and local leaders. The day of the dedication, Berik people from several villages crowded into the new Somanente church building with all the officials. Essau conducted the entire service in Berik, including the singing of recently written Berik hymns. After the service, non-Berik-speaking people—including the chaplain for the military, the chief of police, the county commissioner's representative, and two local pastors—gave enthusiastic comments. Even though those men didn't speak or understand Berik, they strongly encouraged the Berik people to read the Scriptures in Berik. *Thank You, Father, that Your Word has found favor in the sight of these men.* Seeing the Berik people excited to have more of God's Word in Berik brought us a deep joy. Is it any wonder that I thrived in the life God had given us in the jungle?

First Drafting Workshop

Having finished drafting and doing the UNS (uninitiated native speaker) checks on *Philippians*, I was ready to attend our first drafting workshop to speed the translation of the rest of the New Testament letters. Peter and I were one of five translation teams who were able to attend. Jan and Fay, senior translation consultants who had completed a New Testament translation project in PNG, came to Danau Bira to lead us. Every morning, we met as a group, with Jan and Fay guiding us in studying the meaning of the passages we would translate with our helpers in the afternoon. It was imperative that we work with a native speaker of the language, for one of our primary translation goals was that the resulting translated Scripture be NATURAL, that the reader would recognize, *God speaks MY language.* We wanted the translation to be as delicious to the reader as a slice of hot, freshly baked bread is to a baker.

The next morning, we discussed our work as a group, sharing any stumbling blocks we had encountered, before going on to study the next passages. By the end of the workshop, we were all jubilant that more Scripture had been translated in the branch in one month than ever before. However, that wasn't all. Several of us appealed to Jan and Fay to do the consultant checks on other letters that were ready for the final check. They graciously accepted, and Fay checked *Philippians* with me.

A consultant check is an arduous, intense experience. How, you may ask, does someone check the Scripture of a language he or she doesn't speak or understand? Actually, it's quite simple. Referring to the English back translation of *Philippians* I had given Fay earlier, she first developed the questions she would need to probe to be sure the passages were exegetically correct, that is, if the original meaning of each passage had been conveyed and that there were no omissions or extraneous thoughts. The back translation helped to reveal to Fay the Berik passages and expressions that might need to be changed. Then sitting with me and Sefnad, Fay asked me a question in English, which I then asked Sefnad in Berik. He'd answer in Berik, which I translated into English for Fay. She then evaluated the acceptability of Sefnad's response that there were no misconceptions. Finally, she advised me regarding any revisions that were needed.

Remembering my encounter with satan trying to discourage me, I was particularly comforted when I received a note from Fay after she had checked *Philippians* 3:1–11 with me:

Good work, Sue. Keep it up. You feel you are going slow, but you are making good progress, and everyone is cheering on the sidelines, including the Lord, I'm sure. Hope these notes are some help. Love from Fay.

I thanked God for her and her sensitivity and for being there to help us. In fact, the workshop was such a tremendous success that Peter and I sent a letter to our directorate, thanking them and requesting that they make arrangements for more workshops and to help us finish the Berik New Testament draft within the year.

As we reviewed all the goals in the four academic disciplines—anthropology, linguistics, literacy, and translation—that consultants had guided us in setting in the seventies when we began our Berik translation ministry, we were greatly encouraged to confirm that our goals in three areas were 99% complete. Only translation goals remained incomplete. *Thank You, Lord, for orchestrating all the details these many years!*

A True Friend

To my dismay, I received another angry and vile letter from my mother. One day, I was spouting off to my friend and colleague, Joyce. I went on and on, venting my feelings. When I was finally quiet, she gently asked, "Are you angry and bitter about your mom?"

I clenched my teeth, setting my lips in a straight line, and, with a firm voice, said, "I AM NOT." Joyce didn't say another word. But God went to work on me, and finally two weeks later, I admitted that I was very angry and needed God's help and forgiveness. Joyce was—and is—a true friend. With loving courage, she was honest and gently challenged me. She was willing to say what I needed to hear, but she didn't accuse and tear me down. She confronted me with the truth, in love. To this day, I thank God for giving me such a friend.

"Went" or "Drowned"?

With Fay and Jan's help, we continued to move along quickly, meeting our translation goals. Peter finished the *Gospel of John*, and Fay helped me ensure the consistency of the parallel passages found in *Ephesians* and *Colossians*. Next came the consultant check of *Matthew*, and I completed all the revision work on *Galatians*, *Ephesians*, *Philippians*, and *Colossians*, which we published in one booklet in 1990. Fay and Jan were willing to come to Somanente with us for further checks and to guide us.

Spelling checks were another major undertaking. Just as in English, changing one letter in a Berik word can change the meaning of the word. We worked to find any errors that had escaped previous checks. We praised God when we found this one in *John* 6:16. I had typed, *Jei fonap aalbitini*, meaning, "He went and drowned in the lake," instead of *Jei fonap aarbitini*, which means "He went down to the lake."

While we were in Somanente, we were pleased to observe that the government literacy program, *Kejar Paket A*, was now functional in Berik villages. The Packet A Program was designed to teach Indonesian, literacy, mathematics, and basic technology and living skills, including agriculture, fish and chicken projects. Bird of Paradise University students had trained the Berik tutors to continue teaching Berik students who had completed the Berik primer series, enabling them to transfer their Berik reading and writing skills to learning to read and write in Indonesian. It thrilled our hearts to know that the university students had supervised the reestablishment of literacy classes, enrolling 139 Berik students from five different villages.

Planning for Interface

When HIS (Hillcrest International School) announced its plan to initiate a summer program for students who had finished their junior year of high school, we were overjoyed that David would be able to take part. The intent of Interface was that, by spending June and July in their home country, the student would be exposed to and thus better prepared for the things that would be important to them when they return for college the next year: gaining work experience, receiving a regular wage, opening a bank account, managing money, and getting a driver's license.

It was important for us to have a family meeting, so since Peter and I were at a workshop at Danau Bira, David and Scott came out to the lake for a weekend so we could make plans for the upcoming summer. We decided it would be best for David to be in the Minneapolis area where he was familiar. From there, he would be able to make a visit to Moody Bible Institute in Chicago. Next, we needed to seek a nonrelative family with whom David could live those two months. Right off the bat, we all thought of our special friends, Dave and Jan, whose son, Bryan, had been David's best friend during our last year in the US.

Visits to the US

HIS activities, including the first graduation celebrations, ended on May 23. The next day, David flew to Los Angeles for a visit with family before going on to Minneapolis to begin his Interface Program. Dave, Jan, and Bryan gave him a warm welcome. They helped him open a bank account and got him signed up for a driver's education course. They had researched possible jobs for David. He had his interview, was hired for six weeks, and started work on June 8. Back in Irian in August, in time for school to start on August 4, David shared with the leaders of Interface that it was a very positive experience for him, being part of the youth group at our supporting church and visiting family and friends. His summary statement: "The family I stayed with was a very big highlight of my whole stay. They made the whole experience quite a plus for me."

Since our family had already completed four years of our fourth term in Indonesia, and Peter and I would need at least one more year to complete the draft of the Berik New Testament, God led Peter, Scott, and me to take our one-month summer vacation in the US—for two major reasons. It was essential that we spend time with my mother. Also, we really wanted the opportunity for face-to-face contact with all our family, church, and other supporters to elicit intense prayer coverage for the coming year as we neared the finish line of celebrating the dedication of the Berik New Testament with Berik believers.

We had a calm and peaceful time with my mother and were surprised and pleased when she wanted to spend more time with me and also visit Minnesota while we were there. Peter and Scott went ahead to Minneapolis to visit our church and relatives, including Yaufun, Sharon, and five-year-old Nathan. A week later, Mother and I flew to Minneapolis, rented a car, and visited her old and dear friends. Mother flew back to LA with Peter, Scott, and me for a final two days together before we returned to Indonesia.

It had been a good visit with Mother. But I recognized that I was still in need of God's healing hand, for I suffered from headaches most days while on the trip. I realized I was tense, dreading and expecting an unpleasant event. Once we were settled in Indonesia again, the headaches were gone. I prayed for God's perfect and full healing.

What Do We Do Now, Lord?

On August 12, the Indonesian government informed our SIL leadership that they would not be extending our work agreement when it expired in April of 1991. We all felt this was disastrous news—we called it a bomb-shell. Our directorate, of course, began to make plans and dialogue with government officials.

We wondered, "How will this affect the Berik translation program and our family plans?" We had another family meeting, prayed, and asked God to show us His will. After discussing all possibilities, giving it a rest for a couple of days, and then more prayer and discussion, we decided on the following plans for the coming three years. We would:

> ➢ trust God to enable us to finish the draft of the Berik New Testament by May 1990, when David graduated from high school. We remembered Dr. Jim's advice back in 1973 when we began our work with the Berik people, "Peter and Sue, I urge you to plan your translation program so that you finish before Baby David graduates from high school. It's important that you are in the US with him at least for his first year in college."

> ➢ sell our Danau Bira house in May 1990.

> ➢ give our Somanente house to the Berik community in May 1990.

> ➢ take a 12-week trip through Asia, the Holy Lands, and Europe as we returned to the US for furlough.

> ➢ hopefully be allowed to return to Indonesia for Scott's last year of high school. It was important to him to be with his classmates and to graduate with them.

Finally, we realized that, unless the authorities changed their decision to not renew our contract, we would not be able to finish the final checks of the Berik New Testament in Indonesia. We began to investigate the possibility of bringing two Berik men to the US to finish the checks and revisions of the final six New Testament letters. Never in our wildest dreams had we ever before thought of such a thing. To pull it off would definitely be an act of God. We prayed and asked our colleagues, family, and supporters to join us in seeking God's plan.

Malaria became another major challenge to confront us in the fall of 1989. Both David and Peter succumbed. In fact, Peter experienced what turned out to be his worst episode of this disease during all our 26 years in Indonesia. Doctors treated him first with the routine drugs to which Peter had, in the past, responded. When his malaria attacks kept getting worse, they realized the parasite had become resistant to the drugs. They gave Peter nasty-tasting quinine and called for the elders to pray and anoint Peter with oil. After further consideration, the doctors decided it would be best to also give Peter the powerful drug, Fansidar. It took Peter a couple of weeks to recover. We praised God for restoring him. The malaria beast hit David a couple of months later—on New Year's Eve—and kept him in bed, in agony, for most of one week.

The Sunarjo Family Visits Indonesia

"Mom and Dad," George wrote. "We're coming to Indonesia in October (1989). It's important that Doris and our children become familiar with the country of my birth." This was great news! We hadn't seen George and Doris since their wedding in Switzerland in June 1982. But we had been in contact with them and had seen pictures of Benji when he was born in 1984, of Jonny after his birth in 1986, and finally of little Rebecca when she joined the family in 1987. But pictures, as everyone knows, aren't enough.

We were together for several days in Jayapura and then in Somanente. The Berik people welcomed them with singing, dancing, and beating of drums. Many remembered George from his first visit to the Tor River area in 1973. Little Rebecca stole everyone's heart, especially mine for she was the first one to ever call me "Grandma Sue." I loved it then and even today just love being called "Grandma."

Half a Century!

After my "unbirthday" when I turned 40 the day after my dad's funeral, I said to Peter, "I want a BIG party to celebrate my fiftieth. It seems to me that living half a century is a big deal." He responded, "I'll give you a party you'll never forget." He wasn't kidding. He brought it all together on Friday, November 17, 1989, at Danau Bira, when he elicited lots of help and planned a "*This Is Your Life*, Sue event" for all our colleagues on center. They divided the stage in our group meeting hall by hanging a curtain across center stage. They positioned me seated on one side of the curtain while mystery guests, using disguised voices, gave me clues about their identity from the other side of the curtain.

The mystery guests were our colleagues who lived in town and who had, unbeknown to me, secretly flown in to Danau Bira that day for a weekend of fun. After I correctly guessed the name of each secret friend, each of whom was dressed in a silly costume, he or she came out from behind the curtain. The audience was roaring with laughter as I struggled and needed extra clues. Toward the end, I was mystified by a distorted voice saying, "I've known you since I was born." I was completely puzzled but finally figured it out that David and Scott were also there for the celebration.

Concluding that portion of the evening, Peter said, "One more thing. Your sister Mary really wanted to be here tonight, but since it wasn't possible for her to come all the way from Los Angeles, she sent a recorded message for you." He turned on a recorder and played a lovely message from Mary. So very special—I got tears in my eyes. Then as he began to thank everyone for coming to the lake and joining in the fun and was about to announce refreshments, I heard a high-pitched, squeaky voice calling, "Hey! What about me? Don't forget me. Why do I have to always be the last one?" Even with several more clues, I couldn't imagine who it was—until the voice squeaked, "When I was seven and you were 14, I thought you'd always be twice as old as me." I couldn't believe it! It was Mary! She came out from behind the curtain, and I burst into tears. Everyone loved it. I could hardly breathe. Peter really had kept his word.

Someone had put 50 candles on the cake and managed to get them all lit before some of the candles burned down to melt the frosting. There was so much smoke when I blew out 50 little flames all at once that you can't see me in the picture that was taken.

A Dani feast, held the next day on Saturday, was happy and sad at the same time. Happy because Dani feasts were always exciting community events. Sad because it was our farewell to our life at Danau Bira. The pig killed for the feast weighed in at 241 kilos; that's 530 pounds!

For Mary's forty-third birthday on Sunday, we celebrated with an all-day party on the supply barge on the lake. Monday morning, we all flew to Jayapura—the boys back to school, Peter to work on translating *Romans*, and Mary and I were able to spend a little more time together. She had read some of the mission books about the Dani people and their great turning to the Lord. Having also been enticed by a tourist brochure about the "Wamena Mummy," she really wanted to visit the Dani area in the mountains. So Mary and I enjoyed a two-day excursion in the highlands together before she went home.

Two Berik Men to the US?

We were nearing the end of a long, joyous, trying, exhilarating, five-year-term on the field. God had led David to Moody Bible Institute for college, majoring in international ministry, starting in the fall of 1990. Scott said he'd like to return to Meadow Creek Christian School for his junior year of high school. We scheduled our next furlough to run from July 1990 to June 1991.

Believing the coming Christmas could very well be the last time we would ever be in Indonesia as a family, we all wanted to spend it with the Berik church in Somanente. Life had returned to normal, and the people were planning celebrations for Jesus's birth in a brand-new church building. It was a wonderful time as we experienced the indigenous church functioning well.

Because of the government's decision to not renew SIL's working agreement in April 1991, there was a strong possibility that we would not be able to return to Indonesia after furlough. And we realized we wouldn't be able to complete the consultant checks before leaving on furlough in May.

We prayed about it and felt we should have an in-depth discussion with Essau and his nephew, Sefnad, about the idea of having them spend six months in the US with us during our furlough. Even so we wondered how such a plan could possibly work out. *Oh Father, there are so many details that need to be worked out to bring such an audacious idea to fruition! Would Essau and Sefnad be willing and able to go? Could they get passports and visas to the US? Would there be consultants available in the US to work with us? How would Essau and Sefnad adjust to living in a house and culture so very different from all they've ever known? Are You truly leading us in this way? Show us Your will and what to do next.*

The Countdown Begins

Amazingly, all the details began to fall in place. We had described the many differences in climate and culture that Essau and Sefnad would encounter and the emotional stress of being separated from family and friends. But they prayed about it with their families, and because they were 100% committed to working toward the day of the dedication of the Berik New Testament, they agreed to the plan, even stating that they would confirm their commitment by contributing a small amount of their own funds to the costs. Our consultants and branch director put in a request for a consultant to work with us in the States, and applications were submitted for passports for the men. *Lord, it seems You are really working to make it all happen. WOW! Thank You for Your clear leading and provision.*

Peter and I worked together on the book of *Jude,* and by early December, I had finished drafting *1 Corinthians* and had started on my last book, *2 Corinthians.* In January 1990, my calendar was full of notes showing my excitement about finishing my last book: "80 verses left," "25 verses left," "15 verses left," "six verses left." And on January 24: "11:35 a.m. Sue done with all forward translation!" *Hallelujah! Praise You, Lord, for Your enabling and endurance.*

Another major event in January—we sold our Danau Bira house, also selling or just distributing all our household supplies. Our colleagues, who had been our neighbors for the past many years, blessed us with a farewell party. Saying good-bye to all but our wonderful memories, we moved to Jayapura. Fay and Jan graciously stuck with us, daily assisting as Peter finished drafting, checking, and revising *Hebrews.* By the end of February, there were only two New Testament books remaining to be translated—*1* and *2 Peter.* Since Peter had had several added assignments during this five-year term, we worked together on those books.

We had been in continual contact with Wayne and were pleased when he came to visit us again in March for a couple of weeks, this time bringing his son, Erik, along. It was a great visit, for they were both given permission to visit Somanente with us for three days.

Once again, my calendar displayed our excitement regarding our daily translation progress on the road to completion. At the end of March, I noted, "256 verses left." The word spread to all the Berik villages that the last progress thermometer was about to be filled in. What would it be like to reach that milestone? We were soon to find out.

The Last Verse

April and May 1990

Say to God, "How awesome are your deeds!"
—Psalm 66:3a, New International Version

"256 verses left," "199 verses to go," "134 left!" "109 to go!" "50 to go," "28 to go."

Thus read some of the notes I made on the April page of my 1990 calendar. Other notes recorded that Peter finished drafting *Romans* and then went right on to start translating *1 Peter* while I worked on translating and checking *2 Peter*.

The leaders of the Berik church were making use of the Scripture they already had, as demonstrated by the fact that Musa, one of our tutors and co-translators, preached on Easter Sunday, April 15, using *Luke* 24 about Jesus's resurrection as his text. Musa ignited enthusiasm in the hearts of the congregation, as did the other Berik men who were preaching that Lord's Day, saying, "We have a lot of God's Word in Berik now, but very soon, we'll have the whole New Testament in our own language. Mr. Peter and Sowenso will be translating the last verse of our New Testament next week. Plan to come to Mr. Peter's office on Thursday, April 26, to be there for this big event. We'll have a ceremony and a time of worship and praise to God for giving us all the power to accomplish His plan and will."

Since we had continued to work at the rate of each of us translating 10 verses a day, Peter had been able to calculate when he and Sowenso would be ready for the last verse. It seemed we had butterflies in our hearts and tummies all day, every day, all through the month of April. We were excited, to say the least. The Berik planned the ceremony and celebration.

We asked that John, one of our pilots, and his wife, Irene, who had been our prayer partners for several years, be invited to fly to Somanente that day to take part in the occasion.

April 26 dawned at 5:45 a.m. as usual, with a bright-blue clear sky. Berik people, coming from other Berik villages up and down the Tor River, began to gather in the homes of the Somanente villagers, chattering and gathering wood and all they'd need to cook lunch for everyone. Excitement was in the air.

John, Irene, and their two daughters, Tanya and Danielle, arrived about 10:00 a.m. They were there at this historic event to represent all the people who had been part of the Berik translation team with us for the past two decades:

- our families, friends, and supporters in the US who had prayed and given financially—many sacrificially—for 20 years to keep us on the field
- our boys' schoolteachers
- the pilots and mechanics who had flown us and many Berik people in and out of the village, cheerfully and sacrificially serving us all
- the secretaries and bookkeepers in Indonesia and in the US
- the many doctors and nurses who had aided in keeping us able to serve
- our directors and leaders
- everyone in the computer and printing departments who prepared the printed Word for the Berik
- our Indonesian friends and employees
- all the members of Wycliffe Associates who selflessly worked and contributed to our needs, through prayer, providing our linens and my microscope, the high school for our boys, hospitality during our furlough travels and were committed to raise funds to print the Berik New Testament.

As many guests as could fit squeezed into Peter's office, with a large crowd standing outside. Essau stood in the doorway so everyone could see and hear him and gave a welcome, opening prayer, and introduction to exactly what was about to happen.

Peter and Sowenso sat down at the translation desk. Peter read the first sentence of *1 Peter* 5:14 in Berik—loud enough for everyone to hear—

"Greet one another with the kiss of love" (English Standard Version), which he and Sowenso had translated the day before. Then Sowenso read the second and last sentence of that verse from the Indonesian Bible, "Peace to all of you who are in Christ." The two of them talked about the meaning of the verse, agreed on the Berik rendering, and Peter wrote the sentence in Berik.

Then Peter stood up, and Irene came forward and sat on the translation chair. Oh, dear reader, I wish you could have seen her. Serious-minded but with a look of joy on her face, at 12:45 p.m. on April 26, 1990, Irene picked up the pen, and holding it high in the air, with a flourish spiraling it down to the page, she placed a period:

- after the last word,
- of the last phrase,
- of the last clause,
- of the last sentence,
- of the last verse,
- of the last chapter,
- of the last book that we translated in the Berik New Testament.

Everyone present, inside the office and out, many with tears in their eyes, cheered and whooped and clapped and praised God for His enabling to reach this milestone, accomplishing so great a task!

We all made our way to the church building where there was room for everyone who had gathered. Several Berik men led a time of singing, worship, thanksgiving, and prayer. The congregation disbanded to village homes where they enjoyed a meal together; Pilot John and his family returned to Jayapura, and Peter and I gathered with all the tutors and co-translators for a joyful time of sharing.

Telegram

The assistant director for language programs in Irian sent the following telegram (a system of sending message over long distances by using wires and electrical signals) to our supporters abroad:

To: All on the Lord's team providing His
Word for the Berik people in Indonesia

This morning, Friday—April 27, 1990, Peter and Sue gave an important announcement during the daily check-in time for the translation teams on our single-side-band radio network. They asked us all to praise God and rejoice with them that yesterday at 12:45 p.m., the last verse of the Berik New Testament was translated!

Let us praise and thank our wonderful God for His enabling grace and many provisions for the Berik translation assistants and the Westrums as they served God in His work here. We in the administrative office join Peter and Sue in their gratitude to God that you have responded to God's prompting and have faithfully supported them through the many years in prayer, with finances, and by other helps.

With Peter and Sue, David and Scott, we who work with them here thank you for being part of the team that is reaching the Bibleless people of the world with God's Word. I know that Peter and Sue would want me to close this letter with the words of the last verse that was translated yesterday, the words that the Apostle Peter used in closing his letter (1 Peter 5:14), "Peace to all of you who are in Christ."

Buckets of Tears

Because of the government declaration to not renew SIL's work agreement, we didn't know if we'd be issued a visa to return to Indonesia after furlough. We didn't know if we'd ever again be able to be back in the village with the Berik people. They had told us that when someone comes to stay and help them for a couple of months, they have a festival to say good-bye. So they decided to have a two-day farewell for us. People began coming to our house Thursday afternoon to say good-bye. I did my best to talk to each one; many of whom brought up remembrances of our years of living in the village with them.

The next day, Friday, I thought maybe we'd have a bit of a rest day to be able to pack and slowly walk around the village visiting Berik homes to say good-bye to our friends. Early that afternoon, Mama Sara came to visit us. She threw her arms around me and began to cry the death wail, saying, "Oh, my child. Oh, my child! You're leaving me! Bwis died and left me. I'll never see her again. Bintang died, and I'll never see her again. And now, my child, you're leaving me! I'll never see you again. Maria died and left me. Now you're leaving me." That was the beginning of such emotional strain as I've ever known. My heart was breaking as I stood there holding her.

At 4:00 p.m. on Saturday, the farewell activities began with a meal and church service. The singing went on well past midnight. I said to Peter, "Do you remember that first all-night welcome celebration the people gave us in 1973?"

"Yes, of course," he responded.

"I was just thinking how different it is now. At that time, the music making was accompanied by beating drums and frenzied dancing and included a frightening high-pitched screeching by one or more participants. No one would tell us the real meaning of the words they were singing. Now I see joy on each face, with music played on guitars, accompanied by clapping and singing Berik hymns in words everyone understands, words of praise and thanks to God. Just think of what God has done—and He brought us here to watch Him work. Peter, life doesn't get better than this."

Peter had tears in his eyes and just shook his head in agreement.

On Sunday, April 29, we attended what we considered could be our last church service with the Berik. The sermon was about farewells and being apart from one another and included an admonition to not be sad. I sat there on the bench in the church, surrounded by a crowd of Berik believers, my throat choked up, and I cried—tears of joy for being with these dear people and tears of sadness, not knowing when, or if, we'd be able to experience worship with them again on this earth.

Peter was given five minutes to share, summarizing our lives with the Berik people the last 18 years! He gave all glory to God and thanked everyone who had worked with us. The chief of police, the senior military leader, the county commissioner, and Essau all reviewed the changes that had taken place all along the Tor and challenged the people to keep studying and growing spiritually.

The rest of the day involved more packing, visiting, saying good-bye . . . and attending a funeral, listening to the people wail for a baby that had passed away during the night.

We were up all Sunday night singing with the people and enjoyed watching them dance. In the morning, they surprised us by taking us down to the river and soaking us with water! Then taking us, dripping wet, they sang and danced beside us all through the village, walking with us from house to house, stopping as we shook hands, said good-bye to each person, and had a final prayer at almost every house. They cried. We cried. We all prayed.

When the plane came for us at 11:30 a.m., the pilot found that the people had lined up along both sides of the airstrip, and while the pilot waited, we shook each hand once more. Then sitting in the plane, the FINAL prayer was said.

Waiting for takeoff, I took a deep breath and realized I was numb. I seemed to be empty of physical or emotional feeling. Empty. Thoroughly spent.

Peter and I had opposite reactions to the state of our emotions that day. After the plane took off, Peter started to talk. All I wanted to do was sit and stare out the window. I didn't want to talk—or listen. Finally, I said, "Peter, I'm sorry, but I can't think. I can't follow what you're saying. I feel numb. Empty. I need to just be quiet." I know it wasn't easy for him, but I was grateful that he let me silently regroup.

Love and Rejoicing

When we arrived at the airport in Jayapura, we were exceptionally tired and exhausted. We hadn't made plans regarding where we would stay or how we'd get there. To our surprise, all the aviation personnel and Indonesian employees met our plane, laying out a red carpet for us. We were shocked. "We're here with you celebrating the completion of the draft of the first Wycliffe New Testament in Indonesia," they said. Then Pilot Dave presented Peter with an honorary pilot's certificate, reminding us of the hundreds of safe flying hours in and out of Somanente in the past 17 years. Though finding it hard to speak, Peter thanked the aviation and radio department for their valuable service and help in bringing us to this point in the Berik translation program. Then one of our Indonesian colleagues led in a stirring prayer of thanksgiving, following which everyone broke out in a song of praise.

The response of our branch colleagues on this occasion was totally unexpected and overwhelming. Friends invited us to their home for dinner that evening. It turned out to be an open house for us. Emotionally drained after leaving the people we had known and loved for 17 years, we were calmed and healed by our colleagues' outpouring of love and rejoicing. *Thank You, Father, for Your love expressed through Your body of believers.*

Typing the Last Verse

Truly, David and Scott were part of the Berik project from beginning to end. They were a bridge to establishing relationships with the people as they saw that we were parents, just like them. The boys played with and loved their children, becoming friends all through their growing up years. They learned to speak Berik. They celebrated happy events and grieved with the people in their sorrows. And then, in May 1990, David and Scott shared with all of us the joy and excitement of God's enabling us to complete the goal of finishing the draft of the last book of the Berik New Testament just before May 1, the eighteenth anniversary of our arrival in Indonesia. It had been a good life for them.

Many activities claimed our time and attention those three weeks before we departed Irian for furlough. I attended the biannual medical-nursing seminar, thankful that the information taught would be accepted as continuing education credits for me by the Minnesota State Board of Nursing. I was able to complete the consultant check on *2 Peter* and, with great pleasure, typed *1 Peter* into the computer—all except the last verse.

We saved the last verse for David and Scott to type. On May 19, at 6:33 p.m., our sons sat together on one chair in front of the computer, and David, with his left hand, and Scott, with his right, together typed the last verse into the computer.

Peter kept busy. He planned a New Testament celebration with and for the Berik people who were living in the greater Jayapura area and another for the SIL employees. Their service was a major aid in helping to complete the task.

Berik Project Officially Closed

Before we could leave on furlough, one last ceremony was on our agenda. Since we had completed all our branch-required goals in the three academic disciplines of anthropology, linguistics, and literacy; had reached the major translation milestone of completing the draft of the entire Berik New Testament; and because it was uncertain whether we would be able to return to Indonesia under an SIL contract with the Indonesian government, it was decided that the time had come to officially close the Berik project.

The closing ceremony—attended by SIL leaders, university staff, and Indonesian civic leaders invited by the university president—was held at Bird of Paradise University on May 21, 1990. Following the introductory speeches, Peter reviewed our work through university sponsorship during the previous 18 years, including several humorous stories. In conclusion, he made a presentation to President Agus, handing him copies of all our academic papers, published Berik books, and the keys to our Somanente house, thus officially returning auspices of the Berik academic work over to the university. A video summarizing the Berik work was then shown.

After 18 years in Indonesia, we were quite familiar with Indonesian etiquette. We understood that holding one's head higher than a superior is not acceptable. Thus, we were shocked when President Agus, the most senior official present at the ceremony, remained seated as he began his speech, saying, "I will not stand and raise my head higher than these two dear friends of mine. I will sit for the duration of my speech." Peter and I were stunned. We found ourselves on the emotional roller coaster once again, overwhelmed with such a public declaration and demonstration of friendship and respect.

President Agus shared that he had worked with us during all those 18 years. "I was the first interpreter for SIL," he said. "We laughed at Peter's stories, but imagine how hard it was, year after year, to study the language and to produce the results of that study as you see here today. When I was one week old, my mother, frightened by a bomb dropped on our village during World War II, jumped into the water with me. So I know what it was like for Peter when their boat capsized at the mouth of the river. I was pleased to be the one who closed the Berik literacy program, and now it's a miracle that I am the one receiving the results of Peter and Sue's work. There are 250 languages spoken here in Irian Jaya. If it took the Westrums 18 years to document the Berik language, how long will it take to do all 250? It's important to document all the languages and to provide health and education services to the people of Irian and Indonesia. I hope that our leaders in Jakarta, Indonesia's capital, will change their minds and SIL will be able to continue working in our great country."

Peter and I prayed that President Agus's desire would become a reality, even as we were in Jakarta the next week and made a presentation of all our Berik project work to an official in that great city.

David Graduates

We were both involved in the closing-of-the-school-year activities for both our sons. Scott's band concert and family sports day and picnic. David's high school graduation banquet. David's baccalaureate at which Peter and I played the organ and piano together. David's commencement exercises during which he addressed the audience as valedictorian of his class.

In a prayer letter to our supporters, we wrote:

> How well we remember that day in 1973 when our family first stepped from the dugout canoe that had carried us up the Tor River to the village where we would begin the work to which the Lord had called us. Sue was carrying Baby David. The villagers, dancing with their bows and arrows and some beating their drums, escorted us to our new home in the center of the village of Tenwer. There they continued to dance and celebrate all through the night until dawn of the new day.
>
> And now David is a young man, graduating from the international high school here . . . Please

pray for the Lord's guidance for him as he makes the adjustment from living here on the field to entering his home culture as a college student at Moody Bible Institute in Chicago.

And the Lord has brought us to this major milestone in our work with the Berik language project. It's exciting! The Lord has marvelously enabled . . . Some consultant checks, revising of the final books translated, and polishing of the entire New Testament as a whole all remain to be completed before the New Testament is approved for publishing . . . Thank you for being part of the team giving the Word to the Berik people. Thank you for standing behind us in prayer and in so many other ways as we have served the Lord here . . . Please pray for us as we plan to spend a full furlough year in the US. Pray that God will move so that we'll be allowed to return to Indonesia for at least one more year, so Scott can attend his senior year of high school with his class. We'll be bringing two Berik men with us for a portion of the year to enable us to finish the consultant checks and any necessary revisions on the last books translated.

Exhausted but full of joy, we looked forward to the adventure ahead of us with Essau and Sefnad joining us in the US and to that marvelous day when the Berik people would celebrate the dedication of their New Testament. I wondered, *If completing the draft of all the Berik New Testament books caused this much emotional turmoil for me, what will I feel when I see the Berik people holding and reading the published book?*

Our Fourth Furlough

May 1990 through July 1991

> *But Jesus said, ". . . tell them everything the*
> *Lord has done for you and how merciful He*
> *has been." So the man . . . began to proclaim*
> *the great things Jesus had done for him; and*
> *everyone was amazed at what he told them.*
> —Mark 5:19, 20 New Living Translation

From the Equator to the Arctic Circle and Home to Minneapolis

When Peter completed his two years of service with the Peace Corps in 1964, instead of traveling east to return to the US, he went west, thus making an around-the-world trip. Peter and I followed suit in 1969 when we left Borneo, and then in 1990, anticipating that this would be the last opportunity for us and our two sons to travel together, we decided to again go west, instead of east. We left Irian on May 25 and landed in Washington DC 10 weeks later on August 8.

After stops in Jakarta, Singapore, and Bangkok—which we reached by overnight express train—we made our way to the Bible lands. We thank God for our time there together—in Egypt, riding a camel by the pyramids and Sphinx, cruising on the Nile, and crossing the Suez Canal; in Israel, walking where Jesus, Abraham, Moses, and Paul walked and reading the appropriate Scriptures related to the events that occurred in each place; in

Turkey, touring underground catacombs where Christians sought refuge, and at the Acropolis in Greece "listening" to Paul tell the men of Athens:

"I was going through your city, and I saw the things you worship. I found an altar that had these words written on it: 'TO A GOD WHO IS NOT KNOWN.' You worship a god that you don't know. This is the God I am telling you about!" (Acts 17:23, International Children's Bible).

An added blessing was that my sister Mary and her family joined us for 10 days. After Sunday worship outside the Garden Tomb, we went inside, and then turning to exit, my heart skipped a beat, and my eyes filled with tears when I saw the sign, "HE IS NOT HERE—FOR HE IS RISEN." *Oh, thank You, Lord, for that glorious truth!*

After Mary and her family left us, we journeyed on by bus, boat, ferry, minibus, ship, and train, sleeping in our seats, in sleeper coaches on trains, on the floor, even on a porch under vines heavy with grapes hanging from the lattice work overhead. We made stops in the Epistle lands, and after almost 36 hours riding a train the length of Yugoslavia, we took a break from that incessant rocking with a three-day visit to incomparable Venice.

And then we were on our way to our primary European destination—Switzerland. At the end of a week there with George and Doris in the Alps, enjoying their family, especially four-month-old baby Lucas, they loaded their van with camping gear, maps, bags of food, and sent us off—to the Arctic Circle. Because Peter could speak some German, we had incredible experiences in East Germany where we stayed in local campgrounds. The demolition of the Berlin Wall had begun just one month earlier. We felt the emotion of the now-free people standing on the wall with arms raised in triumph and watching revelers on the ground on both sides of the wall tearing it down with sledgehammers, axes, and metal crowbars. We walked right through the wall itself, praising God for this historic event.

Sometimes sleeping in the car but mostly camping in campgrounds, we made our way through the Scandinavian countries, the land of our roots, all the way to the Arctic Circle where we experienced just one hour of dusk between 1:00 a.m. and 2:00 a.m. each day.

After returning George and Doris's car to them in Switzerland, we said good-bye, made our way to Holland, and, on August 8, flew across the Atlantic—to our home country.

House Hunting

Peter's sister Gloria and her family received us for a three-day stay with them in Washington DC before David made a one-week trip to California to visit Grandma and his friends. Peter, Scott, and I flew to Minneapolis where Evie and Nancy welcomed us into their home. Since Scott had said he wanted to sleep at least one night in our own home before he started school, we were chomping at the bit to start house hunting.

After worshipping once again with our dear friends at Meadow Creek Church on Sunday, we bought the Sunday paper and circled ads for houses that were for sale in the areas near the church. Evie loaned us her car, and we spent the afternoon driving from house to house to see the lay of the land. Monday, August 13, we met with a Wycliffe representative who was living in Minneapolis and had also been working as a real estate agent for the past 13 years. He had arranged for a car for us through the Wycliffe office in Chicago and was available to help us find the house God had planned for us. Peter, Scott, and I had great fun wandering through house after house for three days, exclaiming in each place about the features we liked and didn't like. We toured "928" on the fifteenth and, on the sixteenth, asked several of our close friends to see the house and give us their advice. On the seventeenth, we made an offer—which was accepted. God had worked in a miraculous way! In fact, a couple of months later, when outside talking to a neighbor, the woman said, "Charlie, who lives down the block, asked me after you moved in, 'Who bought that house—number 928?' I told him I thought God bought the house because the sale had fallen through twice before you came along. I told him you're missionaries, so God must have kept the house for you." WOW!

During the two-week period between submitting our bid on the house and closing the purchase, we spent time with my brother Jim and his family, thus meeting little four-year-old Tasia for the first time. With delight, we also connected with Yaufun and Sharon, their seven-year-old son Nathan, and one-month-old son David. After being away for five years, our excitement while driving north to Moorhead, Peter's hometown, knew no bounds as we anticipated being with Mom and Dad Westrum and many other relatives and close friends once again. We made arrangements for our furniture and other stored possessions—which we had left at Mom and Dad's, with Peter's brother and his wife, Don and Dianne, and with Peter's cousin and her husband, Rachel and John, in northern Minnesota—to be sent to us in Minneapolis.

On August 30, having received the keys to our home—the first we had ever owned in the US—Peter, Scott, and I took a couple of carloads of things to the house, picked up some fast food, ate sitting on the dining room floor, and slept on the floor in our bedrooms that night. Our belongings, shipped from northern Minnesota, were delivered on Friday, August 31. The three of us cleaned, painted some rooms, laid shelf paper on the kitchen shelves, and Scott and I hung wallpaper in the master bedroom. On Labor Day, September 3, we got our new waterbeds set up—and slept in them the night before Scott began his junior year of high school at Meadow Creek Christian School the next morning. *Thank You, Father, for leading and for the strength and energy we needed to place us in our home so quickly.*

Yes, it had been another whirlwind month, but it was also wonderful and exciting. We all settled into new routines—Scott at school and starting his driver's education course, Peter preparing to work with Essau and Sefnad on the New Testament books still needing various checks, and I got busy unpacking all our boxes. For the first time in our married life, we were able to unpack everything we owned and place it all for easy access on shelves and in cupboards. Peter and I made the rounds of garage sales and thrift stores and bought the remaining furniture items we needed, including twin beds for David's bedroom, thus readying a place for Essau and Sefnad who would be using David's room while he was at Moody in Chicago.

Though Peter had malaria again while they were visiting, we were delighted when Mother and Mary came to visit us in our new home for five days. I enjoyed going with them to get together with "old" friends, and Scott, since he had just received his driver's license, was pleased to take them out for drives to areas now important to him.

Essau and Sefnad Arrive

The first week of October, I flew to Los Angeles to spend a relaxed week with Mother and Mary before going to the sprawling LA airport to meet Essau and Sefnad when they arrived. Two SIL couples had traveled with and guided the men all the way from Irian. I had wondered how they would react to the long trip, the huge aircraft, having food served in flight, and the cool weather—relative to the equatorial island from which they had come. I wondered what they would say about the height of the buildings they would see and about the busy LA freeways and winding mountain roads.

They smiled and hugged me when we met at the airport, but those first couple of days, they just slept and basically said nothing, not to us and not to each other. And then the third day, as Mary drove past a hotel as she took us to the airport to catch a flight to Minneapolis, I pointed to the hotel elevator that was on the OUTSIDE of the building and said, "Let's ride that elevator." Essau's and Sefnad's eyes popped wide open, and they began to talk and to share, not at all sure that riding in that glass bubble was a good idea. But overall, the men did very well in adjusting to American society and culture and in learning to speak English.

Received with Open Arms

We arrived in Minneapolis on October 13. The men were the stars of the week during our Meadow Creek Church annual mission conference, which ran from October 14 through the 21st. Essau brought the news that 47 more Berik believers had been baptized on September 30, and several small children had been dedicated to the Lord. We all spoke and shared at several events—Sunday services, Sunday school classes, in home meetings, at the women's luncheon, and at Awana. Everyone who heard Essau and Sefnad testify were amazed to learn what God had done in their lives. During their whole stay in Minnesota, Essau went to Sunday school with us, and Sefnad joined Scott in his youth group.

I remember one Sunday, as people were gathering for Sunday school in the sixth-grade classroom, Essau stood staring at a bulletin board full of pictures of a remote people group in South America. "Essau, what are you looking at in those pictures?" I asked. "Oh, Mama Sue," he responded. "They are so poor. Look at their small houses, and there's no clean area around each house." All things are relative.

The people of the church were so gracious to the men. One dear couple, had noticed what they were wearing on their feet and took the fellows out shopping one day to buy shoes and socks. It was a red-letter day for them—never in their lives had they had NEW shoes or socks.

The next weekend, all of us went to be with one of our supporting churches in Pine City, Minnesota, to take part in a three-day mission conference. The men were received with open arms. Staying with special friends, Essau and Sefnad marveled not only at their beautiful home and gardens but also at their generous hospitality.

Apples

As you can imagine, the men encountered things that were new and confusing to them. Since fall is apple harvesttime in the Minneapolis area, I served apples in many ways, shapes, and forms—raw apples, sliced apples, baked apples, apple pie—to name a few. Peter and I well remember the evening at the dinner table when Essau sat staring, with a look of dismay, at a dish of applesauce I had placed before him. "What is it?" he asked. "Applesauce," I responded. And then, suddenly, with a sparkle of new insight in his eyes, he said, "I get it! Now I know why you call this big town MANY APPLES!"

Meeting Peter's Parents

Before leaving Irian, we had been careful to plan which translation checks we would work on with Essau and Sefnad in the US. Since translation guidelines demanded that checks on each New Testament book needed to be done by a native speaker who had not had prior experience with the Berik translation of the book being checked, we had made sure that Essau and Sefnad had not been involved with the books we'd now be working on: *John, Romans, Hebrews, 2 Corinthians, 1 Peter,* and *Revelation.* But before we could get down to serious daily work, we needed to do a bit of traveling. The first week of November, Scott stayed with friends in Minneapolis, and Peter and I and the men drove to Chicago to reunite with David for a weekend at Moody where he was majoring in international ministry.

Mom and Dad Westrum's church, and the churches of our other relatives and friends in other parts of Minnesota, also wanted to meet Essau and Sefnad and hear their stories. So off we went. I'll never forget the day we arrived in Moorhead. As we drove down the street to Mom and Dad's home, honking the horn as usual, Peter's mother came out onto the front steps of the house, waving a welcome. After embracing the men, she took us inside and stood by Peter's dad who was sitting in his lounge chair. Mom and Dad, Essau, and Sefnad all had tears in their eyes as Sefnad took Dad's hand and, looking straight into his eyes, said, "Meeting you, Mr. Peter's father and mother and also Mama Sue's family is one of our main purposes in coming to America. You allowed your children to travel across the great Pacific Ocean to Irian Jaya to a little village on the Tor River to minister to our people for 17 years. Thank you."

All through November, the first half of December and in January 1991, we diligently worked on our translation checking tasks, getting ready for our scheduled consultant checks in Dallas, Texas, in February. The days were long—the work tedious for the men. We needed to provide diversions for them. They had come from their equatorial home to spend the winter with us in Minnesota, so during our break times, we would tell them that winter was coming, that it would be very, very cold. People from church loaned them sweaters and jackets. We were all eager for the first snowfall of the year. "Soon, you'll see and FEEL snow," I told them. They just stared at me. I imagine they were thinking, *How can she know that?* In Berikland, there's no such thing as weather forecasting. Every day is the same: 90 degrees with 90% humidity—and rain.

Is That Snow?

We always had the local Christian radio station on in the kitchen during the day. One day at noon, I heard the radio announcer say that snow was forecast for that afternoon. Quietly, I went around the house and closed the curtains and blinds, and I watched. Sure enough, about 3:00 p.m., big white fluffy snowflakes filled the sky. Periodically, I checked the backyard. After supper, I saw that the grass was covered; there was a little cap of snow on each twig and branch of the trees, and the roofs of the houses were sparkling white in the light of the streetlights.

We took the fellows into the family room, opened the drapes that covered the sliding doors, and turned on the outside light. "Oooooooooooooooooohhhhh!" they exclaimed. "Is that snow?"

"Yes," Peter said. Then he opened the door and took them outside. They were astonished! And so excited. Their eyes danced with delight; they shuddered from the cold and turned around to come inside.

As we all stood there together looking out at the winter wonderland, the fellows both began to share at once. They said, "You told us about snow. But we couldn't imagine it. We couldn't understand when you said the snow would cover the trees and houses. We couldn't imagine a white blanket big enough to cover a house. Now we understand, for we've seen it with our own eyes. But how will we tell our friends and relatives in the village when we go back? There aren't any Berik words for this!"

Essau and Sefnad came to love being outside in the snow. They built snowmen with us, went tobogganing, and drove snowmobiles! One weekend in mid-December, we stayed overnight with special friends near a lake in Alexandria, Minnesota. We had told Essau and Sefnad what they must have thought was another wild story—that cars could drive on the lake in the winter when the water was frozen. The only frozen water they had ever seen was ice cubes in a drinking glass, and they wanted no part of it. The first time I gave Sefnad an ice cube in his hand back in the village, he dropped it and shouted, "Oh! Hot!" Since extreme hot from fire was the only extreme temperature they had experienced, he had interpreted the extreme cold as hot. After breakfast in the morning, Dave asked the men, "Would you like to go out and walk and ride in a car on the lake?" The men said a hesitant yes. After sliding around out there on their heavy boots, they said, "Our friends in the village simply won't believe this."

Mother's Birthday and Christmas

December 24, 1990, was my mother's seventy-fifth birthday. We made plans to be with her and to honor her for this special event and to be with her for Christmas. At the same time, we also wanted to celebrate Christmas with Essau and Sefnad and with our Minnesota relatives and friends. So, after David came home from Moody, we went to Moorhead for a celebration with Mom and Dad Westrum and Peter's siblings and their families. Back in Minneapolis, we got together with Evie, Nancy, and Jim and his family. Such events sustained us on the field when loneliness hit during the holidays.

The assistant pastor and his wife at Meadow Creek had become close friends. They had reached out to Essau and Sefnad on several occasions and befriended them. The men felt comfortable in their home and so accepted an invitation to live with them for two weeks while we went to California.

Mary and I had planned well in advance and had arranged for a private room and catering service for an elegant meal in Mother's retirement community. Our boys planned special entertainment, including skits, speeches, and songs. We had games and individual presentations of gifts, and after it was all over, we all had copies of the video recording of the festivities. On January 2, we once again honored Mother with lunch on the occasion of her twenty-second spiritual birthday. *Thank You, Father, for this opportunity to show our love to Mother and for the gracious appreciation she expressed to us all.*

Working in Dallas

Leaving the balmy weather of "the Golden State," we returned to the Minnesota deep freeze. We were eager to get back to work and finish preparations for our upcoming consultant checks in Dallas. Essau and Sefnad were so very happy to have us back and to be living at home together. By the end of January, we had completed the necessary New International Version checks—that is checking translated Scripture against the New International Version (or Revised Standard Version or other fairly literal New Testament versions) to ensure nothing had been omitted or added in the books of *2 Corinthians, John*, and *Revelation*. For a recreational break, Scott and I took Sefnad outside in the ice and snow to attend the internationally famous St. Paul Winter Carnival, especially to see the massive and beautiful ice sculptures.

On February 7, I flew to Dallas to be trained in using Fiesta, a computer program designed to help us in our upcoming checks of the Berik New Testament as one whole unit. Fiesta would enable us to review our translation of 208 New Testament key terms and 130 parallel passages. *Thank You, Lord, for our wise colleagues who can design such helps for us all.*

Peter put Essau on a plane on February 10, and I picked him up in Dallas so we could finish the consultant check of *2 Corinthians*. It was amazing to work with Dr. Pam. She came to the consultant session armed with only her *Greek New Testament* and the Berik back translation I had sent to her. Her knowledge of Greek was awesome. As we finished one section of a chapter, I remember her, saying, "Well, Sue, the next verse has a word that only occurs once in the New Testament. Let's see how you rendered it." I held my breath—until she said, "It looks like you handled it well. Now let's ask Essau this question." When he answered correctly, I whispered in my heart, *Thank You, Lord, for guiding and guarding the accuracy of Your Word.*

Dr. Pike and his wife, Evie,—who had led our grammar workshop at Danau Bira in 1975—were living there in Dallas at that time. I was speechless when I received a phone call from Evie, inviting Essau and me to their home for dinner. Though internationally famous, they were truly humble servants of all. Essau seemed to really enjoy visiting with them and sharing his testimony of all God had done and was doing in his life. In fact, this was true wherever we went with Essau and Sefnad in the States. Many times, Peter and I could hear sniffles and see tears in the eyes of the congregation as Essau shared how God had revealed Himself to him and had enabled him to forgive the five men who had beaten up his older brother. He would often refer to *2 Corinthians* 4:11, saying, "Jesus allowed problems in my life so people could see Jesus in me." *Thank You, Father, for the truth You are revealing to Essau.*

Because Jesus Loves Us

When Peter and Sefnad arrived in Dallas on the thirteenth, having driven the car down from Minneapolis, we rejoiced in being together again. I heard Essau say to Sefnad, "Isn't it great to be here where it's WARM?" At dinner that evening, I said, "Tomorrow I have a surprise for you two. We're going to the Wycliffe boutique to get some things for you to take back to Indonesia with you." Just as when I had told them about snow before they experienced it, they didn't really understand when we had told them about the boutique when we were still in Indonesia. "Don't buy any clothes before you come. There'll be plenty for you in the US," I had said. "There's a store called a *boutique*. Wycliffe people bring things to the store that they no longer need and take home with them the things they need." The men just looked at us. It made no sense to them at all. But when they arrived in Los Angles, they had brought just one suitcase each. Essau had packed only one shirt and a set of underwear.

The next morning, I took the fellows to the *boutique*. I picked up two paper bags from the pile just inside the door and gave one to Essau and one to Sefnad. Then I said, "Follow me." And I led them on a tour around the shop. "This area has clothes for men," I said. "Here are things for women. And over here, you'll find clothes for children. Household supplies are in this corner. Now you can go around and take the things you need for yourself and for your families at home. When your bag gets full, place it over here and get another bag."

The ladies in charge of the store had overheard my monologue and had come from the back room and were standing in the doorway watching us.

Essau and Sefnad were just standing there, staring at me. Then Essau said, "You mean I can take what I want?"

"Yes."

"I don't have to pay?"

"That's correct."

"Why not?"

"Because Jesus loves us. So we love one another and you."

Essau broke down and cried. He put his head on my shoulder, with tears flowing, and said, "THANK YOU, Jesus! THANK YOU, Jesus!"

I looked up to see that the dear ladies, who gave selflessly to volunteer day after day to minister in the shop, were also crying. Then, wiping their tears, they smiled and approached the men to greet and to bless them. Essau and Sefnad began to choose clothes for their children. Soon, the ladies were coming to them with items they thought the men would like, including suitcases to put it all in. It was a good thing I had driven the car to the boutique, for we would never have been able to just carry it all back in paper bags to the dorm where we were staying.

Back to Minnesota

I flew back to Minneapolis on February 15. Peter, Essau, and Sefnad stayed on in Dallas, completing consultant checks with Dr. Pam before beginning their drive back on the twenty-second. Our friend, Wayne, who had met Essau and Sefnad in Indonesia when visiting us there, had written, inviting Peter and the men to make a stop at his home in Missouri. They were pleased to do so, and much to the delight of Wayne's church, they presented a program sharing how God had moved in their lives. Scott and I were thrilled when they got home.

Working full-time all during February and March, we made the necessary revisions on most of the books we had checked in Dallas and completed the remaining New International Version checks and back translations on *1 Peter*, *Romans*, and *Hebrews*. When our church held its spring mission conference, Essau and Sefnad had many friends in the congregation and were pleased and felt comfortable sharing their testimonies throughout the week.

We continued to provide a variety of new diversional experiences for the fellows, such as attending Scott's high school basketball games with us and visiting farms—learning how to milk a goat, which would be useful back home in their village.

New Agreement and New Plans

Our director in Indonesia notified us they were praising God that a new umbrella agreement for SIL to continue working in Indonesia, under the Department of Foreign Affairs, was in the offing. *Oh, THANK YOU, LORD, for this wonderful gift!* When David came home from Moody for Easter, we held another family meeting to pray and discuss our plans for the coming year.

Essau had been given six months' paid leave from his government job in Irian, so in April, he was the first to return. I traveled with him to Los Angeles and helped him check in for his flights, with three FULL suitcases, all the way to the island of Biak, off the coast of Irian.

Scott took the ACT and SAT exams and, like David before him, received very high scores. *Thank You, Father, for the excellent education our sons received overseas and in the US, in both public and private schools.* When Peter and I completed preparing *Romans* for the upcoming consultant check, we made a trip to Moorhead so Peter could say good-bye to his parents.

May Plans Executed

God had led and provided—we were able to execute our earlier decisions. On May 4, Peter, Sefnad, and I set out to drive back to Dallas. Working once again with Dr. Pam, we completed the consultant checks on *1 Peter*, *Hebrews*, and *Romans*, and I received further training in using the Fiesta New Testament checking program. Scott had become interested in possibly attending LeTourneau University, which is located 125 miles east of Dallas, so he flew down to Dallas, and one day, he and I drove over to LeTourneau for a look around. At one point during the campus tour, Scott said, "Yeah, I could see myself attending this university."

The next week, all four of us jumped into the car, and leaving Dallas at 5:20 a.m. and though battling extremely bad weather all the way across Iowa, we drove straight through to Minneapolis, arriving at 11:31 p.m. We were determined to get there before David arrived home from Chicago the next day. Sunday was Sefnad and Peter's last time to be with our dear friends at Meadow Creek Church. They gave the morning message together, and Peter baptized Sefnad. He shared with the congregation, "I want to be baptized here, with all of you who sent Mr. Peter and Mama Sue to my people with the news of Jesus. You have prayed for me these many years. Thank you." There wasn't a dry eye in the place. Two days later, Peter and Sefnad flew back to Irian. Just as in 1966, Peter and I were once again 10,000 miles apart—and feeling lonely.

Closing Our Furlough Year

Though David, Scott, and I were living together at home, rarely were all of us there at the same time. David was busy with a great summer job at the post office. After Scott finished his junior year of high school, he took a 10-day mission trip to Mexico. He had said, "I'm going as a missionary in my own right, not just tagging along after my parents." After the trip, he was pleased to have a job helping friends sand and paint their garage.

I was busy preparing our home for renters who would live there from the end of July 1991 through May 1992. After learning that we would be able to return to work in Indonesia, we had sent letters to various mission organizations and churches in Minneapolis, wondering if there was a mission family who would be on furlough and could make use of our home. Peter and I had been able to work out a contract with a family who had served with the navigators in Jordan for 11 years. *Thank You, Jesus, for this wonderful provision.*

On June 7, I received a cable from Peter telling us that SIL's new working agreement with the government had been signed. Hallelujah! We also received exciting news from Germany. George and Doris were applying to join Wycliffe and SIL through the Swiss home division and were attending linguistic classes in Germany during the summer.

Mother Visits

God gave me another wonderful gift at the end of our furlough. Mother was well and happy and wanted to visit and suggested we take a trip together. At the end of June, she came to Minneapolis, and we flew to Chicago. There, we rented a car and went sightseeing together, driving through Grandma's old neighborhood and by the home where I had stayed with her so many times. We toured Moody Bible Institute with David and then went to Joliet to spend time with Mother's cousins whom I hadn't seen in 40 years. Finally, we reminisced when viewing the hospital where I was born and the orphanage where Mother had lived between the ages of three to 10 years old.

Looking Ahead

It was with tears that I said good-bye to Evie, and then on Sunday, July 28, David, Scott, and I attended Meadow Creek together, feeling weepy as we said farewell to our friends. I brought greetings from Peter at both services and implored the congregation to pray for us as we strived during the coming year to ready the Berik New Testament for printing. Scott and I finished our packing that night but didn't get to bed until 2:00 a.m. David took us to the airport in the morning. First stop—Los Angeles, for a closing visit with Mother and Mary. On August 4, we boarded our plane to cross the Pacific, reuniting with Peter on August 6, our twenty-third wedding anniversary.

The plans God had led us to pursue had come to pass. Scott would be able to be with his lifelong classmates on the field for his senior year of high school at HIS school, that is, Hillcrest International School. Peter and I felt encouraged that we would be able to finish the final checks on the last seven chapters of *Revelation* and complete all the prescribed New Testament prepublication checks before Scott's graduation day. Our goal: to submit the Berik New Testament to the printshop in 1992.

God had been providing the way for us for the past 20 years. We had no doubt but that He would bring us through to the end.

Approaching the End

August 1991 to November 1993

Without counsel plans fail, but with
many advisers they succeed.
—Proverbs 15:22, English Standard Version

God had worked through our leaders and the Indonesian government. Scott, Peter, and I had renewed visas and were back in Irian together for a final year of service—to jump through the remaining required hoops leading to approval to print the Berik New Testament and to allow Scott to graduate from high school with his class.

But Peter and I were feeling lonely again—9,000 miles now separated us from David, who was a sophomore at Moody. On the other hand, we were blessed to have a phone in our rented home, so we were able to talk with David every two weeks, without making a three-hour excursion downtown to call on a public phone.

Just as Sefnad had settled into a routine as a tenth-grade student at a mission-sponsored school after he and Peter returned to Irian, so too Scott quickly settled in as a senior at HIS (Hillcrest International School). He was on the student council, played on the volleyball and basketball teams, was editor of the yearbook, and often played his trumpet for church and school events. He enjoyed having one of his classmates living with us for the school year.

Struck Down by a Cough

Unfortunately, I changed Peter's routine immediately upon my arrival. I was quite ill with a severe cough that I had inherited in mid-July from David and Scott and other friends in Minnesota. I had tried to see the Wycliffe doctor when Scott and I were in Los Angeles on our trip back to Irian, but the poor man was in the hospital with a heart attack. So I pushed on and, by the Lord's enabling strength, made it back to Irian—and was sick in bed the first week. Peter was wonderful, giving me no responsibilities. "Sue," he said, "you don't even have to unpack your suitcase if you don't feel up to it. Take as long as necessary to get well." But neither of us got much sleep the first week—I was up most of the night with such severe coughing that I would vomit. My throat became raw and sore, and I had laryngitis. Peter did all the cooking for the four of us for the first five days I was home. Then, feeling some better, I left the house for a couple of hours—and immediately relapsed.

"Sue, you have a nasty virus," our SIL doctor said. "You need to go really slow in becoming active. You don't want to get malaria on top of your rundown condition. Rest. Force yourself to drink plenty of liquids. Don't talk at all, or just whisper." So for two weeks, I whispered, and for three weeks, I didn't leave the house again. We sought the prayers of our colleagues and shortly were praising God that with reduced activity I was able to work on the computer, typing the revisions Peter had made on the books that had been consultant checked in Dallas.

By November, I began to call that vicious cough "the perfect illness" because every time I relapsed, Peter would say, "Sue, I insist, you must just stay home!" By following his advice, I progressed to the point of being able to cook and clean and do our translation and computer work—eight to 10 hours a day. In a letter to our supporters, I said, "It's really neat the way the Lord has restricted my outside activities but allowed me to keep up with the New Testament revisions and checks that are still before us."

In a letter to my sister Mary, I wrote:

> We put a small air conditioner in my office where I'm typing now. My, what a blessing! It makes my days sooooo much easier. I'm sure one reason I've been able to work and continue to get better at the same time is that I save so much energy by working in this room where the humidity is low,

and the temperature is 80 degrees, instead of 90 to 95! . . . God's creatures still get in this room, however. As I type, every now and then, I need to stop and get rid of the little bugs that are attracted to the light of the screen.

The electricity in this area of town goes off one to three times a day for an undetermined period of time. Maybe 10 minutes, maybe two hours. In fact, it went off while I was typing this paragraph. I thank God for this computer, which will run off its battery for a couple of hours. I can finish typing a paragraph and then print later when the power comes back on. Oh, the marvels of modern technology!

I guess I should mention the ants with which we share this house. Each day, I go around each room and visually check the walls, the tops of the walls around the ceiling, in the corners, and around the windows, etc.—for ants. Then, with my spray can in hand, I make the rounds inside and out, spraying the columns marching up and down the walls and parading back and forth across the counters. I sprinkle a medicated powder on the edge of the desks and shelves—ants are greatly hampered by the slippery powder. A grain of sugar, or any food, on the counter brings them within 30 minutes—in the window, down the wall, across the floor, up the cupboard, and across the counter to a feast—this in spite of washed counters and scrubbed floors. They probably nest above the ceiling and under the roof. Oh well, pray for us to have the endurance to continue the battle cheerfully. The most annoying is the way they march in and out of the fridge! We do have ways to keep food ant free—a *bowl of water with a can or glass in it and the container of food on top works* beautifully—did you know ants can't swim?

With the help of our colleagues, within the first three weeks of being back, I got my systems set up for getting food. On Thursday, our house helper goes to a farm and gets grapefruit and lemons for lemonade. A couple of times a week, one of the workers from the aviation department brings a lettuce substitute, carrots, tomatoes (if available), cauliflower, and green beans. Potatoes come through another aviation worker. We found a store 15 miles away that occasionally has hot dogs and luncheon meat, so Peter checks that out whenever he goes there. One of the pilots is willing to buy cheese and margarine for us all when he goes to Papua New Guinea every other month. I'm on the pork list with one of our translators. Every four to six weeks, I should be able to get a piece from them. There's a chicken farm run by the Bible school—they butcher every couple of months—I got four from them when they butchered in late August. And so it goes. It's a challenge but fun when I can function smoothly.

On December 31, I was finally able to say that the cough, and the accompanying laryngitis and sore throat I had acquired in July, was finally gone. Satan had slowed us down, but God had once again intervened and foiled the enemy's attack.

August 28, 1991

Even though Peter had spent considerable time helping me those first three weeks of August, he and Oskar had been able to schedule time with Marge to finish checking *Revelation*. On August 28, 1991, the consultant check of the last verse of the Berik New Testament, *Revelation* 22:21, was completed. Marge wrote to the branch leadership: "This concludes the verse-by-verse check of the Berik New Testament. All praise to God!"

On the twenty-ninth, the administration responded:

> CONGRATULATIONS! On behalf of the Irian Jaya administration, I want to congratulate you on the attainment of this new milestone. Although there is still much to do before you see the Berik

New Testament in print, having all the consultant
checks finished is a significant accomplishment . . .
Our prayers are with you as you bring this
project to completion . . . Together in His service.

Yes, there was still much to be done, but we, and our Berik co-workers, were energized by each milestone reached. We were delighted that
Sefnad's afternoon school schedule allowed him to be available to work
with us each morning. Other helpers also came regularly, and soon we were
ready for the next step.

Melding Twenty-seven Books into One

In October, it was time to begin all the New Testament final checks—
polishing and melding the 27 books of the New Testament into a cohesive
whole. *Oh Lord, there's so much to do! So many details I haven't thought of
before. Please give us the strength and stamina to keep focusing, one step and
task at a time. Thank You that I know You are faithful and will bring everything that You've purposed to pass.*
How to begin? I started by making a chart with nine thermometers—
the first nine of 15 different final checks to prepare for typesetting:

1. Ensure 208 key Biblical terms are consistently translated throughout whole text
2. Harmonize 130 parallel passages
3. Revise first 14 books translated
4. Write introductions for each book and for New Testament—send to consultant
5. Draft and check glossary—send to consultant
6. Check section headings
7. Choose pictures and illustrations, write captions—send to consultant
8. Read New Testament out loud with Berik leaders
9. Check spelling of 15,500 words

In January 1992, we made a final two-and-a-half-week visit to
Somanente. It was so very good to be with our Berik friends again. The
frosting on the cake was that our house was in good condition and the
fridge ran well. Pretty amazing in that hot, humid, buggy climate.

We had made good progress on the first seven checks on our chart and were ready to begin number 8. Berik leaders and literacy tutors from all the villages came to see us and to form the Berik Translation Finalizing Committee. Peter explained to them, "The work of our committee is very important. Before we can print the Berik New Testament, we must read it together—out loud. This is your New Testament. We need to be sure that every verse of God's message to the Berik people has been expressed in the clearest and most natural way. As a group, we'll check the spelling of all the names of the people and places in the New Testament." I showed them the computer and said, "However you say to spell the words, we'll type it in, and the computer will be sure every word is printed correctly." They were fascinated.

Peter continued, "Our committee will also choose the pictures that you want, how you want the pages formatted, and what color you want for the cover." The men listened carefully and took the responsibility of their committee very seriously. They decided on dark blue for the cover color and the formatting details they wanted—such as one column per page, not two, and having bold face verse numbers.

Since the *Gospel of Mark* is basically a book of short stories and we wanted the 14 men to become comfortable with one another, taking turns reading out loud, we began with reading *Mark*. Each day, we also brought up various discussion topics. One afternoon, Peter told the team, "There are 240 different people groups here in Irian Jaya. Only 12 of them have God's Word in their own language. Two New Testaments are being printed right now in the printshop. The Berik New Testament will be number 15." The men smiled from ear to ear and broke into enthusiastic applause.

Later that day, one of the Berik tutors said to me, "Chief Petrus would have had a very warm gallbladder [would have been very happy] if he had been here today to hear about our New Testament. He loved Jesus and followed Him well. After you and Mr. Peter left Somanente two years ago, the chief said, 'I'm not going back to the airstrip until Mr. Peter and Mama Sue come back!' And it's true, he never went back. But God took him home to heaven. Our gallbladders are fallen [we feel sad] because he will never hold God's Book in his hands."

After excellent daily sessions with the committee—making progress on each of the checks—Peter and I went back to Jayapura. By mid-April, we had completed the first six items on our chart, and we welcomed members of the finalizing committee to Jayapura to continue the work we had started in Somanente in January. The Berik New Testament was their book, in their language. They were eager to finish the responsibilities we had set before them.

We arranged for housing and meals for us all so we could work without interruption. At least 11 men met with us daily. Excitement reigned within the team as we began to choose which David C. Cook pictures and illustrations they desired. It was an exciting time. As word spread through the grapevine; other Berik people who were living in town also came to the meetings. We served 21 for lunch one day. *Thank You, Father, for such strong involvement among the Berik community!*

Each day, we took time to check the spelling of all New Testament names. The hours committed to scrupulously reading each verse, looking for any remaining errors or spots needing improvement, were well spent. Our goal was for each of us to feel fully satisfied that the New Testament was ready for the Berik people to read. Of course, I had made a thermometer for each task, and at the end of each day, we filled it in, enabling us all to visualize our progress.

Our last committee meeting was held on May 1, 1992, 20 years after we had set foot in Indonesia for the first time. The Berik leaders returned to their villages along the Tor River. I set my sights on the goal of typing all the needed corrections in the Berik computer files and on revising and correcting the English back translations. Of course, it was also necessary to print and proofread my work when I finished.

I approached the very last New Testament check with determination and thanksgiving for the computer and the program that could alphabetize all the words in a document. One or two Berik speakers sat by the computer with me, and we read through the entire list of alphabetized words— all 15,607 of them—in the Berik New Testament, checking the spelling and looking for nonexistent words.

Approved for Publication

As a translation team approaches the end of a translation project, the question arises: "Where will we typeset and print the New Testament?" The answer about printing was settled by Indonesian law, which requires that all books printed in an Indonesian language be printed in Indonesia. Our US and Indonesian leadership discussed the question of where the Berik New Testament, the first being done through SIL in Indonesia, should be typeset. They decided it would be best for us to work with SIL's printing arts department in Dallas, Texas.

And so it was that after we reported to Marge that we had completed all the required New Testament checks, on May 12, 1992, she wrote a letter to our administration and to the printing arts department in Dallas:

> I hereby give my approval for the publication of the Berik New Testament. All parts of the manuscript, including footnotes, glossary, table of contents, and picture captions, have been consultant checked and approved.

What a huge, huge relief and milestone! All praise to God for bringing us through!

During our next weekly meeting with our SIL colleagues, Marge commented, "If anything should happen to Peter and Sue, the New Testament is complete, and someone else could print and distribute it." And Peter shared, "The Lord has been so faithful these past 20 years. He supplied over 38 Berik men and women to work with us as language and translation assistants. More than 60 SIL members—pilots and mechanics, administrators, bookkeepers and accountants, schoolteachers, IT personnel, printers, doctors and nurses, buyers, secretaries, and consultants—have worked to make it possible for us to keep going. We've all been supported by an army of God's people in our home countries who have offered up the prayers and financial gifts necessary to keep us all at work here on the field. God raised up and provided all this so that one more of the world's language groups could have the New Testament in their own language. It's all about God's faithfulness."

Family Life

On December 15, 1991, we received word that Peter's father had passed away in a US hospital. Many of our colleagues came to our home in Jayapura to comfort and encourage Peter. Dad's funeral service was on the nineteenth, but because a winter burial is not possible in that frozen tundra in northern Minnesota, his burial was postponed until May 1992, when we were able to join the family for that event.

God had enabled, so all through the first five months of 1992, we kept busy with our project goals and other activities. Peter taught a course at the university and was a sub at the high school. I had two piano students and filled in for the translation coordinator when he was away. Peter and

I both enjoyed being fully involved at the high school and in Scott's activities. We were very proud of him as the valedictorian of his class when he graduated from HIS high school in May. The next day, we took a very early morning flight, the first of several taking us back to the US.

After a busy, fun summer living together in our Minneapolis home while David and Scott had summer jobs—David at the post office and Scott at Taco Bell—in September, we separated again. David returned to Moody in Chicago as a junior. Scott began his studies at Taylor University in Indiana. The printing arts department (PAD) in Dallas notified us, "We've scheduled you to typeset the Berik New Testament during the months of September through November 1992. Please send us your computer diskettes so we can load the manuscript into our system before you get here." By mid-August, Peter and I had finished proofreading the New Testament printouts we had brought with us from Irian and had entered the corrections on the diskettes. We shouted, "Hurrah! Praise the Lord!" when we sent those invaluable spheres by registered mail to Dallas. We were another step closer to the end.

Our official assignment with Wycliffe was then changed from "Indonesia—Linguists-Translators" to "USA—Representatives." Specifically, we would continue the work we had done on our last furlough, reaching out to the students on the 22 college campuses in the twin cities of Minneapolis and St. Paul. Wycliffe asked us to attend an orientation meeting at the regional office in Chicago on our way south to Dallas. We were pleased to become reacquainted with our stateside colleagues and, following the meetings, to also stop by and visit Wayne, who had by now become a very dear friend, at his home in Missouri.

The Sunarjo Family

George and Doris Sunarjo had been accepted by Wycliffe Switzerland as members of Wycliffe Bible Translators in September 1991. In January of 1992, they came to the US as *Members in Training* and settled in at the SIL center in North Carolina for training. We were delighted in June when they were able to come to visit us for 10 days. In fact, on Father's Day, we celebrated both Peter and George as fathers and also David's twentieth and George's forty-fifth birthdays.

After speaking at our church, Meadow Creek, on Sunday, the church voted to also take the Sunarjo family on as their missionaries. In the thank-you letter to their supporters, George wrote:

I've been convicted to give my life as a missionary to people of my country . . . Through my time in Switzerland, God has not only given me a lovely family but also led me to an open door for my vision of becoming a member of Wycliffe Bible Translators. Twenty years have gone by since the first encounter (with Westrums in Jayapura). The blond baby, David Westrum, has now completed his third year at Moody Bible Institute while preparing himself to serve for one year in the former Soviet Union with the CoMission Project. While Peter and Sue are in the final stages of preparation for dedicating the Berik New Testament, I am at the starting line, with five more helpers, beginning our countdown toward a July move back to Indonesia . . . There is much work for us to do there. Aren't God's plans awesome!?

Yes, awesome plans, which included the Sunarjos being in Dallas for management orientation courses the fall of 1992, during the same time Peter and I were there to typeset the Berik New Testament.

Peter Hits Half a Century

Fifty years. I was determined that Peter would have wonderful memories of this major juncture in his life. One afternoon in August, when we were staying with Peter's parents in Moorhead, Peter's brother enticed Peter to go with him to visit their aunt Ruth. Since it was two months before Peter's actual birth date, we were able to totally surprise him when he came home. As Peter walked into the festively decorated living room, most of Peter's family popped out, shouting, "Happy Birthday!" Peter was most taken aback when he saw my mother and sister and Mary's son, Chad, come forward to greet him. They had secretly flown in from California that morning.

In October, George and I pulled off another surprise party for Peter in Dallas. Fifty people had gathered in a friend's home before Peter walked in. He was shocked speechless. It was the first time in my life I saw Peter just standing there, not being able to make any kind of quip. George and I were giddy that we had actually caught him unaware. George and Doris cooked an Indonesian meal for everyone, much to the enjoyment of all our colleagues, who had served with us in Indonesia and who were there with us that night.

Knowing that Peter was a great fan of the TV game *Wheel of Fortune*, one young couple planned and led a *Wheel of Fortune* game for the crowd. Peter was one of three contestants. They dressed me up like Vanna White. With prizes and recordings, the night was a great hit with everyone.

The Road to Publication

Our good friend, Bob, who had set up the printshop in Irian back in 1978, had become the head of the Dallas printing arts department. What a delight it was to work with him once again. When we met with Bob, reporting in to begin the task, he warned us, "Peter and Sue, be aware that preparing the text of a New Testament for publication is a detailed rigorous process with multiple proofreading tasks at each step. You'll need physical, mental, emotional, and spiritual endurance during the next three months. It's exacting work but dynamic error-free Scriptures are worth it. And we're here to cheer you on and to guide and help. Welcome to the team."

Bob introduced us to the typesetting team with whom we would work. Ted, the team leader, explained, "Peter and Sue, we've already loaded the Berik New Testament into our computer system. We'll be giving you a printout of each New Testament book, one at a time. Your job will be to sit together and read the book out loud. One of you will read from the computer screen. The other will read from the printout and note any needed corrections. Before you leave here, you will have read through the entire New Testament three times. During your first read through, you'll especially be checking for accuracy of verb tense, hyphenation of syllable breaks, punctuation, and paragraph length. You'll also check the formatting of the nine letters—two in *Acts* and seven in *Revelation*.

"We've scheduled a room for you to use here in PAD, 8:00 a.m. to 5:00 p.m., Monday through Friday, from now through mid-December. Do you have any questions?"

Overwhelmed, we stared at Ted and quietly said, "Not right now."

"Good," he said. "Let's go to your room, and we'll get you set up."

Alone in our little eight-by-eight-foot windowless room, we sat down and prayed, "Oh God, You've brought us to this point in time, and to this place, for a very special, specific job. We've never done this before. The responsibility of finalizing this translation project feels overwhelming. We need You now. Be here with us as we read. Keep our minds alert. Enable us to find and correct any errors that would mar the translation. Give us keen eyes and keep us focused, verse by verse, word by word—and yes, letter by letter."

On October 1, we received a printout of the *Gospel of Matthew*. And we began—reading every single word and verbalizing every punctuation mark and reading for accuracy, meaning, and fluency. It was an exciting time sitting there in that little room from eight to five o'clock Monday through Friday, all through October and November.

We praised God when PAD agreed to our request, "We'd like to have a bound book containing the back translation of all 27 Berik New Testament books. Please would you help us set up the database and get a printout when we're done here?"

Delays

Bob, PAD director, made a trip to Indonesia and made it a point to visit the printshop where the Berik New Testament would be printed. It was a good thing he did. The formatting standards that PAD had so diligently set up regarding external book size, margins, page size, font size, and spacing had all changed. It took the PAD staff a week to redo it all.

Because of the delay, we weren't able to start our second read through of the New Testament until two days before Thanksgiving. David and Scott came to Dallas to be with us and the Sunarjo family for a great long weekend together. On Monday morning, Ted notified us of the December schedule. "Peter and Sue," he said, "you should plan on working through December 9. Then take a break at home in Minnesota until the New Year. Plan to be back here to start work again on January 11."

Actually, it was a relief to have a break from our intense daily reading schedule. We made it 90% of the way through our second read through and, with joyful spirits, left for Minneapolis where it was a great blessing to be home for Christmas, our first in our very own US home. My mother came with Mary and her family to celebrate with us. *How we praise You, Father, for Your gifts of Jesus, home, and family!*

Red-letter Day

On January 11, 1993, we were back in our little room in Dallas, busy at work steadily reaching for the goal of completing all the prescribed New Testament typesetting checks. On the twenty-ninth, Ted encouraged us, "Peter and Sue, congratulations. You've finished the second read through, scrutinizing the footnotes, book introductions, and the glossary. And now that you finished your week-long task of reading the word list, you're ready for your third—and final—read through."

"Yippee!" I interrupted.

Ted continued, "Here's another printout of *Matthew*. This time you read, be diligent to check the preface and other "front matter," and the opening and closing verses of all the Apostle Paul's letters. We'll also have you review all the words on the maps. Enjoy!"

Oh, happy day! The notation for February 10, 1993, on my calendar reads:

"2:15 p.m.—all proofing of NT DONE! PTL!"

A fax to David at Moody revealed our thoughts and emotions:

"Praise the Lord and rejoice with us!"

"I will praise the Name of God with song, and shall magnify Him with thanksgiving" (Psalm 69:30).

At 9:45 a.m. today, February 12, 1993, we "signed off" the 1,300-plus pages of the Berik New Testament. We stated that we are grateful to God in that we have completed ALL checks and proofreading of the New Testament, that we are satisfied all is correct to the best of our ability, and that we will not make any more changes.

This is a "red-letter day" for us and for our supporters, completing the task that the Lord gave to us in 1970, when we first heard of Wycliffe and the need of Bible translation. After training, we arrived in Indonesia on May 1, 1972, and went to live among the Berik people on May 1, 1973.

Before that decade was out, there were Berik believers, reading and being nourished by portions of God's translated Word in their own language. On April 26, 1990, the draft of the New Testament was completed. In August 1992, the detailed check for content and meaning by a consultant was completed. And today, all further checks such as formatting, spelling, hyphenation, punctuation, etc.

are complete. This means that basically our task of polishing is done.

But God's work goes on! Now the text will be paginated, the pictures inserted, printed out, and filmed. These films will be sent to Indonesia to be printed as a colorful, well-laid-out 1,300-page bound book and later dedicated and distributed among the Berik people. Thank you for your part in all of this.

Continue to pray with us that the process will go smoothly. And pray too as we close this chapter of our lives and as we turn our thoughts and attention to recruiting more people (young and old) to becoming involved in this awesome task of providing God's Word for the peoples of this earth.

David, we began this task when you were born—and now it's finished, 20 years later. Hallelujah! As we go on to a new era of our lives, you also move out to follow our awesome God. We are confident that He will supply all you'll ever need as you live in His will. Please share this fax with your friends and prayer group. We love you.

Rejoicing in Him, Dad and Mom. Psalm 86:8–12.

A New Era of Our Lives Begins

From the emotional high in Dallas to a return to mundane living in Minneapolis was a letdown to be sure. We had been warned, "Translators wonder what their future will hold once the New Testament is published. Postpartum depression can easily settle in. Be sure you pray earnestly for the Holy Spirit to give you peace and to lead you to ongoing significant ministries." We prayed, and God gave us a full and busy life.

Exciting news from Yaufun was that he had made a trip to China and to his home in Sabah, Malaysia. There he learned that his mother had also accepted Jesus as her Savior. When the Sunarjo family came to Minneapolis for a farewell visit before they moved to Indonesia for a four-year term of service, Yaufun and Sharon and their boys joined us for a backyard barbeque. Peter and I treasure the picture we took that weekend—the first picture we have of David and Scott with both Yaufun's and George's families.

David finished his preparations and, within two months, had 100% of the support he needed to leave for Moscow in August. He was one of the 12,000 students that would be sent to Russia with Co-Mission, a five-year project to help teach Christian morals and ethics in public schools.

Scott had transferred to LeTourneau in Texas for the spring semester of his freshman year. But because of a delightful young lady he had met at Taylor, he transferred back to Taylor for the fall 1993 semester.

Planning for the Dedication

On August 6, 1993, we quietly celebrated our twenty-fifth wedding anniversary while busily making preparations to go to Indonesia to celebrate the dedication of the Berik New Testament with the Berik people.

We thought that the New Testament negatives had been sent to Indonesia in February, but in fact, they weren't sent until May. The evil one was NOT happy about this New Testament going to print. Though the machine PAD used to produce the New Testament negatives had previously been used for multiple non-Scripture documents, when the PAD team began to run the Berik New Testament, the film melted in the machine causing extreme damage and a major repair delay. Further difficulties developed in the printshop in Indonesia, so it was decided that the dedication of the Berik New Testament would not be able to take place until late in the year.

However, we received word from the secretary of the Berik organizing committee that 80 people had met in the county commissioner's office to elect and appoint members to the organizing committee and to the subcommittees to ensure a smooth-running dedication day celebration. We chuckled as we read the names of some of the subcommittees: program, decoration and documentation, publicizing and information, health, social activities and welcome dance, keeping the peace, food, and finally a committee of 12 persons to make sure all the other committees were complete and would have what they needed to plan and function well.

Dear reader, can you imagine how exhilarating this was for us, knowing the enthusiasm of the Berik people as they planned the celebration for the arrival, into their midst, of the greatest book ever written?

In September, we received confirmation that 400 Berik New Testaments were ready to be airfreighted to Irian Jaya. Amazingly, Peter was able to talk with the county commissioner on the phone. They were able to decide that, Lord willing, the dedication celebration of the *Berik New Testament* would take place on December 2, 1993. Peter and I made plans to fly to Indonesia on November 16, my fifty-fourth birthday.

The First Copy

"Peter!" I called out. "Come quickly! There's a small package in our mailbox today!"

Peter came running to the living room. We tore open the package and, for the first time in our lives, held a copy of the *Berik New Testament* in our hands. *Oh, Jesus! Thank You! Thank You! Father, You did it! You brought it all to pass. Oh, thank You. Thank You.*

Our eyes closed, we visualized being with our Berik friends when they held their New Testaments for the first time.

The Dedications

1993

*So is My word that goes out from My mouth: It will
not return to Me empty, but will accomplish what I
desire and achieve the purpose for which I sent it.*
—Isaiah 55:11, New International Version

Essau stood at the side of the Somanente airstrip, staring into the bright morning sky watching for the SIL plane—which was carrying valuable Berik cargo. By the time the plane approached for landing that Monday, November 22, hundreds of excited Berik people had lined up on both sides of the strip, eager to meet the plane and rejoice that the first load of Berik New Testaments and dedication celebration supplies were arriving.

After Peter and I disembarked, the pilot began to unload the precious boxes. Essau was first in line. With tears streaming down his face, he received the first box, and referring to his wife Aksamina's deathbed command, he said, "She told us to do it. **And GOD gave us His power. And it's done!**"

Essau led the parade as members of the Berik New Testament dedication organizing committee came forward and, each taking one of the cartons, followed Essau to our house where he led in prayer, "Thank You, our Great Father, that we are here today with Mr. Peter and Mama Sue and Your Book for which we've been waiting for 21 years. You've shown us Your love and power. We say thank You."

After a period of visiting, lunch, and a short nap, Peter met with the committee for the rest of the afternoon while Magdalena helped me open up and settle into our village house, which was in much better condition

410

than we had expected it to be. Built with ironwood posts and joists, the house had foiled the termites in their attempt to live there. Yippee.

Peter had four-hour-long meetings daily with the various committees. By Thursday night, he confided to me that he was overwhelmed with all the demands. The next morning, the plane brought several government officials to the village, and Peter went back to Jayapura to put out the red carpet for our guests from the US who were due to arrive on Sunday.

A Miracle—Together for the Dedication

In April 1993, our family was widely separated. Peter and I were in Minnesota, having just arrived there after finishing the typesetting of the New Testament in Dallas. David was at Moody in Chicago and was responding to God's call to serve one year as a missionary in Russia. Scott was in Indiana, applying to transfer to LeTourneau University in Texas. The Sunarjo family was taking part in an SIL jungle training program in the Philippines.

None of us knew how long it would take to print the New Testament—it could be three months or two years. Each of us had a deep desire to attend the New Testament dedication with the Berik people, but not knowing when it would be, we had to just move ahead, prayerfully following God's leading.

In June, David received all the support he needed for his Russian assignment, and in August, he left for Moscow. It certainly appeared that he wouldn't be able to be at the dedication. Also in August, Scott began his studies at LeTourneau, and during the orientation, the staff said, "This is a place of serious study. Don't ask to be excused for every family activity that comes along." Peter lamented, "Scott won't be able to come either." Then when George and Doris and their four kids left for the Philippines in September, we also gave up on our dreams of having them with us on the momentous dedication day.

But God didn't. .

Each of us willingly did what God led us to do, and God provided and cleared the way. David's supervisor in Russia, Scott's in Texas, and George's in the Philippines—all said, "This is a once-in-a-lifetime event. GO!"

Our church called and offered to help financially. Friends responded to God's prompting and sent gifts.

And so it was that on Tuesday, November 30, I stood at the side of the Somanente airstrip, staring into the sky watching for two SIL planes that were bringing my family to me there in the jungle. David had flown from Russia to Turkey to Amsterdam and then across the North Pole to Los Angeles. There he met up with Scott, Darryl—the chairman of the missions committee from our home church in Minneapolis who was representing the church that had been supporting us for nine years—and Wayne who had been our faithful supporter for the past eight years and was making his third visit to Irian from his home in Missouri. Wayne wrote a report of his experience of landing in a single-engine plane on the 900-foot-long Somanente airstrip:

The Tor River surrounds the village on three sides, so landing is a challenge. Land too soon means landing in the river. Going too far on landing means going into the water. Landing is definitely a thrill for first-time passengers.

As the plane approached for landing, I couldn't even see all the people standing with me on both sides of the airstrip—I was blinded by tears of joy. And then when first Peter, followed by David and Scott, stepped out of the plane, I just burst into shoulder-shaking tears. As I hugged our sons and didn't want to let go, I just kept saying, "Thank You, Jesus. Oh, I can't believe you're really here. Thank You, Jesus! Thank You for this great blessing of bringing us together."

When I finally gained control, I was all smiles as I greeted Wayne and Darryl, two dear friends who had sacrificed dearly to be able to join us.

I was already feeling emotionally spent when the second SIL plane landed bringing the Sunarjo family to us. More hugs and tears all around followed before we set out for home.

Truly, it felt like a miracle that we were all together in the village. God had provided beyond what we had imagined could happen! "Now to Him who is able to do above and beyond all that we ask or think—to Him be glory in the church and in Christ Jesus to all generations, forever and ever" (Ephesians 3:20–21, Holman Christian Standard Bible).

The excitement continued to build the next day, December 1, when 10 of our SIL colleagues flew in from Jayapura. We were so very grateful that Dr. Bill and his wife, Mary, were able to come, for with the influx of Berik people from all the villages, the number of those seeking medical help was greatly increased. David also became quite ill that night. *Thank You, Jesus, that Dr. Bill was here for him!*

After reporting in at the police station, the group toured Somanente, and then as they hiked through the jungle, hoping to visit Tenwer—the village where we had first lived in 1973—they met columns of smiling

Berik people carrying baskets of vegetables, stalks of bananas, and squawking chickens, which were probably aware of the contribution they would be making to the feast the next day. It was quite difficult to find Tenwer—it had long since been swallowed by the jungle.

Wayne wrote his impression of what village life was like for the newcomers:

> Daily life in the village was quite basic. Somanente has no electricity, no streets (just paths), no running water (the Tor River is drinking water, bathing water, sewage disposal, all combined). Safe drinking water is obtained by filtering and boiling river water. A 25-foot deep well was completed by the Westrums, but it has no cover, and Berik people go into the well to retrieve containers accidentally dropped. There are no wheeled vehicles, no stores, no telephones, no TV, no radio. The sun rises at 6:00 a.m. and sets at 6:00 p.m., 365 days a year. The location is two degrees south of the equator. A thermometer placed in the direct sun registered 120 degrees Fahrenheit—that's as high as the thermometer went. Humidity stays at 95% or higher all the time.

We helped our colleagues get settled in the Berik homes where they would spend the night, introducing them to their host families and orienting them to the newly built outhouse and shower facilities. The younger folk preferred a swimming bath in the river. Magdalena and her crew of helpers were amazing as they prepared a meal for 22 of us that evening. Visiting, with the overseas guests sharing their travel adventures and joining our voices for an evening Singspiration, kept us going for a couple more hours—until we all turned in for the night, full of joyful weariness.

December 2, 1993

Twenty-three years after God first gave us the vision, the day we had been waiting for was about to dawn. Some members of the Berik community had stayed up all night putting the finishing touches on the order of the dedication program and the final decorations in the large room where several hundred people would gather. At 8:00 a.m., the sound of two air-planes could be heard.

As the passengers emerged from the aircraft, they were welcomed by Berik dancers—barefooted, bare-chested men dressed to the hilt in jungle finery—knee-length grass skirts with long leafy palm fronds tucked into the back of the skirt's waistband and tight upper-arm bands holding deco-rative leaves in place. Those leaves, and the palm fronds that flowed upward over each dancer's head, fluttered in the breeze and swayed every which way as the dancers jumped forward and back while beating their drums and singing and whooping a welcome to Berikland, home to over 1,200 Berik-speaking people, 450 of which were baptized believers. Truly, the guests had never before had such an experience.

Some of the official government guests who came that day had become close friends of ours through the years. Dr. Agus, president of the only university in Irian Jaya, had given up an invitation to a function in a coastal town in order to be with us and the Berik people. Sangga, the med-ical worker who had lived in the village with the Berik for many years and had named his children after us and with whom I had conducted the medi-cal survey, gave up valuable time to join us. Mr. Rudi, a government official and personal friend who had served with us in Somanente for several years, also came. Larry, our SIL branch director, and Dick, our Irian director, were included among our honored colleagues who arrived that morning.

As I stood outside the grouping of the new arrivals watching the dancers circling around them, and realizing that all these people were there to celebrate the coming of God's Word to the Tor River area, my tears of joy and gratitude to God flowed once again. When Mr. Rudi saw me, he came over to me and held me with my head on his shoulder and said, "It's OK. Just go ahead and cry."

The dancers gave flower hibiscus leis to each of the nine honored guests and, along with a growing crowd of local Berik residents, ushered them through a palm-branch welcome arch and between rows of singing school children to the festively decorated elementary school building where the celebrations would be held. The interior walls of the six classrooms in the building had been removed, resulting in one large meeting hall. As I looked around, I saw that the room was packed to overflowing. People stood, four and five deep, looking in all the windows.

One of the primary school teachers served as the master of ceremo-nies, and the program began with everyone standing and singing "This Is the Day that the Lord Has Made" in Indonesian, followed by singing the Indonesian national anthem. The school choir sang a hymn, led by the police chief's assistant who regularly taught Sunday school. When the visiting pastor spoke, emphasizing the importance of people having the Scripture in their own language, he read a Bible verse first in Berik and then in Indonesian and asked, "Which did you best understand?"

Peter was overcome by emotion several times when he spoke—first, when he welcomed and thanked all the guests from the US and Jayapura for being there with us and the Berik people on this momentous day, and then he presented an overview of our years living and serving with the Berik people. Once, as he paused and allowed his tears to flow, I also broke down, and looking over at David, I saw that he was holding his quivering chin as his eyes overflowed. Exquisite tears of love and joy.

Two middle-school students, a boy and a girl from each of the five village areas, recited memorized verses, one in Berik and the other the same verse in Indonesian. It had been my joy to work with these young people as they prepared for the occasion.

The White Cloth Lifted

The central event of all the pomp and ceremony took place amid clapping, cheering, beating of drums, and the tears of many. The white cloth, which had been concealing the books, was lifted—revealing five copies of GOD'S HOLY WORD IN THE BERIK LANGUAGE to the Berik people for the first time! The five beautiful blue-covered Berik New Testaments were designated for the leaders of the five Berik village areas. Symbolizing that God's Word was now going out into all Berik communities, one by one, the five village area leaders came forward and stood between the two students from their area who had recited their verses. Dr. Agus made the first presentation of a New Testament to one of the leaders and four other dignitaries followed with presentations.

Short messages were given by four guests, and Mr. Sangga closed the ceremony in prayer.

New Testament Distribution

While refreshments were being prepared, about 20 of us—expats and Berik leaders—worked together to place Berik New Testaments into 200 waterproof bags that the women of Meadow Creek Church in Minneapolis had made for the Berik. Darryl captured all the action on video for his report to the church when he returned.

The previous weekend while Peter was in Jayapura, hundreds of Berik had come to me and to the Berik tutors to sign up and pay for the New Testaments they would receive on dedication day. Based on the conviction that people appreciate and more greatly treasure items for which they sacrifice, the committee had set an appropriate cost. As the pile of New Testaments in their tan bags grew on the distribution table at the front of the meeting hall, the Berik gathered around eager to receive their copies.

Our family, Doris and Sunarjo with Berik New Testament

Just before the distribution began, as pictures were taken of our family standing behind the table piled high with *The Book* that's of greater worth than gold, my heart was bursting with joy and gratitude to God. *Indeed*, I thought, *all the hardships we faced were worth it. Now the Berik have a permanent missionary, one who doesn't need a visa to enter the country, one who will never leave them.*

As the emcee called out the names of those who were to receive their copy that day, Peter and I, David and Scott, George and Doris, and all the guests took turns handing the New Testaments to the Berik one by one. It was my delight to place a copy in Magdalena's hands and to hug her tight.

Magdalena receiving her New Testament from Sue

Upon receiving his New Testament from Peter, as the entire assembly watched, Sowenso just clutched his copy of that book of all books to his breast with loud, uncontrollably deep groaning, and crying sobs. After 13 years of working so faithfully with us, he was overwhelmed that he not only held God's Word in his gallbladder (heart) but now also in his hands.

Another Berik man stated, "I need five copies—one for my wife, one for each of my three children, and one for myself. My whole family needs God's Word in our OWN language!"

All-night Celebration

The pilots, who had been recognized and honored by all during the ceremonies, then began their massive job of transporting 18 dignitaries and guests back to Jayapura. They also made a trip to Danau Bira and brought in 400 pounds of tilapia fish for the evening banquet.

Dispersing to homes throughout the village, the Berik women set about cooking for the 500 people who were there that momentous day. By evening, all was prepared, hopes and dreams had been realized, and those who had been sitting and reading their New Testaments, discussing the stories por-

417

trayed in the pictures, carefully put their treasures aside and delighted in feasting together. And then, as was their custom, the all-night dancing began.

Bonding Demonstrated

At 4:45 a.m., we were awakened by cheering, clapping, singing, and shouting. The Berik were coming for us. Oh my, we remembered the Berik custom of showing those you love and with whom you've bonded how much you care. The strong young men called for David, Scott, and George; and running to them as they came out onto the porch of our house, they lifted them up onto their shoulders and carried them off down the path. The crowds of dancers and villagers followed as if in a parade down to the river, where out in the waist-deep water, the three were thrown into the cool water.

Smiling and joining in the exuberance of the group, Peter and I had followed along. I was taking a video of it all. And then I heard my name and looked over at a group of women who were pointing at me. "Peter," I said, "quick! Take the camera from me."

"Oh, they wouldn't throw you in the river," he responded.

But they did. With great abandon, they came running to get me, four of them picking me up, and under the water I went. I loved it. *Thank You, Father, for this expression of their love for me!* As I walked up onto the rocky beach, Darryl, who had continued to video it all, said, "You're all wet, Sue." I smiled with joy.

By then it was daylight. Two planes were scheduled to arrive at 10:00 a.m. to pick up all the rest of the non-Berik people, except for Peter who would stay for the weekend to aid Berik leaders in plans for continued New Testament distribution. We took advantage of the last hours we had to walk around the village, visiting every house and shaking hands, saying good-bye to each person. It was sooo hard. At one point, the people had Peter, David, Scott, George, and me stand in a receiving line, and the people came and shook hands—to say good-bye again.

Finally, after the last person passed by, I gave a closing Scripture to the group assembled there: "Carry the light-giving Message into the night so I'll have good cause to be proud of you on the day that Christ returns. You'll be living proof that I didn't go to all this work for nothing" (Philippians 2:16, The Message).

No One Will Call My Name

Peter had to say good-bye to David and Scott that morning, for they needed to fly back to the US on Sunday. Before dawn on Monday morning, the Berik came, calling for Peter and—you guessed it—took him for a dunk in the river. Afterward, as Peter got dried off and was making his final preparations before the plane arrived to pick him up, Bular came to the house for a private good-bye. Peter wrote:

> I'll never forget Bular's parting words with me. I would soon be leaving with no definite plans for return. Sue, David, and Scott had already gone back to Jayapura, and so it was that I would be alone in our now-empty house. Bular, my best personal helper, asked to spend the night. We talked of many memories, things we had done together, things he had done with our sons, David and Scott.
>
> Suddenly, he broke down, weeping uncontrollably. "Father," he said (he always called me "Father"), "I will miss you very much when you leave, very, very, much!"
>
> I would miss Bular and his wife Magdalena too, but I was curious as to just exactly what he would miss most about me. Just think about it—what do you think he might say? Would he miss the gifts I had given him in exchange for his faithful work? Would he miss our travels together in and out of the area? "What will you miss most about me?" I asked.
>
> "There will be no one to call my name," he said softly, his heart nearly breaking.
>
> "No one to call his name"—yes, I understood. Often, I would stand at the window of our home facing the neighbor's home and call out Bular's name when I needed him for something. Sometimes I felt reluctant, thinking he may resent being summoned from across the village. One neighbor would pass the call onto the next until it got down to Bular's house, and he always came—quickly. And now

there would be no one who needed him—who would call his name.

"Oh, Bular," I said. "It may be true that no one here will regularly be calling your name, but remember to always be a good follower of Jesus. He's always here for you when you call to Him, and one day when He returns to this earth, He will call your name."

Other Celebrations

I'm Going to Read Every Word!

Peter and I had flown from Minneapolis to Dallas, to Los Angeles, to Biak, and on to Jayapura on November 19, 1993. Our hearts and minds were full of praise and excitement for the days ahead. We had sent word that we were coming to celebrate the dedication of the *Berik New Testament*. The day after our arrival, we went to the SIL hangar at the airport where the boxes of New Testaments, having been shipped from Jakarta, were being stored. We took a box with us to the house where we were staying.

That afternoon, many of the Berik people who were living in the Jayapura area came to visit us. Our friend, Oskar, was among them. After visiting for a while, sitting in the cool breezes on the porch, Oskar asked, "Is it really here?"

"Yes," I replied. "Do you want to see a copy?"

Emphatically, he answered, "Oh YES, I do."

So I broke protocol that states that the item that is most central to a celebration is kept hidden until the designated moment during the planned proceedings. But I saw that Oskar's eyes were sparkling with anticipation, so I brought out a copy of the *Berik New Testament* and gave it to Oskar.

He took it and placed it on his lap—and began to stroke it, like you would pet a little puppy or kitten.

After a time, he pointed to the title on the cover and read, *Taterisi Uwa Sanbagirmana Irbimiserem* (*The Great Father's New Promise*). And he read the words in the publisher's logo.

Opening the cover, he read all the names on the map of Palestine. Turning to the title page, he read the title, the publisher's logo, and the publisher's full address. On the back of the title page, he read it all—even the page numbers of the illustrations!

And then he began to read the preface. Finishing the first paragraph, he stopped, looked at me, and said, "Mama Sue, I'M going to read every word."

Turning to a colored picture, he started to read the story on the opposite page. Then he stopped and distinctly said, "Mama Sue, I'm GOING TO READ every word."

Flipping the pages one more time, he emphatically declared, "Mama Sue, I'm going to read EVERY WORD!"

Dear reader, I submit to you that God Himself had placed a love for His Word in Oskar's gallbladder. God was building His church.

Celebrating with Our SIL Colleagues

On Sunday, November 28—the day that David, Scott, Wayne, Darryl, and the Sunarjo family arrived in Irian—Peter introduced the new arrivals to our SIL colleagues at their regular Sunday evening gathering. During the meeting, the group—made up of other translation teams who had experienced many of the same struggles we had and support teams in various roles—celebrated the completion of the *Berik New Testament* program with us. They had prayed with and for us and the Berik people for years, and that night once again gave total praise and thanksgiving to God for His strength and faithfulness in carrying us through to the end. Several prayed that God would be glorified through the Somanente dedication later in the week.

Celebrating with SIL Employees

We knew that it was only with God's power and strength that the *Berik New Testament* was completed, but we also recognized that God had used many individuals to help complete that huge task. Many of our national employees had helped in various ways behind the scenes. Secretaries had typed letters and forms to help us keep our visas and other official documents up-to-date. Buyers had purchased supplies when needed and loaded them onto airplanes destined for Somanente.

At noon on December 7, we included them in a celebration of the New Testament in which they had played a part. We sang hymns of praise together and prayed, after which Peter gave a summary of the Berik ministry, and thanked each employee personally for the way that they had been involved. Closing our program, we all gave an energetic "clap offering" to the Lord for His goodness and faithfulness.

Jayapura Dedication

Since the Berik believers who lived in Jayapura, including Essau and Sefnad, were not able to make the trip to Somanente for the New Testament dedication there, months earlier, they had started to plan for a Jayapura dedication to follow the Somanente festivities. Peter met with Essau and the Jayapura committee to discuss the details of their plan, assuring them that we very much were looking forward to celebrating the New Testament with the Jayapura believers.

The evening of December 7, 125 Berik men, women, and children gathered under a canopy in the front yard of Essau's house to rejoice in God's gift to them. This time, Essau was the master of ceremonies. Since 99% of those attending spoke Berik, the dedication was conducted entirely in the Berik language. What a thrill to worship with these believers by singing hymns—in the Berik language—which the Berik people themselves had written. Sefnad gave the opening prayer; then Peter and several Berik men spoke, and the congregation enjoyed a singing presentation by George and Doris and all four of their children. As dusk fell, Essau lit five candles, symbolizing that the Word of God was reaching out to the people from all five Berik village areas.

Three Berik men reading their New Testament

As the New Testaments were distributed, the people cheered, clapped, and rejoiced with tears as they held God's Word, · IN THEIR OWN

LANGUAGE, for the first time. After the closing prayer, the women went into the house to prepare the refreshments. I was kept busy translating for Wayne and Darryl as they visited with our Berik friends. Then I noticed a group of young Berik men sitting on the cement floor in the main room of the house, under the light of a lantern hanging above them. They all had their New Testaments on their laps and were reading God's Word. What a precious picture! *Thank You once again, Father, for using us, for allowing us to watch You work in Berik gallbladders and lives, establishing Your church here, at the end of the earth.*

Dedications in Los Angeles

At 10:00 a.m. the next day, Peter, Darryl, Wayne, and I boarded a plane to take us back to the US. After an eight-hour layover in Biak where we spent the day relaxing and touring interesting World War II sights, we took off from the Biak airport at 8:00 p.m. on December 8 and landed in Los Angeles at 9:45 p.m.—also on the eighth—29 hours after arising that morning. Mother, Mary, and Chad met us. After a snack in the airport restaurant, and seeing Wayne and Darryl off on their planes to return home to Missouri and Minnesota, Mother, Peter, and I went home with Mary and Chad. We were physically and emotionally drained and oh so grateful for a soft, clean, dry, bug-free bed.

Staying with Mary and her family was such a relief and comfort to us. They had prayed for us and the Berik people all through our 21 years with them. They supported us financially, visited and served with us in Irian, and hosted us during our numerous visits to California when we were on furlough. And there we were again with them, tired and spent—and floating on cloud nine.

We were thrilled when they graciously opened their home to have a minidedication for 12 of our SIL colleagues who had served for years with us in Indonesia and who were now living in LA. After an evening of praise, prayer, celebration, and refreshments, Peter and I presented a copy of the *Berik New Testament*, with a personalized note of appreciation inside the front cover for the part each had played in the Berik project, to Mother and each couple present. All our hearts were full of joy and deep thoughts of God and His goodness and many blessings to each of us.

The final celebration of the Berik New Testament dedication was held at our Wycliffe office in Los Angeles on December 15. During the weekly chapel time, we summarized the Berik language program and the impact

God's Word had had in the lives of many Berik speakers. All Wycliffe members who had been involved in the work in Indonesia were recognized, as were all those working there in the home office who daily support field laborers in countries on all continents. We joined in worship and praise to God whose faithfulness continually enables New Testaments to be completed for language groups all around the world.

The Berik project was finished. God had reached into Berik gallbladders (hearts) and established His church. Father, Son, and Holy Spirit would lead Berik believers in their hearts and through His Word.

It had been an amazing month, much more wonderful than we imagined. It was time for Peter and me to return to Minneapolis—to begin a new era of our lives. We wondered when we'd be with the Berik again.

Three, Five, and Fifteen Years Later

1996, 1998, and 2008

I planted the seed. Apollos watered it. But
God has been making it grow. So the one
who plants is not important. The one who
waters is not important. It is God who makes
things grow. He is the important one.
—1 Corinthians 3:7, New International Reader's Version

October to November 1996

Samfer Fortia!

Over and over, hearing this greeting from groups and from individuals, our hearts burst with elation as the Berik people called out, "Welcome back!" After three wonderful years continuing to serve in the US as representatives of Wycliffe, recruiting on the college campuses in the twin cities of Minneapolis and St. Paul, God brought us back to Indonesia. Before proceeding to our new assignment on the island of Borneo, we were thrilled to be able to spend time in the village with the Berik people in Indonesian New Guinea. Visiting. Laughing. Reminiscing. Worshipping and reading Berik Scripture together. Mourning the loss of those who had passed away during our absence. Just being with the people was immensely satisfying.

There were no pressures on us to translate or check verses, no ceremonies to plan and prepare. For me, the three weeks we had with our Berik friends were the most pleasurable and rewarding I ever had.

Sadly, Peter fell victim to pneumonia and wasn't able to be as involved as he had hoped. I gave him penicillin injections, and he spent the better part of a week lying down on the air mattress we had brought into the village with us. Though Peter initially recovered, he continued to be plagued with fever and weakness throughout the following month, losing 16 pounds in the process. *Thank You, Father, for Your sustaining grace and healing power.*

"Tell us about your sons, David and Scott" was a common request we heard. We shared about their weddings, and their wives, Tanya and Chris. "Ooooh!" they exclaimed. "Our gallbladders are very warm to know about them. David and Scott are Berik children; they belong to us. When will they bring their wives to visit us?" they asked.

The day after we arrived in the village, I announced that I would be in the church daily to read the *Berik New Testament* with the people and to help them practice reading and writing. I had prayed, asking God to give me a facility to speak Berik again, and it was amazing. As I read Scripture and then wanted to comment on the passage, the words were there. *Thank You, Lord, for that wonderful gift. Thank You for all who came—an average of 15 men and women—each day. Thank You for fostering their interest in Your Word and for planting a desire in their hearts to be more fluent readers.* Although formal literacy classes were no longer being held, the number of Berik readers had greatly increased. What a great answer to prayer.

Our living situation was difficult, making it necessary to carry out our activities of daily living in quite primitive conditions, bringing back memories of Jungle Camp. Most of our former house had just rotted away in the hot, humid environment. But dear Magdalena and Bular opened their home to us. It had six small rooms under a LOW corrugated zinc roof. It was like a sauna bath in the afternoon, but we had a great reason to thank the Lord. After three years sitting untouched in the jungle, our Electrolux kerosene refrigerator did the job for which it had been created. We enjoyed the clinking of ice cubes in our glasses.

Sunday church services . . . always an encouragement. Sowenso, the man who worked on the translation with us for 13 years and who cried when he received his New Testament in 1993, gave the message. A dream come true. During the service and in their homes as I visited the Berik, I was on the lookout for used "dirty"—soiled because handwashing wasn't a cultural value—*Berik New Testaments*. There were many, and some had verses underlined and circled. I cheered. But yes, I found that in some homes, copies of the New Testaments had been kept protected and were perfectly clean. Inwardly, I groaned and encouraged the people to read them instead. *Thank You, Jesus, that these people treasure the Book and have kept it safe. But I'm asking You to implant the desire to read it in their hearts.*

As we prepared to leave once again, we realized that we had outlived a whole generation of Berik people. All those who were our age when we first arrived in the village in 1973 were deceased. But we rejoiced that most of the people were generally healthier than they were in the early eighties. Tears—especially Bular's, Sowenso's, and mine—flowed once again when we departed, promising to return.

Those tears gave way to delight when we were able to spend time with Sefnad and Dina while we were in Jayapura. God had so arranged it that we would be near them when their little eight-month-old baby girl named Susie passed away. Our tears of grief mixed with theirs at the funeral, but we had tears of joy hearing Sefnad testify, "My strength and peace are in Jesus."

July to August 1998

Tradition! Tradition! Married on the island of Borneo in 1968 and returning in 1978 and 1988, we had set a tradition. In 1997, David and Scott agreed with plans to continue the custom, and they wanted their wives to be included. They wanted to introduce them to the land of their birth and the culture of their growing-up years. The six of us made plans to visit Asia in July and August 1998. David and Tanya traveled from Moscow, Russia, and the four of us were able to be together with the Berik people in Somanente for over a week. Journeying from Indianapolis where they had full-time jobs and were entitled to just two weeks' vacation per year, Scott and Chris joined us in the village for part of the week.

Earthquake!

"Scott! Help! What was that?" yelped Chris on her first night in the jungle.

"It's just an earthquake," Scott sleepily responded. And just then, their mosquito net fell down on top of them. What a rude awakening for Chris for whom the shaking of the earth was a new experience. But she was a trooper as she held a flashlight for Scott while he got up and relocated the net's corner loops onto the large roofing nails in the four corners of their room.

Essau had given us his house to stay in. What a blessing to be in that sturdy government structure by the airstrip. Though the house shuddered, it wasn't in danger of falling down. Magdalena and Bular came daily to help us and rejoiced in being with the boys they had cared for as babies and their wives.

The Really Old lady

As I walked along the side of the airstrip one afternoon, having made a house call to help a sick child, I heard a group of small children playing in a nearby yard. I think they didn't realize I could understand the Berik language, but I smiled with pleasure and waved to them when I heard them say, "*Jeiba wibakgirsus!*" In other words, "There's that really old lady!" *Thank You, Jesus, for preserving me to this grand old age, able to see the grandchildren of the Berik people who first welcomed us to live among them.*

Blessings

We spent our days in the village visiting the Berik in their homes and taking part in village life. We again found many worn and marked New Testaments and watched with joy as New Testaments were purchased in the market, which was then functioning three times a week. Once again, the Sunday church service blessed us all. Essau preached, and David also gave a message.

"Let's go for a boat ride to Tenwer and find the location of our first house. Let's go on a memory trip." We discussed the idea during breakfast one morning, and off we went, accompanied by helpful Berik adults and vivacious children. We knew we had found the spot where our 1973 house had been built because the cement boulders—that had supported the base of the stair stringers of that house when little Scotty had fallen down those stairs in 1978—were still lying there on the jungle floor. We found the sight where the first communion service had been held and the logs in the nearby stream where the boys played with their friends. *Thank You, Lord, for such wonderful memories.*

David was able to spend his days, before Scott arrived, with the young men of his age with whom he had grown up. They played volleyball and soccer and spent their evenings singing hymns in the church. One night, he and Tanya kept going from 9:00 p.m. to 3:00 a.m. And the night before we all flew back to Jayapura, the singers kept going until dawn.

Jayapura

Sefnad and his wife Dina, who was expecting another child, were living in town and welcomed us with hugs and tears. We later learned that they named that baby Scotty.

"Are you really ready for us, George and Doris?" we queried. The Sunarjo family had returned to Indonesia from their furlough in Switzerland, but they graciously welcomed all six of us into their home for a wonderful family reunion and celebration of our thirtieth anniversary. George and Doris also regularly welcomed and nurtured many of the Berik people who were living in Jayapura, celebrating Christmas and other special events together.

Sandakan, Sabah

Peter and I and David and Scott and their wives closed our Asia visit by traveling together to Sandakan to celebrate our anniversary with many friends and Peter's students who had been with us for our wedding 30 years before. However, one especially memorable evening was reserved for just the six of us. After enjoying a nine-course Chinese feast, David was our emcee for a time of sharing as we also celebrated Scott and Chris's third anniversary and David and Tanya's second year together. Our evening ended with a time of commitment to our great God with Psalm 57:9–11 (English Standard Version):

> I/we will give thanks to You, O Lord, <u>among the peoples;</u>
> I/we will sing praises to You among the nations.
> For Your steadfast love is great to the heavens,
> Your faithfulness to the clouds.
> Be exalted, O God, above the heavens!
> <u>Let Your glory be over all the earth!</u>

June 2008

Visiting Asia once again in 2008 to celebrate our fortieth wedding anniversary, we included time in Papua. One day, God made a way for us to spend an entire day with 65 Berik people who were living in the greater Jayapura city area. Sefnad—as happy, energetic, and busy as ever—and his wife Dina and their two children joined us. Sefnad had graduated from Bible school in May 2001. He had remained strong in the Lord's strengthening power—even through the heartache of having four of his six children die in infancy. Essau, who was currently serving as a representative from his county in the state congress, aided in planning and leading our time together.

Though we investigated every avenue, we were quite disappointed that it wasn't possible for us to visit Somanente—the airstrip had fallen into disrepair. The cost of flying there by helicopter was prohibitive, and we didn't have the strength or stamina to go by boat followed by a hike through the jungle. But we thanked God that some of our closest Berik friends made the trip from the village to town to be with us. Magdalena and Bular expended considerable energy to make the four-day trip. God answered our prayers and gave us the joy of seeing and being with them once again.

What a day it was—talking, sharing, reminiscing, singing, praying, eating, crying, rejoicing, taking pictures, reading Scripture, and declaring what God had done and was doing in our lives!

We talked about the generation of Berik, most of whom had passed on to heaven, who had received us to live among them in 1973. We fellowshipped with many of our friends from the next generation—those who had worked with us to translate the Berik New Testament and had become the leaders of the Berik church. We met their grown-up children who had played games with David and Scott when they were little. And we met the toddlers, the great-grandchildren of the generation that had received us. Amazingly wonderful.

What a surprise when one of the young mothers came up to me and asked, "Mama Sue, can I have my picture taken with you?"

"Sure," I said while I wondered how I'd get a copy to her. Then she whipped out her digital camera and called to a friend to take the picture for her. We watched in amazement as some of the Berik exchanged cell phone numbers! Change. God's hand had enabled them.

WOW After WOW

During a semiformal program, the Berik emcee said, "God not only gave us His Word in our own language but He also instilled in us a desire for education!" We learned there were 13 young Berik men and women attending six different institutions of higher education in Jayapura. Think of it. In 1973, there were no schools in the Berik area, and there was just one college-level school in all of Irian Jaya (named Papua in 2002). But by 2008, 13 young men and women had passed primary and secondary level schools and were enrolled in tertiary level schools—Bible school, seminary, teachers' college, science institute, nursing school, and one young man was attending the government university studying economics and law. WOW!

I asked these young people to stand, one by one, give their salvation testimony, and share the name of their school, their year, and their major. When Matthias stood, he said, "If it's OK, I'd like to give my testimony in English." WOW! Talk about being stunned. Matthias was a senior, set on a path to be an English teacher. I had never dreamed of such a future for the Berik children.

"And now," the emcee announced, "a trio will sing for us." Matthias stood with his guitar, his two friends on either side. Dismayed, I thought, *Oh no, they're going to sing some secular Indonesian language song.*

What little faith you have, God reprimanded me. Tears streamed down my cheeks as the young men sang Berik hymns they had written, challenging all who would listen:

Jesus is Good
Oh Jesus, take my hand. I've fallen into sin.
So I come to You, forever to You.
Come to me . . . into my gall bladder (heart).
I've already opened my gall bladder to You.
Enter . . . into my gallbladder.
Oh Jesus, You are good!

Listen!
Listen! Listen! Oh, listen well!
Everyone, everyone, listen well!
Jesus is calling us, you and me.
To come to Him . . . forever.
For our sins, He has died.

He has died, for our sins.
And because of that, listen!
All of us must follow Him!

WOW again! *Oh, thank You, Jesus, for these young men who are willing to take a stand for You. Bless and grow them in their walk with You and in their witness on the college campuses.*

At the end of the meeting, a group of eight Berik men, including Essau and Sefnad, introduced themselves as the Berik scholarship committee. This was not our doing, nor had we even suggested it in the past. God did it. On their own initiative, without outside prodding or help, the Berik leaders had established the committee to provide funds for needy Berik college students. They had raised more than US$300.00 and had already provided the means for one gal to start her university studies.

One hundred fifty *Berik New Testaments* had been in storage there in Jayapura for such a time as this. We turned these over to the Berik leaders for further distribution. One man, Nehemiah, received his copy then and there and sat reading for the rest of our time together.

Nehemiah reading his New Testament

In the seventies, there were about 1,000 Berik people living in isolation in the jungle. In 2008, the government census listed 1,600 Berik citizens. God was continuing to save, lead, guide, bless, and enable the Berik people. They were following Him and His Word. His church was growing. He was sustaining the work He had started as the church was fed by the Scripture in their own language. WOW!

God grows and nurtures His work above all we ask or think. He's the important one.

It's ALL about Him.

Was It Worth It?

1993 to 2009

So you also, when you have done all that you were commanded, say, "We are unworthy servants; we have only done what was our duty."
—Luke 17:10, English Standard Version

"But, Sue, was it really worth it?" asked a woman one morning after I had made a presentation in her Bible study class about our work with the Berik people.

"I'm not sure I understand what you're asking," I responded with a frown on my face. "Was what worth it?"

"Well, you know—leaving all the comforts of the US to live in that terrible place, where it was so hot, where it wasn't safe for your children, with people who had been cannibals. How could you do that?"

Obviously, though I had told stories about the people and interesting things that had happened, I hadn't relayed God's motivating, caring, and sustaining love. The woman's question impacted me, and I thought much about it. Soon, I began to end my talks with the question, "Was it worth it?"

Was it worth it to leave my own culture to struggle in another culture? Was it worth it to risk the lives of our children with tropical disease? Was it worth it to suffer through the agony of exotic illnesses like malaria and dengue fever? Was it worth it to live with all of God's creatures in our house? Was it worth it to be separated from family and lifelong friends—not even being there when Peter's dad passed away?

You bet it was!

434

It was worth it to witness the Berik people as one after another took hold of Jesus and their lives changed. Fear was overtaken by hope, revenge replaced with love. They became bold in proclaiming Jesus and reached out to the unsaved in other villages. It was worth it to observe that, as the Berik tutors learned about health and hygiene and the people became interested in reading, writing, and education, the official government census grew from 1,000 speakers in 1973 to 1,458 in 1993.

It was worth it when I came to understand that God loved me before I responded to Him and that He had His purposes in mind for everything that happened to me in my early years. God provided Evie, and others, to love on me during Mother's periods of struggle, resulting in the empathy and compassion that I feel for others in similar situations. And when I felt abandoned and rejected, Jesus was the *Hound of Heaven*, leading me to receive His love, forgiveness, and salvation. In spite of the emotional turmoil surrounding my departure from Los Angeles after my first year of nurses training, God kept me focused and instilled peace in my heart, enabling me to become a nurse—ready to minister to the Berik people and our SIL colleagues. Amazing provisions—all before I understood my need.

It was worth it to see our two sons baptized in the river with Berik believers who wanted to publicly declare their faith in Jesus, to see God release His power through His Word, to weep when Sowenso clutched his New Testament to his cheek and sobbed uncontrollably for joy when he received his copy, and to hear Oskar say he would read EVERY word. And that's only the beginning.

God Changed Me

Following God's leading to the jungle was worth it, as I experienced how God changed me and my life.

- ❖ In the early sixties, I was a timid city girl from Chicago and Minneapolis (I've been told I was afraid of my own shadow). By the eighties, I had been transformed into a New Guinea jungle mom.
- ❖ In the sixties, I worked as an intensive care nurse at the University of Minnesota hospitals and as a rehabilitation nurse in Washington DC. In the eighties, I sewed up wounds, set broken bones, and delivered babies on the bark floors of jungle huts and on my wooden desk in a thatched-roof jungle house.

❖ In the sixties, I was a stewardess for United Airlines, flying out of San Francisco, all over the Continental US and to Hawaii, and later for Pan American Airways, flying out of New York City to the Caribbean, Europe, and Africa. In the eighties, I was a linguist-translator working with an isolated group of 1,000 Berik-speaking people, hiking muddy jungle trails, and traveling jungle rivers in dugout canoes.

❖ In the sixties, I didn't know what it meant to be a <u>follower</u> of Jesus Christ; by the eighties, I had a growing love for Jesus who is my personal Savior.

❖ In the sixties, I was single—until August of 1968. In the eighties, I was not only a wife but also a mom to two school-aged boys and two grown "unofficially adopted" young men, and when dozens of Berik men, women, and children called, "Mama Sue," I happily answered.

❖ In the sixties, I had neither recognized nor experienced the power of God. By the eighties, I had witnessed God at work and had seen His power displayed and at work, in my life, and in the *gallbladders* (hearts) and lives of the Berik people. Indeed, God gave Peter and me the distinct privilege of living there, in the jungle, watching Him change a jungle society.

Living where God led us was worth it when I had the firsthand experience of seeing God heal baby Scotty of malaria, thus revealing His power and care to Chief Petrus. And, based on his testimony, many Berik took hold of Jesus—and began their prayers saying, "God, You have all the power." Essau testified, "God gave us His power, and it's done!"

But God didn't just dump me into those changes and new roles. He prepared me to be able to handle ALL He put on my plate. As I faced the overwhelming tasks of learning to speak Berik, write primers, and translate, I realized God had gifted me with an affinity for picky details and organization, enabling me to enjoy the work—to thrive in that for which I felt inadequate. God proved I could trust Him, even with the lives of our children—whether moving to live with ex-cannibals, living with all of God's creatures in our house, or suffering from malaria. God loved me through Peter's gentleness and patience when my lack of athletic prowess was clearly demonstrated in my attempts at hiking in Jungle Camp. God proved I could always depend on Him for the strength and stamina I needed to accomplish whatever He put before me.

He taught me to forgive the abandonment I felt from my mother. When I pondered the power and results of Essau's action in forgiving the men who had beaten up his older brother, I realized my sin of hating and not forgiving my mother. It took several years, but I finally gave up, realizing I was hurting more by my unforgiveness than she was—and my sour heart was keeping me from the relationship with God that He wanted with me. I had allowed my childhood hurts to turn me from God—to nothing. But He was there all the time, planning my life with His love. God showed me He had truly forgiven me for those years when I lived a life displeasing to Him—years I confessed were times of seeking my own pleasure and will, not His. God used a man of the jungle as an example to me.

I learned to forgive the hurts—real and perceived—I felt Peter had inflicted on me. Before our wedding, the pastor talked to us about forgiveness. I was so starry-eyed I said, "I'll never need to forgive Peter for anything!" I learned from my current pastor that a good marriage is two imperfect people who are good forgivers.

God taught me to ask Him for forgiveness regarding a critical attitude, and I found forgiving brings healing and joy. He has transformed me by renewing my mind (Romans 12:2). *Oh why, Lord, did it take me so long to understand and to give up?*

Remembering

Reviewing the past as I've written this book, God has enabled me to understand how He manifested His power and care in my life—even in the many instances when I didn't realize it at the time. When someone comments to me, "Oh, everything you did is so wonderful!" I want to say, "Why do you stare at us as if by our own power or godliness (Acts 3:12), we did this? It's not about us. It's all about Him."

All the changes God made served me well for all the events of the nineties. As the years following the dedication of the *Berik New Testament*—1994 through 1996—flew by, we continued to experience God's power and care and had ample opportunity to share the stories of what God had done in and through us. Local Gideon camps and state leaders invited me to share my testimony at their annual pastor appreciation dinners. "Your work around the world spreads out, like ripples from a pebble thrown in a lake," I would declare. Then, after sharing how God had called Essau and Chief Petrus to Himself, I would add, "A Bible in my language spoke to my heart, and heaven rejoiced! The New Testament in the Berik language has spoken to hundreds of Berik hearts, and heaven rejoices." An update on our family was printed in *The Gideon* magazine in June 1995, and I was again delighted to speak to the pastors at the International Gideon convention in Los Angeles in July 1996.

As Wycliffe representatives and recruiters, we were engaged with colleges and churches in Minnesota and Iowa, and we again witnessed God at work attracting and convicting those He was calling as we presented programs about how God had powerfully drawn the Berik people and had worked in our lives as linguist-translators.

The New Testament for Unwritten Languages

We also became active as speakers on the Wycliffe Associates banquet circuit, traveling in Minnesota and to North Dakota, South Dakota, Iowa, Nebraska, Kansas, and Missouri.

"Tonight, I'd like to read some verses to you from this New Testament," I said one evening, holding up a paperback, as I was bringing my portion of our 30-minute talk to a close. "What verse would you like me to read?"

Invariably, someone would say, "*John* 3:16."

After leafing through the book with a confused look on my face, I would look at the crowd and say, "I would REALLY like to read that verse to you. But I can't."

Holding the *New Testament for the Unwritten Languages* up high—revealing all blank pages—I would continue, "THIS is God's Word for 400 million people! It's been 2,000 years since Jesus gave His life for those people, but NO ONE has gone to them to give them God's written Word. And that's why Wycliffe Bible Translators exists. God is in the business of calling His people to go to the villages to live with the people, learn to speak their language, teach them to read and write, and to give them His Word in the language of their hearts."

By then, seeing the tears in the eyes of many listeners while I myself had tears and would sometimes be choked up, I'd say, "But it's a team effort. It's impossible for a translator to accomplish the task alone. Every translator needs a support team of prayer partners—50 or more committed warriors—and those who will back them financially. In addition, support workers are needed on the field—administrators, doctors and nurses, teachers, finance managers, pilots and mechanics, to name a few. Will you pray about what God would have you do to change this (holding up the blank New Testament) to this (holding up the *Berik New Testament*)?"

One evening, an unusual thing happened. As I was challenging the audience, God spoke clearly to me, deep in my heart. *Sue, I want you and Peter to return to Indonesia. The need is great.* What a surprise! God wasn't done with us yet.

When I shared this revelation with Peter after the banquet was over and we were alone, Peter surprised me. "I too have been thinking about that, Sue. I agree God has something new for us." How neat of God to speak to us both.

David and Scott

Serving all those years overseas was worth it to observe God work in David's and Scott's hearts and lives, to know they were saying yes to Him and responding to His leading. David graduated with honors from Moody Bible Institute in May 1995 and committed to long-term mission ministry. Three months later on August 12, Scott married his sweetheart Chris in a beautiful ceremony in northern Indiana. It was the occasion for a wonderful reunion, with dear friends coming from Minnesota and Missouri, and with family members, including Peter's mother who made her last trip away from Minnesota to be with us. *Thank You, Jesus, that you allowed her to attend Scott's wedding before You called her home to heaven just four months later, in December.*

Uncle Ray gave us the gift of coming to the wedding from California, and George came from Indonesia to join David as a groomsman. Scott, who majored in business administration, and Chris both graduated from Taylor University and have continued to live in Indiana, where their three children—Carlie, Josh, and Nate—were born. Scott works in the computer field and is active in his church's mission outreaches in the US and on trips overseas.

Ever since that day Mother, Mary, and I arrived in California back in 1956, and I saw, for the first time, a place that was so very different than Minnesota, I had a deep interest in learning about foreign people and places. I believe God planted that fascination within me. After many successful moves from city to city, and on to the jungle for 21 years, we were ready for another move and new adventure—leading a new SIL advance into Central Borneo—just south of where we were married 29 years earlier in North Borneo.

A new question arose, "How should we get there?"

"Peter," I said, "let's go by way of Moscow and Siberia!"

"Really? You're kidding, right?" Peter retorted.

"No. Think about it. David has proposed to his honey, Tanya, and they want to set their date for later this year. What if we packed all we need to take to Borneo and went to Moscow to be with David and Tanya on their wedding day? Then it seems a good idea to keep traveling east. The Trans-Siberian railway can take us from Moscow to Beijing in China. We could fly from there to Indonesia. What do you think?"

"Let's pray about it," he replied.

And we did, and God led. Scott and Chris, George and Doris, our sisters, Mary and Sally, and Mary's son, Chad, and David's best friend, Jeff, were all able to be there on September 21, 1996. Talk about miracles. God is so good—all the time.

Three days after the wedding, at 7:30 p.m. on a Tuesday, David and George helped us load our suitcases onto the Trans-Siberian railway. We got off the next Monday morning in Beijing! It was an amazing trip across seven time zones, through miles and miles of birchwood forests, riding an electric train—where all the stations were on Moscow time—and then across the whole of the Gobi Desert in Mongolia.

In due time, we arrived in Palangkaraya, the capital city of Central Kalimantan, where we rented a house that needed some help. We sent an SOS to Meadow Creek, our home church in Minnesota: "Please pray that we can quickly find carpenters who can put up some shelves in the kitchen of the house we just rented. At the moment, the kitchen sports only a thigh-high sink with a cold-water faucet. Also, we'd like to convert a large storage room into needed office space for both of us." The church mission team notified the congregation, and within the month, three men offered to come to do the work for us. Upon arrival, they said, "We're not going to put in shelves. We'll build cupboards, drawers, and counters." Within two weeks, we not only had a beautiful kitchen but offices as well. God and His servants had provided far beyond what we asked for or imagined (Ephesians 3:20).

By the end of our first month in Palangkaraya, government officials, business owners, and students contacted us with the same request, "Please will you help us learn to speak English?" We were quite happy to hold informal conversational English classes and very much enjoyed developing relationships with our new friends with whom we kept in touch until our service there ended in May 2000. I also kept busy teaching and running the office and guesthouse in town. Peter led newly arrived translation teams in surveying the language groups living along the many rivers in the heart of the Bornean jungles. George, in his new role as survey coordinator for all our SIL work in Indonesia, joined us in conducting a seminar for the new teams and for our government and university colleagues.

In 1998, during this challenging period of our lives, we thanked God for His special gift of family—for the refreshment of visits by Mary and Chad and for George, Doris, and their four children coming to celebrate Christmas with us. I don't know what we would have done without George and Doris to help us serve our Christmas guests. Unlike our first Christmas in Indonesia when we were unprepared for our Muslim friends, this time we were ready to receive our friends, we were surprised when we realized we fed 50 visitors on December 25 and 64 on the twenty-sixth.

Struggling Again

As I lived my distinctly human life, reveling in God's blessings—like the birth of our first two grandchildren, David's son, Stephan, and Scott's daughter, Carlie, in 1999—God's grace flowed around us—supporting, enabling, providing. Jesus had become my Savior and my Lord. He's my commander. Just as soldiers jump to action when their centurion commands—"For I too am a man under authority, with soldiers under me, and I say to one, 'Go,' and he goes, and to another, 'Come,' and he comes, and to my servant, 'Do this,' and he does it" (*Matthew* 8:9, English Standard Version)— so too I strive to respond to Jesus's commands. And like nurses carry out doctors' orders and just as stewardesses respond to the captain's command in an emergency—without questioning or arguing— so too I have come to believe I should obey when Jesus leads me, when He commands. It's not always easy. I often failed. I forget.

Yes, in spite of all the good happenings, seeds of turmoil reappeared and began to plague us. We struggled and disagreed. In 2000, by the end of our four-year term, we knew we needed renewal and rejuvenation—again. We felt God calling us to return to the US permanently. *Oh Jesus, where do you want us to live and serve now? Where is the best place for us to get the help we need?*

We felt God leading us to one of Wycliffe's three major US centers: the academic center in Dallas, the aviation and radio center in Waxhaw, North Carolina, or to the administrative center in Orlando, Florida. After spending several weeks at both the Waxhaw and Orlando centers, God confirmed that Orlando would be where we could best serve at that stage of our lives. And it was there that God once again provided counselors to work with and guide us. And again, He led us through a period of growth and healing. Sigh. I needed a refresher course in forgiveness. *Why, Jesus, does it take me so long to learn? Why do I so easily forget?* I prayed. And Jesus was patient and gentle and just kept leading me step-by-step to really lean on Him until I learned that He fills unfulfilled longings. It's incredible, but I've found I can even rejoice in hunger or desire because Jesus sustains me and provides for me. *Thank You, Jesus, for being there for me, for us. Always there.* Though I surely wouldn't pray to go through it again, it was worth it to know Jesus better, allowing Him to heal—as He'd done so many times before.

In addition to Mother developing Alzheimer's, her cyclic periods of depression and euphoria had become increasingly more serious. It became necessary for me to visit her and Mary in California every three or four months. I cried at her hospital bedside one day as she squeezed her eyes shut tight, gritted her teeth, and pounded her clinched fist on the bed in frustration as she tried to communicate her feelings. She had suffered much. I prayed for God's peace to fill her and once again placed her in His keeping. She passed away on December 8, 2002, Carlie's third birthday. *Thank You, Father, that You've released her from her agony and she's with You now. Thank You for providing for David, Scott, and their families—including David's year-and-a-half-old daughter, Nadia, and Scott's six-month-old son, Joshua—to be at Mother's funeral with us. And thank You that You've taught and enabled me to not let the bleak portions of my past overshadow what You're doing now in our lives and will continue to do in the future.*

It's About God's Grace

When I came up out of the waters of baptism in 1968, the congregation sang, "Turn Your Eyes upon Jesus." I've found words from that hymn—"things of earth will grow strangely dim"—to be so very true. I've learned that the Christian life isn't about me helping God; it's about me <u>letting</u> God use me in what He's doing. I'm committed to letting God choose the path He has for me; I've learned I can choose how I travel on that path, even as I walk with Him on it—I can let myself be miserable, or I can trust and experience His peace and joy.

"Abide in me, and I in you. As the branch cannot bear fruit by itself, unless it abides in the vine, neither can you, unless you abide in me" (John 15:4, English Standard Version). Pondering that verse, I ask myself, "How does one—how do I—abide in Jesus?" Like a fish abides in water. Like a bird in the air. In what way does water enable fish? How does air support a bird?

Human Resources and the Clinic

From 2002 through 2008 while serving in Orlando, I enjoyed an assignment in HR, allowing me close contact with our Wycliffe staff all over the US. And then in January 2009, I began my dream position as the nurse-administrator of the Wycliffe clinic. It brought back wonderful happy memories of Rehab 5 at the University of Minnesota, where Peter and I had met 43 years before as I had had the fun and privilege of setting up the 20-bed ward for handicapped children.

Sabah in 2008

There was no need for Peter to ask the question, "Where shall we celebrate our fortieth wedding anniversary, Sue?" For 10 years, Peter, David, Scott, and I had been talking about, anticipating, and planning our 2008 "Asia Adventure." This time, there would be nine making the trip with Peter and me: David and Tanya with their children, eight-year-old Stephan and seven-year-old Nadia; Scott and Chris with their children, eight-year-old Carlie, six-year-old Josh, and four-year-old Nate. Time and financial constraints determined that the boys and their families would meet us on the island of Bali in Indonesia to celebrate and to introduce the children to the land of their fathers' birth. Peter and I would go alone to visit the other Asian locations where we had lived between 1968 and 2000. It was an amazing time together, especially since George was able to join us. It's true that God just keeps blessing and blessing.

After our family left us, Peter and I went on to Sandakan, Sabah, eager to meet with our friends and Peter's former students, many of whom were also now grandparents and retired from their life's careers. We joined in the year-long one hundredth anniversary celebrations being held by the Basel Church, where we were married. We realized God had blessed beyond measure as we learned about all the daughter churches that had been established all throughout Sabah.

I'll never forget the trip to Mile 86, the location of the small mission station where we had served in the late sixties. Traveling in an air-conditioned Jeep, I was surprised when I saw our driver pull out his cell phone to talk with the pastor in one of the interior churches. After hanging up, he explained, "We'll have to take a detour. There have been some heavy rains, and the road we normally take is closed. About 30 minutes later, he pulled off the road, saying, "Come along, we'll leave our jeep here, cross the river using the footbridge, and the pastor will meet us on the other side with his jeep."

Sue and Peter enjoy the thrill of crossing the river

That sounded great—until I saw the footbridge. It was a 300-yard-long bridge suspended 100 feet above the racing river waters. As five of us walked single file on the wooden planks, some of which were no longer tied down, the bridge swayed and bounced this way and that with each step each of us took. Hanging onto the "railing" made of jungle vines, I exclaimed, "Whee, Peter! This is much more fun than Disneyland!"

Arriving at the distant riverbank, as the pastor warmly welcomed us, we praised God for our safe crossing. "Everyone's waiting for you," the pastor said. I was surprised, but when we pulled up to the church at Mile 86 that Saturday morning, I was shocked. We heard singing and the clanging of gongs. Entering the church, we found 125 people waiting for us; they had planned a celebratory worship time.

After 30 minutes of worship, with the praise team using microphones and electric guitars, the dancers began. My heart skipped a beat when two teenage girls came and took me by the hand. I must have looked scared to death, for Peter said, "Come on, Sue. It'll be fun." So there we were on the platform, mimicking everything the dancers did, accompanied by cheers and clapping of the congregation.

And then, after singing "In Jesus We Are Siblings," Pastor Gustamin went to the podium to give his message. "I was nine years old in 1967, when Mr. Peter came here to our village to help the doctor from Canada who ran the medical clinic for us. And then, in 1968, Mama Sue came too. Mr. Peter, if you and the doctor hadn't come to us, we wouldn't know about Jesus today. Thank you!" WOW! Hearing his testimony of the fruit of the work four decades earlier, my eyes were blurred by tears. God had worked mightily in Gustamin's life. He had started multiple little churches throughout the remote interior jungle and was mentoring the younger pastors. That very afternoon, he was leaving to join in starting another church several hours' drive away.

A Surprise Invitation

Back in Orlando in 2005, a co-worker contacted me, saying, "Sue, several *Perspectives* courses will be conducted in Central Florida next spring. We've been encouraged to hear the stories you present about what God did among the Berik people in Indonesia and think you'd do a great job teaching lesson 10 of *Perspectives*. Would you be able to do that?"

"What's *Perspectives*?" I responded.

"Oh, haven't you taken the course?" he asked. "It's fabulous. The course is being offered right here at the Wycliffe office at least once a year."

"Well, Andy, I'd have to understand the course and what's presented in lessons one through nine before I could make a decision. Can you provide the information for me?"

And so it was that I found myself being blown away by the 15-week course, *Perspectives on the World Christian Movement*. *Perspectives* is a dynamic experience, taught by 15 different instructors—pastors, professors, Biblical scholars, theologians, missiologists, and missionaries—all of whom teach in the area of their expertise, relating their own global experiences. Students gain an in-depth view of God's perspectives and plan for His Kingdom, especially His passion for ALL nations. As I studied, I found myself wishing I'd become familiar with this material before we began serving among the Berik people. But then I remembered God had always had His hand on my life, and 2009 was the time He had set to bring *Perspectives* into my life.

With joy, I began to teach lesson 10, "How Shall They Hear?" using the stories written in this book of God's work in Berik gallbladders (hearts) as examples in presenting the objectives of the lesson.

Working, learning, serving, teaching—near family and lifetime friends in the US—we were continuing to experience the good life. I won't deny having struggles or facing hardship. But it's been worth it because God is there walking with me on the paths He chooses for me, and I'm convinced His purpose is to work good in my life.

Is It Worth It?

2010 to 2017

As long as I'm alive in this body,
there is good work for me to do.
—Philippians 1:22a, The Message

"**B**ut, Sue," you may be thinking, "it's fine to say your unusual life overseas has been worth it. How can you say that all that's happening to you now living in the US is worth it? How can you still say that it's worth it to follow Jesus no matter what, to obey no matter what? Do you really think you can permanently walk that kind of path through life?"

Yes, I do. God continues to lead, guide, and provide. Sometimes I'm still surprised. But why should I be? God's proven Himself. I forget. Then He forgives—again.

Time to Scale Down

"Sue, more and more of our Wycliffe staff are being dispersed across the country—only one-third of us work in Orlando," Peter said one morning during our sharing and prayer time together. "I think the time has come for us to scale down and simplify our living situation. We need to find a smaller home and yard that will be easier for us to care for and thus allow us more time to spend with others."

"You're right, Peter. I've been thinking the same thing. Should we look for something else here in Orlando or perhaps move to another area of the US as others are doing?"

We prayed about it and spoke with our supervisors, who assured us that there were open positions for us that we could fulfill in another location. We soon sensed the Lord leading us to return to the central part of the US. Many of our friends were making trips to Branson, Missouri, for their vacations. "Whatever is in Branson that you want to go there?" I asked.

"You'd be surprised," our friends responded. "Branson's a small town—only 10,520 residents according to the last census—but as many as six million visitors yearly enjoy that city in the Ozark Mountains. Why don't you go there on vacation and have a look for yourselves?"

We followed their recommendation and were indeed surprised—but not as they expected. Just three days into our visit, we felt God leading us to move there! As Peter and I talked about it, we listed three things that would need to fall in place for us to be serious about a move to the mid-West:

1. confirmation of assignments with Wycliffe
2. someone to take over my work in the clinic
3. sell our Orlando house

We told Scott and Chris, and our Orlando friends, about it and asked them to pray. Scott exclaimed, "But, Mom and Dad, Branson's for old people!" But we all prayed and were amazed to watch God work. Within the month, God provided new positions for us, a clinic manager—who was more qualified for the job than I, and a Wycliffe member moving back to the US from overseas to purchase our house. *We praise You, Father, for making Your will evident once again. Please show us the house You have for us in Branson.*

And He did. During another visit to Branson, He miraculously led us to our current home, where we've lived since February 2011.

Perspectives

"Who's coordinating the Branson *Perspectives* course?" I asked our new friends in Branson.

"What's *Perspectives*? Never heard of it" was the response.

I was surprised because I knew 150–200 *Perspectives* courses were conducted around the US every spring and fall, and I had assumed Branson would be included. And then, clear as a bell—just as when God said to me in California at the Wycliffe office in 1970, *Sue, I want YOU to translate My Word for one of those 2,000 groups of people.* God spoke again, saying, *Sue, I brought you to Branson so you would bring Perspectives to Branson.*

What? But, God, I don't know anything about coordinating such a course. And we're new in town. I'm not familiar with the churches and Christian leaders here. How can I do that?

With Me, Sue, God whispered in my heart. *Don't you know yet that I can do all things? Don't you remember that I'm your enabler?*

I'm sorry, Lord. Forgive me. Stay close to me. Show me the first step.

In October, I had my first meeting with the north central regional director of *Perspectives*, and he explained the hoops I'd have to jump through to run the first Branson class from January through April 2013. Peter and I jumped the hoops together. Yippee! We took the course online January through April 2012 and the coordinators' training in June 2012. God raised up interested Christians to be involved, and I enjoyed teaching lesson 10 again. We all rejoiced when the 2013 course came to a successful completion.

As usual, God did more than we had imagined. "Sue, I believe God's calling me to coordinate a *Perspectives* class in Harrison, Arkansas, next spring," one of the students shared one day. "Please advise me on how to proceed." I was amazed when yet another student said, "I'm from Nebraska, and there's never been a *Perspectives* course held there. I feel God's leading me to introduce the course in my state." In the spring of 2014, he oversaw three courses in three different Nebraska cities.

God led, fulfilling His purposes.

As the 2013 class came to a close, our course team immediately started working on preparing for another course in 2014. More courses in our part of the country were introduced. Besides coordinating the Branson course, I was kept busy indeed, teaching lesson 10 in seven different cities and speaking at banquets hosted by the Gideons and Wycliffe Associates. God had miraculously changed me, and I loved telling the stories of what God had done. Many times, people said to me, "Sue, you should write all those stories down. You should write a book."

"Not me!" I retorted. "I've never written anything. God's not gifted me in that way." I should have known better than to say that.

Not Coordinate in 2015?

In April 2014, as the course was coming to a conclusion, God again spoke deep in my heart as I was having a quiet time with Him one morning. *Sue, you're not to lead a course in 2015.*

I don't understand, Lord, but I hear You. I look forward to learning Your plans.

After much prayer, I rejoiced when a friend agreed that God would have her lead the next Branson course. I was happy to assist—until August 2014.

Peter Gets an LVAD

"I'm never going to eat again!" Peter said.

Alarmed, I asked, "Why, Peter? Why would you say that?"

"Even when I eat just one bite of food, I can't breathe." I saw he was leaning back in his lounge chair, gasping for breath. "I'm in agony," he whispered.

It was Thursday, September 18, 2014. The next day, we had an appointment with Peter's cardiologist. When we got to the office building, Peter said, "There's a wheelchair by the door. Would you push me in it? I don't think I can walk to the elevator and make it to the waiting room on the fourth floor."

When the doctor saw Peter in the chair, he exclaimed, "What happened, Peter? Why are you in that chair?"

Peter was not his happy, smiling self. "I'm not doing well," he explained. And I added, "He told me he's not going to eat again."

"That's it," the doctor responded. "You've deteriorated quickly and have advanced to end-stage heart failure. This is your window of opportunity. We can offer you the LVAD, or we can put you on hospice. We need you to tell us on Monday what your decision is."

The Disease Had Progressed Quickly

Actually, though we didn't recognize the symptoms, Peter had first had trouble breathing in 2013 when we were visiting David and his family in Moscow. Then in April 2014, when we were visiting Scott and his family in Indianapolis, Peter came down with a severe cough. Back in Branson three days later, he was treated for bronchitis but didn't improve. In June and July, he became increasingly short of breath and would tell me that he could only walk about 20 feet before sitting down. "My legs hurt," he'd say. In early August, we flew to California to spend some time with Mary and her husband and to attend Wycliffe meetings at a beautiful retreat center in the mountains. Peter was unable to enjoy visiting or to be actively involved.

It was then that I remembered a selfish thought I had had as a teenager, *I want to marry someone younger than me so that when I'm old, he can take care of me.* But during my morning quiet time on April 17, 2012, God clearly said in my heart, *I know you thought that as a child, Sue. And I know Peter is three years younger than you, but I want you to take care of Peter.* I wrote it down and didn't think of it again until one day in the mountains when Peter was so uncomfortable.

During those mountain meetings, Peter's condition exacerbated. He was up much of the night, unable to breathe. I carried his meals to our cabin for him. On August 9, he was in acute distress in Denver where we changed planes on our way home to Branson. Upon landing, I wanted to take Peter to the emergency room, but he declined, saying, "If you do that, they'll put me in the hospital. I want to sleep at home." But he couldn't sleep, and on the tenth, he said, "I've taken a turn for the worse." The emergency room doctor reported, "Peter, it's not your lungs; it's your heart." He was admitted to the hospital, had a heart catherization, and was diagnosed with failing kidneys and severe congestive heart failure. His heart was functioning at just 10 to 15% of capacity; three coronary arteries were blocked, and his mitral valve was dysfunctional. They sent him by ambulance to Mercy Hospital in Springfield, Missouri, where he was admitted to the intensive care unit.

Scott immediately came from Indianapolis, and we were told that Peter was a very high risk for surgery. They planned to treat him medically and then explained the various options that might be available, including the possibility of receiving an LVAD—a Left Ventricular Assist Device—to help Peter. On August 15, three stents were inserted in his heart, and the next week, the doctors released him to go home wearing an external defibrillator, saying, "We'll see how Peter does for the next three months; then we'll evaluate how his heart is doing."

One month later while George was visiting us, on September 15, the three of us watched a DVD explaining the LVAD, and we spent several hours talking about it. George left us on the eighteenth to return to ministry in Indonesia. It was that afternoon that Peter said, "I'm never going to eat again."

Implantation Day

September 25, 2014. Peter received his titanium jet-engine "pump." It was implanted just below his heart and revolves at 9,000 revolutions a minute as it assists the left ventricle in pumping his blood throughout his body. Scott and his son, Josh, and many of our friends from church sat with me throughout the day in the waiting room. After eight and a half hours, we were able to see Peter in the ICU. Six days later, he was moved to a cardiac floor and, two weeks later, came home. It was mandatory that I live in the hospital with him during those two weeks so that we could both learn how to care for the needed equipment that goes with the pump. An LVAD runs off the power from two lithium batteries that Peter carries in a holster under his arms. At night, he transfers to the 20-foot cable attached to the "power module" that is plugged into the wall. One day as Peter and I were practicing various procedures, one of the nurses asked, "How come you two are taking this so well?"

I smiled. "Because God is so real. He's here with us. He allows everything in our lives for our good. He gives us the grace to cope, joy and peace that passes understanding [Philippians 4:7]. Let me tell you what He's done in the past."

On October 18, Peter told David, "I'm back from the shadow of death to the land of the living." The last three years have been quite a ride, but Peter is doing well—unlike before the implant, he can breathe, eat well, sleep at night—and is active in church activities and with friends. When asked, "How's Peter?" I respond, "Except for the fact that we plug him into the wall at night, he's in good health!"

Adventures and Retirement

Before Peter's heart disease made itself known, he and our four "boys" had been planning a seventy-fifth birthday party for me. (With the passing of Peter's mother, Yaufun had become one of our boys.) After Peter healed well with his new pump, they decided to go ahead with all of us gathering in Branson Christmas week, 2014. How I thank God for that very special time as 19 of us gathered, praising God and thanking Him for a fulfilling life dedicated to Him and His service.

For five years, Peter and I had been talking about what we'd do when it came time for us to retire from active service with Wycliffe. We had planned to travel to be with all our family and friends who had loved on us, prayed for us, and supported us financially for decades. When Peter became ill in 2014, we prayed asking God to show us how to plan. After consultation with Wycliffe leadership, it was decided that our retirement date would be August 1, 2015—45 years to the day after our acceptance as Wycliffe members.

Contrary to everyone's expectation, God enabled us to travel, executing the plans we had started years before. We made a total of five trips: driving to Minneapolis; with an RV—which we'd never done before—to Iowa, South Dakota, North Dakota, northern Minnesota, Wisconsin, and Illinois; driving throughout the southeast portion of the US; by plane to California; and finally driving to Indianapolis. With Peter driving 11,030 miles—I drove 20—we contacted 386 people. At a Celebration of Life luncheon given by Mercy Hospital, one year after Peter received his pump, Peter shared the story of our travels and commented, "It's astonishing neither of us was sick even one day." Peter's surgeon called out, "Most unusual." A gal seated at the front table added, "Only God could have done it!" Amen.

Stretching Me Again

In January 2016, God surprised me again. *Sue,* He said, *friends have suggested you write a book. I want you to do it. Type up all the stories about how I worked in the Berik society, about how I planned and nurtured your life, how I've taught you to glorify Me with thanksgiving.*

Oh Father, You're not kidding, are You? But I'm not a writer. Isn't there someone more skilled and experienced You could use?

Sue, Sue. Listen to yourself. Didn't you say things like that when I called you to be a translator? And when I called you to speak at banquets and then to teach and lead Perspectives?

Yes, Lord. I did.

And didn't I teach you to walk with Me as I enabled you? And haven't you thrived through it all?

Yes, Lord. Each step of my way, You've led me beyond myself and then provided all that I need and have given me Your joy and peace.

Then just say yes to Me. I'll write the book. Be My instrument, just as you were in Indonesia and in the 15 years since I brought you back to the US. I'll lead you, give you the ideas I want in the book.

OK, Lord. I'll trust You.

To My Grandchildren

In preparing to write this book, I came across a suggested exercise I thought would help me get started. The idea was to write a letter to a grandchild but with no plan to mail it, sharing what I've learned from living my life, giving insights or wisdom I've learned and want to pass on.

On May 5, 2016, I wrote the following:

> Dear Stephan, Carlie, Nadia, Josh, Nate, Benji, Jonny, Rebecca, Looki, Nathan, Betsy, and David,
>
> As the years go by, I want to get to know each of you better, and I want to share with you the things God has taught me in the 76 1/2 years I've lived on this earth.
>
> First and most important, God is real, and He loves me so much He gave His Son to die for me. He had a plan for me from eternity past. He pursued me. He has led me, guided me, sustained me, provided for me, motivated me, healed me, taught me, loved me. Jesus is my friend. He listens to me, comforts me, and gives me peace and joy.
>
> People have loved me, cared for me, helped me, made me laugh, and made me cry. They have hurt me and abused me. The only being I can depend on 100% is Jesus, that is God. I've learned to not place my trust in people or to depend on them for happiness and joy. People aren't perfect; God is. I can fully place my trust in Him and depend on Him. In that way, I'm not disappointed when people fail me. My foundation is in Jesus's love, not in people.
>
> Reality is found in the Bible, in the wisdom God gives us there. This world is not my home— my relationship with Jesus in heaven is my eternal reality. God has placed me here on earth for a period of time so He can glorify Himself through what He leads and enables me to do.
>
> I've learned to not depend on people fulfilling my expectations of them as a basis for my happiness. People will disappoint me—they can't help it because they are imperfect, just as I am. Sometimes my expectations are unreasonable, impossible to fulfill.

I've learned that earthly happiness only comes as a result of eternal joy.

I've learned that God is everywhere—it doesn't matter if I'm in an airplane or on the ground, if I'm in a big city or in the jungle. He's with me when I'm well and active. He's with me when I'm sick. I don't need to be upset when hard things are going on, for God knows His purposes in letting those things happen. He'll care for me through it all because He chooses my path, then walks with me on it.

I've learned God will accomplish with me what He desires, <u>if I let Him</u>. He can work through me even in things in which I don't have natural ability . . . i.e., translating the New Testament for the Berik, speaking in front of people, coordinating *Perspectives*, caring for Grandpa and his LVAD.

I thank God for the life He's given me, and I look forward to eternity with Him.

I love each of you so much. I pray you'll become mighty men and women of God. Grandma Sue.

Is It Really Worth It?

To trust in Jesus to forgive sin, to surrender to Him, to commit to following Him, to thank Him—no matter what?

Yes, it truly is worth it. I've learned the hard stuff polishes me. Trials grow me. God taught me to SIT and LISTEN to Him daily. I've learned pain and disappointment are inevitable, but discouragement and misery are optional. I can choose. I've learned to just whisper His name, and He gives me strength. His grace healed me and Peter. He's brought us through mountaintops and valleys to a new era of life earmarked by giving and forgiving, loving communication, and service. I praise Him daily for our pattern of relating to one another.

Each day, this past nineteen months, as I sat in my lounge chair in the morning for a quiet time with God, I prayed, *"Father, when I put my hands on the keyboard today, put Your ideas for today's chapter into my head. Use me to type what You want—about Your plan and love for the Berik people, how You changed them, how You prepared me to live with them, to speak and teach—and to write."*

I was recently contacted by an organization dedicated to producing audio recordings of Scripture for isolated people groups. I detect that God's not done with the Berik. He showered His gifts on them. He won't abandon them but will keep seeking the younger generations.

I've come to realize that my life wasn't, hasn't been, and isn't—the good life. It's THE BEST LIFE—walking with the One who loves me and us, like no other—being in the center of His will for me. In the early sixties, I thought I was living the good life. In the eighties, and every year since, I've allowed God to transform me to live—and have lived—the BEST Life. That's what this book is all about.

I pray, dear reader, that this book will fuel your prayer life. Do you KNOW my Friend, Jesus? Like Bular treasured having us call his name, like Mary by the empty tomb recognized Jesus when He spoke her name, Jesus called my name and hundreds of Berik names. And He's calling your name.

When you say yes to Him, thank Him, surrender everything to Him, follow Him wherever He sends, you'll soon join me in saying,

"It's worth it. It's the BEST LIFE."

Endorsement

Finishing Bible translation for a people group has always come down to at least three things:

- God's love for the people living at the ends of the earth with no knowledge of his love and no Scripture;
- His commitment to himself, his Word and call in the life of someone who he sets apart for reaching a remote group;
- and the perseverance in faith of the one he calls to facilitate translation of the Bible.

Sue Westrum, along with her husband, Peter, is a living example of what God can do through the dedication of his people and their commitment to accomplishing the Great Commission through the translation of Scriptures. May your faith be encouraged as you read this book. Most of all, celebrate what God can do through the life of someone willing to hear his voice and follow his call.

Bob Creson
President/CEO
Wycliffe Bible Translators USA

"The Best Life" is a testimony of God lovingly reaching out to the Berik people. This book depicts Peter and Sue Westrum living, working, loving, sharing God's truth, and translating Scripture among the Berik people. The Best Life is fascinating to read about experiences that tell the story of the Berik people, their ways, and their desire to learn to read and write, and most of all to cherish the precious gift of God's Word in their heart language.

Brenda McIntyre
Pelican Rapids, MN

You will love reading this book because it reveals more of God, showing His love, His care, His faithfulness, and more, to our missionary family living on the island of New Guinea for a period of more than 20 years providing God's Word for the Berik language group in their own language. Each chapter emphasizes a verse from Scripture, and how it can be applied in individual lives, enticing readers to discover *The Best Life* for themselves. This book will inform and inspire some to be involved in the ministry of Bible translation. It also demonstrates the power of Prayer, our communicating with our great God, and His leading by the Holy Spirit to motivate and guide us.

Peter Westrum, Sue's husband

Branson, MO

This story will bless you and encourage you. It begins with ONE faithful servant providing ONE Bible, placed by ONE Gideon in ONE hotel room waiting on ONE young lady named Sue to be drawn by the Holy Spirit into ONE hope, ONE Lord, ONE God (Ephesians 4:4-6) and ONE Savior, Jesus Christ.

You are about to enter into a journey planned in heaven, placed in the hearts of a faithful couple willing to walk in faith and obedience to God's calling in their lives. A story full of difficulty, struggle, disappointment and gut wrenching decisions as they follow God into the jungles to spend their lives with a people group with a history of cannibalism, a language only known by the natives with no written word and no way to understand the love of Christ. This amazing story includes every imaginable human emotion of raising a family in an isolated world. Many times risking their lives, yet fully trusting God to protect and guide them. You will be drawn into their fascinating lives full of surprises, unsuspected twist and turns that includes romance, love and suspense as they spend a lifetime following God's will.

Bill Matlock - Past President Gideons International State of Missouri

Reading Sue's testimony is an intriguing journey through Acts 26:18 and God's call to bring His word to the Berik people. This book presents a real life opportunity to walk through a many year process of faith and trust in our Almighty God, the endeavors and adventures required to establish an alphabet and a reading course, and translating the New Testament into the formerly unwritten Berik language. On page after page you'll see the hand of God at work and become curious as to what might happen next. This we know – it's all about Him in this compelling journey. Stepping into the world of Bible translation, you'll find a new perspective on life.

Susan Newman, Branson, Missouri

This book gives powerful insight into the way the Lord uses ordinary people to do His extraordinary work! From being a "city girl" to a wife, mother and Bible translator in the jungles of Irian Jaya, Sue vulnerably shares various hard and painful situations, and gives glory to the Lord for how He orchestrated the details of their lives and ministry. We definitely see that God is the sovereign controller of all things! I strongly recommend it to anyone interested in getting an inside glimpse into the life of a missionary— if you are either interested in missions or just want to know better how to pray for and support your missionary family or friends!

Mary Lathrop, Sue's sister
Women's Ministry Director of Lake Gregory
Community Church, Crestline, CA

In her book *The Best Life*, Sue Westrum recounts a lifetime of struggles and successes, from a turbulent relationship with her mother to faith refined in the jungles of Indonesian New Guinea. The tie that binds every chapter of Sue's story is the presence of Jesus walking beside her, even when she didn't know He was there. *The Best Life* shows what it means to give up one's life to God and let Him work miracles, even in the most remote places on earth.

Kim Rensch, BA, MA; National Board Certified educator, North Dakota.

Whether you are being led to full-time mission work overseas, planning an evangelistic ministry at home, or just in need of some motivation and encouragement, Sue's book will open your heart, delight your soul and challenge you to service! Her mix of emotional ups and downs, hilarious stories and examples of great faithfulness will keep you reading on to the very end!

Teresa Potter - Branson, Missouri

Sue Westrum, despite a troubled childhood in a broken household, prevailed to become not only a registered Nurse and an international airline stewardess but ultimately--and most monumentally--a disciple for Jesus Christ who, in concert with her gifted husband, gave the ultimate blessing--an ingeniously-translated New Testament--to a needy tribe near the eastern rim of the world's most populous Muslim nation. Indonesia's Berik people, recent émigrés from the stone-age, at last are also rebirthed by the Gospel due to Sue and Peter's willingness to confront difficulties surpassing anything they had ever faced. What a captivating narrative!

Don Richardson
Author of *Peace Child, Eternity in Their Hearts, Heaven Wins, and Secrets of the Koran*

I first met Sue and Peter after they retired and moved to Branson. Through the years I had only gotten bits and pieces of the story of their adventures in the jungles of Indonesia. But now, we all get the firsthand account of God bringing His Word to the Berik people through the perseverance of the Westrum's. Their story is an inspirational account of the actual work of God among us, all while utilizing ordinary people like them. Don't be surprised if God uses their story to call you into a deeper faith leading to an adventure of your own!

Dr Neil Franks
Former Pastor First Baptist Church Branson, MO
President of the Missouri Baptist Foundation

Have you ever said to God, "Please don't send me to the mission field! I am happy where I am."? If you have even had that thought, this book is for you. Sue Westrum left the city life she was used to in order to serve God in the jungles of Papua, Indonesia. She then experienced the great joy and blessing and fulfillment that can only come from God. She discovered God's way is the best way.

Steve Douglass
President, Cru/Campus Crusade for Christ, International
Author of several books, including *Enjoying Your Walk With God*
Host of the radio program, *Making Your Life Count*

ENDORESMENT

I love stories, and this book is a captivating, real life narrative of the Lord's faithfulness! It will challenge your perspective of what *The Best Life* really is! If you're looking to have your value system turned upside down and to fuel your passion for the heart of God, look no further!

Sadie Voth, Student in Pursuit of Missions

I was overjoyed when I learned that the story contained in this book would finally be written. It would be easy for me to commend this book to you, with all its thrilling contours. However, let me instead commend to you the magnificent God whose purpose leaps off its pages. This book is the story of God sending Sue and Peter as Bible translators, so that a remote jungle people might hear, believe and be saved in the name of Jesus Christ. Anyone exploring God's purpose for all the nations, and what it can look like for individuals to participate with Him in that purpose, would be strengthened and encouraged by reading this book. Sue and Peter's story gives us a testimony of real people, like you and me, faithfully living life in accordance with God's purpose.

Andrew Herbek - Instructor Development Department,
Perspectives on the World Christian Movement

If God has spoken to you through reading this testimony of His work in the lives of the Berik people, and in Sue and Peter's lives, they would love to hear from you by writing sue_westrum@gmail.com

As this book was in the final stages of the publishing process, Sue was diagnosed with inoperable pancreatic cancer. She and her family are truly experiencing the peace that passes all understanding as she continues to hold tightly to her Savior's hand. This book has been about The Best Life. Now Sue is looking forward with joy to The VERY BEST LIFE with Jesus in heaven.

About the Author

In the early sixties, Sue was a timid city girl, who was born in Chicago, raised in Minneapolis, and was a Registered Nurse in a hospital intensive care unit. By the eighties, she had been transformed into a jungle mom, sewing up wounds, setting broken bones on her wooden desk in a thatch-roofed house, and delivering babies on the bark floors of jungle huts. In the sixties, she was a flight attendant jetting around the world from New York City. In the eighties, she was a linguist-translator with Wycliffe Bible Translators, serving an isolated group of 1,000 Berik-speaking people, hiking muddy jungle trails, and traveling jungle rivers in dugout canoes.

In the early sixties, Sue was single and didn't know what it meant to be a follower of Jesus Christ. By the eighties, she was passionate in her love for Jesus, her personal Savior, and was not only a wife but also a mom to two school-aged boys and two grown "unofficially adopted" young men. And when dozens of Berik men, women, and children called her "Mama Sue," she happily answered. In the sixties, Sue had neither recognized nor experienced the power of God. By the eighties, she had witnessed God at work and had seen His power displayed in her life and in the gallbladders (hearts) and lives of the Berik people of Indonesian New Guinea.

After marrying and ministering with her husband, Peter, for 15 months in Malaysian Borneo, Peter and Sue served with the Berik for 21 years. Returning to the US in 2000, God expanded Sue's ministries to include public speaking and teaching. In 2015, after 45 years, Peter and Sue retired from active service with Wycliffe. They now make their home in Branson, Missouri.

Readers can view more pictures of persons and activities mentioned in this book by accessing http://thebestlifebook.com/

CPSIA information can be obtained
at www.ICGtesting.com
Printed in the USA
FFOW02n0309070718
47281670-50224FF